Praise for *Queer African Reader*

The Queer African Reader *serves as an amc*　　　　　　　*...ɟ*
the struggles faced by African LGBTI people both in Africa and in the diaspora.
From personal narratives written by individuals like the late human rights
defender David Kato to in-depth academic and feminist analysis of the
discourse concerning sexual orientation and gender identity in traditional
African contexts, this publication contains a wealth of knowledge that can act
as a starting point for various discussions concerning queer Africans around
the world. Hopefully this book will allow others from all walks of life to share
their unique African LGBTI experiences.
Victor Mukasa, Ugandan human rights defender and long-term LGBTI activist

The Queer African Reader *is a revelatory, path-breaking collection of*
writings drawn from across the continent and its diaspora. Ekine and Abbas
have achieved a huge task in compiling and editing so many contributors
who courageously share what it means to inhabit the precarious space that
opens up between the patriarchal heteronormative regimes of the past and
the radical possibilities heralded by so many personal-political struggles for
sexual freedom. The Queer African Reader *offers timely testimonies, a bold*
and defiant cacophony of voices that variously subvert the sexual-political
despotism that relies on normative fear and hatred to resist radical non-
conforming ways of being and enjoying sexuality and desire. The first of its
kind, the collection offers a rich festival of material including analytic and
expressive prose, theoretical discussions, erotic fiction, journals, documents
and representations from visual and performance artists, which work to
share the disquieting realities of LGBTQI experiences, contradictions and
political perspectives to life. The Queer African Reader *is a rich resource – a*
milestone in the self-narration of Africa by people who will be silent no more.
Essential reading for the 21st century!
Amina Mama, professor and director, Women and Gender Studies,
University of California, Davis

Long awaited and overdue, written amidst burn-out and premature death, in the front lines of empire and gender violence, this first collection by queer Africans is no quick or easy read. The Queer African Reader *demonstrates that urgency was never an excuse to leave anyone behind: unlike the depressingly streamlined movements of the global/ising North, it has ample space for impossible subjects that complicate the single story and expand who belongs in the movement and what it demands, from transgender to disability to healing. Written by and for Africans, this assembly of leading and emerging activists, artists and academics from the continent and its diasporas takes a leadership in sustainable, accountable community building that non-Africans, too, should learn from – while hearing the signal that queer and trans Africans have always been able to represent themselves.*
Jin Haritaworn, PhD, trans/queer of colour activist, York University (Toronto), author of *The Biopolitics of Mixing* **and co-editor of** *Queer Necropolitics*

A richness of voices, a multiplicity of discourses, a quiverful of arguments. African queers writing for each other, theorising ourselves, making our movements visible. This is a book we have hungered for.
Shailja Patel, award-winning Kenyan poet and activist, author of *Migritude*

All too often we read about African queers as monolithically victimised or as passive recipients of modernity from the West. What a great antidote the Queer African Reader *provides to that narrative, with its diversity of styles, stories, memoirs, scholarly theory, art, photography and deliciously combative polemics and petitions as rich as the diversity of Africans themselves! Listen to the poetry, feel the passion – love, rage, sadness, pride – admire the beauty, grow from the insights of Africans speaking directly to us about their struggles to be true to themselves, to their families, their lovers, their nations. This brave volume should be essential reading for all human rights activists far and wide in Africa and the diaspora.*
Marc Epprecht, author of *Hungochani, Heterosexual Africa?* **and** *Sexuality and Social Justice in Africa*

Queer African Reader

Through the voices of the peoples of Africa and the global South, Pambazuka Press and Pambazuka News disseminate analysis and debate on the struggle for freedom and justice.

Pambazuka Press – www.pambazukapress.org

A Pan-African publisher of progressive books and DVDs on Africa and the global South that aim to stimulate discussion, analysis and engagement. Our publications address issues of human rights, social justice, advocacy, the politics of aid, development and international finance, women's rights, emerging powers and activism. They are primarily written by well-known African academics and activists. Most books are also available as ebooks.

Pambazuka News – www.pambazuka.org

The award-winning and influential electronic weekly newsletter providing a platform for progressive Pan-African perspectives on politics, development and global affairs. With more than 2,800 contributors across the continent and a readership of more than 660,000, Pambazuka News has become the indispensable source of authentic voices of Africa's social analysts and activists.

Pambazuka Press and Pambazuka News are published by Fahamu (www.fahamu.org)

Queer African Reader

Edited by Sokari Ekine
and Hakima Abbas

Pambazuka Press
An imprint of Fahamu

Published 2013 by Pambazuka Press, an imprint of Fahamu
Dakar, Nairobi and Oxford
www.pambazukapress.org   www.fahamu.org   www.pambazuka.org

Fahamu Kenya, PO Box 47158, 00100 GPO, Nairobi, Kenya
Fahamu Senegal, 9 Cité Sonatel 2, BP 13083 Dakar Grand-Yoff,
Dakar, Senegal
Fahamu UK, 2nd floor, 51 Cornmarket Street, Oxford OX1 3HA, UK

British Library Cataloguing in Publication Data
A catalogue record for this book is available from the British Library

ISBN: 978-0-85749-099-5 paperback
ISBN: 978-0-85749-100-8 ebook – pdf

Cover photo: Thobe and Phila, Pietermaritzburg, KwaZulu Natal, 2012.
© Zanele Muholi

Manufactured on demand by Lightning Source

Contents

About the contributors

Hakima Abbas has been active in struggles for social justice around issues of self-determination, race, class, gender and sexuality for over 15 years in Africa and the diaspora. She is a political scientist by training and has worked as a researcher, trainer and strategist. Hakima is the editor and author of various publications on aid and development, the African Union, peace and security, gender and sexuality. She is a board member and advisor to several global philanthropic and civil society initiatives.

Shelley Barry is a South African film-maker, writer and activist.

Gathoni Blessol is a queer social rights activist and human rights defender whose main focus is the socio-economic struggles in LGBTI-Q communities. She is currently working with people living with disabilities and who have diverse sexualities. She recently graduated from the Fahamu Pan-African Fellowship Programme and is a member of the Anarchist Society, Pasha AfriQ and MWITO, all in Kenya.

Douglas Clarke is a graduate student in the social justice and equities programme at Brock University, Canada. He has a previous MA in philosophy and studies representations of the Black body in popular culture. This includes theories of gender and sexuality as well as racism and the mythologising of Blackness.

Kaitlin Dearham is a feminist researcher, anthropologist and consultant based in Nairobi. She is the East Africa programme manager of None on Record: Stories of Queer Africa.

Pamella Dlungwana is a television writer, researcher and producer. She has collaborated with visual artists using the media to educate, liberate and incite. Pamella has published in online journals (Poetry Potion, Itch).

Sokari Ekine is a feminist writer, blogger and educator and is founder and principal author of Black Looks. She has been active in struggles for social justice for over 20 years and has written for various online and print publications, including Pambazuka News, *Feminist Africa* and *New Internationalist* on issues of gender, sexuality, organising and art and militarisation in Africa and the diaspora.

Charles Gueboguo is the author of two books addressing the issue of same-sex practices in Africa: *La Question Homosexuelle en Afrique* (Paris, L'Harmattan, 2006) and *Sida et Homosexualités en Afrique* (Paris, L'Harmattan, 2009). He has co-edited with Marc Epprecht the special issue of the *Canadian Journal of African Studies* on 'New perspectives on sexualities in Africa'. He is currently enrolled in a PhD programme in the Department of Comparative Literature at the University of Michigan.

Jessica Horn is a feminist writer, poet and women's rights activist whose work focuses on questions of sexuality, health, violence and embodied liberations.

Jessie Kabwila is a Malawian feminist academic activist who holds a comparative literature PhD from Binghamton University, New York. She heads the department of English at Chancellor College, University of Malawi, where she teaches various literary courses. Jessie is editor for *WAGADU* and reviewer for *Culture, Health and Sexuality*.

Julius Kaggwa is the programme director of SIPD Uganda, a grassroots, not-for-profit human rights organisation in Uganda, which through community outreach and engagement provides reliable and objective information on atypical sex development issues (also known as intersex conditions).

Mouhamadou Tidiane Kassé is a Senagalese journalist. He teaches journalism and is editor for the Press Group Wal Fadjri and of the French edition of Pambazuka News. He works as a consultant on the training and networking of journalists. Tidiane specialises in media and development, HIV/AIDS and sexual reproductive health.

Happy Mwende Kinyili's struggle is to identify, name and confront the evil that permeates our realities. Thus, her daily toil is to build a world where the oppression of different evils is overcome and an alternative community based on a revolutionary love, effervescent hope and emancipatory truth is realised.

David Kato Kisule (born 1964 – died 26 January 2011) was a Ugandan teacher and LGBT rights activist, considered a father of Uganda's LGBTI movement. He served as advocacy officer for Sexual Minorities Uganda (SMUG). David was murdered on 26 January 2011, shortly after winning a lawsuit against a magazine which had published his name and photograph identifying him as gay and calling for him to be executed.

Gabrielle Le Roux is a South African artist and activist for social justice. Her current work with transgender activists focuses on portraits and narrations of lived experiences. It is rooted in the conviction that we change each other's lives with our stories and that people who speak first-hand about an issue do so with authority and are the ones who should be listened to most closely.

Keguro Macharia teaches English at the University of Maryland, College Park. His academic and popular work has appeared in *Wasafiri*, *Criticism*, the *East African* and the *Guardian*. He blogs at gukira.wordpress.com and is a member of the Concerned Kenyan Writers collective (CKW).

Zandile Makahamadze is a writer and a human rights and social justice activist. Zandile has represented the Africa region in the International Lesbian and Gay Association and was a chairperson of Gays and Lesbians of Zimbabwe. Zandile's poetry and short stories have been published by Zimbabwe Women Writers, and aired by the Zimbabwe Broadcasting Corporation.

Valerie Mason-John, aka Queenie, is the co-author and editor of the only two books, *Making Black Waves* and *Talking Black*, to document the lives of African and Asian lesbians in Britain. She has published a collection of poetry, plays, poems, *Brown Girl in the Ring*. Her first novel, *Borrowed Body*, won the MIND book of the year award. Her plays *Sin Dykes* and *Brown Girl in the Ring* received critical acclaim. She was named as one of Britain's Black Gay Icons, and was artistic director of the London Mardi Gras Arts Festival for five years. She is an ordained Buddhist and works as a meditation teacher and life coach.

Zethu Matebeni obtained a PhD at Wits University, Johannesburg. She currently occupies a research position at the Institute for Humanities in Africa (HUMA), University of Cape Town. She is the co-director of the documentary film *Breaking Out of the Box*, as well as the co-curator of the exhibition 'TRACKS: Sexuality in the City', and is involved in ongoing projects addressing the intersectionalities of race, class, sexuality, gender and politics in South Africa.

Audrey Mbugua is project and monitoring and evaluation officer of Transgender Education and Advocacy (TEA) Kenya, a human rights organisation working towards defending the human rights of transgender and transsexual people in Kenya.

Zanele Muholi has been engaged in creating a visual history of black lesbian identity and politics in post-apartheid South Africa. She is the recipient of a number of awards including, in 2009, the FannyAnn Eddy award for outstanding contributions to the study and advocacy of sexualities in Africa. Three books have been published on Muholi's work: *Only Half the Picture* (2006), *Faces and Phases* (2010) and *Zanele Muholi: African Women Photographers #1* (2011). Muholi's award-winning documentary *Difficult Love* (2010) has been shown at various film festivals in South Africa and abroad.

Kagendo Murungi is a Kenyan video producer, activist and writer with a background in international sexual and gender rights advocacy as well as community organising for political, social and cultural empowerment with LGBTGNC Africans, and for social and economic justice with working class and poor LGBT communities in New York.

Bernedette Muthien is co-founder and director of Engender, South Africa, which works in the intersectional areas of genders and sexualities, human rights, justice and peace. She co-convenes the Global Political Economy Commission of the International Peace Research Association, is a member of Amanitare, and serves on the advisory board of *Human Security Studies* journal. Bernedette has recently published a collection of her poetry, *Ova*.

Kenne Mwikya is a queer blogger and writer currently studying law in Kenya.

Sibongile Ndashe is a feminist who works with the law but believes in justice. She is currently employed as a lawyer at Interights in the equality programme and writes here in her personal capacity.

Mia Nikasimo is a creative writer, essayist, poet and playwright. She is currently working on a novella and other stories entitled *Trans*.

Awino Okech is a researcher who has been involved in development work for the past 12 years in eastern Africa, the Great Lakes region and South Africa. Awino's research interests lie in the areas of gender and sexuality, culture and nationalisms. She holds a PhD in critical gender studies from the University of Cape Town.

Ola Osaze is a Brooklyn-based Nigerian queer transfag activist, feminist and gender liberationist of Edo and Yoruba descent. He has organised with the Audre Lorde Project, Queers for Economic Justice, the Sylvia Rivera Law Project and with Uhuru-Wazobia and Liberation for All Africans. His articles have appeared in blogs such as Black Public Media, the Trans Atlantic Times, and anthologies such as *Yellow Medicine Review: A Journal of Indigenous Literature, Art and Thought*.

Diriye Osman is a Somali-born British writer, visual artist and editor. His collection of short stories *Fairytales For Lost Children* will be published in September 2013. He is deputy editor of *SCARF* magazine.

Lyn Ossome is based in the Political Studies Department at Wits University, Johannesburg. A feminist researcher, she has contributed extensively to research and advocacy projects in eastern, southern and Horn of Africa countries. She has also served in consultative and advisory capacities within a number of civil society organisations in eastern and southern Africa. Her scholarly work, in the areas of feminist theory and politics, land and agrarian studies, post-colonial theory, queer theory and African politics, is widely published. She remains committed to struggles for social justice across the Global South.

Olumide Popoola is a Nigerian German writer who presents internationally as author, guest lecturer, speaker and performer. Her novella *this is not about sadness* was published in 2010 (Unrast Verlag). She is currently a PhD candidate in creative writing at the University of East London and a visiting lecturer in creative writing. See www.olumidepopoola.com.

Raél Jero Salley PhD is an artist, cultural theorist and historian. He is senior lecturer in painting and discourse at the University of Cape Town. Salley's work is focused on contemporary art and visual production, primarily visual practices related to blackness, Africa and the African diaspora.

Busisiwe Sigasa (23 December 1981–12 March 2007) was a young lesbian-identified woman living in Soweto. In April 2006 Busisiwe was raped and subsequently contracted the HIV virus. She was already diabetic and, without sufficient funds to receive the full medical care she needed, her life was always on the edge. On 12 March 2007, after falling into a diabetic coma, Busi passed away.

Liesl Theron is co-founder and director of Gender DynamiX. Gender DynamiX published its first book, *TRANS: Transgender Life Stories from South Africa*, in 2009. She is author of '[Un]accessible shelters for LGT people in Cape Town' in *Tapestry of Human Sexuality in Africa* (2010). She also has a chapter, 'Orientation quiz', in *Reclaiming the L-Word – Sappho's Daughters Out in Africa* (2011).

Kylie Thomas is an ACLS African Humanities Program Fellow at the Centre for Humanities Research at the University of the Western Cape, South Africa. Her book about visuality and mourning post-apartheid is published by Bucknell University Press in 2013.

Nancy Lylac Warinda has a BSc in biomedical science from Egerton University, Kenya. Even with a geeky science background and a budding busy career, she still has time to indulge her creativity. She has written and published several poems and stories, including writing articles for the *Guardian*, Tanzania.

Introduction

Sokari Ekine and Hakima Abbas

The journey of this reader began in January 2010 at a critical moment in African queer history. A Malawian transgender woman, Tiwonge Chimbalanga, 20, and her male partner, Steven Monjeza, 26, were put on trial for the crime of gross indecency and unnatural acts, punishable by up to 14 years' imprisonment with hard labour. The international media and international advocacy groups went into a frenzy of activity reporting on the violation of 'gay rights' in Africa. The president of Malawi, the late Bingu wa Mutharika, joined the chorus of rhetorical transphobic and homophobic violence. Embassies and diplomats of the global North were in turn stirred into action, fuelled by the advocacy of lesbian, gay, bisexual, transgender and intersex (LGBTI) organisations in their countries, and demanded the release of the two 'men', threatening the withdrawal of aid should their human rights not be respected.

And, with this, all the topics of muted discussion among a growing group of queer African activists, thinkers, artists and communities came to the fore in a dazzling display of the quagmire of LGBTI lives on the continent. There was the obliteration of non-conforming gender identities, trans lives and beings in the insistence on referring to Tiwonge as gay even though she stated that she identified as woman. There was the violent rhetoric of populist homophobia used to silence dissent across a whole nation not only by a ruling elite drawn from the political and economic gentry, but also resting on the power of an imported religion. There was the use of independence rhetoric, including the defining of what is African and a rejection of Western imposition, to mete out violence by African against African (those identifying with dominant sexuality and gender proscriptions against those embodying dissident gender and sexuality definitions) with the intent of disappearing gender non-conformity and non-heterosexual identities from the national project. There was the 'gay international' – the international lesbian and gay advocates and organisations – flying into the country with little or no contextual understanding to frame the issues but with a firm conviction that they were saving the persecuted victims of Africa's brutal barbarianism by (merely) consulting with 'local groups' and reprimanding African leaders for their failure to embrace liberal ideology complete with human rights siloes, and their accompanying neoliberal economic strangleholds. There were the Western governments and embassies, who flexed their muscles to come to the rescue of the persecuted minority, while emphasising the continent's continued colonial dependence and reinforcing the skewed power dynamic between the global North and South. Using the withdrawal of aid as a lever for saving LGBTI Africans, these 'international development partners' created a wave of paradoxical dread at this threat despite widespread recognition that aid has never served African peoples' interests. There was South Africa, who we turned to in expectant anticipation, because of our clung-to memories of a liberation party led by principle, waiting for the party to speak out boldly, but whose long silence left us with heads hung in shame. There was another of our 'leaders' cajoled to provide a presidential pardon but still insisting on the denial of queer belonging with a 'we'll get you next time' attitude. There were the brave Malawians from all spheres of life who stood either in their homes or in front of the national media to denounce the oppression meted out against us all and targeting the few; Malawians who didn't get international air time because their message was too complex but who tried to warn their nation of the impending stranglehold of a growing democratic regression; the same Malawians who found themselves imprisoned or driven into hiding only months later when the people's dissent finally hit the streets and the universities. There was the LGBTI movement in Malawi, whose voices couldn't rise above the cacophony of interests speaking for, about and against them but whose communities were driven deeper underground in fear. There were the Africans around the world organising, looking to each other for strategy and support and failing to make a dent in the theatre of the absurd played around African lives. But, just as the phenomenon of mediocre politicians looking for some limelight and finding it in the presentation of fundamentalist persecution of an already fearful community seems to spread across the continent, so has the African resistance, which grows, learns and is strengthened by each battle.

Wanting to give voice to this resistance and carrying the history of the multiple identities that we embody, we two editors, Sokari Ekine, an African from Nigeria, and Hakima Abbas, an African from Egypt, joined forces with a community of Africans around the globe to pay testament to the unrelenting power of queer communities across Africa and her diaspora. The *Queer African Reader* brings together academic writings, political analysis, life testimonies, conversations and artistic works by Africans that engage with the struggle for LGBTIQ liberation. The *Queer African Reader* breaks away from the homogenisation of Africa as the homophobic continent to highlight the complexities of LGBTIQ lives and experiences with contributions that explore issues of identity, resistance, solidarity, pinkwashing,[1] global politics, intersections of struggle, religion and culture, community, sex and love.

Understanding the magnitude of what we were proposing to document in the *Queer African Reader*, we knew that we could not attempt to do this alone. So, we took to the wires to elicit discussion from our multiple communities and prospective contributors on how to document not only the resistance in the daily lives and struggles of Africa's queer communities but to valorise the complexity of how queer liberation is framed in Africa and by Africans. We also hoped that the collectivising of the reader would ensure that the publication was responsive to the needs of the queer African movement in the discussions it encompassed rather than being a voyeuristic insight for 'other' eyes. What we unearthed through this process, and at the root of queer resistance in Africa, is a carrying forward of the struggle for African liberation and self-determination from the body to the collective.

We use the term 'queer' here and in the title to denote a political frame rather than a gender identity or sexual behaviour. We use queer to underscore a perspective that embraces gender and sexual plurality and seeks to transform, overhaul and revolutionise African order rather than seek to assimilate into oppressive hetero-patriarchal-capitalist frameworks. Queer is our dissident stance, but we use it here knowing the limitations of the terminology in relation to our African neocolonial realities. Contributors throughout this volume use an array of identifiers to denote dissident genders and sexualities. As editors we believe that this diversity provides the flavour with which this reader is spiced. It is this very multiplicity that we embrace in the perspectives, experiences, ideas and strategies put forward in this book.

While we wanted to portray the full spectrum of the black rainbow in this volume as well as to give voice to progressive pro-queer and pro-feminist voices from an array of Africans identified in different sexual and gender spheres, we recognise that there are distinct gaps in the material that is collated here. For instance, the absence of submissions from Africa's North and the lack of older-generation voices in the experiences documented produce gaps in the tapestry that this reader seeks to document. For these we take full responsibility and we hope that this will only spur other Africans to take up the challenge. We hope that others will produce more that affirms not only the existence of sexual and gender political dissidence in Africa, but which also strengthens reflection and highlights the important contribution of these voices to the liberation of our continent.

In looking for the finances to make this reader a reality, we were grateful that it was a feminist African funder, Urgent Action Fund – Africa, that was the first to support this work. We would therefore like to thank UAF-Africa for their generous support of and belief in this project in its nascent stages. The *Queer African Reader* was also made possible with the generous support of the Arcus Foundation and we would especially like to offer gratitude to their international programme officer, Carla Sutherland, for her support of Fahamu's 'Reclaim' initiative, from which the *Queer African Reader* is born.

A few months after we began the process that has culminated, three years later, in the *Queer African Reader*, David Kato, a teacher and prominent LGBTI activist in Uganda, was murdered. David, a few weeks before his murder, submitted an article to us for consideration in this volume. We have included David's article as the first in the reader in memory of a fallen soldier. We humbly dedicate the *Queer African Reader* to all the survivors and victims of multiple oppressions and to the resisters who fight every day with body, spirit and mind to free us all. We salute you.

Note

1   A deliberate obscuring of continued injustices, usually between the global North and the global South, behind an image of liberalism identified through a particular form of 'tolerance' of homosexuality and, to a lesser extent, other gender and sexual identities.

An essay

David Kato Kisule

David Kato submitted this short essay to the editors of the Queer African Reader *just a month before he was murdered on 26 January 2011. David Kato was a teacher and prominent LGBTI activist in Uganda who served as advocacy officer for Sexual Minorities Uganda (SMUG). Just weeks before his death, David won a landmark case against a Ugandan tabloid newspaper that published pictures of 100 people, including David, in an article calling for the hanging of lesbian and gay Ugandans. This essay is published here, with very few edits, in remembrance of David Kato and all those who have fallen in the struggle for LGBTI equality.*

In this country, it is absurd that as the LGBTI community strives to liberate its community to attain not special rights but equal rights like others, they are caught up in a dilemma. Having sodomy laws and oppressive laws (which have long been repealed at their countries of origin!), the massive investment by foreign religious groups in African communities, the recent spread of homophobia promoting sustained hatred and the global reproduction of homophobia institutionally by American Evangelicals, has made matters worse for the survival of the LGBTI community in such countries.

In the name of protecting a traditional family, the Evangelicals recently prompted the drafting of the anti-homosexuality bill in the Ugandan parliament as a private member's bill which affects not only the LGBTI community but, if passed, will have global repercussion to the entire community.

This is why there is need to approach and confront the bill as a global problem with global repercussions. There is also need to use vibrant and outspoken ways to speak about the bill not simply as 'expressing homophobia' but as promoting sustained hatred and violence. There is a great need to raise debate about global systems that currently work to reproduce homophobic authoritarianism throughout the world.

In Uganda, as the LGBTI community has become more visible in regard to demand for inclusion in government health strategies, in the fight to close all gaps of HIV spread, legislators have come up with legislations of criminalising even consensual same sex proposing a death penalty!

This has made many return to the closet and made more vulnerable to the scourge. Some have been arrested, harassed, detained and some have died in the process. Many thrown out of homes, houses, schools and others humiliated (canned in public, raped) like there is institutionalised homophobia since fueling it is by policy makers and the perpetrators have gone on with impunity! Lesbians raped by family members and others in the name of curing them from lesbianism and in process catching HIV!

Such allegations have been made once at Mbale court where Late Brian Pande and Wasukire Fred were charged with carnal knowledge against the order of nature and the police surgeon had this to tell court:

He found one of them with no STD but on second test he found both with STDs.

He found one with a wound at his anus

He found one bleaching his face

So with this concluding that the two guys had had sex together.

In response as the magistrate asked for sureties to give the two court bail, one prominent advocate in court asked the magistrate not to bail the two since within a week the whole town of Mbale was to be full of homosexuals and so the two should die in prison! No wonder Pande died weeks after getting out of Maluku prisons where we had been refused to see them when we visited. Contradicting reports from hospital, his death certificate saying he died of meningitis, which they had not checked for yet, and police surgeon saying that, with a well nourished body, he died of anemia!

It is strange that as we followed up the Mbale case and had not known who Fred was, as we asked for Fred as we had seen in the media, we were told that the person we wanted was a man but has always lived looking like a woman! One wonders if he had lived in the same community up to more than 30 years, what harm had he done! Only fuelling of hate in public by religious fundamentalists and policy makers have sparked off such hate!

Legislation created without the inclusion of the marginalised community is undemocratic, the bill itself is unconstitutional since advocates for discrimination, has not followed or respected the international principles and not followed Ugandan law.

Generally the state and situation is alarming and much there is a great need to fight to deter the bill which is complicated since any civil society to lay a hand in this fight is taken to be promoting homosexuality which is to be criminalised according to the last communication by the minister of foreign affairs!

Thanks to the efforts, courage and struggle of the LGBTI community in Uganda, activists, artists, religious leaders, allies and policy makers across Uganda, Africa and the world, the anti-homosexuality bill in Uganda has not been passed at the time of writing. However, the danger and threat still looms as more and more countries across the continent continue to threaten similar legislation and incite violence and persecution of those perceived to be of non-heteronormative sexualities and transgressing gender identities.

2

'In sisterhood and solidarity': queering African feminist spaces

Awino Okech

This chapter seeks to examine the space for and place of queer organising within 'mainstream African feminist spaces'. This is an ambitious task, given the multiplicity of spaces, actors and agendas. The possibilities of 'mainstream feminist spaces' suggest a multiplicity of vanguard or other sites operating in the periphery of the main. This in itself is a position worth interrogating but does not fall within the purview of this chapter. My objective is not to critique specific feminist movement building sites but rather to offer a theoretical through-line, trace disjunctures and reflect on possibilities. This chapter begins a theoretical conversation that is in no way designed to be comprehensive or representative of the wealth of experiences and literature available.

For my analysis in this chapter, I draw on personal experience – read here as my participation in diverse spaces, some named as feminist activist spaces, others as feminist academic sites, conversations with diverse actors with histories in different forms of organising, some feminist, some explicitly named as Lesbian, Gay, Bisexual, Transgender, Intersex (LGBTI). I draw on these conversations as sites within which various individuals identified as women, feminist, lesbian, researchers have grappled with the meaning of finding a theoretical space, within activist sites to make meaning of the struggle[1] of living and occupying one of many identities that renders them vulnerable not only to specific attacks by the state but also to a particular isolation amongst 'sisters' where 'safety' is constructed as a core component of the space.

The charge of homophobia[2] within the women's movement[3] or latter-day autonomous feminist spaces in various parts of

Africa is not new. These charges were evident in the aftermath of the UN Fourth World Conference on Women in Beijing in 1995, with many an African woman activist flagging that matters 'sexual' were not the priority of African women (Jolly 2000). Sex and sexuality only became a priority in as far as they impacted health, mobility, employment and inheritance (read reproductive rights and violence against women). Debates around bodily autonomy and sexual integrity continue to remain tenuous sites of legislation and activism in many African countries.[4] This can be seen in the development of public discourse and/or legislation on abortion, which continues to draw angry sentiments from both policymaking bodies and the public alike (Klugman and Budlender 2001, Center for Reproductive Rights 2010). In addition, the onslaught of violence against women and men who perform their sexuality differently – against normative heterosexuality – has also recrafted discourses on autonomy. Sexual orientation as an 'advocacy' subject has been cited as holding the potential to hijack the struggle, as has been evident when choices are made over which issues to foreground publicly as political and, I add, ideological within women's rights lobbies.[5]

The distinct organising that occurs across most of Africa between LGBTI work and feminist/women's rights lobbies is equally telling given that LGBTI work has historically drawn on the large body of work I will call, for the purposes of this chapter, feminist theory. Jackson makes a useful distinction below in noting that:

> Queer and feminism converge insofar as both question the inevitability and naturalness of heterosexuality and both, to some extent at least, link the binary divide of gender with that between heterosexuality and homosexuality. Beyond this they differ in emphasis. Queer theorists seek to unsettle heteronormativity, but are relatively unconcerned with what goes on within heterosexual relations. Feminists, because they are concerned with the ways in which heterosexuality depends upon and guarantees gender division, are far more interested in the institutionalisation and everyday practice of heterosexual relations (Jackson 2005: 2).

As a result, choices have been made[6] by individuals and organisations around which political identity to foreground, with some arguing that while they retain a strong connection to feminist theory, ideology and spaces as core to the impetus of their activist work, their lesbian political identity is centred because of the 'silence', lack of 'solidarity' and sometimes overt 'homophobia' within the spaces where it should not be the norm – feminist spaces and/or the women's movement (Hames 2003, Kraak 2002).

In this chapter, I assess whether the conceptual and ideological tools that feminism offers have been used in ways that are neither homogenising nor essentialising within movement building processes. I examine the conceptual approaches that have been deployed in building movements within autonomous feminist spaces. In doing so, I interrogate how ready they are to respond to a growing queer[7] movement.

This is important for three reasons. The first is grounded in the history and uptake of feminism on the one hand and the cause of women on the other. Where feminists and feminism have been ghettoised and labelled in various ways is noted by Adeleye-Fayemi:

> It is very difficult to create and sustain feminist space in many African countries, for several reasons. Feminism is still very unpopular and threatening. The word still conjures up bogeys of wild, naked white women burning their bras, imperialism, domination, an undermining of African culture, etc. Feminists are subjected to ridicule and insults, and in some cases, receive threats to their lives. They are called 'frustrated', 'miserable spinsters', 'castrators', 'home wreckers' and many other undignifying epithets (Adeleye-Fayemi 2000: 8).

Some of the responses to challenging these labels were admittedly reactionary rather than proactive. While they were useful in troubling a Western epistemological hegemony, the emergent discourse instead re-embedded patriarchy and specifically its heteronormative[8] roots (Mikell 1997, Oyewumi 1997, Steady 1981). It also produced a discourse on African feminism that was constructed in opposition to what Western feminism was seen to represent. It did not necessarily evolve new discourses that meaningfully engaged with the contextual realities of Africa. Rather, it became culturally relative. The result was a slew of projects designed to excavate narratives and histories to counter dominant constructions of Africa and 'African women'. African feminism defined in this way remains oppositional and, shaped by imperial constructions and admittedly re-definitions of Africa, it does not evolve organically.[9]

The second recognises that African feminist scholarship in particular and feminist scholarship in general have been largely unavailable to the majority of African students and citizenry interested in engaging in gender analysis beyond the gender and development bytes made popular by the development enterprise. Consequently, some of the epistemological imperatives that I will locate here in terms of their centrality to challenging heteronormativity remain under-utilised in movement building spaces. The mantra of needing to respond to real problems and being relevant to the lived realities of women 'on the ground' has resulted in the construction of a feminist epistemology, which is inaccessible and irrelevant to understanding and responding to women's lived realities. This is a tension that, while consistently recognised, is hardly ever resolved in praxis.

The third considers the current context, which is characterised by massive reversals of both the conceptual and activist gains that feminism offered to understanding socio-economic and political injustices. The developmental and depoliticised manipulation of gender as the conceptual framework that should shape interventions that seek the transformation of gendered norms is often based on principles of equality that seek inclusion rather than transformation.[10] This has contributed in part to energies directed towards remobilising a political stand that centres dismantling patriarchy and associated power both theoretically and in praxis. The reclamation of autonomous spaces where such reflection can occur is a factor of this larger political context. How, therefore, have these latter-day reclamations led to an effective and renewed understanding of patriarchy and a destabilisation of heteronormativity in order to respond to diversity[11] and the transformation of hierarchies of power within the movement and outside?

Thinking movements

> The term 'movement' has become so au courant and loosely used in current discourse as to become almost devoid of meaning ... we need to revisit our definition of movements and be clear about what is and is not a movement. For, it is somewhat troubling how many different phenomena are described as movements (Batliwala 2002: 398).

Batliwala's concerns above reflect not only the imposition of the term movement on any activity that brings together a coalition of organisations but is also indicative of a growing preoccupation with the idea of building people's movements through programmatic interventions by international development organisations. The 'developmentalisation' of movement building is a growing trend that warrants some conceptual interrogation, particularly in as far as these Africa-wide processes actively think through the notion of organising, what models of organising are critical to their social justice objectives and the place of ideology in these agendas.[12]

Social movements emerge as popular contestations of the legality of participation. They therefore aspire to redefine and extend the space and limits of 'acceptable' forms of political, social and economic engagement within society. There is a constant tension between 'the legality of participation' as defined and regulated by powerful institutions and individuals, and popular wishes of the majority of people whose involvement in the governance of their societies is limited by rules of participation. In the last decade, this tension has been heightened by the decreasing space for citizen participation by governments and supra-state institutions and has presented major threats to the space that citizens have for autonomous action.

There are a number of theories that have informed analysis around the development of social movements. Resource mobilisation theorists, for instance, explain collective action in terms of structural opportunities, leadership, ideological and organisational networks (McClurg Mueller and Aldon 1992: 12–16). New social movement theorists offer 'collective identities' as a way of examining how people act in concert, often with the object of achieving a new, distinct or semi-autonomous kind of presence and cultural recognition.

Scholars writing from the perspective of 'new social movements' are interested in the construction, contestation and negotiation of collective identities in the process of political activity. Collective identity refers to 'the (often implicitly) agreed upon definition of membership, boundaries, and activities for the group' (Laraña et al 1994: 15). The existence of collective identity, just like the notion of 'collective consciousness' or 'false consciousness', is difficult to substantiate. The very nature of social movements means that collective identity is a 'moving target', with different definitions dominating at different points in a movement's trajectory.

The 1990s[13] in particular saw an evolution of movements, especially in countries facing transition or going through democratic consolidation processes that led to a change in their logic, dynamic and emphases. According to Alvarez (1998), one of the significant changes has been the modification of an anti-statist posture toward a critical negotiating posture in relation to the state and formal international arenas. This has also meant a shift from a defensive sort of autonomy and a confrontational dynamic toward a logic of negotiation (Alvarez 1998).

Non-governmental organisations have consequently come to be regarded as the vehicle of choice – the magic bullet – for fostering development strategies (Gruhn 1997: 325). The gradual liberalisation of the political environment in which social movements operated and the introduction of gender to the state, prompted in part by some opposition-controlled state governments in the early to mid-1990s, resulted in the need for growing numbers of feminists to formalise their organisations and develop greater policy expertise (Hassim 2004, Salo 2005). The terms of this incorporation was often not feminist-inspired and contributed to a deviation into a discourse on 'gender'. Hassim notes that the impact of institutionalisation of interests led to the creation of a set of specialised institutions that led to 'the consideration of gender out of the realm of politics and into the technical realm of policymaking challenges' (Hassim 2004: 18). This raised a peculiar set of challenges, key among them being that the women's movement does not constitute self-evident subjects, interests and ideological forms. Hassim notes that 'women do not mobilise as women or simply because they are women'; in other words, woman is not a stable subject for mobilisation (Hassim 2004: 5).

Several theorists have pointed out that attempts to disaggregate gender identity are futile, as the cultural meanings of 'woman' shift in relation to the numerous other markers of identity and in different contexts (Butler 1990, Rubin 1975).

> The combination of theoretical and practical difficulties of defining the movement's interests and political identity on the one hand, and the suspicion with which feminism was treated … affected the women's movement's ability to develop political identity relatively autonomous of the ideological power of nationalism (Hassim 2004: 7).

Hassim, while speaking specifically to the South African context, raises a set of conceptual and practical concerns that frame approaches to the development of 'women's movements'. These concerns are encapsulated in the distinction she makes between inclusionary and transformative goals of movements. The former are concerned with:

> inclusion in the state in a piecemeal and often de-politicised fashion, seeking to include women into existing policy frameworks without questioning whether the overall policy directions are appropriate for women, or how new areas of policy or lawmaking should be placed on the agenda (Hassim 2005).

Underpinning the inclusionary approach, according to Hassim, is the desire to maintain some minimal conditions for unity among women through a reluctance to tamper with the structural roots of gender inequality. In addition, the influence of liberal ideologies within this project contributes to fostering the perception that the market and the family lie outside the realm of state intervention (Hassim 2004: 12).

The transformatory approach, on the other hand, pays attention to the ways in which power operates within and between the political, social and economic spheres of specific societies. In effect, it is a political project of transformation (Hassim 2005).

Salo (2005) challenges Hassim's approach as being reliant on distinct binaries (reformist or transformatory) and therefore fails to consider the multiplicity of spaces and challenges that emerging and existing women's movements encounter. Salo argues, therefore, that the reformist and transformatory goals are not mutually exclusive. Both Hassim's (2004) and Salo's (2005) arguments point to the complexity inherent in mobilisation of any kind let alone that named as feminist. Salo (2005) and Hassim (2004) allude to the importance of examining how people come to occupy movements and the meanings attached to particular spaces. It is the tension between mobilisation and the value attached to how spaces are occupied that I am interested in, particularly the ways in which feminist spaces in Africa have sought to cohere ideologically around queer politics generally and movements specifically.

Building feminist spaces

> This space [the feminist movement] is made up of our friendships, networks, our bonds, organisations and our individual and collective feminist energies. This is the space we use to mobilise around our feminist principles, where we hone our analytical skills and where we seek (and sometimes find) answers to our many questions. The belief that this space is needed to make our lives better and easier. This is manifested in our processes of self-discovery, our hopes, our dreams, our aspirations, our yearning for more knowledge and revelations (Adeleye–Fayemi 2000: 6).

> The AFF [African Feminist Forum] was designed as a medium for sharing African feminist thought and practice, providing 'safe spaces' for critical reflection on personal and collective progress, and a springboard for action. People participate in the regional forum and its sister initiatives in their personal capacity. This was an intentional strategy to enable individuals to share and grow their activist beliefs and commitments beyond the limitations of their institutional positions or roles (Horn 2008: 122).

> The 1 in 9 campaign's ideological stance reflects the basic tenet of feminism that the personal is political. Recognising that fundamental truth, the campaign acknowledges that in order to eradicate sexual violence against women, it must actively combat all forms of oppression, including, but not limited to racism and classism as all of these impact women's access to equality and justice. The campaign recognises that manifold forms of oppression, including but not limited to, sexism,

racism, classism and homophobia, converge to deny women access to equality and justice. The campaign will incorporate this consciousness into its policy and practice such that it will shape the manner in which we understand and respond to sexual violence against women (1 in 9 Campaign n.d.).

The excerpts above are drawn from three pieces that reflect broadly on the trajectory of different movement building processes. All of them do so from a conceptual/theoretical basis by thinking through the contexts and triggers that led to particular decisions around how feminist spaces would be constructed. Adeleye-Fayemi (2000) discusses the meaning of building a feminist movement in Africa and the priorities of such a space. In her paper, she reviews the broad spectrum of challenges, both epistemological and methodological, and seeks to bring together the diverse energies, primarily organisational, that have contributed to building a women's movement across Africa. She emphasises the lobbying and advocacy work conducted by women's rights organisations and the gains therein. She also takes a critical stance on transnational feminisms conceptualised through an examination of the notion of global 'sisterhood'. Adeleye-Fayemi (2000) considers the Western intellectual and financial hegemonies and infers how these have in turn led to the need to evolve 'local feminisms'. The questions of class, ethnicity, race and gendered identities do not emerge as core challenges in sustaining an African feminist movement.

Horn in her piece eight years later reflects on the creation of and deliberations within the second African Feminist Forum (the AFF is an autonomous feminist space for individuals self-identified as feminists).[14] She examines the ethos as well as the guiding principles for inclusion in this space. She also highlights, albeit briefly, the discursive tensions that emerge in a space of this nature which brings together diverse groups of women; these largely revolve around sexuality, from the questions of abortion to those of sexual orientation.

The third excerpt, derived from the 1 in 9 Campaign, is representative of a bold attempt to defy the (South African) state through a deliberate grouping of organisations (even though individuals may have spearheaded the work) to offer solidarity to the plaintiff (Kwezi) during the Jacob Zuma rape trial.[15] The ideological basis of the campaign's work, its interpretation as well as in its broader terms of reference, is evident in the excerpt. The 1 in 9 Campaign also sets itself apart – given the 'sporadic' nature of its evolution necessitated by the case and the fact that it brought together organisations and individuals while creating space for working with allies – by maintaining clarity on the place of women's leadership and voice in the campaign (see www.oneinnine.org.za). I suggest that the 1 in 9 Campaign represents, to the extent that is possible, a departure from the inclusion and transformation binary by on the one hand seeking to consciously engage with the spuriousness of gender as a fixed identity from which organising can spring and, on the other hand, overtly acknowledging the reality of homophobia as a form of violence against women and confronting it as one of the intersecting oppressions.

I have selected these three excerpts not because they are representative of a trend but because they offer for the purposes of this chapter a narrative that defines both the evolution of and the continuity in approaches to building and sustaining feminist movements. Two are pan-African in orientation and one national with sub-regional aspirations. All of the pieces, when read in full, allude to the theoretical imperatives that have shaped the evolution of each space or where the ideas that shaped spaces such as the AFF were developed.[16] I draw specifically on the concepts of friendship, sisterhood and solidarity to analyse the ways in which they have been conceptually deployed in the organisation of feminist spaces and/or the mobilisation of diverse actors. I rely on European and American feminist scholarship in the rest of this chapter for two main reasons. The first is informed by the long history of queer organising and subsequent theorising in these contexts. Secondly, while contexts may differ, these scholars at different moments have been embroiled in the same set of political issues that this chapter addresses in addition to being relevant to the current moment in Africa.

Theorising friendships

> Friendship was/is seen as political solidarity; as constitutive of feminist movements and the basis of collective identity. It is seen as a mode of personal support, intimacy and care as such productive of self-identity (Roseneil 2006: 324).

Core to the theory of second wave feminism was a belief that solidarity amongst women was vital. Contrary to Beauvoir's (1968) position around the inherent difficulties of women transcending to true friendships, the emphasis on women's friendships as based on principles of equality rather than inequality, as evident in patriarchal heteronormative structures, was emphasised by Adrienne Rich (1980) and Mary Daly (1978). 'Friendship was argued to offer feminism a focus on the agentic, non-institutional, emotional and pleasurable aspects of social life' (Roseneil 2006: 323).[17] It suggested a different theoretical worldview from one which attended primarily to the structures of gender oppression, to the institutional arenas through which domination and subordination are reproduced:

> Men's homorelational affiliation and preference have historically grounded nation-states, but friendship is characteristically and distinctively interstile, unregulated, voluntary and driven by the pursuit of pleasure. It contrasts with formal, legally regulated and institutionalised personal relations between husband and wife, parent and child and the state (Roseneil 2006: 323).

Importance was placed on friendship by earlier generations of feminists and it became the root or base of feminism as an inherent and fundamental part of feminist movement building (Roseneil 2006: 323). The lens of friendship enabled a challenge to heteronormativity and required that attention was paid to the radical transformation of the organisation of intimate life (Roseneil 2006: 323).

Scholars in analysing the importance of friendships to the suffrage movement argue that friendships became an important part of the suffrage discourse because they differed from the notion of comradeships, which served as the mobilising discourse in the male-dominated socialist movement (Roseneil 2002, Roseneil 2006: 327). The positive attributes of women's friendships had been pathologised, where a passionate love for one's friend came to signal deviant sexual identity. This descriptive deviancy could be associated with the possibility of increased economic independence from men and the identification of patriarchy as an attempt to reign in heterosexual bonds (Roseneil 2006: 327).

The emergence of strong lesbian feminisms led to the interrogation of women's same-sex friendships and whether they could be read as erotic. Smith-Rosenberg (1975) suggests that some of these love relationships were in every sense that except the genital. She argues:

> The essential question is not whether these women had genital contact and can therefore be defined as heterosexual or homosexual. The twentieth-century tendency to view human love and sexuality within a dichotomised universe of deviance and normality, genitality and platonic love, is alien to the emotions and attitudes of the nineteenth century and fundamentally distorts the nature of [these] women's emotional interaction. These letters are significant because they force us to place such female love in a particular historical context. There is every indication that these four women, their husbands and families – all eminently respectable and socially conservative – considered such love both socially acceptable and fully compatible with heterosexual marriage. Emotionally and cognitively, their heterosocial and their homosocial worlds were complementary (Smith-Rosenberg 1975: 8).

Rich (1980) develops this analysis through her work on lesbian histories through her proposal on a lesbian continuum. Rich argued for a view of women's same-sex friendships as falling within this continuum and therefore evidence of same-sex 'loverships'. She challenged clinical definitions of lesbians, arguing for a move beyond the actual sexual genital experience (Rich 1980: 51–3).

I suggest that the analytical approach taken by both Rich (1980) and Smith-Rosenberg (1975), albeit differently, plays into dominant constructions of women as passionless in the emphasis of these relationships or loverships as asexual. The erasure of sexuality as key to lesbian identity as well as the denial of the specificity of lesbian lives and history have been raised in several critiques of her work (Roseneil 2006: 330). I argue that the continuum that both Rich (1980) and Smith-Rosenberg (1975) suggest is one that pervades current activist discourse and is manifest in the construction of women's friendships – the fundaments of 'sister' comrade – as central to mainstream feminist autonomous spaces. The emphasis on the individual, safety and rejuvenation as critical elements for creating and fostering autonomous spaces is critical in this regard. Consequently, same-sex relationships among women are situated as part of a heteronormative continuum and not as distinct performances of 'other' sexualities. The erasure of sexuality as part of women's friendships on the one hand and the conflation of women's friendships with lesbian sexualities on the other raises a set of challenges in the conceptualisation of queer identities and how solidarity across movements is in turn offered.

Building solidarity

The evolution towards adopting solidarity as opposed to 'sisterhood' was based on a critique that surfaced the absence of race and class as analytical through lines in building movements (hooks 1984, Mohanty 2003). The concept of 'solidarity' was argued to be strategically more powerful. Scholars such as hooks (1984) and Mohanty (2003) argued that solidarity rested not on the assumption of sameness of oppression and allowed for a greater differentiation (for instance, as far as class and ethnicity were concerned) of the roots of oppression. The inner bond that would naturally lead to solidarity was not a pregiven, stable phenomenon, so they maintained, but should be constructed in practical political struggles.

However, 'solidarity', as it is used today, claims to rest on unconditioned foundations. An essentialist approach to solidarity suggests that relationships are a manifestation of something authentic; a foundationalist perspective holds that women should feel solidarity because of the inner bond between women (hooks 1984: 59). Understood as such, solidarity creates a pre-discursive subject, but most importantly, it stands as a precondition for action. In other words, a group has to feel solidarity before it can successfully act. I argue that, while useful, the way in which solidarity and sisterhood are deployed is limiting in fostering a politic that challenges patriarchy in meaningful ways.

There are two distinct ways in which solidarity offered around the crisis of violence directed towards people identified as gay and lesbian is constructed. The first is conducted within a human rights framework that deals with it purely on the basis of a broad spectrum of rights, which if revoked by a rogue state renders the claimants powerless. The second set of responses are those that are willing to confront the possibilities of these relationships as part of a heterosexual continuum, as an area where historically women's friendships have always 'strayed' but not stayed, where the erotic acts as a mechanism for dealing with the 'limitations' of the primary heterosexual relationship bonds of marriage and family, thereby simultaneously invisibilising and/or 'understanding' lesbian relationships as extensions of heterosexual female bonds.

Women's friendships are recognised for their ability to challenge heteroreality – a reality not dependent on men. This draws on the discourse of sisterhood of the 1970s where elective bonds of friendship between women proved vital in sustaining feminist communities. The destabilisation that these friendships caused in terms of discourse was to move away from a heterorelational frame. As opposed to devaluing them it gave those bonds primacy, they were not seen as frivolous and that in itself was transgressive and radical. It showed that care and support could occur outside the family, within the spaces where friendships and solidarities are forged (Roseneil 2006: 331). It nonetheless resulted in the conflation of that discourse with lesbian sexuality and related political organising.

The homorelational friendships (among women) that have progressively been perceived as an imperative to building and sustaining feminist movements occur within the confines of a heteronormative framework, where feminist spaces provide a reprieve from the constraints of marriage and heterorelational structures such as the state, university and religion, which activists encounter on a daily basis. Heteronormativity remains under-problematised and the homorelational friendships developed in these spaces as part of solidarity remain at the level of support and do not move towards destabilising the heteronormativity from which reprieve is sought. The binaries of man–woman, heterosexuality as sexual orientation and not as an organisational principle for labour, economics and power, shape the analysis of the state, the economy and the transformation envisioned.

This approach, like Adrienne Rich's (1980) lesbian continuum, decentres sexual identity and undervalues the centrality of sexuality as a core part of lesbian relationships, thereby leaving heterosexuality and heteronormativity as intact analytical and organising frameworks. A cursory examination of feminist responses aimed at countering and/or interrogating state tyranny against 'deviant sexualities' views state responses as diversionary tactics that are geared towards moving us away from pressing democratisation concerns by recalcitrant and autocratic states on the one hand or as private affairs that should not be 'regulated' on the other (Tamale 2010, Nakaweesi and Mugisha 2009). The efficacy of such an argument in silencing detractors cannot be underestimated but its limitations are glaring for three main reasons.

The first is that it dismantles the feminist dictum of the personal is political as well as analyses that have sought to dismantle the public/private dichotomy. It does this by situating same-sex relationships within the private domain and as a space that should not be 'regulated'. This flies in the face of the theories and experiences of domestic violence, one of the most successful sites of feminist activism across the globe. Secondly, it limits the 'performance' of these relationships to the 'private' and not the 'public' domain through a 'don't ask don't tell' approach. Finally, these analyses underproblematise heterosexuality – its role in organising family, labour and the economy, its function in institutionalising heteronormativity and through this 'arranging' an 'acceptable secular' state. The destablisation that same-sex sexualities portend – in a context where the state, the church and governance rely on male homorelational friendships as the basis for nation-state social contracts – demands a violent counter response, which is what state-instigated violence is about. Heterosexuality therefore acts as a means for maintaining oppressive patriarchal societal order via the family, the church and 'culture' (McClintock 1995, Burton 1999, Stoler 2002).

Heternormativity also becomes the means to reinforce particular hierarchies within heterosexualities. Seidman (2005: 40) notes that heteronormativity 'not only establishes a heterosexual/ homosexual hierarchy but also creates hierarchies among heterosexualities', resulting in 'hegemonic and subordinate forms of heterosexuality'.

These distinctions ignore the refusal to collaborate with heteronormativity, as Rich notes:

> The history of women who – as witches, femmes seules, marriage resisters, spinsters, autonomous widows, and/or lesbians – have managed on varying levels not to collaborate [with heterosexual norms]. It is this history, precisely, from which feminists have so much to learn and on which there is overall such blanketing silence (Rich 1994 [1980]: 50).

Queering[18] feminist spaces

Feminist movements have had a long history of attempts to overcome the exclusions of women in mainstream feminism – women of colour, lesbians, bisexuals and transgender, indigenous women, non-English-speaking women, women of the global South (Johnson 2005: 21–37). According to Harcourt (2009), dealing with exclusion can only be possible through an acknowledgement that feminism is built on the 'politics of difference' that can exist alongside the 'politics of friendship'. However, there are multiple, even conflicting, identities among feminist movements (Harcourt 2009: 73). This approach takes seriously the theory of intersectionality that looks at how different socially and culturally constructed categories interact, causing the complex levels of inequalities.

Intersectionality is an 'analysis claiming that systems of race, social class, gender, sexuality, ethnicity, nation, and age form mutually constructing features of social organisation, which shape Black women's experiences and, in turn, are shaped by Black women' (Collins 2000: 299).

Intersectionality draws on postmodern theoretical discourse, in particular its critique of essentialism and the deconstruction of stable subjects, including a feminist subject ('women'). It therefore poses a challenge to essentialist feminist theory and politics: if 'there is nothing about being "female" that naturally binds women' (Haraway 1991: 155), then who should feminist movements represent? hooks argues that solidarity cannot grow of itself but needs a sustained, ongoing commitment. Mohanty, writing on transnational feminism, adds that solidarity should not be seen as a pregiven phenomenon but should be constituted in practice, through the process of working together. Thus the challenge is 'to construct the universal on the basis of particulars/ differences' (Mohanty 2003: 7). Haraway (1991), hooks (1984) and Mohanty (2003) move away from a politics of essentialism to propose a politics of coalition building and affinity.

> The idea of affinity groups comes from the anarchist and work-ers movements of late 19th century Spain, who later fought against fascism during the Spanish Civil War. At the same time that the affinity group model was being adopted by the Anti-war movement in the 1960s, small 'consciousness raising' groups of women were forming. From the late 1960s onwards there was a 'transformation of feminist notions of political intervention'. Feminists were breaking with 'both traditional lobbying tactics and to some extent (…) left-wing opposi-tional politics', which were dominated by men and offered no space for women's agendas. This was recognised as the sort of political practice and organising that would make the women's liberation movement 'self-starting, self-regulating and self-directing' (Whelehan 1995: 8).

Affinity groups have most recently been associated with the anti-globalisation movement and the ways in which young people get involved in social movements. The movements' direction and momentum would not come from following trusted leaders or experts, but rather from getting people to interact and ana-lyse their situation themselves (Coote and Campbell 1982: 23). Contrary to the identity based on solidarity, affinity does not have to be founded on an underlying consensus among members of the group, but political identities are formed in an act of negating the constructed 'them'[19] (Lloyd 2005: 163). To negate the constructed 'them' means drawing a political frontier between 'we' and 'them' through the act of articulation. New subject positions are named and accounted for through the negation of certain 'them', for example, as anti-racism, anti-sexism, anti-capitalism.

Postmodern feminism that challenges the validity of organising primarily on the basis of gender identity has been perceived as a dead end for political feminism as a movement. Gender is seen as a construction and therefore challenges the existence of 'woman' as a category. According to this argument, due to the lack of 'a shared experience of oppression – an identity – political demands cannot be articulated' (Lloyd 2005: 55). However, if affinity groups are a model that can be effectively deployed to destabilise heteronormativity and gender as organising principles, what kind of political identities are we speaking about? Wieringa (2009: 36) asks: 'Do resistance or oppositional identities form a better vantage point from which to organise feminist politics? This seems indeed most likely, but then the next question is how to move from opposition, resistance, negation, to positive demands, to an agenda for change?'

The challenge remains how to create an affinity group model that is sustainable and is able to deal with the inevitable hierarchy of professionalisation that funders require, yet remains flexible and transparent and able to mobilise the enthusiasm of diverse groups. This not only requires theorising political mobilisation that the affinity model allows for, but also a new feminist politics: idealist yet pragmatic, professional, transparent, able to build alliances with diverse groups as well as established interests.

The potential for effective solidarity[20] between an emerging queer movement and mainstream autonomous feminist spaces can only occur if the fundamental theories that structure the spaces shift. These theories have to be able to reconceptualise the meaning of homosocial friendships and the tenuous relationship with queer identities and sexualities. The 'solidarity' offered towards the growing queer movement in Africa cannot be seen as one that is simply key to building bridges across movements but as one that destabilises heteronormativity by dismantling how the family, the state, the economy reproduce normative heterosexuality. This approach begins to separate same-sex friendships/'experiments' and same-sex desires, thereby giving credence to the sexual and political identity ascribed to being queer and separating it from one that co-exists neatly within a heteronormative paradigm. Rather, it has to be one that troubles the primary theorising within feminist activist spaces, which takes as given gender identity (man/woman) as a framework from which to understand, confront and dismantle patriarchy.

Notes

1 Struggle is used to refer to the tensions manifest in navigating multiple identifies, some political, some viewed as personal, some labelled as risky and in conflict. For instance, where a gay woman holds public office but her gayness is not a political issue, the result is often a muting of her sexual identity or making it public and turning that into a political issue. In most African contexts the two do not neatly co-exist.

2 This could mean anything from a 'silence' on sexual orientation and heteronormativity within feminist activist discourse to overt references to an othering – 'they' – or the reticence in overtly identifying and engaging with LGBTI political struggles when called upon. In Kenya, for instance, the most vocal pro-choice lobbies have been gynaecologists rather than women's rights activists.

3 I do not delve into a discussion on the existence and viability of a women's movement. This has been ably discussed most recently by AWID through their movement building research project (see www.awid. org). I make the distinction between a women's movement and feminist spaces based on further analysis in this chapter, which traces the division between a women's movement that draws on feminism as its organising ideology and those who distance themselves from it.

4 Women's rights activists have been latecomers in pro-choice debates and, in negotiating with the state and other sites of power such as the church, choice has effectively been erased.

5 I draw here from conversations with queer women who have had to negotiate for mention of sexual rights and choice in meaningful ways within conference statements and declarations. The candidness about the distraction that sexual orientation portends was offered because their queer identity was not foregrounded as being political.

6 I draw here from conversations with activists in sub-Saharan Africa who work with LGBTI organisations or are self-identified LGBTI activists as opposed to being women who are lesbians.

7 The word queer here is similar to Jolly's interpretation of it as constituting a rejection of the binary distinction between homo and heterosexual, and therefore a conceptualisation of sexualities as non-essential and transitional (Jolly 2000: 84).

8 'Heteronormative' is used here to refer to institutions, structures of understanding and practical orientations that make heterosexuality seem not only coherent, i.e. organised as sexuality, but also privileged.

9 More recent scholarly work in this arena has produced more nuanced analysis (see among others Bennett 2008, Lewis 2003, Mekgwe 2008, Mupotsa 2008, Pereira 2009, Salo 2005).

10 See a fuller discussion on this by Hassim (2004).

11 I use diversity here to highlight existing binaries that ascribe otherness to homoerotic desires, for instance.

12 For a fuller discussion on this, see Batliwala (2002) and AWID's movement building research project and extensive resources on the subject at www.awid.org.

13 A factor of the end of the cold war.
14 While Horn in her piece is careful in her use of non-gender-specific language through the word 'people', the space targets people who are self-identified as women, both biologically and in performance, in the sense that even if they were lesbian they would identify as lesbian women rather than lesbian men.
15 In 2005, the then South African deputy president, Jacob Zuma, was charged with the rape of Kwezi. He was later acquitted of all charges. The formation of the 1 in 9 Campaign was spurred by this case.
16 Adeleye-Fayemi's contribution to a number of African feminist movement building initiatives can be gleaned from her piece.
17 Roseneil is privileged here for the extensive analysis she offers on the theories of friendship based on a history of feminist analysis around the British suffrage movement among others. The theoretical literature on women and friendships unfortunately remains limited to a Northern context (see also Roseneil 1995, Roseneil 2000, Roseneil 2002).
18 Queer is used here to mean impact on/affect.
19 See Honor Ford-Smith's (1997) candid account of the meaning of building a movement through the praxis of an organisation. Her experiences as a founder member of Sistren – a Jamaican women's theatre collective – are useful in thinking through the meaning of negotiating power, class and funding.
20 Solidarity is used here to refer to the possibilities of a merger of ideological and political interests in the pursuit of equity and non-discrimination on the basis of sex, gender, sexual orientation, creed, race or ethnicity as outlined in a multitude of rights-based frameworks.

References

Adeleye-Fayemi, B. (2000) 'Creating and sustaining feminist space in Africa: local global challenges in the 21st century', paper prepared for the 4th Annual Dame Nita Barrow Lecture, Toronto

Alvarez, S.E. (1998) 'Advocating feminism: the Latin American NGO "boom"', paper presented for the annual Schomburg-Moreno lecture, begun by the Latin American Studies Program at Mount Holyoke College

Batliwala, S. (2002) 'Grassroots movements as transnational actors: implications for global civil society', *Voluntas: International Journal of Voluntary and Nonprofit Organisations*, 13(4): 393–410

Beauvoir, S. de (1968) *The Second Sex*, New York, H.M. Parshley

Bennett, J. (2008) 'Editorial: researching for life: paradigms and power', *Feminist Africa*, 11: 1–12

Burton, A. (ed) (1999) *Gender, Sexuality and Colonial Modernities*, New York, Routledge

Butler, J. (1990) *Gender Trouble: Feminism and the Subversion of Identity*, New York, Routledge

Center for Reproductive Rights (CRR) (2010) *In Harm's Way: The Impact of Kenya's Restrictive Abortion Law*, CRR, New York

Collins, P.H. (2000) *Black Feminist Thought: Knowledge, Consciousness, and the Politics of Empowerment*, New York, Routledge

Coote, A. and Campbell, B. (1982) *Sweet Freedom: The Struggle for Women's Liberation*, Oxford, Basil Blackwell

Daly, M. (1978) *Gyn/Ecology: The Metaethics of Radical Feminism*, Boston, MA, Beacon Press

Gruhn, I.V. (1997) 'NGOs in partnership with the UN: a new fix or a new problem for African development?', *Global Society*, 11(3): 325–37

Hames, M. (2003) 'The women's movement and lesbian and gay struggles in South Africa', *Feminist Africa*, (2), http://agi.ac.za/sites/agi.ac.za/files/fa_2_standpoint_4.pdf, accessed 30 November 2012

Haraway, D.J. (1991) *Simians, Cyborgs, and Women: The Reinvention of Nature*, Free Association Books, London

Harcourt, W. (2009) 'Sexual and bodily integrity', in Dütting, G., Harcourt, W., Lohmann, K., McDevitt-Pugh, L., Semeniuk, J. and Wieringa, S. (eds) *The European Feminist Forum: A Herstory 2004–2008*, Amsterdam, Aletta Institute for Women's History

Hassim, S. (2004) 'Voices, hierarchies and spaces: reconfiguring the women's movement in democratic South Africa', part of the research project 'Globalisation, marginalisation and new social movements in post-apartheid South Africa', University of KwaZulu Natal

Hassim, S. (2005) 'Terms of engagement: South African challenges', in *Feminist Africa*, (4): 10–28

hooks, b. (1984) *Feminist Theory from Margin to Center*, Boston, MA, South End Press

Horn, J. (2008) 'Feeding freedom's hunger: reflections on the second African Feminist Forum', *Feminist Africa*, (11): 121–6

Jackson, S. (2005) 'The social complexity of heteronormativity: gender, sexuality and heterosexuality', paper presented at the conference 'Heteronormativity – a fruitful concept?', Trondheim

Johnson, R. (2005) 'Gender, race, class, and sexual orientation: theorising the intersections', in MacDonald, G., Osborne, R.L. and Smith, C.C. (eds) *Feminism, Law, Inclusion. Intersectionality in Action*, Toronto, Sumach Press

Jolly, S. (2000) 'Queering development: exploring the links between same-sex sexualities, gender and development', *Development*, 8(1): 78–88

Klugman, B. and Budlender, D. (2001) 'Advocating for abortion access: eleven country studies', Women's Health Project, University of Witswatersrand

Kraak, G. (2002) 'Homosexuality and the South African left: the ambiguities of exile', paper presented at WISER, Johannesburg

Laraña, E., Johnston, H. and Gusfield, J.R. (1994) *New Social Movements: From Ideology to Identity*, Philadelphia, Temple University Press

Lewis, D. (2003) 'Editorial', *Feminist Africa*, (2): 1–7

Lloyd, M. (2005) *Beyond Identity Politics. Feminism, Power and Politics*, Sage Publications, London

McClintock, A. (1995) *Imperial Leather: Race, Gender and Sexuality in the Colonial Contest*, New York and London, Routledge

McClurg Mueller, C. and Aldon, M. (1992) *Frontiers in Social Movement Theory*, New Haven, Yale University Press

Mekgwe, P. (2008) 'Theorising African feminism(s): the "colonial question"', *QUEST: An African Journal of Philosophy/Revue Africaine de Philosophie*, (20): 11–22

Mikell, G. (1997) *African Feminism: The Politics of Survival in Sub-Saharan Africa*, Philadelphia, University of Pennsylvania Press

Mohanty, C. (2003) *Feminism Without Borders: Decolonising Theory, Practicing Solidarity*, Chapel Hill, NC, Duke University

Mupotsa, D. with Mhishi, L. (2008) 'This little rage of poetry: researching gender and sexuality', *Feminist Africa*, (11): 97–107

Nakaweesi-Kimbugwe, S. and Mugisha, F. (2009) 'Bahati's bill: A convenient distraction for Uganda's government', Pambazuka News, (453), http://www.pambazuka.org/en/category/comment/59556, accessed 30 November 2012

One in Nine Campaign (n.d.) 'Terms of reference', http://www.oneinnine.org.za/23.page, accessed 27 December 2012

Oyewumi, O. (1997) *The Invention of Women: Making an African Sense of Western Gender Discourse*, Minneapolis, University of Minnesota Press

Pereira, C. (2009) 'Interrogating norms: feminists theorising sexuality, gender and heterosexuality', *Development*, 52(1): 18–24

Rich, A. (1994 [1980]) 'Compulsory heterosexuality and lesbian existence', *Blood, Bread, and Poetry*, Norton Paperback, New York.

Roseneil, S. (1995) *Disarming Patriarchy: Feminism and Political Action at Greenham*, Milton Keynes, Open University Press

Roseneil, S. (2000) *Common Women, Uncommon Practices: The Queer Feminisms of Greenham*, London, Continuum International Publishing Group

Roseneil, S. (2002) 'The heterosexual/homosexual binary: past, present and future', in Richardson, D. and Seidman, S. (eds) *The Lesbian and Gay Studies Handbook*, London, Sage Publications

Roseneil, S. (2006) 'Foregrounding friendship: feminist pasts, feminist futures', in Davis, K., Evans, M. and Lorber, J. (2006) (eds) *Handbook of Gender and Women's Studies*, London, Sage Publications

Rubin, G. (1975) 'The traffic in women: notes on the "political economy" of sex', in Reiter, R.R. (ed) *Toward an Anthropology of Women*, New York, Monthly Review

Salo, E. (2005) 'Multiple targets, mixing strategies: complicating feminist analysis of contemporary South African women's movements', *Feminist Africa* (4): 64–71

Seidman, S. (2005) 'From polluted homosexual to the Normal Gay: changing patterns of sexual regulation in America', in Ingraham, C. (ed) *Thinking Straight: New Work in Critical Heterosexuality Studies*, New York, Routledge

Smith, H.F. (1997) 'Ring ding in a tight corner', in Alexander, J. and Mohanty, C. (eds) *Feminist Genealogies, Colonial Legacies, Democratic Futures*, New York, Routledge

Smith-Rosenberg, C. (1975) 'The female world of love and ritual: relations between women in nineteenth-century America', *Signs*, 1(1): 1–29

Steady, F.C. (1981) *The Black Woman Cross-Culturally*, Cambridge, MA, Schenkman

Stoler, A. (2002) *Carnal Knowledge and Imperial Power: Race and the Intimate in Colonial Rule*, Los Angeles, University of California Press

Tamale, S. (2010) 'Human rights impact assessment of Uganda's anti-homosexuality bill', Pambazuka News, (465), http://pambazuka.org/en/category/features/61423, accessed 30 November 2012

Whelehan, I. (1995) *Modern Feminist Thought: From the Second Wave to 'Post-Feminism'*, Edinburgh, Edinburgh University Press

Wieringa, S. (2009) 'From solidarity to affinity and feminist communal identities', in Dütting, G., Harcourt, W., Lohmann, K., McDevitt-Pugh, L., Semeniuk, J. and Wieringa, S. (eds) *The European Feminist Forum: A Herstory 2004–2008*, Amsterdam, Aletta Institute for Women's History

3

Postcolonial discourses of queer activism and class in Africa

Lyn Ossome

Introduction

Africa is at present confronted with neo-colonial phenomena of globalised capitalism and globalised racism (Schuhmann 2007: 122), a fact that more than ever suggests the need for ingenious strengthening of movements around a politics backed by a conscious engagement with diverse locations and histories of suffering. The shift by African states towards democratisation, beginning in the structural adjustment period of the late 1980s, is historically important for, among other factors, the impact it had in creating visibility around queer activism and class struggles. The democratic period was underlined by an intensified demand for liberties, which on the one hand facilitated a 'coming out' of lesbian, gay, bisexual, transgender and intersex (LGBTI) rights,[1] and on the other unleashed a wave of competing fundamentalist and moralistic claims that are still facilitating a veiled backlash.[2] On this Neville Hoad writes:

> In interesting relation to their transnational circulation, lesbian and gay human rights have emerged as a new but vulnerable factor in the postapartheid national hegemony of South Africa, where their provisionally successful institution can be accounted for by activists' insistence on their national character against their transnational form. Their temporality is equally baffling. They have surfaced at the moment of transnationalism, although in southern Africa this moment is also the delayed moment of postcoloniality. Zimbabwe became independent in 1981 and Namibia in 1991; South Africa held

its first democratic elections in 1994. These rights have been committedly staged as a legacy of colonialism and as a means of facilitating a new identity form that threatens national values. They have become a relic of the colonial past that must be transcended and/or a sign of the transnational future that must be feared (1999: 561–2).

One unfortunate casualty of this opening up of political spaces has been the diminishing engagement with class analysis by social justice activists. While religious fundamentalists have aligned with state power, LGBTI groups have been left out in the cold: the intensification of homophobia, largely existing in the context of economic liberalism and religious fundamentalism in Africa, speaks to this state of affairs. Many oppressive social relations such as those of racism and homophobia involve systematic misrecognition. While this shift from distribution to recognition has been progressive in highlighting hitherto ignored forms of oppression, some observers have regretted the fact that it seems to have been coupled with an abandonment of concern for class politics, which has been associated with the politics of distribution (Phillips 1999). The retreat from class was not merely illogical but decidedly untimely, for it coincided with the rise of attempts by neoliberals to legitimise class inequalities.

Among many discourses framing the renewed wave of homophobia across Africa at present is one which locates itself broadly within two conservative strands of thinking. One strand is a civil conversation engaging with questions of the very right of existence of queer people, and is primarily political in context. The other, while tacitly recognising this right, additionally constructs same-sex relations around its materiality and ties freedom and choice to issues of accessibility: this thinking implicitly speaks to social and economic rights as the emergent frontier of struggle for LGBTI groups. I seek in this chapter to demonstrate the urgent necessity to foreground this latter strand, and illustrate the ways in which the political, albeit important, is being used by queer activists in Africa to submerge an all-encompassing socio-economic rights struggle.

We can observe in many countries that in times of socio-economic tension, citizens' rights and specifically the protection of groups thought to be more vulnerable, such as women, immigrants and other minorities, become scapegoats in the name of patriotism, which often includes references to an assumedly shared homogenous tradition. It is the abject 'other' (immigrants, perverts, criminals, HIV/AIDS positives, prostitutes, homeless – the dangerous classes) that is made responsible for threatening the inner peace rather than, for instance, hegemonic notions of violent masculinity or specific class interests (Schuhmann 2010: 100). Although there is a tendency to lay the blame on states alone, nationalist and ethnic processes too, depending on their objectives, might project forces that are hegemonic within society, and in so doing disrupt the state's own power to protect minorities. Nationalist, ethnic and morally bound hegemonies (espousing fundamentalist religious and puritan ideological notions of decolonisation) employ a variety of tactics aimed at displacing and rendering invisible the active voices of non-conforming groups. The effect of this is to eschew them from class struggles and, effectively, from political participation.[3]

In Africa, such tactics have included the widespread use of alienating myths, violence and outright discrimination in ways that directly destabilise and undermine participation of those members of LGBTI communities who are also members of oppressed and disadvantaged classes. In addition, heterosexist solidarity has been used to obscure class differences, much to the detriment of poor people of all cultural identities. These tactics also severely circumscribe the ability to access and legitimately establish rights claims even in countries that have achieved nominal success with legislation that prohibits discrimination, such as South Africa. I shall illustrate all three points, drawing examples from ongoing conversations and contestations on the continent.

Destabilising myths, queer activism and erasure from memory

A growing body of research, activism and art has comprehensively demonstrated the falseness of the 'fact' of Africans' exclusive heterosexuality.[4] Worth interrogating, therefore, are the ways in which 'elitist' and 'westocentric' labelling is being directed towards queer activism and activists. Highlighting this strand of thinking in scholarship, Amory (1997) observes that the studied avoidance of research on homosexuality and the downright heterosexual panic concerning the issue are best captured by the recurring and insistent refrain, 'There is no homosexuality in Africa!', often accompanied by the similarly insidious accusation that homosexuality is a 'western perversion' imposed upon or adopted by African populations. This view of queerness partly stems from an exclusionary heterosexual citizenship that ignores the fact that queer represents a resistance to anything that is socially defined as normal, and in that sense queer may exclude some gay and lesbian practices that have a 'normative perspective' or may include other experiences that are not explicitly sexual (Jagose 1996: 98). It is a highly prejudicial view that alienates from the mainstream and invisibilises legitimate claims of economic and political inclusion and diversity by queer groups.

There is a dialectical process in the seeming hegemonic economic location of sexual minority groups within states. Evans observes that there are legal and moral constraints which prevent a variety of marginal or minority groups from pursuing their religious and cultural beliefs or economic needs in equal measures. The state's management of these 'moral aliens', who are to be found in the marginal matrix of citizenship, is exercised in social, political and economic arenas and results in both formal and informal discrimination. This is the twilight zone between the liberal and republican constructions of citizenship, where religious, ethnic and sexual minorities are located – outside the national 'moral community' but inside the civic nation. To those who can afford it, this is not a completely closed-off system (1993: 6). Sexual minority groups developed, as a result, socioeconomic 'community' infrastructures of varying degrees of complexity around their identities. They organised to obtain further housing, insurance, medical, parenting, marital rights and so on, and spent a significant proportion of their income on, for example, gay commodities and distinctive lifestyles in segregated or specifically gay social and sexual territories (1993: 8). Among African LGBTI activists, retreat into similar enclaves[5] has been enforced largely by high insecurity in the form of sexual, physical, emotional and psychological brutalisation. At the heart of this retreat is the imperative to survive economically as well as socially and culturally. Strict moral boundaries in society generate communities bounded by immorality and illegality, and which in negotiating their citizenship claims adopt economic mechanisms which appear paradoxically to eschew active participation within broader political and social rights paradigms that most legitimately represent their claims as citizens. Popular movements are particularly vulnerable to reductionist tendencies, the result of 'identity politics'. The problem with those who pursue identity politics is that they end up obscuring class issues and in the process lose strategic focus and potential for broader alliances. As Yuval-Davis notes, identity politics tend not only to homogenise and naturalise social categories and groupings, but also deny shifting boundaries of identities and internal power differences and conflicts of interest (1997: 119).

Destabilising myths

Class struggles represent one site within which myths regarding homosexuality are reproduced and retrenched. The perpetuation of homogenising notions that subsume all queer people under an alienating and contentious category is, to this extent, curious. The myth of homosexuality as being elitist, itself a prejudicial and racially manipulated classification, seeks to strip sexual identity of its intersections with gender, racial or ethnic subjectivities, and in so doing essentially diminishes the range of issues upon which sexual minority groups might ground their struggles. The effect is to deny LGBTIs who are poor the support and solidarity of other constituencies that are similarly economically marginalised – for instance the extent of lesbians' specific vulnerabilities as women, or as wage labourers, or as ethnic minorities, may be concealed under such homogenising discourses of elitism. The resulting distortion is the appearance of an independent history of cultures that inform institutions, systems and ideological conceptions of the nature and location of our oppression as African people on the continent and in the diaspora.

It is important to ask who benefits from the production of these myths and distortions.[6] It may be argued that the ruling elites with the support of state power seek through this divisive discourse to isolate a minority elite class, identified by sexual orientation, which they falsely identify with global forces of oppression. The majority marginalised groups whom they target though this type of moralising are sold into the belief of fighting, together with the state, a common enemy – an oppressive global force. Queer people are targeted not so much because of their identity, as to deliberately continue the ideological conscription of subjects, subvert the reality of shared struggles, and sustain the class oppression of the majority. There are many tactics at the disposal of the state and ruling classes to achieve this end, of which the most dramatic being witnessed at present is physical and institutionalised violence.[7]

Violence

Sexualised forms of violence that penetrate societies derive from a structural base that profiles those it targets along lines of class, gender, race and ethnicity. Sexual violence directed towards queer individuals may be understood in one sense as a political weapon in the hands of disenfranchised groups that are themselves victims of the structural violence in an unequal economic system which induces violence among the excluded or economically marginalised. However, the effectiveness of this violence in reality functions within a system that sub-profiles individuals within these categories: thus, heteronormative identification of individuals within racial, ethnic and class categories places self-identifying queer people outside of the matrices within which structural violence is understood and addressed.

Marxist feminists have critiqued violence against women in relation to capitalist production and reproduction, and its capacity to disrupt the reproduction of labour power. Though this reproduction is predominantly pegged on wages, it has also been shown to rely on the attainment and enjoyment of certain fundamental rights and freedoms. This type of understanding has enabled the emergence of a holistic response towards the economic oppression of women that spans micro/macroeconomic policy, political representation and legal encoding in national, regional and international statutes and conventions. Yet the sub-profiling mentioned above, and the heteronormative ideological reproduction of labour, mean that lesbian and bisexual women, for instance, remain circumscribed from claiming similar victories by the deliberate segregation or failure to link homophobic violence to overall patterns of economic violence in society.

One clear demonstration of this point is the recent denial of observer status to the Coalition of African Lesbians (CAL) in the African Commission on Human and People's Rights (ACHPR). The commission declined the application without giving any reasons. By ignoring CAL's stated objectives, which are rooted in the advancement of gender equality, social justice and the protection of the rights of particularly vulnerable individuals (CHR 2010), this ruling illustrates one of the ways in which the pursuance of convenient, conservative political aims can serve to deepen economic discrimination against all women, and not just those ostensibly targeted by it, for in this case how does the law calibrate the claim to rights other than through its non-discriminatory application on the basis of gender? The precise definition of the term 'gender' itself remains unspecified within the statute books of the ACHPR.

Erasure

Another illustration that should be related to economic violence is the vote in 2010 at the United Nations General Assembly in favour of an amendment which removes sexual orientation from an anti-execution resolution. Morocco and Mali, two socially conservative Muslim African countries, introduced in the General Assembly's human rights committee an amendment to the resolution, which comes up every two years, to condemn extrajudicial, summary and arbitrary executions and other killings. This vote is significant if understood within the context of economic scarcity and violence. Even though the net number of new conflicts arising out of Africa has significantly decreased over the last two decades, the threat of civil wars looms large in our shaky democracies and struggling economies, from Sudan to Ivory Coast, Kenya to Zimbabwe. Recent popular movements against unemployment, poverty and corruption of the ruling elite in North Africa paint an even more profound picture of the class struggles gaining momentum on the continent. Within the economic contexts of conflicts, many observers have noted that poverty and violence go hand in hand, and that there is a strong negative relationship between economic growth and crime across countries. Sexual minority groups become particularly vulnerable to scapegoating and witch-hunting during times of economic hardship.[8] Their explicit exclusion from the General Assembly resolution, which specifies violence as being a function of race, nationality, ethnicity, religion, language, refugee/indigenous status, denies structure to the broad nature of homophobic violence. In addition, replacing the specification of discrimination on the basis of 'sexual orientation' with the more generalising phrase 'discriminatory reasons on any basis' is demonstrative of a deliberate erasure and obscuring of the nexus that exists between violence, sexual identity and class. In the event of economic shocks such as highlighted above, it can also strip homophobic violence of its economic and social contexts, restricting resistance to a political battleground (of rights) and isolating it from its economic roots and validity as a class issue.

Economic liberalism and fundamentalisms

Today more than ever, the reality that individuals occupy multiple identities that can shift, merge or emerge is acknowledged, as is the need to map class struggles within this complex reality. Arguably most contentious among these is sexuality, at the heart of which lies the principle of choice, which is in turn based upon the principle of freedom. As such, any limitation on choice is an assault on the idea of freedom. At the nexus between freedom and choice is presumed the ability of individuals to access, express and enjoy rights, the most basic ones relating to issues of survival. This ability is at present circumscribed for many working class populations in Africa, disenfranchised by neoliberal economic policies. One outcome of this state of affairs is increasing cultural and religious fundamentalisms that manifest in exclusion, false compartmentalisation, separation and silencing of oppressions.

For LGBTI groups this silencing has been subsumed within the classical struggle between progressive social movements and nationalist hegemonies, especially conservative political parties and ruling elites, to control popular support and retain power in the face of global economic and social challenges. Social movements exist primarily as a counterweight to bureaucratic excesses: as an alternative voice they appeal to a conscious majority that is marginalised economically, politically, socially and culturally by dominant individuals, institutions and processes within society. Yet at the same time social movements respond to and articulate their demands through means that are (necessarily) tactical and may be exclusionary if expedient. As groups constantly vigilant of shifts in global priorities, in ceaseless conversation with and interrogation of national prerogatives for development, and in perpetual search for mass appeal, social movements are bound to eschew, albeit tacitly, themes and contestations that might compromise their critical broad reach and dilute their effectiveness. Inevitably too, the thematic issues defining struggles are bound to be swayed by hegemonic notions of 'good' or 'bad' as they instinctively react in opposition to the mainstream.

It is therefore not surprising that at a time when Africa and Africans are assailed from scores of media outlets with the 'un-Africanness' of homosexuality, a highly politicised claim sanctioned and agitated through apathetic states, the most visible reaction from social movements has been weak rejoinders in the same politicised breath, and in the process submerging core issues of economic hardship, livelihoods and survival around which these polarising discourses are structured. Simply put, states and societies need social movements to self-identify from among themselves diversionary sacrificial lambs, and Africa has witnessed a number in the past: Asians in Idi Amin's Uganda, foreigners in South Africa, albinos in Tanzania, witches in Kenya, Mozambique, Tanzania and Uganda.

Difference has always been deployed to divert society's anger when economies did not favour the majority, and as African governments lean increasingly towards the same market-based economic policies that have disenfranchised large populations in the past, the manufacturing of 'difference' and the perpetuation of fundamentalism are bound to go on, with social movements – unless willing to change tactics – remaining at the centre of this balancing act (Jagose 1996: 94–5). Paradoxically, despite the seeming appearance of a backlash, queer activism is at present experiencing a resurgent push on the continent: the visibility created by public awareness and discussions carried in the media, debates within academia and, for the general public, curiosity around the subject are resources that can once again be harnessed towards pursuing the aims of social and economic justice.

Transcending difference; refocusing class struggles

What is the importance of sustaining this conversation? What is at stake? From a political perspective the impact of queer activism on post-liberation evolution in Africa and the diaspora is an area that has received scant attention in post-colonial discourses. Its contribution to studies related to gender and sexuality, as well as violence and representation, remains under-theorised or altogether ignored on the continent.

One significant contribution relates to the rise of HIV/AIDS and its links to Haiti and Africa. In the early discovery of the epidemic, the scapegoating of Haitians and then later Africans brought a certain diaspora consciousness and sensibility into at least one encounter with the disease – the twinning occurred of anti-racist and queer activism (Walcott 2007: 30). From the early 1990s, the multidirectional pressures which the AIDS epidemic placed on categories of identification, power and knowledge necessitated and nurtured new forms of political organisation, education and theorising, which were largely produced under the rubric of queer theory. Notably, this contribution spanned the coalition politics of much AIDS activism that rethought identity in terms of affinity rather than essence (Saalfield and Navarro 1991) and therefore included not only lesbians and gay men but also bisexuals, transsexuals, sex workers, people with AIDS (PWAs), health workers, and parents and friends of gays. The AIDS epidemic also necessitated the rethinking of traditional understandings of the workings of power in cross-hatched struggles over epidemiology, scientific research, public health and immigration policy (Halperin 1995: 28).

In Africa, as in many poor countries in other continents, the impact of the AIDs pandemic has been most profoundly felt at the point at which it ruptures the economic bases of families and communities, but also in the ways that it disrupts dominant social and scientific responses to treatment. The reality of men who have sex with men (MSM) has gained firm recognition as being crucial to HIV/AIDS treatment campaigns in many African countries. The currency of the MSM phenomenon lies in the fact of the largely middle-class demographic it affects, along with the potentially devastating impacts on the developing economy's labour force. As such, important, positive shifts in employment policies that now recognise HIV as a basis of discrimination have occurred, despite attempts at separatism and erasure. Marc Epprecht (2006) urges us to consider whether, even if homosexual practice is not commonplace, or recognised as such, homophobia, transphobia, heterosexism and other 'invisibilising' discourses could be significant cultural influences on the majority population. If so, interventions aimed at the majority population today (for women's empowerment and for sexual health, notably) cannot, he argues, afford blithely to ignore insights coming out of queer scholarship and activism.

A highly moralised African past, a society not marked by decadence, is imagined, and set as a stage for decolonising projects that are invested in movements such as Pan-Africanism and African feminism, both of which are guilty of a particular identity politics that, in normalising heterosexuality, excludes certain subjects in the name of representation. There is a need to restart a more honest conversation within movements and among activists, and in particular to transcend differences that polarise, weaken and compromise activism aimed at creating a more just society. Carrying the voices of LGBTI groups effectively in class struggles demands that their activism be seen as rooted in different sites of struggle that should not be seen as being contradictory to one another and, as Judith Butler (1993) argues, do not need to be reconciled with one another. This, for example, means engaging with the positions taken by queer activists participating in women's movements (as feminists), as workers within labour unions and on other social and economic justice platforms, all of which can be engaged with at the same time, as intersecting and at times confluent. This is not to wish away difference, but rather to acknowledge and build on diversity. Nira Yuval-Davis (1997: 131) urges us towards 'transversal politics', in which perceived unity and homogeneity are replaced by dialogues which give recognition to the specific positioning of those who participate in them as well as to the 'unfinished knowledge' that each such situated positioning can offer. Transversal politics, nevertheless, does not assume that the dialogue is boundary free, and that each conflict of interest is reconcilable. The boundaries of a transversal dialogue are determined by the message, rather than the messenger.

Whereas the political stage remains abstracted (by structures of power) for the majority of Africans, the 'bread-and-butter', socio-economic stage is one that is immediately accessible to most, on which daily lives and struggles for survival are mapped and dramatised in remarkably similar ways across ethnic, sexualised or racialised boundaries. There is a higher likelihood of achieving unity on this latter stage so, not surprisingly, it is more crucial for hegemonic powers to seek to eliminate this stage as a basis for unitary campaigning, as is already being witnessed by the attempts to wipe out LGBTI rights and our participation in supra-bodies such as the African Union and UN and at national levels through legislative processes such as the attempts in Uganda since 2009 to legislate in extreme ways against homosexuality. It is equally crucial, then, for activists to recognise the currency of this socio-economic stage and work towards consolidating it as a core base for class struggles.

Conclusion

Amory (1997) observes that our analyses need to be informed by an awareness of the multiple and intersecting causes of political persecution and oppression: gender, race, ethnicity, class, religion, as well as sexuality. We need to work to form alliances with other scholars and groups who share these goals. It is also important to remember that historically the failure to link struggle issues as a continuum has weakened solidarity and delayed progression and is a fertile source of internal divisions. Making choices about sexualities transcends class, race and geography, and ought not to form the basis upon which continental struggles for equality continue to suffer setbacks. Any resurgence in homophobia is bound to refocus queer activism on the personal and political, which, albeit important, might also be self-defeating in as far as this might prevent the necessary engagement of queer activism with intersecting class issues and, further, would prevent queer activism from gaining firm voice to challenge patriarchal, sexist and heteronormative discourses in society. The dangers of retracting into identity politics at a time when a deepening of social and economic problems on the continent compels strong alliances for social justice cannot be ignored. It is not ironic that the current politics of otherness in post-colonial Africa is so deeply embedded within a discourse of class and sexuality: many aspects of daily life in Africa retain the connection of sexuality to questions of political economy. In the end, the idea that queer activism might actually recuperate class analysis in Africa is not too farfetched.

Notes

1   Democratisation processes in different African countries provided the context within which gay rights formally emerged. For instance, South Africa's democratic transition provided a political opportunity and structure amenable to gay mobilisation (Cock 2003; Croucher 2002). This emergence, however, was not marked by purely positive processes: Zimbabwe's 'Stonewall' moment happened in the aftermath of Robert Mugabe's banning of Gays and Lesbians of Zimbabwe (GALZ) from the Zimbabwe International Book Fair in Harare in July 1995; and at the Second SWAPO Women's Congress on 6 December 1996 President Sam Nujoma reaffirmed this stand when he vowed to 'uproot' homosexuality from Namibian society.

2   As Mukhopadhyay notes, the universalistic promise of liberalism, while fuelling struggles for equal rights, has also been the reason for limiting rights to formal guarantees, because liberalism does not recognise difference and inequalities (in terms of resources and power) between people arising from these differences. Within the liberal framework, an individual is conceived of as the human subject who does not have a gender, class, caste, race, ethnic or community status (2007: 270). Even when this notion is extended to include identities, liberal discourses are easily manipulated by those hegemonic groups in society that have real access to resources and power. This is seen in practical terms in African countries where sexual identity is sacrificed at the altar of conservative religious or ethnic identities that are being positively manipulated for political and economic mileage.

3   From the perspective of political diversity and representative democracy, the invisibility of LGBTI groups in formal sites of class struggles delegitimises their claims for substantive equality.

4   As noted in Epprecht (2006: 188), Moodie (1994), Harries (1994), Gevisser and Cameron (1994), Murray and Roscoe (1998), Kendall (1999), Lockhart (2002), Njinje and Alberton (2002), Epprecht (2004), GALZ (2002) and

Morgan and Wieringa (2005), for example, thoroughly document the presence of diverse expressions of same-sex sexuality in Africa – in traditional societies, in colonial institutions and in present-day settings. A growing, pan-African network of LGBTI associations also attests to diverse, indigenous, same-sex and bisexual cultures and practices in Africa. A range of images written or produced by Africans in fiction, theatre and film further destabilises the stereotype of the 'pure' African heterosexual.

5   This retreat has included prolonged periods of exile of activists from their countries of origin, residence in secluded safe houses, and the need to secure compounds of residence. Many are robbed of day-to-day means of economic survival and as a result depend entirely on donations and goodwill. This enforced removal of an active workforce from wage labour may distort unemployment figures and weaken class struggles.

6   Alluding to this question, Mark Gevisser (2011) contends that 'as many Africans become increasingly uncomfortable with their countries' dependence on the West, they look to find a place to put their pride: they might be poor, but at least they have values! In all the world's global indicators of wellbeing, they can at least lead one: morality. With ineffective states and moribund economies, what better way to maintain popular support than through the scapegoating of an unpopular minority in the name of a battle against western decadence?'

7   Violence should be understood here along a continuum that begins with the isolation, stigmatisation and overt discrimination against homosexuals, usually in the end manifesting in physical brutality and even murder.

8   Miguel (2005) in his study of witch killings in Tanzania, Oster (2004) analysing witchcraft trials in Europe, and Berman's 2003 study of radical religious militias all use empirical findings to demonstrate the power of economics to rationalise phenomena that have previously been understood almost solely through a sociocultural lens.

References

Amory, P.D. (1997) '"Homosexuality" in Africa: issues and debates', *A Journal of Opinion*, 25(1): 5–10

Berman, E. (2003) 'Hamas, Taliban and the Jewish underground: an economist's view of radical religious militias', unpublished manuscript, University of California, San Diego

Butler, J. (1993) *Bodies that Matter: On the Discursive Limits of Sex*, London, Routledge

Centre for Human Rights (CHR) (2010) 'African Commission should reconsider decision on Coalition of African Lesbians', Pambazuka News, 22 November, http://www.pambazuka.org/en/category/features/68946, accessed 24 November 2010

Cock, J. (2003) 'Engendering gay and lesbian rights: the equality clause in the South African constitution', *Women's Studies International Forum*, 26(1): 35–45

Croucher, S. (2002) 'South Africa's democratisation and the politics of gay liberation', *Journal of Southern African Studies*, 28(2): 315–30

Epprecht, M. (2004) *Hungochani: The History of a Dissident Sexuality in Southern Africa*, Montreal, McGill-Queen's University Press

Epprecht, M. (2006) '"Bisexuality" and the politics of normal in African ethnography', *Anthropologica*, 48(2): 187–201

Evans, D.T. (1993) *Sexual Citizenship: the Material Construction of Sexualities*, London, Routledge

Gays and Lesbians of Zimbabwe (GALZ) (2002) *Sahwira*, Harare, GALZ

Gevisser, M. (2011) 'Homosexuality and the battle for Africa's soul', http://africanarguments.org/2011/03/homosexuality-and-the-battle-for-africas-soul/, accessed 9 March 2011

Gevisser, M. and Cameron, E. (eds) (1994) *Defiant Desire: Gay and Lesbian Lives in South Africa*, Johannesburg, Ravan

Halperin, D.M. (1995) *Saint Foucault: Towards a Gay Hagiography*, New York, Oxford University Press

Harries, P. (1994) *Work, Culture and Identity: Migrant Laborers in Mozambique and South Africa, c. 1860–1910*, Portsmouth, NH, Heinemann

Hoad, N. (1999) 'Between the white man's burden and the white man's disease: tracking lesbian and gay human rights in Southern Africa', *GLQ: A Journal of Lesbian and Gay Studies*, 2(4): 559–84

Jagose, A. (1996) *Queer Theory: An Introduction*, New York, NYU Press

Kendall, K.L. (1999) 'Women in Lesotho and the (Western) construction of homophobia', in *Same-sex Relations and Female Desires: Transgender Practices across Cultures*, Blackwood, E. and Wieringa, S. (eds), New York, Columbia University Press

Lockhart, C. (2002) 'Kunyenga, "real sex," and survival: assessing the risk of HIV infection among urban street boys in Tanzania', *Medical Anthropology Quarterly* 16(3): 294–311

Miguel, E. (2005) 'Poverty and witch killing', *Review of Economic Studies*, 72: 1153–72

Moodie, T. with Ndatshe, V. (1994) *Going for Gold: Men, Mines and Migration*, Berkeley, CA, University of California Press

Morgan, R. and Wieringa, S. (eds) (2005) *Tommy Boys, Lesbian Men and Ancestral Wives: Female Same-Sex Practices in Africa*, Johannesburg, Jacana

Mukhopadhyay, M. (2007) 'Situating gender and citizenship in development debates: towards a strategy', in Mukhopadhyay, M. and Singh, N. (eds) *Gender Justice, Citizenship and Development*, Ottawa, IDRC

Murray, S. and Roscoe, W. (eds) (1998) *Boy-Wives and Female Husbands: Studies in African Homosexualities*, New York, St. Martin's Press

Njinje, M. and Alberton, P. (eds) (2002) *Everything Must Come to Light*, Johannesburg, Out of Africa Films

Oster, E. (2004) 'Witchcraft, weather and economic growth in renaissance Europe', *The Journal of Economic Perspectives*, 18(1): 215–28

Phillips, A. (1999) *Which Equalities Matter?* Cambridge, Polity Press

Saalfield, C. and Navarro, R. (1991) 'Shocking pink praxis: race and gender on the ACT UP frontlines (inside/out: lesbian theories)', in Fuss, D. (ed) *Gay Theories*, New York, Routledge

Schuhmann, A. (2007) 'Exoticising the erotic: white on white via the black body: collecting artefacts within German dominant culture', in Wright, M. and Schuhmann, A. (eds) *Blackness and Sexualities*, New Brunswick, Transaction Publishers

Schuhmann, A. (2010) 'Taming transgressions: South African nation building and "body politics"', *Agenda*, 83: 95–106

Walcott, R. (2007) 'Somewhere out there: the new black queer theory', in Wright, M. and Schuhmann, A. (eds) *Blackness and Sexualities, New Brunswick*, Transaction Publishers

Yuval-Davis, N. (1997) *Gender and Nation*, London, Sage Publications

4

Disability and desire: journey of a film-maker – life story

Shelley Barry

In 1996, at the age of 24, I found myself in hospital, with empty walls and broken dreams colouring my days. My partner at the time, Janine Clayton, and I were caught up in local taxi violence in Cape Town, South Africa, with members of rival taxi organisations firing at each other. The driver of the taxi we were in died, and my spine was severed by a bullet. My body told me long before doctors had the courage to admit it. I was paralysed from the chest down. During those endless afternoons with little else than my mind to entertain me, I contemplated the extent of my loss. Perhaps what struck me deepest at the time was my conviction that I would never be desired or loved again. I felt that my body had become damaged goods, my sexuality erased.

As time went by, I began to dismantle my perceptions by analsying their origins. I recognised that my mental picture of a person with a disability was that of someone in need of care, someone to be pitied, someone who certainly had no real claim to love or any kind of fulfilling life. The basis of my beliefs was largely informed by society's consensus on people with disabilities … these were people who were mostly invisible, unless as beggars on the street or patients in hospital. This invisibility was entrenched by the media.

My political consciousness grew within the disability rights movement. I began to acknowledge that it was society that had placed my body in a box with a label and stuck it away on a dusty shelf. I had a different body, yes, not a damaged one. The process of reclaiming my body was an exceptionally powerful and liberating experience. I understood desire and sensuality from a completely different perspective. I realised that passion is something that everyone can access (it is not reserved for the young and the able-bodied), and it can suffuse every aspect of our lives. I recognised the importance of self-love as opposed to requiring affirmation from others in order to love myself.

I felt pride. I even dared to feel beautiful. I cruised around on my wheels feeling that I had every right to be in the world, as much as anyone else did. And I began to live with a passion and fervour that fundamentally changed the course of my life.

My spiritual explorations into Eastern philosophy also came back to me with more force and power. I had always made a distinction between the body and the spirit, and this period gave that belief more clarity. For me, the body houses the spirit and is merely a vehicle. This does not mean that one does not honour the body – quite the opposite!

I truly believe in the power of a positive mind – something we can all access, and which begins with awareness of your thoughts. Our thoughts are energy, and energy manifests itself. It is amazing how much thought dictates outcome! Last year, I finally took the plunge and became a committed Buddhist.

After years in the disability rights movement, I returned to my dreams of becoming a film-maker. I was fortunate enough to receive a scholarship to film school from the Ford Foundation. At 32, I became a full-time student again. In my first writing class at Temple University in Philadelphia, my professor told us, 'Write about something because you *have* to write about it. Write from your soul.' My first film birthed itself with this honesty. *Whole – A Trinity of Being*, a visual doc-poem of three short films, explores my spiritual journey of embracing and celebrating my body. The first segment, 'Pin Pricks', tells the tale of how the fabric of my life was torn apart and the revelations that took me beyond this loss: 'I chose not to wear that garment of bitterness so easily fitted to the wounded body.'

The next segment deals with my second disability – my dependency on a tube that fits into a hole in my throat, allowing me to breathe and speak. In the film, I declare: 'I celebrate this hole. The breath and speech it gives is my life force. So, I decorate it with jewellery, different handmade beads and trinkets because scars should also be crowned. Even if they're not neat or pretty or hard to look at sometimes.'

For me, the power of this film came from the vulnerability involved in openly showing, on screen, the gaping wound in my throat. It had always been very difficult for me to look at it. By making a film about it, I hoped to encourage other women to feel beautiful, scars and all. Our scars are often imposed on us, yet we carry their shame. We are warriors because we have survived those scars, and live to tell their and our tales. I adorn my scar not to hide it, but to protect it and to celebrate it. This holds vital lessons for so-called able-bodied women as well – many have C-section scars, mastectomy scars and other injuries, but are taught to be ashamed of these and to hide them.

The last film of the trilogy is a sequence of images, snapshots of life in a wheelchair – not traditional snapshots, but those that dare to claim a strong sense of sexuality and desire. One of the hardest scenes I did was a shot of my wheelchair next to me in the bath, cutting to a shot of my hands travelling over my body, in a gesture of masturbation. Doing this scene was not at all gratuitous. I made a political decision to present a picture of a disabled woman who has an active sexual relationship with herself. This was because the notion that women with disabilities might claim their sexuality or be sexually active is mostly absent, if not downright taboo, in all spheres of art, media and society in general. Black disabled women are the most invisible of all in this respect. Our cultures teach us to hide our sexuality, to not lay claim to our bodies, to wait demurely for a man to want us enough. Unless we begin to challenge those perceptions by inserting ourselves in this absence, this blank space, the status quo will continue.

In another scene, I depict my partner and myself in a loving embrace. This was difficult to do, because it meant exposing my personal life and relationships on screen, to an audience of strangers. Yet the necessity far outweighed the difficulty. I felt it was important to show that we should not only openly lay claim to loving ourselves, but claim the pleasure of being loved and loving others – in ways that are sensual, intimate and playful.

The film ends with a declaration of discovery: 'I know about this dance of living. This dance is not with the feet. This dance is with the heart. And when I dance with the heart, music comes through me. Music is me. And then all that I am, is the dance.'

It has been two years since making that first film. To date, it has won four international film awards, much to my surprise! My work has continued to focus on re-envisaging a media that makes people with disabilities visible, not only as sexual beings, but as people in the fullness of human experience. I am juggling various stages of post-production on other films and hope to send them off into the world within the next few months. I am also working on the cinematic aesthetics of shooting films from a wheelchair. Unless we as people with disabilities, as women, as black people, as lesbians, become the makers of our own images, our lives will constantly be depicted on the basis of assumptions that others hold about who we are, how we live, and how we love.

This article was first published in Feminist Africa *(2006, 6).*

5

African LGBTI manifesto/ declaration

April 18, 2010, Nairobi, Kenya

As Africans, we all have infinite potential. We stand for an African revolution which encompasses the demand for a re-imagination of our lives outside neo-colonial categories of identity and power. For centuries, we have faced control through structures, systems and individuals who disappear our existence as people with agency, courage, creativity, and economic and political authority.

As Africans, we stand for the celebration of our complexities and we are committed to ways of being which allow for self-determination at all levels of our sexual, social, political and economic lives. The possibilities are endless. We need economic justice; we need to claim and redistribute power; we need to eradicate violence; we need to redistribute land; we need gender justice; we need environmental justice; we need erotic justice; we need racial and ethnic justice; we need rightful access to affirming and responsive institutions, services and spaces; overall we need total liberation.

We are specifically committed to the transformation of the politics of sexuality in our contexts. As long as African LGBTI people are oppressed, the whole of Africa is oppressed.

This vision demands that we commit ourselves to:

- Reclaiming and sharing our stories (past and present), our lived realities, our contributions to society and our hopes for the future.
- Strengthening ourselves and our organizations, deepening our links and understanding of our communities, building principled alliances, and actively contributing towards the revolution.

- Challenging all legal systems and practices which either currently criminalize or seek to reinforce the criminalization of LGBTI people, organizations, knowledge creation, sexual self expression, and movement building.
- Challenging state support for oppressive sexual, gendered, discriminatory norms, legal and political structures and cultural systems.
- Strengthening the bonds of respect, cooperation, passion, and solidarity between LGBTI people, in our complexities, differences and diverse contexts. This includes respecting and celebrating our multiple ways of being, self expression, and languages.
- Contributing to the social and political recognition that sexuality, pleasure, and the erotic are part of our common humanity.
- Placing ourselves proactively within all movement building supportive of our vision.

http://www.blacklooks.org/2011/05/
african-lgbti-manifestodaclaration

'Proudly African & Transgender' – collaborative portraits and stories with trans and intersex activists

Gabrielle Le Roux

The exhibition 'Proudly African & Transgender' is a creative intervention for social justice in the form of portraits and stories of ten transgender African activists who collaborated to be portrayed in this way because they want their faces to be seen and their voices heard around the world.

> Transgender Africans have been silenced for a long time. We have been invisible as though we did not exist. Today, many of us speak, we show our faces, we write and we express ourselves openly.
>
> This exhibition is an extension of that. The portraits are our images and they speak our words, they tell our stories, they express our feelings, they exhibit our pride, even our fears, they are our history, they are us today and the history of the African transgender struggle in future. They are strength, hope and pride to generations after us.
>
> I felt lost for a long time. I thought that there was no other like me. I thought I was abnormal, strange and this made me powerless. My transgender niece or nephew, grandchild or friend's child will not feel lost. They will look at my portrait and they will gain power, hope, peace of mind and pride. They will know that another transgender existed before and that it is okay to be gender non-conforming.
>
> When the world sees our portraits, they will know that Africa has transgender people and that there is a struggle against injustices on our continent.

Thus writes Victor Mukasa, expressing the vision and intention of the exhibition, both as the person with whom I envisioned this project for a number of years, and also as one of the people portrayed. Victor is an internationally respected Ugandan LGBTI human rights defender, whose position in 2008 with the International Gay and Lesbian Human Rights Commission (IGLHRC) made this project possible. He now works as an independent consultant.

In December 2008 the first ever gathering of exclusively African transgender people took place in Cape Town, organised by the IGLHRC and Gender Dynamix, initiated by Victor Mukasa. It was an historic and very significant event, providing space for people to share their specific experiences and language about the meaning and consequences of being gender non-conforming in their countries. As part of the gender identity workshop, Victor and I introduced the possibility of the exhibition and invited participants to take part. Each of the people who wanted to share their experience in this way sat for me to draw them from life, and collaborated by writing whatever they wanted to say about themselves directly onto their portraits. Later they wrote texts about themselves, and the exhibition remains a work in progress in that these texts change periodically. Participants came from Zimbabwe, Uganda, Kenya, South Africa, Namibia, Burundi and Botswana.

In the absence of institutional support the portraits and stories were not exhibited for a year, but all the collaborators felt strongly that they should be, and one by one the doors started to open for the work to be seen. The interest internationally is considerable. There are plans afoot to show it more broadly on the continent.

Flavrina, Burundi

I am 30, born on the 7 April 1982.

I had three brothers and one sister. My father was a politician. My mother was not rich but the little she had she liked to see everyone enjoy. She taught me to share everything.

She would say, 'I don't know if you are my daughter or my son but I love you.' I was always together with my mum. When I made a mistake she wanted to protect me and didn't believe in beating me. She died when I was 7 and my father when I was 12.

Life is hard for me as a transgender refugee in South Africa. I have lived here for four years and been through a lot. I came to South Africa for the Gender Identity Strategic Workshop in 2008, the first meeting ever of African trans activists. While I was here I received a message that it was not safe for me to go home.

I want to return to Burundi and continue my LGBTI activist work, there are no other transgender activists that I know of there, but I can't travel until my papers are sorted out.

Right now I'm working hard at my English. I am involved here as an activist for the rights of trans people, refugees, sex workers and HIV positive people. I am part of the organisations SWEAT and PASSOP. I am working part time as a street sweeper and part time as a sex worker. I have dreams for my future and the contribution I can make.

'I am a child of God. Dieu est grand et il m'aime comme je suis. God is great and he loves me as I am. J'aime les trans comme moi. Je les sens dans mon corp et mon coeur. I love the trans like me, I feel them in my body and heart. Imana ninkuru kandi irankunda kandi ndumwana wimana.'

Text from portrait

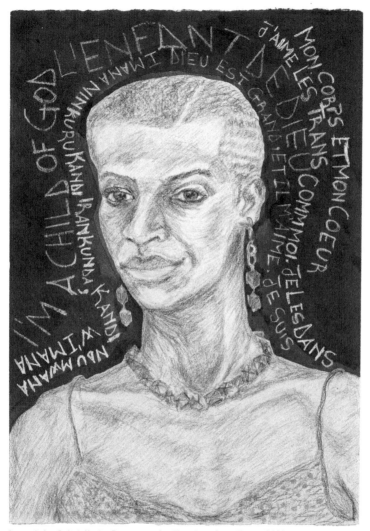

Portrait by Gabrielle Le Roux, text by Flavrina. Cape Town, 2008

Portrait by Gabrielle Le Roux, text by Julius Kaggwa. Cape Town, 2008

Julius Kaggwa, Uganda

I am the founder and director of the Support Initiative for People with Atypical Sex Development, SIPD, which is a grassroots not for profit human rights organisation in Uganda. Through community outreach and engagement we provide support for intersex Ugandans. We also provide reliable and objective information on the plight of persons with intersex conditions and gender non-conforming characteristics in Uganda. SIPD particularly addresses the human rights, sexual health and social support of intersex children and people. Our website is www.sipd.webs.com.

My decision to actively be involved in activism has brought me face to face with some extremely painful experiences – right within the LGBT community. I went through a very difficult time and had to take some time off the public scene and recover.

From the struggles of my life I have never forgotten the love of God and my parents who brought me into this world.

I believe in rights for all. I identify myself as a man but I'm not a threat to women and my respect will always be there because every human being has equal rights. I would never be in this world if it wasn't for a woman who chose to have me.

I am struggling and suffering because my culture expects the opposite of me, but that doesn't mean I will stop being an African. I'm still black with black ancestors and I'm proud to be African.

Julius Kaggwa won the Human Rights First Award in 2010 for his work against the Anti Homosexuality Bill in Uganda.

> *'I'm intersex. I'm transsexual. I'm a man. I'm Ugandan and proud of who I am. It has been a difficult journey but one I don't regret taking because I can only be who I am. A unique creation.'*
>
> **Text from portrait**

Madam Jholerina Brina Timbo, Namibia

I am a trans woman from Windhoek, Namibia. I am 23.

A long way I have come from a young tender age of 12. Transphobia, verbal abuse and assault I have endured because of who I am. Many believe and think being transgender is an abomination and a disgrace to the nation.

Finding my true self and understanding myself was a battle I thought would never end. With the help of Rainbow Project when I was down, stressed and struggling with my physical appearance and the whole thing, I could go about accepting myself as a trans woman. Many friends I have lost when I reached that point. Always trying to fit in but I never fitted in any group or people.

Clearly when we lose the right to be different we lose the privilege to be free.

I would like us to be united as one in the fight against human rights violations taking place in this world. Discrimination, stigma and abuse are not only in Africa but the developed world as well.

In my country Namibia being LGBTI is a crime if you are caught in the act. I hate the way people look at me and laugh. It's because there are no laws to protect me to be who and what I am…

I believe that as Human beings we must speak out for the greater good of the world. But for me as a trans woman in Namibia, and not having all the rights like everyone else, it's not easy.

Long live the movements.

'I'm an African woman. To understand me, get to know me. This is who I am and what I am. I am the modern day Cleopatra. Courage is not the absence of fear but rather the judgment that something else is more important than fear. African beauty that I am.'

Text from portrait

Portrait by Gabrielle Le Roux, text by Madam Jholerina Brina Timbo.
Cape Town, 2008

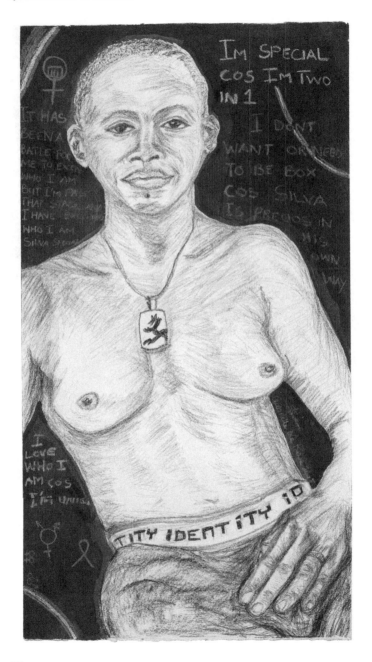

Silva Skinny Dux Eiseb, Namibia

I love my name.

I have lived in Namibia since birth. I see myself as a Trans man. I am the founding Father of the Transgender movement in Namibia, TAMON, Trans Activist Movement Of Namibia. I live in one of the townships called Dolam in Windhoek. I have been an activist for more than ten years in the LGBTI movement, and I am a feminist.

Being a Trans person in Namibia is not an easy thing. You need to have a brave heart to go out there in the streets, you are exposed to lots of attacks physically and verbally if you are not strong enough to defend yourself. It's wrong to be different in these people's eyes than the usual: a man has to look like this and a woman like that. That is why some Trans people are the victims of corrective rape because they want to see if you are a real man, you have to fight to prove that you are man enough. Trans women are beaten up because a 'man' is not to behave in that way.

Letting my portrait be drawn is to let the world out there know that we are there and we exist and that I am proud of who I am. The exhibition will not only benefit me as a person but the whole Trans community, I see it as a way of highlighting issues that normally stand in the background when people talk about human rights. If the portrait of my reality and others in my situation is spread around the world it might create a common ground for a common struggle.

'I'm special cos I'm two in 1. I don't want or need to be boxed cos Silva is precious in his own way. It has been a battle for me to accept who I am but I'm past that space and have accepted who I am. Silva. Special. I love who I am cos I'm unique.'

Text from portrait

Portrait by Gabrielle Le Roux, text by Silva Skinny Dux Eiseb. Cape Town, 2008

Skipper Mogapi, Botswana

I am an activist from Botswana, who has been in the fight for gay rights since 2004. I identify as Trans man and worked as coordinator of Lesbians, Gays and Bisexuals of Botswana [LeGaBiBo] since 2006.

I hold two positions at the moment, the coordinator of LGBTI movement, and as the Prevention and Research Initiatives for Sexual Minorities [PRISM] assistant program coordinator, from 2007 to date.

My interest in LGBT rights started in 2004 when Behind the Mask was doing research in LGBTI rights and movements and I had been a media victim – my sexual orientation was disclosed in the newspapers.

There are so many challenges I face as trans person in Botswana, like having to be stared at all the time and asked to identify yourself everywhere you go, for example using the public toilets or getting into a night club. At school I had a problem with dress: I identified as a man and was expected to wear a dress all the time.

It's also hard to get a job. Although my papers show that I am female, my physical appearance shows that I am a man. The hardest thing is, since I started taking testosterone in 2009, whenever I travel the police and immigration officers have to question my passport or identity card.

'Black African man is who I am ... the man no-one sees. Rejoicing was my mother day I was born, happy to have given birth to a baby girl. Little did she know I am trans.'

Text from portrait

Portrait by Gabrielle Le Roux, text by Skipper Mogape. Cape Town, 2008

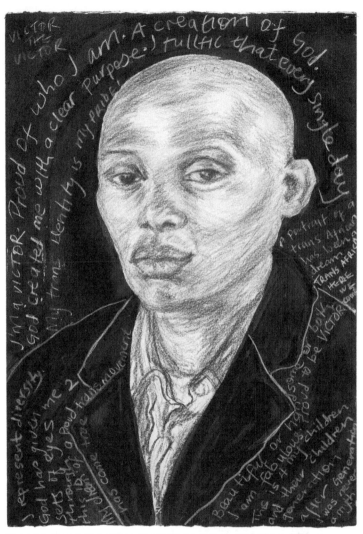

Portrait by Gabrielle Le Roux, text by Victor Mukasa. Cape Town, 2008

Victor Mukasa, Uganda

I am a transgender person. Yes, PERSON! I transgress traditional gender norms. Not to be stubborn, but that is me. It is not of my own making. I was born that way. My childhood, as my parents told it to me, and as far as I remember, was as such. People everywhere I went said that I look like a boy. In fact many addressed me as a boy. Even to date, I am still the same. I dress just as boys and or men traditionally dress. It is in my expression too. That is me. I am a proud transgender person.

My experience as a transgender person in Uganda is not a sweet story. In short, a transgender person in Uganda is constantly surrounded with ridicule, mockery and abuse. For most Ugandans, any person that expresses 'him/herself' as the opposite sex is a homosexual and so this exposes transgender people to all the mistreatment. All transgender people are seen as the obvious homosexuals. Therefore, on top of all the transphobia, there is homophobia, even if you are not gay.

The showing of Transgender Africans' portraits is signifying the need to protect, respect and promote the human rights of transgender people, not only in Africa, but in every corner of the world.

'Victor the victor. I'm the Victor. Proud of who I am. A creation of God. God created me with a clear purpose and I fulfil that every day. My trans identity is my pride. A portrait of a trans African has been a dream. Trans Africa here we come. I represent diversity. God has given me 2 sets of eyes through this ID. My dream of a proud trans movement has come true. This is for my children and their children generation after generation. I was never a myth.'

Text from portrait

Where the exhibition has been seen

The exhibition was first seen on the walls of the workshop in Cape Town when it was being created in December 2008. Since then, 'Proudly African & Transgender' has been publicly shown (in the form of prints) at:

- Amnesty International in Amsterdam, February 2010.
- International Congress on Gender Identity and Human Rights in Barcelona, where six of the ten people in the portraits were present. The exhibition provided a special platform for African activists at that historic global gathering of trans activists.
- Istanbul Pride 2010, at the invitation of Amnesty Turkey.
- Joint exhibition with South African photographer Zanele Muholi's 'Faces and Phases', IHLIA, International Gay and Lesbian Archive, at de Oba, Amsterdam's central library, July–October 2010.
- Transgender Europe, 3rd Council, in Malmo, Sweden, October 2010.
- Madrid during the Stop Trans Pathologisation March, October 2010.
- Pembe Hayat Trans Remembrance Week conference in Ankara, Turkey, November 2010.
- African Same Sex Sexualities and Gender Diversity Conference, Pretoria, South Africa, February 2011.
- Athens Pride, Athens, Greece, July 2011.
- TRIQ Trans Inter Queer Association, Berlin, Germany, September 2011.
- This Human World Film Festival, Schikaneder, Vienna, November–December 2011.
- Café Munck, Hamburg, February 2012.

To see the exhibition online, visit: http://www.blacklooks. org/2010/02/proudly-african-transgender/

7

The vampire bite that brought me to life – fiction

Nancy Lylac Warinda

We like to think that vampires don't exist and if they do in some form they should be vanquished, pierced in the heart with a blunt wooden stake. Well, I like vampires. I like their stealth, dark, mysterious countenance. To me they hold a promise of unfathomable adventure and who doesn't like adventure? I am obsessed with the search for thrill. Blame it on daddy issues or unmanned hours in front of the TV. Whatever, it's just me.

I had had one of those long dull weeks and the much-anticipated weekend was finally here. My girl Debby invited me to a wedding-after party in one of the hottest clubs along Lang'ata road. Naturally, I much obliged, determined to have a very wild night.

Heck, I deserved it. It had been months since I broke up with my boyfriend Fred. Lush, handsome, proud Jaluo man from Rapogi, he was a little rough on the edges because of his impoverished background but had Einstein's brain and fierce ambition that saw him quickly rise up the corporate ladder in the year we dated.

We dated for a whole fucking year. That was the longest I have ever been in a relationship. He developed exquisite tastes which I didn't mind. Until those colossally annoying opportunistic Nairobi gold-digging girls started circling around him like hungry malnourished hyenas.

Whenever he took me out he insisted on having his sautéed beef with red Bordeaux Medoc and his chicken with Italian non-riserva Chianti or Côtes du Rhône. He loved his classic fondue with New Zealand's Sauvignon Blanc. He was getting too much loving and he let it get to his head.

I opted to bow out of the relationship. I just couldn't see myself clamouring and competing for his attention.

Ahh! But he was lush, a treat to many a woman's eye.

I could never date a guy who wasn't lush. In fact my girl always teased me that I only date beautiful men. Even then, I was never truly happy. They ended quickly with me bored to death with the relationship. I always felt like there was something missing, something I could never seem to grasp at.

I was meeting Debby at the club. I put on my little white-buckled, v-necked dress and a pair of suede ankle boots. Threw on a black trench coat, wore my hair down and sprayed on Chloe to keep fresh, I was hot and ready to have a ball.

Awesome DJ mixes thronged the air, the kind that just drive you to shake your booty. The after-party crowd was alive and ecstatic. Everybody was as high as a kite. '*Makaratasi vinoma* the end!'[1] as my good friend Debby puts it.

We danced like there was no tomorrow until I had had enough. I slid past the revellers to my seat to take a breather and to reload on the booze. I had sat for a few minutes when a lady came over to my table. She introduced herself as Veronica. It immediately rang a bell.

Once, Debby had described a girl she worked with who fit her description like a glove. She had long beautiful locks that could reach the middle of her back and which she neatly held up. Her eyes were sexily small and smoky. She wore a classic cool CK cologne, a plaid shirt, a black cropped jacket and khaki pants. She looked as cool as that Smirnoff vodka commercial with water and ice all over.

She sparked an interesting array of thoughts in my head. My wildness radar went scarlet red. She was tall, slim with an athletic build that I, surprisingly, found to be absolutely sexy. She had a striking alpha masculine demeanour. I had to keep reminding myself that she was a girl.

I have always been attracted to men yet I was fixated on her, on the prospect of capturing her attention even if for the night alone. She asked me to go get tequila shots with her and I was immensely thrilled.

Something about her was incalculably intriguing. I don't know if it is the mystery that surrounds such arrangements that drew me, or just my determination to party wild. I found myself staring at her as she took her shots of tequila. There was a glint of mischief in her eyes and I was damn sure it reflected in mine. We went back to our seats and found our friends had finally quit the dance floor. Everyone was talking too loudly as if the heightened alcohol levels in their system had suddenly made them deaf.

Debby was on her usual inciter horse, urging people to drink a little more. Debby and I had been friends for many years. She was great to be around. A smart, beautiful, witty, funny, loving, happy person. She had a kind soul and fabulously free spirit.

On this night she wore a flowery, flowing satin white and pink dress that revealed her generous curves and emphasised her hourglass African shape. She wore it with matching huge dangling earrings and a pink scarf that stretched over her shoulder to partly cover her exposed upper back, finally resting on her voluptuous buttocks.

She made one of her colleagues, who apparently had some interest in me, sit next to me. She was obviously oblivious to the sexy undercurrents between me and Veronica. Everybody who worked with her knew she was gay and of course I wasn't. I made small talk with the guy, which seemed to be such an arduous experience because I kept thinking of Veronica. The guy tried hard to capture my attention, with no fruit. Not even a tiny grape.

What was she thinking? What was she making me think? Who was she going home with? What was she going to do to her? I excused myself and in unsteady steps headed for the ladies.

I didn't know the location so I had to ask for directions from a waiter – up some stairs and around some dark-lit corners. I was surprised I found it in the hazy maze, with alcohol swirling around in my brain.

When I got out of the ladies, I couldn't remember from whence I had come but I walked on trying to act more sober than I was. I found myself out on the balcony and – alas! – there she was, smoking her SM cigarette. It was almost as if some unseen force was driving me towards her. She looked hot, feral and seditious. And the look she gave me made my insides melt. My knees went proverbially wobbly or was it that I was staggering drunk? Anyway, I managed a, 'I think I am lost.'

To which she whipped, 'Are you sure you weren't looking for me?' And indeed I wasn't sure.

'May I join you?' I ignored her query.

'Do you smoke?'

'Sometimes.'

'Enjoying yourself?'

'Not with that guy I am not.'

'Stick with me girl and I'll show you a good time.'

She took my hand and led me to the dancing floor. We danced in a subtle, sexy manner, careful not to arouse the undue interest of ogling lustful men chancing for a threesome. We took a few more shots of tequila and it was time to head home.

Debby had conveniently disappeared with her date.

Out on the parking lot, Veronica put her arm around me since I was giving indications of feeling cold. Then she stopped me in my tracks and squeezed me into a warm hug. She stared into my face for like ten seconds and raised my chin into a kiss. First soft and sweet, then deep with raging desire.

I wanted her and she wanted me just as bad.

'Are you coming home with me?' she whispered into my ear.

'Uh, uh, I don't…,' came the weak reply.

I was looking over at Debby, who seemed pretty busy with her date.

'We are adults, we can do what we want.' It's like she had read my mind and sensed my worry. 'I will take care of you girl, you won't regret this.'

I didn't need more urging, I needed her and I needed to see how this shit would go down.

We got into a cab and conveniently sat in the back. She gave the driver directions as she snuggled next to me. We couldn't wait to get to a more private place. We tried to be discreet but I bet the cab driver knew the silence at the back meant we were getting busy.

He would shift nervously in the driver seat and cough unnecessarily to cover his embarrassment. He made click sounds and covered it up with a little whistling of an awkward tune. At one point I thought he would drive the car to a screeching halt and command us to get out.

He didn't. I guess his homophobia ended where money was concerned. We didn't give a damn. What crime were we committing?

Veronica put her hand under my head and let her lips teasingly brush over mine. She kissed my left cheek, bit my earlobe then gently blew over it.

Frantically back to my mouth, like a love-starved lunge.

She dove in to kiss my collar bone with wet kisses as her other hand searched for me, moving down under my dress to roughly cap my breast, filling her palm with it.

I almost screamed when her cool finger found its way inside me. Instead, what came out was a muffled awkward gulp. I put my arms around her neck and drowned her in long desperate kisses as one ending an era of deprivation.

'Babe, we have to stop,' she whispered, pulling away from my embrace. 'Otherwise, otherwise we won't make it home.'

'Yeah ... right!' I relented and gently stroked the inside of her arm in a bid to lengthen the moment. 'How long till we get there?'

'Not long darling ... not long.'

It was only a few minutes later when we got to her place. She hurriedly paid the cab driver and we practically ran through her gate, past her front porch to her door. She fumbled with her bag to look for her keys as I nervously looked on.

We briskly walked up the stairs and into her bedroom.

'Welcome to my humble abode.'

'Why, thank you.'

And that was more than we ever said that night.

She banged the door behind me and crushed her mouth into mine.

Her tongue, swift and sleek in my mouth, opening it, invading it and spreading the flavour of desire.

When she moved to my throat I was gulping for air. I felt lightheaded, enchanted, like my body was being transported into a parallel universe.

I ran my fingers through her neatly locked hair and moved her head back so I could reach for her lips. My tongue played with hers, darting, folding, shifting and licking, demanding a fulfilment of which I never knew existed in me.

She pressed herself against me, ran her fingers down my back and grabbed my ass, pulling it upwards, smacking it to leave a wicked ache between my thighs. I instinctively started to unbutton her shirt and slipped my hand under to caress her lovely breasts.

They were small, pear-shaped and firm. Her nipples erect, exposing her desire.

She shoved me onto her bed and pounced on me like a hungry lion. She yanked off my trench coat and threw it on the bed.

She undid the straps of my dress and let it slip to the floor. I removed her shirt. She wasn't wearing a bra.

The sight before me was surprisingly breathtaking.

She undid my bra strap and gently caressed my breasts. Our eyes locked in a trance, drawing us to each other.

Her mouth was on me again, frantic, seeking, finding. Our bodies glued to each other, imbibing each other as though we intended entering each other. Locked in the pursuit of pleasure, tongue meeting tongue, breasts pressing on breasts, belly on belly. Rising and falling from grace together. I lifted my knees to welcome her thigh that pressed upon my clit.

She moved mercilessly, eliciting a savage response. I felt like I was floating on the ocean or dancing on a meadow with a sweet summer breeze brushing against my cheeks.

Throaty murmurs escaped from somewhere in me as I fervidly jerked up on her thigh. My hands moved up and down her slender frame. Clutching a breast here, stroking a thigh there, caressing her back, belly, ass, groin, finally sneaking a plunge into her. She released an 'Oh, God!' as she jerked on my hand.

We moved in learned rhythm.

Heat swamped my entire bodice, coating my skin in sweat. She sensed I was nearing the cliff as my breathing had become moist, quick and intense.

A surprise huge bite on my neck that mimicked a vampire's bite shot a multiplicity of pain and pleasure, bombarding in an atrocious attack to my system, leaving me in an oasis of pure bliss.

My emancipation only excited her more and she was determined to lengthen my bliss.

She moved down, her mouth and teeth taking me to a zone where normal things don't happen very often. She was driving me absolutely crazy and I didn't even know how I could possibly return the favour.

I slid more of my fingers deep inside her and paced her rhythm with my play, intermittently stroking her clit with my other hand.

Her movements increased in tempo.

I could smell her primal pungent scent as her temperature went a notch higher. Her breathing became quick and her heart began to race. Finally, I heard her cry out a laboured cry to her God again.

We lay on the bed, spent, exhausted, grateful to one another for the magical moments.

Veronica was the first to speak.

'Damn, girl! That was awesome!' she said in a hoarse sexy voice that made me want to kiss her again and again.

'It really was … so … do you do this often?'

'Do what?'

'Meet up chicks in bars. Take 'em home and fuck 'em rancid?'

'That is so crude and grossly inaccurate. I do not. Honestly, you are the first girl I have been with in a long, long time.' She divulged, 'I lost my girl friend in a car accident about this time last year.'

'Am so sorry, dear. Must have been a nightmare.'

'It is still surreal to me. It took me a very long time to accept her sudden death. She was my everything, my best friend, my confidant, my lover, my soul mate. The woman who was going to be my wife, my forever. I had even introduced her to my mother.'

'Really, how did that go?'

'My mom was in shock. Even though I had told her I like girls. She never accepted it. She devised a plan to make me change my mind. First, I had to be prayed for by her pastor, to remove the demons in my head that were lying to me, convincing me that I was a boy. Then I was to see a psychologist to help me deal with the change. If that didn't work, she would enlist the help of a powerful witchdoctor. Brew a love potion that will make me fall in love with her choice of man. I don't blame her. She tried her best in raising me all alone. She didn't understand how I became a lesbian under her careful watch.'

'You must have loved her to bits, this girl.'

'Yes, I did. Sometimes I think I still feel her, smell her perfume and the pain starts all over again. I want to be honest with you. You are a great girl but I hope you understand that I can't really rush into anything serious, not right now.'

Her words tore me up inside. I felt a sharp stab rush through my entire body in a split second.

I needed more of her. She needed me less.

'You need time, I know,' I said, almost in a whisper. She heard me and held me close.

'That's all I ask. You are the type I would love to bits.'

We cuddled up. I lay my head between her breasts and slowly drifted to my own thoughts.

What did all this mean for me? I mean, what the heck did all this mean? The experience I had with this girl was like nirvana. Not just in the physical sense but on a deep emotional level. The yearning I felt for her while we were at it was unlike anything I had ever experienced.

She was gorgeous, lovely, a sight to behold. Soft, yet rough. I could tell from her love-making that she was an incredible person. I had just met her but I wanted to know her more. This wasn't going to be one of my little experiments. You know the ones, the list of things to do before I die. I needed more of this shit. I needed it bad and she was indeed beautiful.

But what did that make me? A lesbian? A bisexual? I never liked those terms. They didn't sound nice. To me they have always been used in a bad light, always derogatory. Godless, perverse people with no proper upbringing. Woman was meant for man. So how can this exist? What did this mean? What was I? All the men I ever went out with had to be extremely handsome, almost beautiful, beautiful like a woman. It was always important for me to like what I see. Here I was liking what I saw in someone like me.

Still, I didn't think I would have liked to be called those names. What business did anyone have defining who I was by someone I sleep with? Who the hell made it so important to define people?

This defining who I was, did it have to be linked to my sex life? Wasn't it rather irrelevant to my personality, the thing that made me me?

To me, sexuality was personal, not a personality. Sexuality is fluid and flexible but as it is, a great conduit of power used to manipulate and control people.

Nobody likes being controlled.

I knew I was so much more, much more than the box used to define gays, bisexuals and lesbians in our society. When it came to it, I wasn't going to let anyone put me down.

I felt like a new dawn had begun in my life, a dawn of limitless possibilities and adventure. I was determined to explore this era to the fullest. Driven to be all I can be, all because of her, stunningly gorgeous Veronica.

When she dropped me off at home, I wondered if I would see her again, feel her and hold her close.

My heart sank when she didn't ask for my number and just bade me farewell.

Note

1   *Makaratasi vinoma* the end!' – Nairobi slang-phrase used to emphasise inebriation.

8

Contesting narratives of queer Africa

Sokari Ekine

Two distinct, yet interlinked, narratives dominate discussions of queer African sexualities: one claims that queer sexualities are 'un-African' and the other treats Africa as a site of obsessive homophobia. The first stems from a mix of religious fundamentalisms, which insist on strict literal interpretations of religious texts, and a culturally essentialist position which pathologises and denies the existence of queerness on the continent. These fundamentalists argue that queer sexualities threaten African social and cultural norms and claim that pro-queer initiatives in Africa by Western countries and NGOs are imperialist. The second narrative on 'African homophobia' is rooted in colonial discourses of deviant and peculiar African sexuality and in a contemporary neoliberal, global 'LGBT'[1] agenda which seeks to universalise white Euro-American sexual norms and gender expressions (Hoad 2007: xii, Massad 2007, Atluri 2009). The tensions posed by these two narratives present a serious strategic challenge for African queer anti-colonialist politics caught at various points between the meta-narratives of LGBT imperialism and homophobic religious fundamentalism on the one hand and indigenous contemporary constructions of sexuality and gender on the other.

The moral panic against homosexuality across the continent is systemic and indicative of an instrumentalised, well-organised campaign which exposes the cosy relationship between religious and cultural fundamentalisms asserted through vigorous nationalist political agendas. Nigeria, Uganda and, to a lesser extent, Malawi have been at the centre of this anti-queer movement, repeatedly driving state homophobia through reoccurring legislations. In Uganda, an anti-homosexuality bill was first tabled in 2009 and since then it has been repeatedly reintroduced, the latest reincarnation being on 7 February 2012. West African politicians must have been on a 'Uganda anti-gay' watch as, within days, politicians from two other countries had released statements against same-sex marriage. The first was made by President Yahya Jammeh of the Gambia during the swearing in of a cabinet minister. It is hard to see this as coincidence as there does not appear to be any other contextual reason why the well-rehearsed statement was made at this time:

> It's not in the Bible or Qur'an. It's an abomination. I am telling you this because the new wave of evil that they want to impose on us will not be accepted in this country…
>
> As long as I am the president, I am not going to accept it in my government and in this country. We know what human rights are. Human beings of the same sex cannot marry or date – we are not from evolution but we are from creation and we know the beginning of creation – that was Adam and Eve (Jollof News, 2012).

The second came from Liberia when in early February 2012, Rep. Clarence K. Massaquoi introduced a draft bill that would criminalise same-sex marriage (*Liberia Times* 2012). This was followed by an amendment prepared by Senator Jewel Taylor, former first lady and ex-wife of Charles Taylor. The amendment to the Domestic Relations Law would make same-sex marriage a felony. Nigeria has also introduced a series of bills on same-sex/same-gender marriage (2006, 2009) and in November 2011 the Same Sex Marriage Prohibition Bill was passed by the Senate. At the time of writing the bill has yet to be signed by the president.

But not everyone has chosen such unambiguous assaults on LGBTI people. The valorisation and affirmation of heterosexual marriage and 'the family' in the national project (as well as the continental one, as can be seen from African Union instruments) are pervasive in countries throughout the continent.

All three countries, Nigeria, Uganda and Liberia, have existing laws criminalising homosexuality that date back to British colonial rule. So the questions are not just why these laws remain, but why are they being expanded and why now? The refusal of the Nigerian and Ugandan bills to die, the potential for copycat legislation in other countries, the international furore around them, and differing queer responses present an opportunity to examine these national and international paradoxes and relationships of power.

The rhetoric around homosexuality being 'un-African' relies on the essentialist notion of an 'authentic Africanness', based on the belief that there is something intrinsic to Africa called 'African culture and African traditions'. But it is more than just a defining of the authentic; it is the power to determine who counts as human and what lives count as lives (Macharia 2010). This essentialist position is problematic for many reasons. As Dosekun argues:

> ...an anti-essentialist position maintains that Africa and thus African-ness or Africanicity are historical and therefore contingent constructs. This means that we cannot meaningfully speak of an essential Africa or of essentially African or un-African things, in which case a consciousness and practice such as feminism cannot be dismissed as un-African in these terms. This anti-essentialist argument does not imply that there is no such thing as Africa. It does not deny the many shared historical, material and cultural conditions across Africa, which are in many ways unique to the continent and which in many ways shape our identities as African. It denies rather that these conditions are inherent, natural or fixed (Dosekun 2007).

Dosekun usefully reminds us of the linkage between the naming and claiming of culture and traditions within kyriarchal[2] structures of power and inequality. Rather than patriarchy, which is concerned with the domination of men over women, kyriarchy allows for a more complicated relationship of power based on multiple intersecting structures of domination such as race, ethnicity, class, sexual orientation and gender (Fernandez Factora-Borchers 2008).

The invocation of a nostalgic African culture as the basis for the 'homosexuality is un-African' position is often countered by the argument that this narrative originated with the imposition of colonial penal codes, namely by the British. However, this does not account for similar legislation in francophone and lusophone countries. It is not my intention in this collection to focus on the past, but as Clarke, Muthien and Ndashe point out later in this book, the reference to the historical origins of homophobia in Africa has limited usefulness as an argument for changing laws and effecting social change.

A further analysis can be found in a reading of what Jacqui Alexander calls 'heteropatriarchal recolonisation' (Alexander 1997: 66), the continuity between the 'white heterosexual inheritance and Black heteropatriarchy'. Alexander's focus is the Bahamas and the states of the wider Caribbean; nonetheless, she provides an excellent framework from which to locate contemporary homophobia in African states. The struggle to break free of colonialism was largely a political project, which involved minimal disturbance to Western economic interests or heteropatriarchal structures. Indeed, nationalist movements used the same colonial, militarised masculinities as a foundation for liberation and post-colonialism, thereby maintaining the non-status of African women.

The heterosexualisation project of nation building is further facilitated through legislation or re-legislation (Nigeria – same-sex marriage bill, Uganda – anti-homosexuality bill). Heterosexuality is consolidated as the only acceptable basis for citizenship and the establishing/re-establishing of order and preventing/ending the chaos brought about by sexual/social deviancy of the queer imposition. Thus the renewed legislation builds on the 'civilising mission' of colonialism by reinforcing heterosexuality as the natural order, existing without complication or contradiction (Alexander 1997, Hoad 2007, Atluri 2009). To quote Alexander:

> The law has now presumably emptied society, emptied heterosexuality of the chaotic, the disorderly, the criminal. Both the law and heterosexuality have now been sanitised to function as the repository of order, returning each to an ordinary moral position. Thus articulated, the law would have presumably satisfied its civilising mission, functioning silently, as early British mandates had commissioned it to do, while constructing and defending its own hierarchies (Alexander 1997: 82).

The language chosen by African religious and political leaders to justify heterosexuality as the only acceptable order is similar to that used in other parts of the world: family, cultural and traditional values, sex based solely on procreation within the sanctity of marriage and endless references from religious texts. For example, as the Hon. Samson Osagie, Nigerian senator, stated:

> It is only appropriate that as Africans we uphold our cherished traditional values. It is scriptural that marriages are recognised between a man and a woman. It debases our value when you begin to tolerate marriage between people of same sex. For me, I believe this is one bill that is popular and will enjoy the support of majority of members of the House (Vanguard Nigeria 2011).

Following the passing of the Nigerian same-sex marriage prohibition bill by the Senate in November 2011, there has been a shift in language from morality to include sovereign national rights and laws, possibly as a response to statements by the British Prime Minister, David Cameron, tying development aid to 'LGBT' rights (BBC, Andrew Marr Show, 2011) (Dowden 2011) and the copycat statement by Hillary Clinton on enforcing 'gay rights' globally (Clinton 2011).[3] Both Cameron and Clinton hinted that in countries that persecuted LGBTI people, monies would be given directly to chosen NGOs – presumably those promising to become LGBTI-friendly. In response to aid conditionality, Nigerian Senate President, David Mark, stated:

> If there is any country that wants to stop giving aid because we won't pass the bill on same sex marriage; that country can go ahead.
> We are a sovereign nation and we have the right to decide for ourselves because no country can interfere in the way we run our country (AllAfrica.com 2011).

Nigerian civil society and human rights activists responded to the bill in a statement addressed to the president and the house by presenting an analysis of the 'grave implications' for all Nigerians irrespective of their sexual orientation and gender identity:

It is worth noting for all Nigerian citizens that the proposed bill aims at:

a) prohibiting any form of de facto cohabitation between two individuals of the same sex or gestures that connote same sex relationship directly or indirectly. If this bill becomes law male–male or female–female holding of hands, touching each other, making eye gestures, hugging or any display of affection will be evidence for conviction and 10 years imprisonment.

The bill also aims to:

b) restrict the right to freedom of expression;

c) restrict the right to freedom of association;

d) restrict the right to freedom of thought, including the freedom of conscience and religion (NSSMB 2006).

On the face of it, both the US and to a lesser extent the British statements have substantial support from among British, US and African activists. Similarly, statements by African countries on sovereignty and the right to determine their own laws carry some weight from an imperialistic point of view. However, below the surface of the rhetoric of Western and African leaders lies an unequal and sometimes precarious relationship. It is one that is grounded in both colonialism, racism, economic exploitation and debt dependency and a neoliberal consensus based on economic imperatives, neither of which allows for any normative contradictions. This consensus is riddled with assumptions that LGBTI Africans live in silos, not as complete Africans, but outside national and international political and economic realities. The implication here is that as incomplete Africans, LGBTI people are not affected by free market structural adjustment policies. Nor are they impacted on by the increasing militarisation driven by the US 'war on terror', which is exemplified by the US military presence, particularly through Africom, or by the actions of terrorist organisations such as the Lord's Resistance Army in Uganda or Boko Haram in Nigeria.

The similarities between the impacts of the US Patriot Act, for American Muslims in particular and people of colour in general, and the Nigerian same-sex marriage bill on personal liberties, censorship and freedom of speech are greater than most people would care to contemplate. For example, both require increased state surveillance supported by citizen vigilantism in order to achieve the intended results. Both Muslims and queers are seen to threaten the perceived religious and cultural values of an agreed Judaeo-Christian heteronormative, implicitly white, imperative. Yet, just as the US manages a materially productive relationship with, for example, Saudi Arabia and Bahrain while at the same time facilitating a growing internal Islamophobia, and certainly not daring to challenge either of these countries on their human rights (and particularly LGBTI rights) record, so too African countries may continue similar relationships with the West while curbing citizens' rights when both are compelled by economic imperatives. Interestingly, the statement by Nigerian civil society criticising the Nigerian bill made reference to the potential negative impact it would have on Nigeria's economy:

> With this bill Nigeria and Nigerians will be shown to be untrustworthy and incapable of upholding and domesticating international treaties and conventions which they have signed and ratified. From the perspective of foreign investors, the inability to uphold international agreements raises the question of whether their investment and personnel can be safe in the hands of such an untrustworthy partner. At a time when the country is on a drive to attract direct foreign investment, this bill also stands as a threat to the economy (Nigerian Human Rights Defenders 2011).

A common argument used to explain the introduction of anti-homosexuality bills is that they are diversionary, a way of distracting the populace from more urgent needs such as the removal of fuel subsidies, high unemployment, corruption or fighting terrorism. While it is true that in many African countries anti-LGBTI religious fervour and state homophobia have been a unifying force, it is hard to imagine that whipping up hatred of queer folk will in the long term distract people from these kinds of issues. For example, the Nigeria Occupy Movement of January 2012, which was focused on the removal of fuel subsidies and political corruption, came about despite these distractions. Further, there has been considerable criticism in the mainstream media and social media in Nigeria following the passage of the bill in the Senate. These remain minority voices but the voices are increasing in number and becoming louder.

At this juncture, the transformation of LGBTI Africans from un-African deviants to a legitimate minority remains elusive. In South Africa the hard work of LGBTI activists like Simon Nkoli, Bev Ditsie, Edwin Cameron and Zackie Achmat, to name a few, ensured that the 1994 constitution gave full protection to LGBTI people. Despite this there remains a high level of homophobia and associated hate crimes, particularly against working class black lesbians and transgender people, highlighting the inter-connectivity of oppressions. Over the past 10 years many other African countries have witnessed the transformation of LGBTI Africans out of unseen closets into visible broken glass cabinets, and the replacement of silences by an active and assertive engagement with the state, civil society, queer communities and international NGOs. Alongside the increasing visibility, and the accompanying activism, there has been a growing presence and intervention by what Massad calls the 'Gay International' (2007) – 'LGBT', white, Northern-based NGOs and activists with an almost obsessive interest in searching for homophobia across the global South. The notion of a 'shared gayness' (Hoad 2007, Massad 2007) is established by these groups while at the same time spectacularising African homophobia as a unique geographical phenomenon, unconnected to local and global histories, and essentially inherent.

Some sections of the Gay International take a different view and seek to provide a historical account of 'homosexuality' or same-sex intimacies. The stated aim is to counter the competing narrative of 'homosexuality as un-African', placing the blame for homophobia, at least in some countries, on colonial laws which criminalised male homosexuality. It is not always clear whether this search for 'anthropological proof' of pre-colonial sexual utopias is for the benefit of us Africans or a justification for their own involvement in saving Africa from its colonial legacies (Tatchell 2010). Either way, both these narratives obscure the diversity and contextual specificity of queer African formations, past and present, which are shaped by multiple factors – religion, ethnicity, nationalism, globalised and indigenous popular cultures and diaspora connections (Macharia 2010).

Responding to these anti-queer legislative efforts, Western NGOs and governments have taken a strong interventionist approach. This has culminated in statements by the British and US governments on withdrawing aid to those countries in the global South that continue to persecute LGBTI people. Following the announcement by British Prime Minister David Cameron referred to earlier, over 100 African social justice organisations and activists issued a public statement expressing their 'concern about the use of aid conditionality as an incentive for increasing the protection of the rights of LGBTI people on the continent'. In particular the activists called for a complete rethinking of the present methods of engaging with Africa, including the primacy of consultation with those affected:

> The imposition of donor sanctions may be one way of seeking to improve the human rights situation in a country but does not, in and of itself, result in the improved protection of the rights of LGBTI people. Donor sanctions are by their nature coercive and reinforce the disproportionate power dynamics between donor countries and recipients. They are often based on assumptions about African sexualities and the needs of African LGBTI people. They disregard the agency of African civil society movements and political leadership. They also tend, as has been evidenced in Malawi, to exacerbate the environment of intolerance in which political leadership scapegoat LGBTI people for donor sanctions in an attempt to retain and reinforce national state sovereignty (African Social Justice Activists 2011).

The statement also pointed out that the legal foundation for persecuting LGBTI people throughout the Commonwealth was laid down by the British Empire, and old ways of engaging with the continent must be addressed by the affected, not simply imposed by interventions of the same powers. However, not everyone is in agreement on aid conditionality and a small number of organisations and activists were not supportive of the statement. Ugandan activists from Sexual Minorities Uganda (SMUG) and Icebreakers, who have been at the forefront of challenging state-sponsored homophobia in their homeland, chose not to sign. Even among those who argue in favour of aid conditionality there is an insistence on consultation and a country-specific approach, as explained by David Kuria of Gay Kenya (one of the signatories to the statement):

Instead of assuming that we can have a 'pan-africanist' approach, we should instead query what challenges and opportunities it presents to us as a country. Gay Kenya's statement on aid noted that each country has had a different aid narrative, and could thus not talk of an 'African' but a contextualised Kenyan response (Kuria 2011).

The dangers of the aid conditionality approach became clear with the backlash surrounding the 2010 arrest of Malawian couple Tiwonge Chimbalanga and Steven Monjeza. The couple were sentenced to 14 years for 'unnatural acts and gross indecency' (Mapondera and Smith 2010) but later given a presidential pardon. The high-profile nature of the case has led to a considerable backlash against the Malawi LGBTI community. In an interview, Malawian LGBTI activists commented that prior to the Chimbalanga/Monjeza case, life was easier:

'It was easier [before],' says Thandeka. 'Things are tough right now.'

'Some time back, you could dance, you could maybe kiss, but not now,' says Amanda. The men all have girlfriends or wives to cover the fact that they are gay (IN Toronto 2012).

Reservation about international interventions remains strong, particularly in view of the lack of consultation and the actions which result in undermining and even endangering local activists and conditions. Even the space to write about and publicly critique unilateral interventions from powerful Western activists comes at the risk of libel cases and withdrawal of publications. Dealing with unassailable personalities whose celebrity rests on a history of struggle that sometimes has consequences more dire for the 'helped' than the 'helper' remains a battle. The white saviour complex is alive and well and thrives on appropriating other people's struggles.

Western interventions which seek to impose a Western narrative on the queer African struggle are part of an uninterrupted history of suppressing the needs and experiences of Africans dating back to colonisation. The African struggle is not only directed at changing existing legislation; it is a struggle in which we seek to reassert our own narrative and reclaim our humanity. The

Gay International, as part of an overall neoliberal agenda, is an obstacle to defining and controlling the strategies and outcomes of a queer African struggle based on intersecting struggles and movement building. It also seeks to place itself at the centre of our struggle, ignoring local resistance and the overall movement for liberation and commitment to justice.

The universalisation of 'gay rights' was officially formalised by Hillary Clinton in her 2011 Human Rights Day speech in which she vowed that the US would actively seek to ensure that LGBT rights existed throughout the world (Clinton 2011). Note that she uses the acronym LGBT and the word 'gay' rather than the more inclusive LGBTI or LGBTIQ used by most Africans. She appears not to have heard of intersex people and their rights in this struggle.

Although Clinton did acknowledge that the US record on 'LGBT' rights was far from perfect, her statement contained a number of glaring omissions, not least how the US intended to enforce global 'LGBT' rights. Would there be sanctions, withdrawal of aid, refusal to sell military equipment or targeted assassinations? The lack of clarity reduces Clinton's position to the murky waters of international diplomacy and double speak. Take this statement from the outgoing US ambassador to Liberia, which was made after the introduction of two anti-homosexuality bills in the country:

> She stated, however, that the issue of gay rights in Liberia was being surrounded by what she referred to as 'misconceptions'.
>
> 'Our policies on gay rights are in the public domain,' she said. 'I think the issue that has appeared in Liberia is the issue of misconception that United States aid is tied to Liberia's actions in these areas, and this is not the case,' she said.
>
> She told the *Daily Observer* that she was surprised to learn that gay rights in Liberia were an issue.
>
> 'I don't know that this is an issue here in Liberia; although I read about it in the press all the time, I was surprised to hear that this is an issue in Liberia' (Binda 2012).

Considering that most African countries are US allies and are of strategic military importance, it is hard to imagine that policing and enforcement would be anything other than selective. As is usual for US diplomats, Clinton did not appear to see the irony in the declaration that the US would now be policing the world on one set of rights while itself engaging in numerous human rights violations at home and abroad.

Clinton also conveniently ignored the growing anti-gay evangelical movement in the US and its ties with similar movements in Africa. However, the real concern for African LGBTI people engaged in building progressive social movements is what kind of world Clinton's 'LGBT' rights invoke. How much will it compromise social and economic justice and grassroots democracy in our respective countries? Framing the narrative in terms of rights creates tensions with other civil society and social movements. Queer Africans are not just queers, they are people who live their lives in the same way as everyone else and as such our struggle needs to align itself with other social justice movements such as those of and for rural women, shack dwellers, climate change, land rights and so on.

These pronouncements conveniently ignore the Western history of racism, colonialism and homophobia and even those that recognise colonial culpability in homophobic laws do so with the idea that European and American versions of sexual narratives and activism are the standard which we should all follow (El-Tayeb 2011).

Those of us living in the diaspora are well aware that Cameron's and Clinton's statements are contradictory to the racial configurations of citizenship as experienced in Europe and America, where even birth is insufficient as a marker of belonging. The only way African queers are meaningful activists in the diaspora is if they are working as certified internationalist advocates. At the point when one is unwilling to become a 'collaborator' in the internationalist agenda, thereby challenging the West's legitimacy as saviours, our voices are silenced by casting us as inauthentic Africans. To be authentic one has to be living on the continent and be framed as a victim. Kagendo Murungi's experience, narrated in this volume (see Chapter 21), of working with the International Gay and Lesbian Human Rights Commission (IGLHRC) in New York provides some excellent examples of how the voices of Africans in the diaspora are dismissed.

African states claim sovereignty but at the same time employ a heightened cultural and religious fascism to fuel state homophobia. Even here, there is a complexity in the relationship between some African states and religious institutions as to where power lies in determining the moral agenda and who is accepted as a citizen. Another tension derives from LGBT imperialism that by now has fledged into a profitable NGO/donor industrial complex built on the premise of saving Africans from Africa. As these conflicting tensions push against each other, they have become internally divisive as the various activists struggle to be heard. Even as African LGBTI people have become the site of struggle between competing but related narratives and as the associated tensions push against each other in internally divisive ways, it is essential they engage on their own terms, with the national and the international, and continue to explore the challenges of a transformative politic.

Notes

1   Note on terminology: the term LGBTI (lesbian, gay, bisexual, transgender and intersex) is the acronym in general use by Africans. I use 'queer' as a broader, more inclusive terminology. Other terms – LGBT (lesbian, gay, bisexual, transgender), 'homosexuality', 'gay' – are used only in reference to direct speech.
2   From the Greek word *kyrios*, meaning 'lord' or 'master'.
3   In this speech on Human Rights Day 2011, US Secretary of State Hillary Clinton called for a worldwide end to criminalisation of LGBT people.

References

African Social Justice Activists (2011) 'Statement of African social justice activists on the decision of the British government to "cut aid" to African countries that violate the rights of LGBTI people in Africa', http://bit.ly/SVB0rr, accessed 19 December 2012

Alexander, M. Jacqui (1997) 'Erotic autonomy as a politics of decolonisation: an anatomy of feminist and state practice in the Bahamas tourist economy', in Alexander, M.J. and Mohanty, C.T. (eds) *Feminist Genealogies, Colonial Legacies, Democratic Futures*, London and New York, Routledge

AllAfrica.com (2011) 'Nigeria: Christians laud passage of same sex marriage bill', 1 December, http://bit.ly/uy0nnc, accessed 28 January 2012

Atluri, Tara (2009) 'Putting the "cool" in coolie: Disidentification, desire and dissent in the work of filmmaker, Michelle Mohabeer', *Caribbean Review of Gender Studies*, 3

BBC, Andrew Marr Show (2011) 'David Cameron moralises on foreign aid', 30 October, YouTube, http://bit.ly/wbMmkO, accessed 4 February 2012

Binda, S. (2012) 'US aid not tied to gay rights, says outgoing US ambassador', *Daily Observer*, http://bit.ly/zNBFJn, accessed 3 March 2012

Clinton, Hillary (2011) 'Secretary Clinton's Historic Speech on LGBT Human Rights – "Gay rights are human rights"' , 6 December, YouTube, http://www.youtube.com/watch?v=MudnsExyV78, accessed 4 February 2012

Dosekun, Simidele (2007) 'Defending feminism in Africa', Center for African Studies, Cape Town, http://www.africanstudies.uct.ac.za/postamble/vol3-1/defending.pdf, accessed 6 November 2012

Dowden, Richard (2011) 'Getting gay rights wrong in Africa', Royal Africa Society, http://bit.ly/wqpLab, accessed 4 February 2012

El-Tayeb, Fatima (2011) 'European others: queering ethnicity in postnational Europe', University of Minnesota Press

Fernandez Factora-Borchers, Ana Lisa (2008) 'Accepting kyriarchy, not apologies', My Ecdysis blog, http://bit.ly/4vhZOS, accessed 28 January 2012

Hoad, Neville (2007) *African Intimacies: Race, Homosexuality and Globalisation*, Minneapolis, MN, University of Minnesota Press

IN Toronto (2012) 'Cruel to be kind', http://intorontomag.com/index.php/insight/item/212-cruel-to-be-kind, accessed 3 March 2012

Jollof News (2012) 'Gambian president renews attacks on homosexuals', http://bit.ly/ADaLEO, accessed 20 February 2012

Kuria, David (2011) 'Aid conditionality – blessing or curse', Gay Kenya blog, http://bit.ly/tsujVa, accessed 28 January 2012

Liberia Times (2012) 'Outlaw gays' right', http://theliberiantimes.com/?p=5662, accessed 20 February 2012

Macharia, Keguro (2010) 'Homophobia in Africa is not a single story', *The Guardian*, 26 May, http://bit.ly/yifxG3, accessed 28 January 2012

Mapondera, G. and Smith, D. (2010) 'Malawian gay couple jailed for 14 years', *The Guardian*, 20 May, http://www.guardian.co.uk/world/2010/may/20/malawian-gay-couple-jailed-14-years?INTCMP=SRCH, accessed 6 November 2012

Massad, Joseph (2007) *Desiring Arabs*, Chicago and London, University of Chicago Press

Nigerian Human Rights Defenders (2011) 'Human rights and legal implications of the Same Sex Marriage Prohibition Bill, 2011 for every Nigerian citizen', http://bit.ly/U8xQQB, accessed 19 December 2012

Nigerian Same Sex Marriage Bill (NSSMB) (2006) http://bit.ly/ZOKclb, accessed 19 December 2012

Tatchell, Peter (2010) 'Evils of colonialism: still wrecking lives', *The Independent*, http://ind.pn/KbeciP, 9 May, accessed 23 February 2012

Tatchell, Peter (2011) 'Don't cut aid over human rights abuses, switch it', 1 November, http://bit.ly/A0M9Sf, accessed 20 February 2012

Vanguard Nigeria (2011) 'Same sex marriage: FG, N/Assembly damn US', http://bit.ly/tet3N6, accessed 28 January 2012

9

African statement to British government on aid conditionality

We, the undersigned African social justice activists, working to advance societies that affirm peoples' differences, choice and agency throughout Africa, express the following concerns about the use of aid conditionality as an incentive for increasing the protection of the rights of LGBTI people on the continent.

It was widely reported, earlier this month, that the British Government has threatened to cut aid to governments of 'countries that persecute homosexuals' unless they stop punishing people in same-sex relationships. These threats follow similar decisions that have been taken by a number of other donor countries against countries such as Uganda and Malawi. While the intention may well be to protect the rights of LGBTI people on the continent, the decision to cut aid disregards the role of the LGBTI and broader social justice movement on the continent and creates the real risk of a serious backlash against LGBTI people.

A vibrant social justice movement within African civil society is working to ensure the visibility of – and enjoyment of rights by – LGBTI people. This movement is made up of people from all walks of life, both identifying and non-identifying as part of the LGBTI community. It has been working through a number of strategies to entrench LGBTI issues into broader civil society issues, to shift the same-sex sexuality discourse from the morality debate to a human rights debate, and to build relationships with governments for greater protection of LGBTI people. These objectives cannot be met when donor countries threaten to withhold aid.

The imposition of donor sanctions may be one way of seeking to improve the human rights situation in a country but does not, in and of itself, result in the improved protection of the rights of LGBTI people. Donor sanctions are by their nature coercive and reinforce the disproportionate power dynamics between donor countries and recipients. They are often based on assumptions about African sexualities and the needs of African LGBTI people. They disregard the agency of African civil society movements and political leadership. They also tend, as has been evidenced in Malawi, to exacerbate the environment of intolerance in which political leadership scapegoat LGBTI people for donor sanctions in an attempt to retain and reinforce national state sovereignty.

Further, the sanctions sustain the divide between the LGBTI and the broader civil society movement. In a context of general human rights violations, where women are almost are vulnerable, or where health and food security are not guaranteed for anyone, singling out LGBTI issues emphasizes the idea that LGBTI rights are special rights and hierarchically more important than other rights. It also supports the commonly held notion that homo-sexuality is 'unAfrican' and a western-sponsored 'idea' and that countries like the UK will only act when 'their interests' have been threatened.

An effective response to the violations of the rights of LGBTI people has to be more nuanced than the mere imposition of donor sanctions. The history of colonialism and sexuality cannot be overlooked when seeking solutions to this issue. The colonial legacy of the British Empire in the form of laws that criminalize same-sex sex continues to serve as the legal foundation for the persecution of LGBTI people throughout the Commonwealth. In seeking solutions to the multi-faceted violations facing LGBTI people across Africa, old approaches and ways of engaging our continent have to be stopped. New ways of engaging that have the protection of human rights at their core have to recognize the importance of consulting the affected.

Furthermore, aid cuts also affect LGBTI people. Aid received from donor countries is often used to fund education, health and broader development. LGBTI people are part of the social fabric, and thus part of the population that benefit from the funding. A cut in aid will have an impact on everyone, and more so on the populations that are already vulnerable and whose access to health and other services are already limited, such as LGBTI people.

To adequately address the human rights of LGBTI people in Africa, the undersigned social justice activists call on the British government to:

- Review its decision to cut aid to countries that do not protect LGBTI rights
- Expand its aid to community based and lead LGBTI programmes aimed at fostering dialogue and tolerance
- Support national and regional human rights mechanisms to ensure the inclusiveness of LGBTI issues in their protective and promotional mandates
- Support the entrenchment of LGBTI issues into broader social justice issues through the financing of community lead and nationally owned projects.

http://bit.ly/SVB0rr

10

Straight to the matter – fiction

Olumide Popoola

You might think that I should've headed straight for the arrival gate. I shouldn't have sat there denying the blazing heat, the welcome that would surely hit me straight on, like a meltdown. Just because there was this air-conditioned not-yet-land I could hide in for now and later on fill it with the philosophical musings of a 30-something. That age group is notorious for the musings and until they're in their 50s one must wait and endure their new found wisdom. Especially should one reside at that point (temporarily) in another age bracket. All of this so their fragile emotional inner lives could deal with transience and the fact that one eventually perishes.

What's the rush, you might say? What's the rush of getting things done, pressing along, tying loose ends? Of bringing this into a nice bundle that from now on can be carried on to patient places where gentle people will carefully unfold and unwrap it? What's the rush? Well, age. Ageing. The invariable charge of infinity and the hotter than July (in some real hot country) question: will we prevail (meaning will we remain beyond death)?

But we're not there yet, nowhere near. You keep interrupting before we've had the chance of coherence. You would say, move on, straight away. Don't hesitate just to take in everything. Just to stare at the clusters of people streaming by me, queuing in animated manner underneath the slightly elevated glass window. It completed the box inside which a couple of sweating men sat. Receiving, inspecting, then issuing in beige uniforms: passport control. The commotion was loud and powerful. I had to take a rest and if you stay quiet I will actually get one too. I found a bench on the wall, lining the swelling sight of travellers. Whole families returning from successful lives abroad, business people who took shopping opportunities after whatever their line of fortune had lifted them westwards; students on leave; other business people from other shores looking to dock onto the fertile harbours of this complicatedness. Searchers. Knowers. Returnees. Few fugitives (as far as I could tell).

I would have smoked had I not been at the airport and had I not been under-age. Together with the toxic fumes I would have inhaled the scenes of elaborated reunions and recent farewells. The losses and gains and the euphoric expectations of what was about to happen beyond the immigration booth. But I didn't smoke; we were after all at the airport.

I too would soon pick up the pieces I had left behind or intertwine new memories with established and tested truths of mine, I would. There was no need to delay, I can hear you say that. Stride along into the future. Those who do, meet their fate early.

I was bending forward on the bench that I was sitting on with my legs apart, my elbows firmly planted on my thighs, right where the knees started, hands loose, dangling and totally nonchalant. In this position all observation was a manner of looking upwards, and casually turning my head, and following the drama. The small girl who I had played with during the crowded flight, or rather she had played with me, sought me out, running up and down the aisle to where business class began, constantly turning her fuzz-ball-crowned head. Her hair partitioned into neat squares, held together by colourful dices and balls that made a faint clicking sound every time she reached the dividing curtain and her eyes looked back. Was I – and I was sure that it was me she was seeking out – following her? Her dimples reaching for me without words, she knew the value of her cuteness already and the impact a smile would impart on anyone, not just a youth like me. I couldn't help it. I darted my arm out when she was on her way back and with high-pitched chuckling she ran towards it, then fell into it, over and over again. Her mother who sat three seats behind me in one of the middle aisles hadn't been too happy about it. I wasn't the type to instil anxieties, but well, I wasn't inducing any confidence in advanced baby-sitting skills either. After half an hour of conversation and game playing between me and the little one, Mum was sleeping, nevertheless. Out like a dog, her head resting on the right neigbour's shoulder. Like that she was producing a false picture of marital bliss with him and he – from time to time – looked at the woman who was passed out on his arm as if at some point in the farther past he had knelt and asked for her hand (or anything similarly appropriate). She didn't move at all, remained with her mouth wide open, feet stretched out, now that finally they were outside the shoes. I had stood the test and the child's mother had eventually given in to the faint buzzing, that all planes seem to give off like unlaboured, even breaths – air-conditioned and altitude frozen into mechanical anonymity – and that would make for a light sleep, above the clouds, as they say.

I never got the girl's name because her mother didn't wake up again until the films were being repeated for the third time and the girl's nappy was full and tears aflood. My tickling power – and overall attraction – diminished instantly. Mum looked astounded and took a moment to return from where her dreams had taken her into the wide tube that was navigating the night sky. She patted her daughter's hair absent-minded, slinging her arm around her small neck to console her but when the ledge of the chair proved to be in the way she pulled the small body up in one confident move. Her daughter ended up on her lap and with her other hand she fumbled for her pumps to help her swollen feet ease back into the blue patent leather.

'OK, OK,' she shushed and they went to the tiny toilet cubicle. When they returned, the girl freshly changed and sleepy, the captain announced the imminent arrival in Lagos.

They were approaching the glass window. The mother's royal blue *buba* and *iro* were finished with a tangerine *gele* and matching cobalt blue shoes and handbag. She handed the passport to one of the pair behind the glass window. I waved but the little girl didn't see me. I should've gone over to say good bye, you may say, but what for? They passed to the other side. What good would it do to prolong this casual encounter as if it were of more significance than it could possibly be?

They had arrived. I however, remained firmly in limbo.

He knew I was coming. He was probably amid the heaving cluster of expecting this-side-bounds, looking out for me. Imagining how I had myself found a similar outfit of matching skirt and blouse and if not a purse then a suitably feminine carry-on bag. Don't laugh. He would be on the other side, his sunken eyes squinting, too stubborn to accept how glasses versus pride would ease his days. He would be there, shorter than myself, stocky but only with a small belly, like I had seen on the picture Ada had emailed. With silvery hair that slowly eased away from his forehead, leaving growing lakes amongst the bountiful sides.

You don't remember Ada, do you? That is because you're always just a bit ahead of yourself. Those who wait might sometimes get the whole story. It's up to you.

The queue was getting shorter and I was attracting attention. Don't say you could've told me so. Say that you understand. At least pretend. That is an option.

It wasn't just the security people who had already told me a few times:

'Sah. Dis place is not for waiting o. Go there and show your passport.'

I had excused myself, pointed at my face from which the sweat was pouring generously.

'Sorry. Don't mean to be a problem. Just a moment, if I may. Please. It's my circulation. I'm a bit dizzy. Just a moment to rest.'

They had left me there when I pulled the plastic bottle of water out of my rucksack. No need to get anyone. Just a moment to come by and chill. That's all I wanted. The guard that had stood in front of me in his impeccably ironed uniform, legs apart, arms folded and thumbs hooked into his belt, towering over my sunken frame, was now pointing at me. He was standing next to the passport box, speaking to a man who had newly arrived. It was a tall, lanky figure, thin and breathless and I instantly thought he must be the supervisor. He looked like he had dashed out from a secret office in the inner workings of the well-constructed and refurbished airport. There had been a fire, a severe one, my flight seat neighbour had informed me before I had gotten absorbed with the girl and ignored him. I hadn't been into talking, my stomach felt too tense to inhale and release words in regular fashion; and he was a first year engineering student. I wouldn't have known what to ask.

The guard moved away from the box with the immigration officials, coming towards me in long strides.

The last time we had spoken was on the phone. I had spoken. Dad had been quiet. I didn't know whether he was on the other end of the line, but the urge to say what I did had consumed me. Riding a wave, a perfect one. At its crest – its highest point – I was gushing out sentiments like no man's business. Laying down arguments really – prophylactic – all across the low and even force that was arriving at the shore, slow and inevitable. I thought they'd be there together, the points I'd made, like waves shoaling towards the beach, where there was understanding. To be met with multiple possibilities, which in my fevered excitement were all positive ones. I hadn't taken into consideration that it also meant one could occupy different spots, in different bays, just as we two are still struggling over the question at what age one learns to sit with one's helplessness.

What I had also miscalculated was that beach was synonymous with holiday, thus unreal and impermanent. The stuff of dreams that slipped through the consciousness and was best observed through its gaps, but not taken for the real deal. I wasn't sure if he'd listened until his voice echoed in his unmistakably guttural timbre inside my ear.

'I have already made myself clear in my email. Have I not?'

I looked this up. This. What happened when my hopes collapsed. The way the water arrives when something is in the way. It says: diffraction refers to various phenomena that occur when a wave encounters an obstacle, the apparent bending of waves around a barrier. It also occurs with matter.

So I too crashed. I fell right through. It wasn't a small obstacle, it was huge. Everything.

I wonder what you would have suggested? With your sure ideas about the simplicity of it all.

'What's the worst that can happen?'

Nothing was worse than this.

'I have already made myself clear.'

Now, looking at it again, I can see that it wasn't diffraction at all. I was quite literally axed.

The supervisor arrived at my side.

'Are you well? If you need any medical attention…?'

'No, no, I'm fine. I'm sorry to keep bothering you. I'm just resting until the end of the queue has moved.'

'Well, as you will see,' he continued in polite fashion, extending both his index and middle finger to the place where only minutes ago there had been a line in front of the booth, 'this is already so. You need to show your passport to the official over there.'

'Yes,' it came out of my mouth warily, 'of course.'

Last time I had been here I had only been a few years older than the girl I'd played with earlier. A friendly stewardess had taken my tiny hand and brought me from the check-in counter into the aircraft. There was no one to hold my clammy hands now. I unscrewed the plastic bottle I was still holding and took a deep swig. Then I shouldered the backpack with sudden leverage. The officer looked pleased. His hands on stand-by, ready to grab me by the side should my body fail after all.

Surprisingly, everything went very quick but I should tell you that there was a suspicious look: a long one that travelled from my shaved head (number 1) to my oversized T-shirt and the baggy three-quarter denims. Another thorough inspection of the red passport.

'Kara Funmilayo?'

'Yes.'

'Are you sure? Kara?'

He was there on the other side, he would be. Like that time when I had been the aircraft personnel's darling. When the stewardess had led me out to passport control, he was waiting right here, right by this place – or, actually, I'm not sure where it was, it was before the fire, but figuratively speaking it was this exact place. He had gotten me through security without queues, without much scrutiny due to a bit of help from a beige-uniformed military man, a friend who was generous towards dad and me. In return dad was generous to him.

'It's not Yoruba. English.'

'Oh, OK. Funmilayo?'

This last bit a question. One that didn't await an answer. Not from me. As I said, all went quick. He showed his box partner my passport and as they were speaking to each other in low voices, debating. Suddenly, he nodded vividly and stamped it. Another lingering look but no more whispering. I was released. Emptied out into the deserted baggage claim area where only a few cases were left on the carousel. Mine stood out. A brand new sports duffel bag, not unlike the blue-robed lady's *gele*, only brighter, a much brighter sort of pumpkin colour with white leather seams and suspiciously small next to the set of four identically clothed trolley cases. I was in no rush.

You might interrupt and mention that I hadn't been so far, anyway. That I had and have been digressing in every possible manner. Ploughing through each detail in a laborious way. I, of course, would have to reject your interference, deny it any grounds for discussions, for surely details are a matter of consideration and hardly have I elaborated on many. Maybe not enough? But wisely, this time, I will keep my peace, join the observation, with you. Searching. Knowing. Returning. Was I a fugitive?

The rucksack fitted onto my back like an extra piece of clothing, as if it belonged. Mine had been the last international flight in and its arrival two hours previous had brought a steady stream of good tips from the cheerful returnees and travellers. The baggage handlers could see that I wasn't a promising prospect. My late coming had confirmed this already, my young age was another clue. The lack of urgency in my stride gave view to my reluctance: I was no achiever, no generous spender but although barely past adolescence, someone with baggage. Other types of loads. A lost wanderer.

'Sah. Sey you na need taxi? Hotel? Transport? Directions?'

They tried, nevertheless, although with little conviction or effort, but my shaking head only confirmed their suspicions. They'd thought so.

His email had of course made everything very clear. Especially the matter of direction and which one my life had gone. Which decision I had made and that I had taken it without consulting with him on the matter. The matter. As if one could palpate it, as if there was such a thing; break it apart even, find within it free-flowing and binding elements which one could designate certain importance to. Onto one more than others. A matter of decision. As if one could exchange them for another order and produce an altogether different matter – or more precisely, form. Have them arrange themselves in a refuting direction to the one I had so independently insisted on. Which, to bring the matter to a close, had opposed in the first instance, directions that should be inherent and a given. That although matter could change, this particular one was inherently made for permanence.

The tote bag felt good in my hand. The soft leather handle in my palm prevented it from slipping. It actually absorbed a bit of the moisture from my clammy hands, soaking up my anxieties with it, which could only mean that things were looking up. My confidence boosted itself into action. One more door, one more wall to pass through.

Finally, with conviction, I walked through, striving forward, silently congratulating myself for choosing the three-quarters, although it had been uncomfortable when the damp wind lifted the legs slightly from the inside when I left London hours ago. There was an almost dull thud, the way the heat was welcoming me and I abruptly stopped in my tracks. The pavement was empty. No one was there. He hadn't come.

Why must we go over this, you ask? Why return?

Sweat was again pouring down the length of my torso, this time no longer in anticipation but with the help of humidity, in full knowledge of the matter.

His word had said: 'Obviously, your time in Europe has taken you away from our way of life. Although you're not yet to be considered a woman, you have proven to me that you are capable of taking matters into your own hands.'

I had broken the form, claimed in youthful need a name that was neither African nor one that could bear his, and he therefore released me to my chosen destiny.

Young men were helping passengers from other flights lug heavy cases into their waiting taxis. A large man with two mobiles, one to his ear, with another gesticulating as two porters heaved an oversized suitcase into the boot of a rusty Peugeot.

'No, I've expected you at the time that I've told you to come here. You come and you wait, you hear? I don't need any apologies now, I'm standing at the airport, without a driver, without my own car. It is unacceptable.'

My feet were heavy and there was no possibility of moving, not even a centimetre. 'But where are you? You are meant to wait. Madam didn't know that I was arriving at this time. You did!'

Four large cases in identical casing and descending size had been stored in the trunk and on the back seat. The large, dark man in beige pants and matching brown and beige checked polo shirt heaved himself into the backseat, next to the smaller two of the luggage quadruple. The driver waved a thank you to his helper and the man was shouting into the phone, the door still wide open.

You're quiet now? Here is where I could need a wise intervention, one of your sure help-alongs. I had called. Like you said, what's the worst that could happen.

'Have I not made myself clear? In view of your decision you are no longer considered part of this family.'

I was released. I wasn't returning, I wasn't searching – I knew – and I was definitely not a fugitive. No one was here to get me, what could I be running from? The crashing waves had split into a magnitude of possibilities. They did not bear space for all matters. Not this one. Aunty Ada had called and said, 'Just keep quiet and have a child. No one will ask afterwards. You're so young. Your father has neglected you when you needed him most. Don't turn your back on him now. Just go and have a child.'

I hadn't turned my back, in fact here I was facing all, although I had not brought a child, simply because I hadn't borne one.

The man in beige stepped out of the car again, now holding each of his phones to both ears before his voice and face calmed down like the rough sea might do once the storm had passed the shore.

'OK, I'll wait.'

He hung up, then spoke quietly to the taxi owner, handing him a generous amount of naira for his wasted time. I placed the tote bag on the dusty cement square. A large car pulled up. The darkened windows didn't allow me to see who was inside and the large man was blocking the view when he nearly ripped the door out of his hinges so eagerly was his opening. Joyful hellos were exchanged and he leaned further inside. A young driver in a cobalt blue and orange XXL basketball shirt jumped out of the front seat and grabbed the waiting bags. The man in beige was finally smiling. In his relief he had forgotten the long wait, the flustered anger and the earlier disbelief at being stranded at the airport. He threw out light sentiments, forgotten was the disapproval, his heavy hand in friendly touch on the younger man's shoulder. Then he helped store the bags.

He hadn't come because I was no longer his daughter. I had chosen carefully, had looked for the words that would make him understand, had asked friends and relatives, older mentors. After listening to all and considering what you said, I had chosen what I thought would be easily understood. When I called, following the email exchange, and said I'd be coming in two weeks he had been quiet.

'I've already booked the flight, I will be arriving on the 19th, the last flight from Heathrow.'

'Have I not made myself clear?' After a long silence he added dryly: 'What about your lesbianism?'

The man in beige opened the back door again and proceeded to enter. Then he turned to me.

'Where are you going, son?' he said. I shook my head. Tears were rolling down my cheeks. He left the door leaning and walked over to me.

'You've been here for a while. No one is coming to get you?'

I said nothing. I couldn't speak. He hadn't come. The magnitude must've been obvious. Waves crushing into me, diffracting all over the matter.

'Where do you need to go?'

In my hand was the address I had memorised more to show off and surprise him than out of need. There were several pieces of paper because everyone knows how easily I forget and lose things and my instructions had been clear: Keep them in separate places. In case. I had them all together in one stack, so sure had I been.

'That's off Ikorodu. We'll drop you on the way.'

He shouldered the tote bag and pulled me by the sleeve.

'Sit in the back, with my wife.'

He himself chose the seat next to the driver. It was so cool after the humid evening air, the air-conditioning humming slightly, the door buzzing to remind us that it was still open. I sneezed. Clumsily I dropped into the seat, mumbling 'Good evening ma' while trying to fade into the leather in order not to disturb anyone. My damp T-shirt stuck to my skin like an already licked lollipop picked up from the ground, sticky and slightly dirty.

'Hello,' she replied in comfortable manner, a flair of someone who had seen the world and moved in it as if it was merely the backyard to one of her townhouses. A generous smile flashed her good set of teeth. It was encouraging and suggested they picked up strangers all the time, but of course her husband explained. He was eyeing me in the rearview mirror and turned around to start a conversation, not interrogative but inquisitively enough to make sure I knew that he only half thought that I was decent.

'Straight from London? That's funny…'

I looked at him and then his wife. She was holding the small girl from the plane, who was sleeping soundly, and now I saw that she was wearing the blue outfit, the orange *gele* placed on the back rest. What is the likelihood? Again, I would have expected you to comment on this. The timing, the coincidence. Twice in close proximity, a blue and orange combination. Me in a stranger's car. Everything fitting so seamlessly, almost nothing in the way of coherence.

'My wife also…,' he looked in the mirror at my face and stopped mid-sentence. My short hair felt shorter and alarmingly exposing. We stopped and the driver handed the money the man in beige had given him to the collector in the small cement hut outside. The car crawled over the uneven speed bumps then accelerated, suddenly released from traffic and road stop. Night scenes flashed by and the husband's eyes kept a steady gaze, trying to figure out how to approach me. The matter of the missing welcome scene, the loose end that my appearance was bidding, the tears that had dried on my cheeks.

'We're not far. Is someone going to be there? They know you are coming?'

He paused.

'I don't mean to be … I mean, please don't take it the wrong way. You are a boy? Or a girl?'

From the other side the driver announced softly, as to not disturb and fall out of favour for the second time this evening, that we were entering the small street leading to the address on my piece of paper. The husband turned towards me again.

'They know you're coming?'

This was it. A return. An unknown. A quest. I had arrived.

It is the form that makes a thing what it is. Change occurs because the same matter can be arranged in different ways.[1] All was the same. All was different. I nodded.

For the heart of the matter is always somewhere else than where it's supposed to be.[2]

'Yes, they know I'm coming.'

To allow it to emerge, people approach it indirectly by postponing until it matures, by letting it come when it is ready to come. There is no catching, no pushing, no directing, no breaking through, no need for a linear progression which gives the comforting illusion that one knows where one goes. Time and space are not something entirely exterior to oneself.[3]

He knew I was coming.

Notes

1 Banach, David (2006) 'Some main points of Aristotle's thought', http://www.anselm.edu/homepage/dbanach/arist.htm, accessed 7 November 2012.
2 Trinh, T.M. (1989) *Women, Native, Other. Writing Postcoloniality and Feminism*, Bloomington and Indianapolis, Indiana University Press: 1.
3 Trinh (1989): 1

The face I love: Zanele Muholi's 'Faces and Phases'

Raél Jero Salley

This essay analyses 'Faces and Phases' by Zanele Muholi, a project started in 2006 and still ongoing. Muholi is a contemporary photographer and performance artist and activist working in South Africa, whose work actively responds to questions about individual being and contemporary social belonging in Southern Africa today. Muholi's work imagines contemporary life with a mixture of awe, excitement and romantic vision. Her works also challenge conventional discourse on blackness, sexuality, gender and class. 'Faces and Phases' is an elegant, technically accomplished project that aims to both empower Muholi's female collaborators and offer outsiders an innovative way of seeing, one that critically engages contemporary visuality in southern Africa.[1] The images discussed here are from a phase of this project in 2011.

Muholi's work is exceptional in the way it pushes new directions and agendas, as through her photography she confronts violence acted upon the female body and the lives and abuses experienced by black lesbians in South African townships. Muholi's oeuvre includes images that reveal hate crimes and oppression directed toward lesbian/gay/bisexual/transgender/intersex (LGBTI) communities, while other images highlight pleasures and intimacies within those communities.

My aim is not to speak for Muholi or her collaborators. Rather, my investment is in supporting the transformative potential of Muholi's work and explicating its impact on contemporary visuality.

My discussion is organised in three thematic sections: documents; images, icons and indexes; portraits and values.

107

My main point is that while Muholi's visual expressions are often described according to the critical terms available (black and lesbian), this project is geared not toward integration into dominant structures, but rather toward transforming the basic cultural fabric of hierarchies that allow quotidian experiences of oppression to persist and operate efficiently.[2] 'Faces and Phases' provides an occasion for critical engagement with 'a regime of visibility' within which black queer marginality achieves coherence. As a result, the project offers a moment for a nuanced and attentive examination, one that has the potential to reconfigure currently exploitative sociocultural relations and produce new arenas of expression.[3]

Look, for instance, at Mbali, who stands to the side, close to a wall, her closely shaven blond head tilted and left arm folded behind her back. Mbali confronts us with a confident gaze and an open, three-quarter pose. The arrangement proudly displays her t-shirt, emblazoned with the iconic superwoman symbol.

Photo: courtesy of the artist

Mbali Zulu,
KwaThema, Springs,
Johannesburg, 2010.
Silver gelatin print
Image size: 76.5 x 50.5cm

Muholi's engagement with Mbali comes after violence – a hate crime in 2008 in which a member of the community (Eudy Simelane) was murdered. Mbali's portrait is made with this event in mind. Muholi describes the picture as a commemoration, memorial and historical record of the roles brave women play in the face of pain and suffering. Mbali's choice to wear an icon of heroism communicates a defiance, resilience and fearlessness in the face of violence, stigma and homophobia.

Muholi insists on a documentary style of image making for her 'visual activism'. She is intent on producing an historical archive of images for and of black lesbians, bisexuals, transgenders and queers. She speaks forcefully when she explains, 'It is about observing and taking action, about taking pictures of herself and other women to heal from their past.'[4]

This observation and action matter dearly to those of us who live in South Africa, where homophobia is widespread and hate crimes are regularly perpetrated. While the images circulate among the audience that serves as her subject, they also reach a broader audience in order to present locally specific, culturally readable visual performances as alternatives to current conceptions of identity.

Visual documents

A history of black photographic image making has been concerned with opening up the apparently fixed meanings of images, and one of the key sites is documentary photography, a form that carries with it a claim to truth, the message of 'this is how it really was'. Constant (self-)documentation, Jennifer Blessing suggests, is an attempt 'to fix identity, to hold up a mirror image of the self, to be who you want to be, to be "real" but, most of all, to be sure you exist'. But the documentary form may also be seen in a wider political framework. For black photographers, using documentary aesthetics is potentially an attempt to reposition guaranteed centres of knowledge, certainties of realism, and struggles to contest negative images with positive ones.[5] Such pictures exhibit an interest in making the private public, and suggest a family album, a community and a struggle with which the viewer is invited to empathise.

Photo: courtesy of the artist

Betesta Segale,
Gaborone, Botswana, 2010.
Silver gelatin print
Image size: 76.5 x 50.5cm

Betesta offers an example of Muholi documenting family, community and struggle. Betesta is a transgender person from Botswana, a country with the only transgender support group on the continent, called Rainbow Identity Association (RIA), founded by Skipper Mogapi, who is also featured in 'Faces and Phases' (2010). Nonetheless, Betesta is still faced with isolation, an experience Muholi describes as a continual process of 'coming out.' Betesta faces the challenge of existing outside a fixed, defined sexual identity, and thereby challenges those viewers who demand such definition. As Jean Genet writes: 'Changing sex doesn't consist merely in subjecting one's body to a few surgical adjustments: it means teaching the whole world, forcing upon it, a change [or reinvention] of syntax.'[6] Genet's notion of a fundamental turnabout of syntax implies an underlying signification beyond transsexualism, one that points to the possible abolition of a fixed 'reality' (and by extension the possibility of documentation) of sex altogether.[7]

The point is that 'Faces and Phases' engages the documentary photographic form against fixed polarities and boundaries. Without a 'real' or essential black lesbian or transgender subject with which to ground signification, we are faced with unfinished visuality, continuously contingent, unguaranteed distinctions.[8] As Baudrillard theorises: where poles cannot be maintained, one enters 'absolute manipulation', and criticises potential forms of 'new authenticity'. Muholi's pictures of South Africans delight in the documentation of what is labelled unusual, and possibly assert the 'realness' of the never-before-seen or the unimaginable, allowing, even provoking, viewers to stare back and ponder.

This critical visual encounter leads us to ask: what sort of looking is this, and how does it work?

Images, icons and indexes

My argument is that 'Faces and Phases' provokes a way of looking that potentially reconfigures sociocultural relations through the movement of images, icons and indexes.

Look at Pinky Zulu, for instance. Here we are confronted with an image – a likeness, figure, motif or form that appears in or through the material support of the medium (in this case, photography), which forms the set of material practices that brings the image and object together to produce the picture which, in this instance, includes the figural subject and symbolic text. As complex assemblages of virtual, material and symbolic elements, the picture communicates and produces meaning.

Photographs, observes Christian Metz, are pictures that offer both indexical and iconic signs. An index commonly refers to a list, a systematic catalogue, an indicator or a way of expressing a relationship or value. Consider this in the context of Muholi's practice, which emerges out of her encounters as an activist at the nexus of black African cultural politics and multiple dimensions of class, gender, sexuality and ethnicity in South Africa.

The index refers to a process of signification in which the signifier is bound to the referent not by social convention, not by similarity, but by actual connection in the world. Pinky Zulu was there in 2010, posing to produce the photographic image in South Africa, which grounds it in a specific space and time.

Photo: courtesy of the artist

Pinky Zulu,
Constitution Hill,
Johannesburg, 2010.
Silver gelatin print
Image size: 76.5 x 50.5cm

Muholi's stated aim is to provide 'positive' visual alternatives to black lesbian marginality, which involves a cultural strategy that responds to reductively iconic images.

The icon is an image, representation, symbol, someone or something famous, or something otherwise with larger than life status. Icons are often perceived to represent universal concepts, emotions and meanings. A crucial function of an icon is to bring out a notion of public and collective effect in the nation state. In fact, a photographic icon may be a form of public art that generates civic action. The icon is an aesthetically familiar form that has the ability to project an 'emotional scenario' to manage a basic crisis, a relational sign that produces affective responses by invoking normative codes, meanings and values. While the index is grounded in space, time and the material world by direct physical connection, the icon is a mere relation between the sign and the thing signified.

While Muholi's pictures may be indexical, I want to argue that a repetitive emphasis on incomplete narratives of black lesbian subjects and communities may emphasise what Nicole Fleetwood identifies as non-iconicity – a counterpoint to over-determined representations of lived experience. Muholi suggests as much by provoking the viewer with complex, open questions:

> What does an African lesbian look like? Is there a lesbian aesthetic or do we express our gendered, racialised and classed selves in rich and diverse ways? Is this lesbian more 'authentic' than that lesbian because she wears a tie and the other does not? Is this a man or a woman? Is this a transman? Can you identify a rape survivor by the clothes she wears?[9]

By asserting non-iconicity, 'Faces and Phases' emphasises specific and particular indexical aspects of the photograph, which reshapes the sort of relations one may form with the photographic objects. These non-iconic pictures critique incomplete narratives of, for and about black lesbian existence, and develop archives, communities and histories as counterpoints to unfinished, troubled and troubling representations.[10]

Distinctive features of Muholi's work include her relationship with her subjects as well as their self-presentation. These portraits are intimate. They come out of time spent together.[11] But they are also public, and have had national and international impact.

Since our interest is with the ways in which this project is geared not toward integration into dominant structures, but rather toward transforming the basic cultural fabric, we must inquire: 'What role does portraiture play in relation to community, nation and value?'

Portraits and values

The portrait has been a symbol for higher human qualities since ancient times. While portraits convey a likeness of an individual, they also demonstrate the imagination of the artist and a perceived social role for the sitter in ways that raise the subject above the conventions of the moment. The historical conventions of portraiture matter to Muholi's work insomuch as they remind us of the traditional features of the portrait: it exhibits personal and

Ziyanda, Cape Town, 2010.
Silver gelatin print
Image size 86.5 x 60.5cm

public qualities, a duality of likeness and type, and stylisation and individuality.

Usually, a portrait is defined as a work of art that represents a unique individual. But this simple definition is not enough because a portrait is complex and contradictory. While it may be concerned with physical likeness in appearance, it may also suggest something about the subject's inner position or life, character or virtues.

Three factors are useful to considering the complexities of portraits, writes Shearer West. First, portraits may show specific and distinctive aspects of a sitter as well as generic qualities valued in the sitter's context or milieu. Second, while all portraits represent the body and face, they also refer to the soul, character or virtues of the sitter. Third, all portraits involve a series of negotiations (usually) between the artist and the sitter, and the impact of these negotiations, and the viewpoint of the photographer, shape the picture.

I would add that portraits have qualities of the object of representation (iconicity), refer to the act of sitting (indexicality) and contain gestures, expressions, and props that can be read with knowledge of social conventions (symbolism). It is the indexical value that seems to transport us into an actual moment in the past when the artist and sitter encountered each other in a real time and place.

In 'Faces and Phases', the images are as much about the individual as about a collective or community presence. The sitters see themselves not framed as the other so much as infiltrating the status quo, bringing their community (or nation) to the forefront. To this point Simon Njami writes:

> Mastering your own image means bringing into the world voices and colours that elude globalisation and uniformisation, it means refusing to be just the fruit of the other's gaze. It means assuming, in a kind of silent contradiction, your own vision of yourself, following your cultural codes and aesthetics.[12]

As Benedict Anderson has argued, a modern nation is not a natural fact: its origin, history and destiny are the stuff of myth, made and not given, but 'imagined communities' always disavow their artificial, constructed character, constructions produced from images and discourses about the seeable and sayable.

Consider these observations alongside Muholi's decision to 'capture images of [her] community in order to contribute towards a more democratic and representative South African homosexual history'.[13] Muholi decries the reduction and sensationalisation of the many different, complex stages, roles and phases within a black lesbian community, so in 'Faces and Phases' photographic portraiture supports nation building.

The project also presents likeness itself as an unstable concept, an idea to 'be balanced against the limitations of representation, which can only offer a partial, abstracted, generic, or idealised view of any sitter'.[14] Whether or not a portrait was actually based on a sitting, the transaction between artist and sitter is evoked in the imagination of the viewer.[15]

These portraits, then, paradoxically present the photograph as the object we look at, but also refer to the photographic session, a transaction between the sitter and photographer – the thing that is always invisible to the viewer. As Barthes writes, '[the photograph] is not what we see'.[16] The photographic portrait redoubles this instability because as an indexical image it seems to freeze a moment in time and aid memory, but it also falsifies experience, or mythically provides an iconic 'natural and universal [visual] language'.[17]

Looking at the images in 'Faces and Phases', the viewer is confronted with questions: is the thing unseen that which shapes black lesbian experiences of political and ethical life? Is it a troubling presence of exclusion? Is this an effective method to form a sense of belonging, kinship or nation in visual rendering? Looking at Muholi's 'Faces and Phases' portraits in the context of portraiture, community and national values, one encounters enigmatic pictures that defy any single thread of explanation.

New narratives

'Faces and Phases' is a group of social images that exude an exhibitionistic self-delight. They appear without self-doubt or sentimentality, and seem to offer a dream of total control and a demeanour of mastery. The pictures either 'speak to us', sometimes literally, sometimes figuratively; or they look back at us silently.[18] Because pictures have this kind of social and psychological force, we talk as if pictures have feeling, will, and desire. What I have tried to do is reflect on how this power is constituted and performed in this context.

In the process, I have moved away from an analysis of politics of representation, and toward increased concern with how subjectivity itself may be constituted through visual discourse, how subjectivity is performed through visual technologies.[19] This is part of an effort to resist overdetermined narratives of black or lesbian identity in favour of noting how these pictures resist imposed labels by linking the visual subject to us as agents of sight and objects of discourse that impact the production of visuality.

When I say visuality I mean the social field of the visual, the everyday processes of looking at others and being looked at. It is this complex field of visual reciprocity that is actively constitutive of social reality. Muholi's figures are not subjects 'captured' on film, rather, these are subjects that capture and bring us into a world where to perform is to control. These non-iconic images refuse to project a prescribed 'emotional scenario' to manage crisis, in favour of a visual presentation that lessens the weight on the black lesbian visual to do so much. 'It is a move away from the singularity and significance placed on instantiations of blackness to resolve that which cannot be resolved. Rather than invoke normative codes, meanings and values, these pictures open themselves to love without 'hypervisibility' or turning into idols, that is, subjects of 'abomination and adoration'. These 'Faces' may demand love, but do not need or return it.

To speak of 'the face I love' in Muholi's 'Faces and Phases' is a way of relating to a (libidinal) object, a picture. Some faces offer a picture of seriousness, others begin to smirk, others appear with a spirit of pleasure and play. In all of these varied modes of self-presentation, I see in Muholi's portraiture work an effort to present – on their own terms – a multitude of visual subjects who have been excluded from dominant South African society and public memory, both during apartheid and today. In this regard, 'Faces and Phases' negotiates complex knots that afflict the subject and object of racism, sexism and gender bias by means of portraits that show complex individuals occupying multiple subject positions and enunciations.[20]

Conclusion

My point has been to suggest a way into these photographs that does not reduce them to social criticism, excessive category or viable commodity. This is important because I do not read these pictures as ridiculing the supposed homogeneity of (the South African) nation, (black, lesbian or transgender) community or even (homo or heterosexual) spectatorship. Instead, 'Faces and Phases' actively reveals how the phenomenon of 'black lesbian' is currently capable of becoming visible in ways that enable (and/or force) a re-vision of existing dominant conceptions of the world. This includes a re-tooling of visual mechanisms, a sort of reinvention that occurs through critical consideration of the needs and interests of the humans that appear in 'Faces and Phases'.

Notes

1 N. Fleetwood (2011) *Troubling Vision*, Chicago, University of Chicago Press: 37.

2 Cohen, Cathy (2005) 'Punks, bulldaggers, and welfare queens: the radical potential of queer politics?', *Black Queer Studies*: 21–51.

3 For further discussion on seeing and looking as it operates in contemporary visual culture, see Marita Sturken and Lisa Cartwright (2001) *Practices of Looking: An Introduction to Visual Culture*, Oxford, Oxford University Press.

4 Personal correspondence between the author and Zanele Muholi, Cape Town, October 2010.

5 Blessing, Jennifer (ed) (1997) *Rrose Is a Rrose Is a Rrose: Gender Performance in Photography*, New York, Guggenheim Museum: 96.

6 D. Bailey and S. Hall (2003) 'The vertigo of displacement', in Liz Wells (ed) *The Photography Reader*, New York, Routledge: 381.

7 Genet, as quoted in Sarah Wilson, 'Femininities-masquerades', in Blessing (1997: 148 and 178).

8 This kind of turnabout is akin to the *détournement* developed in the 1950s by the artists of the Situationist International. In general it can be defined as a variation on a previous visual work, in which the newly created one has a meaning that is antagonistic or antithetical to the original. The original work that is 'détourned' must be somewhat familiar to the target audience, so that it can appreciate the opposition of the new message. See http://en.wikipedia.org/wiki/Détournement and http://www.cddc.vt.edu/sionline/presitu/usersguide.html.

9 R. Salley (2009) 'Unfinished visuality: contemporary art and black diaspora 1964–2008', PhD thesis, University of Chicago.

10 Z. Muholi (2010) 'Faces and Phases', Cape Town, Michael Stevenson Gallery.

11 Fleetwood (2011: 42).

12 Parallels are to be found in Nan Goldin's photographs from the early 1970s, for instance. Goldin photographed drag queens and pre-op transsexuals. Drag queens have been the subject of many 20th century photographers, including Brassaï, Lisette Model, Weegee and Diane Arbus. See 'Queer reality' in Blessing (1997).

13 S. Njami (2010) *A Useful Dream: African Photography 1960–2010*, Silvana Editoriale Brussels, Brussels, BoZar Books, Centre for Fine Arts: 12.

13 Z. Muholi, artist statement, 'Faces and Phases I'.

14 S. West (2004) *Portraiture*, Oxford, Oxford University Press: 24.

15 West (2004: 41).

16 R. Barthes (1980) *Camera Lucida: Reflections on Photography:* 6 as quoted by W.J.T. Mitchell (2005) *What Do Pictures Want? The Lives and Loves of Images*, Chicago, University of Chicago Press: 274.

17 L. Wells, 'General introduction', in Wells (2003: 5); Mitchell (2005: 273).

18 For discussion of the lives (and loves) of images, see Mitchell (2005): 30.

19 Fleetwood (2007: 12) employs this succinct language.

20 Mitchell (2005: 47).

12

Caster runs for me

Ola Osaze

In South Africa, thousands of miles away from New York City, Caster Semenya lives and breathes. Perhaps she is already training for the next race, picturing a victory not overshadowed by questions about her gender. She emerged out of relative obscurity to shatter the world record and win the gold medal at the women's 800-metre final in Berlin in 2009.

Her victory was so astonishing that all the whisperings about her gender were suddenly amplified. A few other runners, who thought the title was rightfully theirs, grumbled publicly. The International Association of Athletics Federations (IAAF) stepped in, refusing to believe that someone so young, new and, some would argue, so black and poor, could win. They did the unimaginable: forced Semenya to undergo a battery of 'gender tests'. Most female-bodied people dread that annual visit to the gynaecologist. Many shudder at the thought of laying on the examination table, legs stirruped with a medically trained individual studying away in between them. What Caster went through at the hands of supposed gender experts, psychologists, endocrinologists, gynaecologists and internal medicine specialists makes the routine pap smear exam look like a nice, peaceful stroll on a sandy shore.

To me, as a Nigerian who defies gender categorisation, Semenya's story is all too familiar. I decided to interview other New York City Africans who, in some way or other, are also gender 'outlaws'. I wanted to learn what aspects of Caster's story they strongly identified with, their analysis of how Caster had been treated, and what the entire world can learn from this moment. I asked NCK, an African man who wanted to maintain anonymity, why there was such a furore around Semenya's gender expressions. '[It's] not only how dare she put herself within the arena of woman, but how

119

dare she come out of those trappings [of poverty] and run the race, cross the finish line, wear the [gold] medal and the South African flag.' He connects the athlete's experiences to the legacy of colonialism in Africa, stating this is the same way labels like 'coloured' and 'Indian' were used to impose and uphold apartheid in South Africa. Words are not meant to impose limitations, he explains, yet words and phrases like 'masculine' or 'hermaphrodite' have been used by other athletes, IAAF officials and mainstream journalists to dehumanise Caster, in spite of her win.

Kagendo Murungi, a Kenyan woman who identifies as gender non-conforming as an act of resistance against society's two-gender system, argues African women's successes are constantly devalued because of pervasive racist and sexist stereotypes. 'There is a long history of the most private aspects of our physical anatomies being paraded around the world for the pleasure of the European elite. The spectacle and outrage of Saartjie Baartman, the "Hottentot Venus", might be the best known example of this phenomenon,' she declares. Similarly, Yvonne Fly Onakeme Etaghene, a self-identified Nigerian-dyke-poet, argues: 'If Caster can be someone who is not fitting into a socially prescribed gender role, then that means our genders' demarcations are not real.'

IAAF officials demanded Caster essentially prove she is a 'traditional' woman. 'Well, what is a traditional woman? What are traditional women's bodies?' queries NCK. 'They are trying to say that this is one body that we can exclude out of the corpus of bodies labelled as women, as opposed to examining the label of woman, and seeing that the experience is so much larger and this person has transcended all of it.' Transcending, in Caster's case, has involved being a natural-born athlete, refusing to obey gender norms in terms of how to dress or act, training endlessly and developing a muscular body that many, regardless of gender, vie for. (Linda Hamilton's muscular build in *Terminator 2* was the only reason I went to the gym in the 1990s.) Masculine women are nothing new, so why are Caster, and gender non-conforming people in general, demonised by mainstream society? Etaghene blames it on people's inability to accept gender expressions falling outside the socially prescribed two-gender system enforced in practically every sphere of life. 'People don't know how to deal with athletic bodies unless they are attached to people who have penises. [They are] not able to deal with ways in which women can be and are masculine.'

Gender non-conformity, Etaghene argues, is a vital part of the tapestry of African experiences and expressions. 'If you look at African cultures and others from the dawn of time, there have always been masculine women and feminine men, and people who have traversed the gender spectrum, whether it be in a spiritual ceremony and someone who is biologically a woman is possessed by a masculine spirit, and is acting in a way that is [perceived as] masculine. That is gender-revolutionary.' The dark-skinned, 'fro-hawk sporting poet has often been vilified for her identity. 'I can relate to people poking at you and making a spectacle out of you. Whether it be what I have to say, or how I look, or being a Nigerian dyke, people make that a spectacle like, "Oh my god, you're a Nigerian dyke, there's only one of you and you're so weird".' Etaghene uses art as a way to heal from such experiences. 'It's about staying grounded and focused and knowing that I am my own normalcy. I am not left of centre. I am my own centre. I don't look at, for instance, heterosexual white femininity as who I should be.'

What has been encouraging is how South Africans, sensing the racist and sexist underpinnings of the IAAF's actions, resolutely stood up for their 'home girl'. Etaghene, Murungi and NCK think this presents the perfect opportunity to increase visibility of, and respectful dialogue about, the interconnectedness of African women and lesbian, gay, bisexual, gender non-conforming, transgender and intersex experiences. 'If nothing else, at least, perhaps the mainstream press will report on intersex people and leave [the offensive term] "hermaphrodite" in the past where it belongs,' adds Murungi. Similarly, Etaghene feels hopeful that more people will ardently support intersex rights, thereby placing intersex issues on a more global scale. Additionally, according to Murungi, mainstream media's 'irresponsible, outdated, knee-jerk racist, sexist, transphobic, exotifying' portrayal of Caster has been repeatedly challenged by an outpouring of DIY journalists and social networking enthusiasts.

People have posted affirming messages on websites like Caster Runs For Me and For Caster Semenya. Others have uploaded videos on YouTube, expressing their solidarity in a multitude of ways. For example, a one-minute-long cartoon piece, also titled 'caster runs for me', by queer Turkish German artist Beldan Sezen urges people to question gender roles and defy any attempts to police gender expressions. In Etaghene's case, solidarity was expressed through the creation of a love poem to honour Semenya as a survivor. In an excerpt from her poem, 'Caster Semenya: praising your name', the poet looks to the past and prophesises about the future:

but it hurts to be a visionary sometimes, to be brilliant,
    to be excellent
sometimes it hurts in ways we could never have imagined
the trailblazers often get yelled at
misunderstood and demonized –
from Jesus to Tupac
Audre Lorde to you, Caster
anyone who is different or exceptional
feels the brunt of unexpected pain & criticism
the children of your critics
will praise your name,
rock t-shirts with your face on it,
have posters of you on their walls to inspire them to be great.[1]

Note

1   The rest of Etaghene's poem can be found on her blog, a dyke of a certain calibre: http://www.myloveisaverb.com.

Transsexuals' nightmare: activism or subjugation?

Audrey Mbugua

With the advent of LGBT activism, concerns have been raised about transphobia among homosexuals. The primary goal of this chapter is to explain the basis of this transphobia, provide examples of transphobia among homosexuals and offer recommendations on how to deal with transphobia and the marginalisation of transsexuals by some homosexuals. But, before I do that I need to issue a disclaimer: some homosexuals might feel the chapter is deficient of the respect they are accustomed to from human rights activists. We have been used to the disproportionate privileging of gays and lesbians, meaning it's an abomination to criticise homosexuals when they are wrong. Why? Because you don't do that. You don't hurt the feelings of homosexuals. Why? Because you don't!!! I will not go off course to offend for the sake of it but neither will I sugar-coat any words in this chapter.

When I talk of transgender or transsexual people, I will be referring to people who experience a long-lasting and persistent discomfort with their assigned sex and seek medical and legal assistance to transition from one sex to another. Note that I will not be talking about drag queens and kings, male sex workers who go around dressing in certain clothes to get attention from clients and I will definitely not be talking about shemale porn actors, cross dressers and effeminate gay boys and butch lesbians.

Abuses and violence by *some* gays and lesbians

Take a moment and reflect on these words:

> A transsexual is a mentally deficient gay man with a fetish for amputation. I, as an out and proud gay man, am disgusted that these people are given legal rights to trick others into believing they are what they are not. Gay people don't pretend to have a 'medical condition'. If you want to treat a transsexual, treat them to intense therapy to get over their self-loathing of their homosexuality.[1]

It is remarkable such a statement can be made by a homosexual. Early in June 2011, I wrote the following untrue paragraph for a small test (remember, the paragraph is hypothetical – it is not true):

> A homosexual is a mentally and sexually deficient skunk with a fetish for sodomy. I, as an out and proud transsexual, am disgusted that these people are given legal rights to trick others into believing they are what they are not. Trans people don't pretend to be sexually deficient. If you want to treat a homosexual, treat them to intense therapy to get over their unnatural orientation.

I then approached a gay friend of mine, told him I got it from a certain website and asked him what he thought of it. He said it was hateful, false, stupid and based on prejudice.

I then showed him the first paragraph of a gay man insulting transsexual people and asked him what he thought of it. Anyone would think the reaction would be the same as for the hypothetical paragraph attacking homosexuals. But, to my shock, this young man recoiled and said that people were not aware of transsexual issues because there wasn't enough information and resources so people ended up 'misunderstanding them'.

I managed to get similar sentiments from others and it is worth reading a few:

> I am a lesbian. I do not like transsexuals. My problem is this: there are people out there born without feet, arms, legs, etc. and yet they somehow come to terms with the body they were born into. To claim that you need surgery, or are somehow

born in the wrong body ... well, shit, aren't we all?! I think to remove your penis, and insert said flesh inside of your body, or the other way around, is a cheap cop-out and a lazy way around the problems that really plague your heart... In India, men often [resort] to castrating themselves as a way to reach enlightenment faster, although I recently saw a video where the men said they were doing this because they feel like women ... which I again think is crap ... I am so incredibly tired of psychologically ill people using cross-dressing, third genders, and transgendered platforms to carry out their own fantasy, while the rest of us have to suffer.[2]

I am gay, and I hate transgendered people. Probably because I watched a documentary about gay people, that resulted in that we are naturally born gay, through the amount of exposure to testosterone whilst in the womb. But I don't see how transgendered people can be natural. I like people who dress as male/female for entertainment ... I find it sickening that transgendered people would want to change their gender. Or that a man would dress as a woman, seriously and not for entertainment.[3]

I find that there are a lot more people in the GL community who dislike Trannies because they find them selfish, indecisive, overly sexually fluid and basically dirty, confused, and dramatic people. To destroy their families and a great base of their friends takes a certain level of being self-absorbed. It takes another level to choose to not be one gender or the other, but in between, and then to have a relationship where the one normal partner has to be constantly supportive of the TG partner takes an even greater level of self-inclusion. Plus every transgendered person I know has had to make some big dramatic production out of every choice they've made, to start doing drag, to not start doing drag, to not identify as gay, to identify as lesbian, it really doesn't matter what they choose, it has to be some big grand thing. It's ridiculous to ask all of the gay community to participate and submit to this level of drama because in comparison to gender reassignment surgery, our drama (regardless of how legitimate) is dwarfed and poo-pooed...[4]

There are a number of reasons why some homosexuals hate and marginalise transsexuals:

First, some homosexuals oppress and marginalise transsexuals because they are desperate to look 'normal' in the eyes of

125

heterosexuals. It is their way of saying, 'Hey, look at me! Don't I look like you heterosexuals? But look at that thing pretending to be something it's not. It's a freak. Let's do something for it to conform to our gender norms'. In an act of desperation, they inflict pain on other minorities. Look at the following excerpts from transgender people:

> Early this morning, I was mis-gendered by a gay man on a bus journey. I ignored his slight but he continued sucking up to his female friend. When I was about to get off he followed me and deliberately swung his bag striking my bottom and apologised … even after apologising, he turned back to his female friend laughing out loud and said, 'didn't I tell you he's a man?' … a gay man or any other man groping a transsexual woman to gain the friendship of a straight woman suffers first from transphobia but also internalised homophobia.[5]

> Trans people often use the argument of them having nowhere else to go, but having nowhere to go doesn't mean you have to go somewhere. Especially if that somewhere is a civil rights group that's trying to earn respect not mockery.[6]

Second, some homosexuals isolate transsexuals because they regard them as security risks. This is a scenario I have seen among some gays in Africa, including Kenya. They don't like to be seen associating with transsexuals in public. And not just all transsexuals but transsexual women who don't blend as women or who are open about their identity. This is common in hostile parts of Kenya.

You see, members of the public were convinced that it is these transsexual women who are the gays and, to be precise, that 'they are the bottoms' (the 'wife' in a male homosexual couple) and if you are seen with one then you are the big spoon (the husband). So most gay men will not want to be seen with these 'bottoms' because they will out them (as gays put it). So they will marginalise and chase them from their LGBT organisations or events to avoid attacks from members of the public.

Third, *some* gays and lesbians are very jealous. They think we are competing for attention, beauty and rights. That's why some will always want to put us down. I once went out in the company of some lesbian friends and I was talking to this girl in the group and, out of the blue, one of my lesbian friends was telling the group that I was a man. And, using such rubbish, she got the girl. Look at the following:

> In my teens, I was friends with Phil, a gay guy … wasn't happy being a male, so I decided to change my sex … Men checked me out and Phil HATED all the attention I was getting … Phil came in my new home, looking jealous … I wasn't getting good vibes from this queen … Somebody called Deshaun's (her boyfriend) job and said that he was living with a man with titties and a dick. Deshaun and I thought Phil was behind it. I passed beautifully and back then, people did not know that much about trans issues. I 'befriended' Tony and Melvin, two jealous queens. God, they were envious of me. They slashed my car tires. Sprayed silver paint all over my auto. Threw eggs on my door. I swear to God, I didn't do anything to these guys. My only crime was being an attractive trans woman, who had a man by my side … I could sit here for hours and share count-less stories about things gay men did to try to screw up my life.[7]

Sometimes, their attacks on transsexuals are based on misconceptions. Some homosexuals think that transsexuals want to be assimilated into their community. And, instead of looking at it objectively and directing their anger to their homosexual colleagues who are to blame for this, they insult transsexuals. For example:

> I am a bi woman and I think we lack credibility as 'mentally' stable people because we're being lumped in with people who in my opinion self mutilate themselves. If that is too harsh a description then I would lump them in with people who like plastic surgery … who are always dissatisfied with who they are physically. but I am told my friends and have read too many articles by transgender people that [their] choice to change their bodies and appearance has NOTHING to do with their sexuality … SO why are they lumped in with gays n lesbians in every argument, parade, policy and whatever else there is when gays and lesbians are fighting for their civil rights. I think transgenders have NO business in the gay and lesbian 'community'.[8]

> Yes they should be in the bloody beauty section if anything, all they care for is looks. We have real problems not just image.[9]

Similar sentiments – from homosexuals – can be accessed on other websites:

> I think the appropriate treatment is to teach people to love themselves as they are, not irreversible hormone therapy and performing hatchet-jobs on one's genitalia.[10]

> I cringe at the 'T' crowd being lumped with gays and lesbians. I mean all the power in the word to them, but I feel that sexual dysmorphic disorder, or whatever its called is just that, a disorder. I think trans people just hate themselves for being gay, whether they know it or not. I've never met a trans person who wasn't a complete car wreck looking for endless attention to boot. I think it drags down the gay rights movement to be attached to the always photo-ready trans circus.[11]

> I agree somewhat that trans people, particularly FTMs, are pretty messed up, that they're not so much ill as deluded. Trans people should have their own community, their own organisations, their own legal defense fund.[12]

> No it's (transsexualism) a complete aberration or abomination.[13]

> I have no problem with gays, or lesbians, or transgenders, but i personally believe there is something mentally wrong with transgenders. I don't hold that against them though. You cant help being gay but you CAN help changing your sex.[14]

There are a number of transgender people who had something to say about lumping transsexuals in with homosexuals:

> YOURE AN IGNORANT BIGGOTED HYPOCRITICAL *****.
> DO YOU THINK I WANT TO BE GROUPED WITH YOU F*GS AND CARPET MUNCHERS???? NO!!!!!!![15]

> [A]bsolutly no transsexuals are born that way with a condition that is medically treatable gay peopl just have a skew sexualityy and dont make the correct choice in gender preferenc for their gender . we should not be in their group in no way shape or form but now transgenders which are a group of cross-dresserd drag queens and other sexual devients do belong in the gay groups.[16]

> It wasn't our choice to be 'lumped in' with the GLB. The problem is that THANKS to EFFEMINATE GAY MALES

cross-dressing, doing drag, feminising their bodies for sex work, etc, the general public has come to regard anyone who presents an atypical gender expression as gay or lesbian. YOUR OWN GROUP created this problem.[17]

These three were responding to the above transphobic attacks. Another noted that:

I am a Transsexual woman who neither seeks anything from, or gives anything to, the LGB community. As far as I'm concerned, if every LGB person vanished from the face of the earth tomorrow, it wouldn't affect my Transsexualism one iota … I have nothing against LGB people, but their condition has NOTHING to do with my condition. Frankly, I don't care what any of these 'communities' do. As far as I'm concerned, they'd be better off looking at my example for guidance and support, than I would be looking at theirs. How are communities full of people like this going to benefit me?[18]

You have to forgive my colleagues' intemperate language, but given the provocation and accusation of invading the homosexual community and transphobia you would have to understand that their message is not any bit unclear; transsexuals are not homosexuals, we are not interested in being homosexuals or people perceiving us as homosexuals, we are proud of ourselves and our achievements. We have no business being in the LGB movement, we know who we are and are proud of ourselves. Furthermore, I wonder what transsexuals would gain from being part of the LGB community; primarily, we lose out because people attack and discriminate against us, thinking they are attacking homosexuals.

There are some transgender people who would attack my logic and resort to non-issues. For example, some would claim that there are transgender women who are lesbians and transgender men who are gay. (By the way, why not say there are transgender people who are drivers, bankers, advocates and so forth?). I wonder what relevance such statements have to the genesis of transphobia in the gay community. Others will blame all these on ignorance of the transsexual concept within the gay community. But if we adopt such kind of thinking, what is to stop all cisgender people from attacking and killing transgender persons and blaming it on ignorance? Ignorance is not a defence. I am sure most of the gays who are transphobic don't know much about transposons? Do they go around insulting transposons or spewing forth hate speech against transposons?[19] In harsh times our minds can have a habit of lying to ourselves before we go out to the world lying to others. We need not to bury our heads in the sand; the problem is not ignorance.

And it is with this in mind that I turn to the topic of gaynisation of transgender people and the gayjacking of trans lives to serve the homosexual agenda.

Gaynising/lesbianising and gayjacking trans lives

Gaynising/lesbianising is the process of homosexuals turning transgender people into homosexuals. Gayjacking is the process of using transsexual issues and struggles to pimp up the gay/homosexual agenda.

Scrutinise this dream of a gay activist:

My dream is a day when no LGBT person has to choose between being openly gay – or being killed.[20]

Then consider the following statement:

The gay community, or LGBT (lesbian, gay, bisexual, and transgender) community, is a loosely defined grouping of LGBT and LGBT-supportive people, organisations and subcultures, united by a common culture and civil rights movements.[21]

Lumping transgender people under the gay label is a common practice among some homosexuals and their allies. It is based on the ridiculous assumption that the LGBT community is the gay/homosexual community. This practice is detrimental to transgender people for the following reasons:

First, LGBT organisations end up neglecting the transgender community and their issues. Gay struggle includes decriminalisation of homosexuality, same-sex marriages and prides, men who have sex with other men (MSM) and HIV, condoms, dental

Table 11.1 Prevalence of HIV in Mumbai

Year	2000	2001	2002	2003		2004	2005	2006	2007
Combined MSM, hijra & transgender prevalence	23.9	23.6	16.8	18.4	Hijra & transgender	49.2	3.9	29.6	42.2
					MSM	9.6	6.0	7.6	8.4

dams and lubricants. The issues of transsexuals include hormone therapy, sex reassignment surgery, electrolysis and changes of names and sex markers on identification and academic documents among others.

There are numerous organisations purporting to work on transgender issues and they don't. Yet donors don't question them – but if it were a mainstream organisation channelling funds meant for homosexual people to cancer patients then there would be a storm. But homosexuals are allowed to get away with it because of the disproportionate privileges they enjoy. Of all the donor officials working with the LGBTI communities I have met, only one is transgender. The rest are homosexual men and women and, of course, most do not appear to like the idea of people such as Audrey questioning imperialist ideologies among some homosexual people. The gays and lesbians take the lion's share while transsexuals eat the leftovers at the periphery. This animus sucks like hell. We need to stop babysitting homosexuals and treat them like everyone else.

The serious effects can be seen in the desegregation of data on HIV prevalence among transgender women from that of MSM where some 'experts' placed them, in their infinite wisdom and with the encouragement of some homosexuals (see Table 11.1). The data was provided by the Mumbai AIDS District Society.[22]

From 2000 to 2003, the medical and social interventions to stem new HIV infections were carried out from homosexual perspectives. But with the desegregation of data from 2004 to 2007 we begin to get a better picture of the magnitude of the problem of HIV among transgender women and can see that the interventions that were earlier being channelled (through a homosexual lens) were counterproductive for transgender women. Similar data and trends are provided in the reference paper. A year ago, I started a campaign to have the data for transgender women desegregated from that for MSM and homosexual men and all the resistance that I face comes from homosexuals. I don't know what they stand to lose if transgender women are not part of their MSM campaigns; they come out so arrogantly and brutishly that you have to feel concern that these are the same people who are forcing transgender women to accept their help.

Second, the habit of gaynising transgender people poses security risks to transgender people. Homophobic people end up violating the rights of transgender people because they have been made to believe that they are the gays. Government officials end up denying transsexuals their rights because they don't want to be seen to be 'promoting homosexuality'. I am not insinuating that it is okay to discriminate against gays and lesbians and wrong to discriminate against transgender people. But it is wrong to make transgender people sacrificial lambs or a shield for gays and lesbians. I would rather be confronted for a 'crime' I am guilty of than for the 'crimes' of others.

Lastly, gaynisation of transgender people is intellectual fraud. It is done to confuse people and is malicious. It is is a mark of self-stigma among some homosexuals.

At times I sense a certain level of desperation among some homosexuals when confronted by the anti-gaynisation campaigns transsexuals are putting up. For example, some LGBs will rush to defend themselves, using the cliché, 'but there are transgender people who are gay'. (Why the obsession about sex and trans; why not say there are some trans who are doctors, engineers, models and accountants?) It is even weirder: for some of them a trans man who is attracted to men is gay and those dating women are butch lesbians. Trans women dating men are gay men whereas those dating women are lesbians – you can see how cunning they can be. Some of us grew up adhering to this model till we knew better. Education is liberating. If you have ever interacted with a section of the homosexual community you will have discovered that there are no straight transgender people. They always twist things for us to be part of them.

In March 2011 I invented a system known as the transsexual nomenclature on sexual orientation (TNOSO):[23] all transgender persons attracted to men are T5,000, those attracted to women are T7,000, those attracted to all are TATA (Transgender Attracted To All) and those attracted to nobody are T0. The system received remarkable support from some transgender people, but most homosexuals abused me for it (as if that was going to change anything). They accused me of using propaganda and science fiction to break the gay movement: so sad. Then there are transsexuals who felt there was a possibility that donors and gays would think of us all as homophobic traitors. I really sympathise with this lot – their desire to be seen as good transsexuals or to fit in the ideal caricature (for trans women) of a woman is incompatible with the secret principles of transsexuals. It is bad enough to believe in other people's lies but a serious misstep to start believing in your own lies.

And, I cannot forget to remind some homosexuals of the following. You overzealously tell people your bedroom activities are private affairs. You tell the church and the state to stop poking their noses in your private affairs. However, you change your tune when it comes to trans people; you assume you have the right to know how transsexuals have sex, with who, when, why and what label is appropriate for them. I urge transsexuals to retaliate against oppressive homosexuals; no more babysitting some people who think the world owes them an apology and special attention because they are gay.

There is a need to go deeper into the topic of why some gays force their labels on others. I posit that such individuals are not proud of who they are; they acknowledge the fact that they are sinners and will suffer torment on earth and in heaven. These individuals get scared and foolishly decide to make other people targets of their torment. Their reasoning is that it is comforting to know you are not the only one who is suffering, there are millions of others in your situation and they are coping well. The mantra is: transsexual people will never be happy if the homosexual community is unhappy.

Misrepresentation and misinformation

Once upon a time in the world of mental health, homosexuality was classified as a mental disorder. It was not until 1973 that homosexuality was removed from the *Diagnostic and Statistical Manual for Mental Disorders of the American Psychiatric Association, Edition II* (DSM-II). We are now seeing some gays and lesbians pushing for gender identity disorders to be expunged from the DSM-V. The International Lesbian and Gay Association is one institution that is zealous on the topic. They are demanding:

> The removal of Gender Identity Disorder (GID) of both the *Diagnostic and Statistical Manual of Mental Disorders of the American Psychiatric Association* (DSM-IV) and International Classification of Diseases (ICD-10), which are related to the World Health Organisation...[24]

And that's not the end:

> Free access to hormonal treatments and surgery (without psychiatric care ... This campaign comes against the stigma that is disqualifying gender identity in both the *Diagnostic and Statistical Manual of Mental Disorders of the American Psychiatric Association* and the International Classification of Diseases.[25]

So, the poor lad in our village laughs at me because he read the *Diagnostic and Statistical Manual Text Revised Edition IV* (DSM-IV TR) and stigmatised me? That police officer who was harassing me in the street the other day did it because he is a regular reader of the DSM-IV TR and knows about GID?

I once met three homosexuals who supported the idea of expunging GID from the DSM-IV TR and I could sympathise with their arguments: 'Transsexualism is not a medical condition and should not be in the DSM ... Audrey, do you know homosexuality also used to be classified as a mental disorder till it was expunged in 1973?' They waxed on.

Do these people think of the consequences of expunging GID from the DSM-V? Transsexuals need medical attention relating to transsexualism and doctors need to be trained on how to manage transsexualism. You lose these once you expunge it from the

DSM-V and you transsexuals and those to be born in the future will never be able to access medical services relating to your sex transitions. We cannot afford to pussyfoot over the issue. Senseless people have to take their crazy ideas where they came from.

But, some gays and lesbians are motivated by selfish reasons:

> 'GID' (DSM-IV) entered into the picture as a potential repressive and dangerous oppressive agent for lesbians and gays. Since many lesbians and gays do not conform to the heterosexual bipolar cultural gender paradigm, they have been and can continue to be oppressed by the APA ... hundreds of LGBT youth are confined to psychiatric institutions and subjected to 'treatment' to change their sexual orientation ... The classification of 'Gender Identity Disorder' as a disease presents a major obstacle to accessing health care.[26]

This is utter nonsense. If gays and lesbians are being forced by medical practitioners to change their sexual orientation then they can sue these medical practitioners or their hospitals instead of pulling the rug out from under transsexuals' feet – the DSM-IV is a diagnostic tool for gender identity disorders not homosexuality/ sexual orientation. Doing away with it jeopardises access to medical services for transsexuals.

Additionally, some gays and lesbians need to stop making false statements. I have heard and read articles by some homosexuals and their allies telling the world that LGBTI people in Africa are criminalised.[27, 28, 29] Homosexuality is criminalised, transsexualism and intersexuality are not. The habit of making people targets for anti-gay hatred and discrimination is unacceptable. If someone is criminalised then they should not implicate others.

The situation is getting to a critical level. There are these homosexuals who are introducing themselves in workshops and meetings as 'LGBTI persons'. When you probe, they say they mean they are gays. This phenomenon is called 'gayflage' (from 'camouflage') and needs to be clipped in the bud. It is disgusting and a very fine form of treachery.

I managed to talk to two transsexuals from Kenya about all these unacceptable behaviours by some gays and lesbians:

TXCRD

What's your opinion about transgender people being forced to work with gays and lesbians? Transsexuals should be an independent group. It is very important for transsexuals to have their own voice in the society and not homosexuals talking on their behalf and pushing them around as if they own them.

Have you ever had your rights abused by some homosexual? Yes, abusing me to the point of calling me a man, another one told me together with my transgender friends that we would go to hell, they have threatened me and stolen from me. I think most are like that.

What do you think of homosexuals? Most are very bad.

Do you like being lumped or associated with homosexuals? I don't like being grouped together with them and I don't like being associated with them. I don't like the way people talk about homosexuals and it's assumed I am in there. Also, they don't get to answer for the abuses they carry out.

What do you think should be done about LGBT activism? Transgender issues should be independent but I don't care what the rest do because they push themselves to transgenders.

TRT101

What do you think about homosexuals? Most are bad people. Their behaviour is bad and ungodly.

Do you like being associated with homosexuals? No. I don't see why I should always be pushed to associate with homosexuals. I should be able to exercise my freedom of association

Have you ever had some homosexuals abusing your rights? Yes, one tried to make me a sex slave in addition to him stealing my Ksh 8,000.

Do you like homosexuals claiming they work on transgender rights? No. It makes me uncomfortable and makes me feel horrible. Most don't do the right thing and we are left to suffer because of their mistakes.

What do you recommend with respect to LGBT activism? Homosexuals should work on their issues and transsexuals on theirs. We can work together when in agreement but they should not force us to work with them.

Conclusion

Transphobia is a reality among some homosexuals. It takes the form of verbal abuse, discrimination, exclusion and hate speech. It runs deep and can be overt or covert, but it has debilitating effects in the transsexual community.

Homosexuals are protected by an abnormally thick wall of respect – undeserved respect. This means that you are not supposed to criticise homosexuals because some assume they are entitled to special rights and privileges. If there is evidence to prove they are wrong then it is for that evidence to be thrown in the trash bin, not them.

Transsexuals don't want to be lumped with homosexuals. This association is normally counterproductive due to the confusion it causes in mainstream society. Additionally, the issues of transsexuals get ignored by LGBT organisations in favour of the homosexual agenda. Transsexuals demand space to voice their own issues independent from the gay rights movement.

Some homosexuals want the LGBT community to be unpacked so that it becomes the LGB community. Transsexuals have expressed similar desires due to the problems involved in working with most homosexuals.

It seems everyone at any level of ignorance about transsexuals has the inherent right to give their 'expert' opinion about transsexuals and transsexualism. Some homosexuals fall under this category. They feel that just because they are homosexuals, they are always right and are qualified enough to give an opinion about transsexuals and transsexualism.

Recommendations

Transsexuals need to be careful of the people, groups and organisations they associate with. They need to be able to know constructive people and should realise they have the freedom of association. They should not be dictated to about who to work with. There is no reason why we transsexuals should be working with other people simply because these other people are homosexual people.

The wishes of transsexuals and homosexuals who want a split from the LGBT community should be respected. The issues of transsexuals are totally different from those of homosexuals, and splitting the LGBT community will enhance greater focus on transsexual issues.

Transsexuals need to be assertive. Most transsexuals are scared of criticising homosexuals; they are scared of being accused of homophobia.

Those homosexuals (and their allies) who have a habit of carelessly jumping into transgender issues and pretending to be experts in this field need to stop doing so. While a few homosexuals have something worthwhile to offer, most homosexuals inadvertently or intentionally create problems for transsexuals due to the misinformation they spread about transsexuals. Some homosexuals impose a superiority complex over transsexuals, they neuter trans folks, misguiding them to engage in destructive sexual behaviour, substance abuse, and encourage us transsexuals to divorce ourselves from the health fraternity and our families.

Transsexuals need to make concerted efforts to educate mainstream society about transgender issues. They need to make mainstream society understand that transsexuals are not homosexuals and are not related, and that the issues (e.g. legal) of transsexuals are different from those of homosexuals. In connection to that, I would advise the mainstream society to take whatever the homosexual community says with a pinch of salt.

Dedicated to the transsexual race across the universe.

Notes

1   'Is a "transsexual" a woman or a cross dressing eunuch?',
    CrossDressingQuestions.com, http://crossdressingquestions.com/is-a-
    transsexual-a-woman-or-a-cross-dressing-eunuch.html, accessed 1 June
    2011.
2   Nathan Tabak (2010) 'Transgender rights are gay rights', Change.org,
    http://news.change.org/stories/transgender-rights-are-gay-rights,
    accessed 1 June 2011.
3   'I hate transgendered people, please convince me not to', http://
    au.answers.yahoo.com/question/index?qid=20080830200855AAB9ZEu,
    accessed 13 June 2011.

4   'Why do gay/lesbian dislike transgendered people?', http://www.
    answerbag.com/q_view/913328, accessed 13 June 2011.
5   Mia Nikasimo (2010) 'Transgender people face hate speech from lesbian
    and gay people', Black Looks, http://www.blacklooks.org/2010/10/
    transgender-community-face-hate-speech-from-lesbian-and-gay-people/,
    accessed 13 June 2011.
6   'Do you think transgender should be lumped in with gays and lesbians?',
    Yahoo Answers, http://answers.yahoo.com/question/index?qid=201010141
    21109AAJH3MA, accessed 13 June 2011.
7   Pamela Hayes (2011) 'Why do some gay men hate transsexuals?',
    Transgriot, http://transgriot.blogspot.com/2011/01/pams-ponderings-why-
    do-some-gay-men.html, accessed 13 June 2011.
8   'Do you think transgender should be lumped in with gays and lesbians?',
    Yahoo Answers, accessed 15 June 2011.
9   Ibid.
10 'Chaz Bono is no longer gay. Well, then it's time for the old heave-ho',
    (2010) The data lounge, http://www.datalounge.com/cgi- bin/iowa/ajax.
    html?t=9212259#page:showThread,9212259, accessed 15 June 2011.
11 Ibid.
12 Ibid.
13 'Do you think transsexualism or transgendered is a sexual orientation?',
    Yahoo Answers, http://answers.yahoo.com/question/index?qid=200811281
    23203AAYICtM, accessed 15 June 2011.
14 'Do you think transgender should be lumped in with gays and lesbians?',
    Yahoo Answers, accessed 15 June 2011.
15 Ibid.
16 Ibid.
17 Ibid.
18 'LGB People, what are your views on transgender individuals?', Yahoo
    Answers, http://answers.yahoo.com/question/index?qid=20101201123307
    AA2TITq, accessed 15 June 2011.
19 A transposon is a chromosomal segment that can undergo transposition
    (*Oxford English Dictionary*).
20 R. Hofmann and R.O. Gutierrez (2011) 'Fearing no evil', http://www.poz.
    com/articles/David_Kuria_HIV_2591_20107.shtml, accessed 16 June 2011.
21 Wikipedia, 'Gay community', http://en.wikipedia.org/wiki/Gay_
    community, accessed 16 June 2011.
22 A.L. Guevara (n.d.) 'The hidden HIV epidemic. Transgender women in
    Latin America and Asia', International HIV/AIDS Alliance, http://www.
    msmgf.org/files/msmgf//Latin%20America/ART_EN_010808_HID.pdf,
    accessed 16 June 2011.
23 'Transsexual nomenclature on sexual orientation', TransgenderKenya,
    http://www.transgenderkenya.com, accessed 16 June 2011.
24 'Groundwork for the campaign against the pathologizing of
    gender identity. Stop trans pathologizing' (2012) International
    Lesbian and Gay Association, http://trans.ilga.org/trans/

welcome_to_the_ilga_trans_secretariat/library/articles/groundwork_
for_the_campaign_against_the_pathologizing_of_gender_identity_stop_
trans_pathologizing_2012, accessed 17 June 2011.

25 Ibid.

26 Tere Prasse, 'Genderevolution sidebars', http://womynweb.net/gendersb.
htm, accessed 17 June 2011.

27 'African LGBTI Manifesto/Declaration' (2010) http://www.priorityafrica.
org/African_LGBTI_Manifesto-FINAL.pdf, accessed 17 June 2011.

28 'MCC call to action: save LGBT lives in Uganda', http://mcchurch.
org/2011/05/10/mcc-call-to-action-save-lgbt-lives-in-uganda/, accessed 17
June 2011.

29 Kiwianglo (2011) 'Ugandan bishop addresses U.N. on tolerance for LGBT
community', http://kiwianglo.wordpress.com/2011/04/11/nigerian-bishop-
addresses-u-n-on-tolerance-for-lgbt-community/, accessed 17 June 2011.

The media, the tabloid and the Uganda homophobia spectacle

Kenne Mwikya

Introduction

On 9 October 2010 *Rolling Stone*,[1] a Ugandan tabloid, outed 100 alleged 'homosexuals'. It printed their names, photographs, home addresses and other contact information – with a line on the front page that said 'hang them'. It further claimed that gays and lesbians and bisexual and gender non-conforming people were planning to recruit one million children. By the end of that week, the tabloid had gained major traction in world news and was featured in a range of publications including the *Guardian* and the *New York Times*.[2]

News of the *Rolling Stone* outings spread rapidly. PDF copies of the issue circulated with comments of the kind of fiercely anti-homophobia rhetoric that dominates the spaces in which the tabloid had gained relevance. That is how the Uganda *Rolling Stone* intrusion came to pass. I call it 'intrusion' because the flood of commentary – most of it against the outings – skipped an important phase, i.e. the details around the outings and analysis of their relevance, which in turn could have limited their power.[3]

In this chapter, I examine the relationship between the media and the queer community in East Africa by focusing on Uganda, which has gained international notoriety for the introduction of an anti-homosexuality bill in parliament and the media spectacle it caused and, as far as the reintroduction of the bill in parliament is concerned, continues to cause as I write this chapter.[4] I look at how the tabloid press in Uganda, the regional and international media, and in particular the pro-queer blogs, approached the queer rights (essentially, human rights) crisis in the country. I argue that such coverage sidesteps crucial ruminations on the crisis by concerned intellectuals and denied the country opportunities to defuse the crisis.[5] I propose critical reflection and rethinking on the relationship between the media and the queer community by queer African activists, intellectuals and spectators.

Background

It was not the first time Uganda had witnessed mass outings by disreputable tabloids. Another tabloid, *Red Pepper*, had started publishing the names, identifying features, places of employment, residences and contact information of activists and other 'out' queers as early as 2007. These events were sparked by a conference arranged by US evangelicals and attended by journalists, police officers, members of parliament and government and other stakeholders that gave the rallying call against queers in the country. It was, I should note, the first time a tabloid had been morphed by its pro- and anti-LGBTI readers into some sort of powerhouse in which ideas, debate and conversation could collate.

In a Uganda where an anti-homosexuality bill had been tabled in parliament by David Bahati MP in October 2009, the allegations and outings were both bizarre and scary.[6] The allegations found a ready population, which had been inundated with anti-LGBTI rhetoric from politicians and religious leaders that blamed LGBTI people for the country's social problems. Worse still, only a small and underfunded group of sexual minority activists existed in Uganda, an activist network that could not keep up with the logistical and financial capabilities of religious and government institutions supporting anti-LGBTI measures in the country. In this context, *Rolling Stone* and its predecessors threatened queers in two crucial respects. First, the normalisation of tabloid media as a viable repository for 'collecting' discourse legitimised the need to open up discourse. Second, however, the tabloid itself, with its severely biased material, encouraged readers to focus not on the quality of reporting and the fact of the outings but on queers living in Uganda. This meant that instead of asking whether it was ethical to 'out' LGBTI people, the discourse revolved around whether or how the information provided by *Rolling Stone* should be acted upon. These two situations acted in concert with each other to produce a scenario in which discourse, debate and conversation were premised on biased, unquestioned information, on which the public (which readily and regularly consumed this information) were encouraged to act.

In the few days that followed, *Rolling Stone* had become a 'newspaper' rather than a tabloid of high disrepute and bad grammar. Giles Muhame, the man behind the murky paper, was deemed a 'journalist'.[7] This redefinition of the paper and its editor became one of the many un-doings by Western liberal media and subsequently by pro-LGBTI blogs and African news agencies, which were giddy about carrying such a controversial story and sourcing news from Western agencies rather than carrying out their own investigation. The redefinition of the Ugandan *Rolling Stone* created an inaccurate picture of the tabloid as the institutionalisation of anti-LGBTI bigotry and homophobia in Uganda and, indeed, Africa. It could be said that *Rolling Stone*'s power lay in its 'tabloidness' and our gullibility in 'condemning' something that had a readership of around 3,000 people.

The proponents of the concept of some sort of 'gay agenda' have always insisted that activism by sexual minorities has been covertly and overtly supported by the increasingly liberalised media.[8] On the other hand – and I see this in a country such as Kenya where we have many people coming out in support of LGBTI people[9] – activists and bloggers have insisted that it is good for the media to paint a picture about queers, whether favourable or unfavourable, premised on the pragmatic view that 'publicity is publicity'. This means that our ability or willingness to engage with highly prejudicial and biased reporting about queers in Africa is directly related to whether or not we appreciate the fact that some 'headway' is being made in trying to spark discourse on sexual and gender variance by such reporting. Hence, the policing of homophobia, transphobia and prejudice in media reporting is scant. As debate can have various ways, ends and means that do not directly aid a more tolerant discourse on homosexuality or gender non-conformity, activists seem to be involved most of the time in a severely unequal relationship with the media to the detriment of the activists themselves and queer people all over the continent.

Indeed, it would be churlish not to point out that we have had many op eds in our newspapers, and features and interviews on television and radio which have highlighted the 'plight of gays and lesbians', especially when it comes to health and basic rights (such as the decriminalisation of private, consensual same-sex relations, anti-discrimination laws and hate-crime legislation). However, such endeavours have been based on misinformation and the wide-eyed perception that queers need 'support' – commonly translated as pity.

Such undertakings have not been totally clean. Newspaper dailies and TV and radio still carry biased and unbalanced news and analysis, sometimes sliding off to tabloid status with lies or misinformation about queer activists, stereotypes and the subcultures emerging out of a tense discourse on sexual identity, the menace from both foreign and local fundamentalist groups and the queer erasure that sometimes stings but also aids the nuanced if not closeted existence of most LGBTI people.

This kind of doublespeak betrays the fact that the media are just using homosexuality to get a wide readership. Thus, the double portrayal of misdirected compassion and contempt or indifference portends a turbulent future on how reporting by the media will be interpreted and debated by the public. It must be noted that journalism, as with other professions in Africa, is still deeply embedded in hetero-patriarchy, still linked to religious doctrine and still governed, more or less, by profit, government censorship and the political rhetoric of the day.

It can thus be said that media coverage of queer issues tends to be incredibly complex within local, translocal and glocal spaces, inhabiting different forms, following different methods and envisioning divergent ends.

The circumstances under which *Rolling Stone* operated were not unique as its outing tirades had been preceded by *Red Pepper*. The only difference with *Rolling Stone* was the overwhelming media attention it received and the muffled analysis inundated by such coverage. Both tabloids thrived on events that had shaped the lives of queers in Uganda for the worse, namely the normalisation of anti-LGBTI sentiment by US evangelicals and local religious and political leaders and the anti-homosexuality bill introduced to parliament by MP David Bahati. One would have thought that this would have been a good time to think about the coincidence between what was being published by *Rolling Stone* and other tabloids and the rising anti-LGBTI sentiment in Uganda, the introduction of the anti-homosexuality bill in the Ugandan parliament and its subsequent featuring in national and international cultural, political and ideological debate. Nothing like this happened.

Since the introduction of the bill, international attention on the country's treatment of LGBTI people has shifted from the wider picture of human rights and sexual freedoms to fighting the bill independently of other human rights abuses. From this separation and the subsequent opposition between fighting the anti-homosexuality bill and larger issues of human rights abuses in Uganda, it can be deduced that the legitimisation of LGBTI rights was the intended outcome once the bill had been defeated – a huge gamble. I doubt media attention on the *Rolling Stone* issue would have lasted as long if the bill were not as menacing or, and this is more telling, if the Western factors in this equation, that is the US far-right evangelicals and the shifting of culture wars from the West to Africa's fertile grounds of religious fervour, had been absent.

Events surrounding queer or 'homophobic' Uganda have followed an almost cyclical pattern of events and reactions since the US evangelical conference, the *Red Pepper* outings, the introduction of the anti-homosexuality bill, the *Rolling Stone* outings, the January 2011 death of activist David Kato and the kerfuffle that surrounded the seeming end of the anti-homosexuality bill in the Ugandan parliament in May 2011 and the reintroduction of the bill in 2012. For people with a genuine concern over what is taking place in Uganda, the intimidation of activists and the normalisation of anti-queer rhetoric which are symptoms of the dehumanisation of LGBTI people, the cacophony does not make sense. Intellectual thought and analysis have been scant and were muffled by the din of blogs and news sites summarily concluding that Uganda is homophobic.

Media machineries in Africa do not get off the hook, as on close scrutiny there is little coverage of the queer and human rights crisis in Uganda. Instead, we see general self-censorship, or supposed censorship by governments, about issues affecting queers in the continent and an over-reliance on Western media for news and reportage about African affairs. This paved the way for Western news sites to handle reporting on queer Africa with an authoritative fervour that concentrated on the pragmatics and drew a picture that would evoke passionate responses about how 'homophobic' Africa is. In the end the coverage of the Uganda homophobia spectacle ended up, in the eyes of most Africans watching the story, as an example of Western governments using their media to overly criticise and impose 'foreign' beliefs upon them. Such an articulation is fallacious, but in a continent where the biggest propagators of ideology are the church and the government, this made sense.

African news agencies have also shown great irresponsibility in their coverage of queers in their own continent. The system for addressing concepts such as balance in the coverage of queer Africa is flawed, so the media in Africa have ended up deeming coverage of LGBTI persons, their stories and their impact, perceived or otherwise, in society as something of a formality. This is evidenced by the fact that although the media publish diverse stories which are both pro-queer and 'socially conservative' if not prejudicial, debate on homosexuality has been precluded by the too easy consensus of an anti-LGBTI stance. The ball is in the media's court to produce material that will generate genuine debate, conversation and discourse and see whether the end will be the usual conclusion that homosexuality is wrong and un-African.

The Ugandan *Rolling Stone* betrayed the similarities with which the news agencies in Africa, Western news agencies and pro-queer blogs handled the news, and the way such reporting in the end went only to serve the needs of their consumer bases. The tone in which these differing media machineries carried their stories was consistent with their core readerships. *Rolling Stone* largely catered for the needs of the Ugandan who wanted to 'be in the know' but could not afford a newspaper such as the *Daily Monitor* or the *New Vision* – the two mainstream newspapers in Uganda. On the other hand, a paper such as the *Guardian* (London), known for its wide reporting on queer Africa, caters to an audience that is – and here I'm speculating – interested in the 'internationalism of queer'.[10] Reporting by a network such as the

BBC was hardly destined to be a viable collation point for debate, conversation and analysis in Africa given the differences between a country which is debating same-sex marriage rights and a continent still grappling to wrest itself from the clutches of sexual minority repression. Much can also be said about *Rolling Stone*. Even in Uganda, there came a time when *Rolling Stone* was just debated with the enthusiasm of an anecdote from the past, losing traction with its core readership. I pit these extremes against each other to point out the similarities between reporting endeavours across the wide spectrum between a tabloid in 'backwater' Kampala and a paper such as the *Guardian* in London.

I want to point out the 'spectacularisation' by both the Western news agencies and *Rolling Stone* and its predecessor, *Red Pepper*. While *Rolling Stone* concentrated on the trumped-up accusations that queers were recruiting children, queer blogs amplified its power. Giles Muhame was, meanwhile, institutionalised and invited to interviews where he demonstrated his flailing mastery of English. The aftershocks of this portrayal are still with us today in that Muhame's comment after receiving news of activist David Kato's death was that it was the work of the government to kill queers and not the public.[11]

Another example of spectacularisation is a documentary by Scott Mills of the BBC that deems Uganda the 'worst place to be gay' – never mind that such a demonstration does not change perceptions about how to approach queer activism in Africa and takes the well-trodden path of 'Africa is homophobic'.[12] Such reporting is exclusively geared at a Western audience keen on insulating itself from the rest of the world. In this way it conveniently ignores its own homophobia and transphobia, including bullying, beatings and even murder, as well as racism and Islamophobia, and summarily uses its findings as evidence to suggest the viability of a concept like 'African homophobia'. Uganda is the new Iran, an African backward state that terrorises queers, who are, curiously, saved from being associated with the homophobia found in spaces which they inhabit. The heroic Western media has imposed itself as the leader in 'helping', or the more job descriptive 'exposing', queer activism on the continent not as it really is but how they want it to be. Activism and intellectual thought around queer Uganda have been pushed onto the backburner, as from reading the media you would think that activism in Uganda is either non-existent or totally disorganised and frantic, with its ultimate goal being defeating the anti-homosexuality bill.

However, some criticism should also be levelled against the strategies which activists use in their work to end state-sanctioned repression against queer minorities in their countries. The totality with which Western paradigms are used in activism in Africa should be suspect given that the feasibility of such strategies in Africa is in question and that even in the spaces in which they were previously employed, the results were wide-ranging and not always positive.[13] With such a 'way of doing things' deeply embedded in paradigms of Western activism, interference by Western news agencies was not only seen as appropriate by Western media but also as an extension of a globalisation of queer rights in which the West was the paragon. But tensions between the aspirations of the West and the needs of places such as Africa and the Middle East cannot be blanketed by internationalism. Their paths are markedly different, as are the immediate needs and challenges that befall countries such as Kenya and Uganda as opposed to the US and Britain. These tensions do not address the normalisation of 'homosexuality is un-African' and blatantly ignore and often threaten bridging attempts by religious organisations concerned over the increasing interpretation of morality as something institutional rather than a cultivated, personal aspect of human nature. Queer internationalism demands that players have 'something' that is 'good' to bring to the table. Queer internationalism is not as binding as it is touted to be, nor as beneficial as it is portrayed as when fighting homo/transphobia in a localised space such as Uganda. The actions of queer internationalism only go to engender the rampant belief that LGBTI activism, just like homosexuality, is a Western import and an imposition on a people's sovereignty. These are issues that internationalism, in its inchoateness, cannot address inclusively or conclusively.

The activist–media 'cooperation' in Africa is a bittersweet affair, with the media taking the upper hand. Thus, objectivity and bias, just like the terms of any debate, are closely monitored and policed by the media, which set them in the first place. An example is an article that appeared in the *Daily Nation* that completely misrepresented David Kato and his wide-ranging work as an activist and a pioneer in the fight for sexual minority rights in East Africa. The article went out of its way to feign a sense of balance by printing lies and quoting non-sources and in the end, Kato was portrayed as a promiscuous, HIV-positive, uppity person – things which, even if true, would be completely irrelevant to his work as an activist.[14] The article received a large number of comments condemning Kato and all queers, with religious zealots enforcing LGBTI stereotypes, and a general agreement that his death was a good thing. Thus people who knew nothing about David Kato or his work were 'invited' to voice their hatred and ignorance of LGBTI issues. Much the same can be said about the reactions from Ugandans who welcomed the outing sprees by *Red Pepper*, *Rolling Stone* and the blog posts and the reporting from Western media on the homophobia spectacle.

In November 2010, a group of LGBTI activists – Kasha Jacqueline, David Kato and Pepe Julian Onziema – petitioned the Ugandan High Court to stop further outings by *Rolling Stone*.[15] Their actions show how their resilience to the repression of sexual and gender variance in Uganda has emboldened activists. These are extremely brave people who have remained in their countries and continue with their work as activists. Only a few weeks after a judge ruled in favour of the applicants of the petition, David Kato was killed outside his house under unclear circumstances. The anti-homosexuality bill was shelved a few months later, in mid-May 2011, amid confusion over whether it would be tabled in parliament.[16]

Where does this leave progressive queer African bloggers, commentators and intellectuals? The Uganda homophobia spectacle is a wake-up call for more in-depth thinking, commenting, critiques and organising. As the guardians of our own narratives and the people called to safeguard our own cultures and beliefs, it is time to seriously reconsider our chequered relationship with the media and call for more objectivity: balance or bust! A new collective in which activist groups cooperate with unaffiliated but nonetheless supportive bloggers, commentators and thinkers must be forged. In a country like Kenya, *Rolling Stone* could have been criticised as highly abusive of journalistic ethics and best practices but nonetheless seen as relevant. These are the rules of engagement that LGBTI activist groups must reconfigure. Cooperation with the media must aim to produce content which serves the public by telling the truth, being objective and telling stories of vulnerable groups and not as a good opportunity to tabloidise reporting for the sake of arousing interest. The concern raised about the commentary of queer stories by Western news agencies, especially the pro-queer blogs, is a symptom of our dependence on Western thought and modes of activism as a paradigm effective enough to work in places such as Uganda and the ineffectiveness of queer internationalism and rights-based imperialism imposed within countries, on governments and on societies.

Witnessing the transfiguration of the Ugandan *Rolling Stone* from a lowly paper to a bastion of queer oppression in Africa, the following has to be asked:

1 How did transnational/international anxieties over sexual orientation affect the reporting of the Uganda homophobia spectacle?

2 How do we address the interference of Western media in queer African affairs, agencies which comment with the air of imperialism and with their own ends in mind?

3 How should Western groups and individuals that aim to provide queer Ugandans with much needed support do so?

4 How do we approach the anxieties of foreign paradigms in addressing activism? Are their stories our stories? To what extent do we see ourselves in the stories that they tell about us?

5 What should be done about the biased reporting of queer in Africa, or is this just an excess of the non-queer mainstream in manipulating uncharted territory in law books and social sanctions?

These questions are just a few which should be asked and answered analytically to pave the way for a new queer rights activist framework that is not only responsive to the needs of African gay, lesbian, bisexual and gender non-conforming persons but which is able to influence decisions in decades or centuries to come.

The dust had settled, David Kato's alleged killer was sentenced to 30 years imprisonment for the crime and David's legacy was solidified, tentatively, with the setting up of a Vision and Voice Award with his name.[17] But at the time of finishing this article, the anti-homosexuality bill had been reintroduced in parliament twice, in 2011 and 2012, with the death penalty having been dropped from the 2012 version.[18] The Ugandan government continues to harass sexual rights activists, infringing on their fundamental freedoms and threatening arrest on dubious or no grounds at all.[19] With this resurgence, the Uganda homophobia spectacle should be tested on how far and to what extent it informed and influenced debate on sexual minority rights in Uganda and Africa. It would seem it has failed that test.

We could only hope that all the participants involved have learned from the spectacularisation and that if they have not, there are people willing to constantly and incessantly expose the failings of the spectacle. We can only hope that the East African, African and global public will not be in for another round of infotainment at the expense of real human rights issues in Uganda and the rest of Africa.

Acknowledgements

I would like to thank Keguro Macharia and Sokari Ekine for general feedback and intellectual, political and emotional sustenance, editing and correcting aspects of this work.

Notes

1   For further information, see Wikipedia entry on *Rolling Stone* (Uganda), http://en.wikipedia.org/wiki/Rolling_Stone_%28Uganda%29, accessed 12 March 2011.

2   X. Rice (2010) 'Ugandan paper calls for gay people to be hanged', *Guardian*, 21 October, http://www.guardian.co.uk/world/2010/oct/21/ugandan-paper-gay-people-hanged, accessed 19 November 2012; J. Gettleman (2011) 'Ugandan who spoke up for gays is beaten to death', *New York Times*, 27 January, http://www.nytimes.com/2011/01/28/world/africa/28uganda.html?_r=1, accessed 12 March 2011.

3   For instance, Box Turtle Bulletin's 'Slouching towards Kampala: Uganda's deadly embrace of hate' (www.boxturtlebulletin.com/slouching-toward-kampala.htm, accessed 12 March 2011), a timeline of events leading up to the introduction of the anti-homosexuality bill, focuses too much on the Western influences that might have sparked debate and conversation on the bill within Uganda's political and clerical class and takes only a casual interest in the internal forces that actually made the bill's entry

into parliament possible. But though certainly biased in this aspect, it is still a useful site if one wants to get hold of relevant news and blog sites that have covered and are still covering the story in Uganda. Another page on the Box Turtle Bulletin site, on the Ugandan *Rolling Stone* (www.boxturtlebulletin.com/rolling-stone-uganda.htm, accessed 12 March 2011), was also helpful in gathering wide-ranging information on not only the attitude employed by various blogs and news sites covering Uganda on this but also the quality of information.

4   C. Ni Chonghaile (2012) 'Uganda anti-gay bill resurrected in parliament', 8 February, http://www.guardian.co.uk/world/2012/feb/08/uganda-gay-death-sentence-bill, accessed 19 November 2012.

5   See Keguro Macharia (2010) 'Homophobia in Africa is not a single story', 26 May, http://www.guardian.co.uk/commentisfree/2010/may/26/homophobia-africa-not-single-story, accessed 19 November 2012; and 'Explaining African homophobia?' (2010) 24 May, http://gukira.wordpress.com/2010/05/24/explaining-african-homophobia/, accessed 19 November 2012. Both are a response to Madeleine Bunting's (2010) assertion of 'African homophobia', 'African homophobia has complex roots', 21 May, http://www.guardian.co.uk/commentisfree/2010/may/21/complex-roots-africa-homophobia, accessed 19 November 2012, a notion based largely on the anecdotal and other aspects of homophobia found in all cultural contexts. Keguro challenges scholars from the West to actually engage with scholarly work and activist collectives that have amassed a wealth of knowledge on African sexualities, information that would dispute any conception of an exceptional 'African homophobia'. Keguro's challenges could be employed many times over when it comes to the Uganda homophobia spectacle.

6   A copy of the Anti Homosexuality Bill, Uganda 2009 can be found at the Warren Throckmorton website, http://wthrockmorton.com/wp-content/uploads/2009/10/anti-homosexuality-bill-2009.pdf, accessed 19 November, 2012. More information about the bill, its publication and subsequent controversy internationally can be found at the Wikipedia entry, 'Uganda Anti-Homosexuality Bill', http://en.wikipedia.org/wiki/Uganda_Anti-Homosexuality_Bill, accessed 19 November 2012.

7   Examples of the Ugandan *Rolling Stone* being misnamed as a newspaper include *Rolling Stone*, USA ('African 'Rolling Stone' impostor spreads hate agenda', http://rollingstone.com/politics/news/african-rolling-stone-impostor-spreads-hate-agenda) and in the UK, Simon Akam (2010) 'Outcry as Ugandan paper names "top homosexuals"', *Independent*, 22 October, www.independent.co.uk/news/world/africa/outcry-as-ugandan-paper-names-top-homosexuals-2113348.html, accessed 12 March 2011.

8   What is now called the 'gay agenda' is a notion deeply embedded in Americanism to the extent that the modalities of its argument cannot hold water in a region such as East Africa where LGBTIQ rights organisations have neither the logistical nor financial capabilities to carry

out the huge ideological campaigns that such a notion can require of the LGBTI community. However, though the arguments are fickle and sometimes based on falsehoods, they continue to be used worldwide to justify the criminalisation of queers, the suppression of LGBTIQ rights and consequent bastardisation of queer rights activism.

9   Denis Nzioka (2011) 'Gays in Kenya causing quiet revolution', 26 January, www.gaykenya.com, http://www.gaykenya.com/3881.html, accessed 12 March 2011.

10 For a summary of this, read Keguro Macharia's 'Africa's queer internationalism', *The New Black Magazine,* http://www.thenewblackmagazine.com/view.aspx?index=2527, accessed 12 March 2011.

11 X. Rice (2011) 'Ugandan "hang them" paper has no regrets after David Kato death', *Guardian,* 27 January, http://www.guardian.co.uk/world/2011/jan/27/uganda-paper-david-kato-death, accessed 12 March 2011.

12 Scott Mills video for the BBC, 'Worst place to be gay', http://www.bbc.co.uk/iplayer/episode/b00yrt1c/The_Worlds_Worst_Place_to_Be_Gay/, accessed 12 March 2011.

13 Keguro Macharia, 'Glocal strategies for LGBTI activism', www.gaykenya.com/news/3769.html, accessed 12 March 2011.

14 E. Rukundo (2011) 'Nairobi: Gay activist in the eyes of his friends and foes', *Daily Nation,* 6 February, http://www.nation.co.ke/Features/DN2/Gay%20activist%20in%20the%20eyes%20of%20his%20friends%20and%20foes%20/-/957860/1102396/-/item/0/-/t11skl/-/index.html, accessed 12 March 2011. A similar article appeared in the Ugandan *Daily Monitor* on the same day.

15 'Judge orders Ugandan paper to stop publishing gay lists', CNN, http://edition.cnn.com/2010/WORLD/africa/11/02/uganda.gay.list/?hpt=T2.

16 It is difficult to say what exactly happened. Details concerning the said 'death' of Uganda's anti-homosexuality bill and whether the Ugandan political class will pursue a similar bill in the new session of parliament still remain sketchy. *Pink News* (2011) 'Confusion over Uganda's anti-homosexuality bill', 5 May, http://www.pinknews.com/2011/05/11/confusion-over-ugandas-anti-homosexuality-bill, accessed 2 June 2011.

17 J. Mayamba (2011) 'Gay activist murderer sentenced to 30 years', *Daily Monitor,* 10 November, http://www.monitor.co.ug/News/National/-/688334/1270664/-/bgvjh8z/-/index.html, accessed 19 November 2012. The David Kato Vision and Voice Award recognises 'an individual who demonstrates courage and outstanding leadership in advocating for the sexual rights of LGBTI people'. The inaugural recipient of this award was Jamaican gay activist Maurice Tomlinson (http://www.visionandvoiceaward.com, accessed 20 February 2012).

18 Sokari Ekine (2012) 'Uganda will pass anti-homosexuality bill this year, says speaker', *Guardian,* 26 November, http://www.guardian.co.uk/world/2012/nov/26/uganda-anti-homosexuality-bill, accessed 16 December 2012.

19 (2012) 'Ugandan minister shuts down gay rights conference', *Guardian*, 15 February, http://guardian.co.uk./2012/feb/15/ugandan-minister-gay-rights-conference?newsfeed=true, accessed 20 February 2012.

15

The single story of 'African homophobia' is dangerous for LGBTI activism

Sibongile Ndashe

As the nascent movement for lesbian, gay, transsexual and intersex (LGBTI) rights grows, staking claims in public spaces and becoming more visible, the next phase requires that attention be paid to the message that helps propel the movement. It ceases to be sufficient to count the numbers of statements and words of support that the movement receives. The starting point has always been that LGBTI rights are human rights and hopefully that is the end point as well. This current phase of activism has to respond to the social context, explain what the movement wants and is asking for, and identify allies and refine activities and strategies in order to respond to the challenges and opportunities faced by the movement. What was once unclear has to be clarified and unquestioned strategies need to be questioned. Movement building remains an integral part of this process. I will focus on one aspect of movement building: the opportunities and challenges of building and sustaining relationships with other movements, local, regional and international.

Different countries on the continent are at different phases of activism. In some countries, there are no movements to speak of and 'don't ask, don't tell' remains the only form of activism: people know that there are LGBTI people in the communities but there is no discussion to be had. There are countries where there have been movements which have remained static, as it has not been possible to expand the circles of activism. There are countries where the movement has been able to entrench itself into civil society. The saying 'Africa is a continent, not a country' is made the more important where a single story continues to pervade LGBTI activism on the continent, i.e. that activism does not exist and that there is only homophobia. Other commentators have eloquently critiqued the single story that is told about African civil society's relationship with the LGBTI movement on the continent.[1]

The single story is indeed a dangerous story that makes it easier to impose ready-made solutions in the sea of 'nothingness'; it makes it easier to undermine local processes because 'they are not happening'; and it makes it easier to co-opt individuals and call them local movements in order to gain a foothold in a country. This gives non-African voices the cover to pursue their own agendas and reinforces homophobic elements within society when they argue that homosexuality is part of a Western agenda. Even with the best intentions, foreign interventions often misunderstand local dynamics and politics and can do much more harm than good. More fundamentally, the attempted foreign leadership of the movement's struggle in Africa subordinates the interests of the local community to those of external actors, reinforcing entrenched racial divides within the global movement and drowning progressive voices and positive developments.

The search for homophobes, in a context where homophobia is known to exist, is pointless unless, of course, the only point is to gather evidence of homophobia and name and shame those who have been 'outed' as homophobes. This fascination with outing homophobes has enabled the silencing of progressive voices. It also denies the opportunity to be heard to those who have changed, voluntarily or otherwise, are undecided, beginning to speak out or are saying things that are progressive.

For example, in talking about how homophobia is tolerated by the state in South Africa, an incident about now-President Jacob Zuma is often quoted. He was speaking to traditional leaders in ways that qualify as incitement to violence by stating that when he was growing up no gay person would have stood in front him.[2] Zuma was rightly and roundly condemned for these statements. At the time, he had been dismissed as the country's deputy president but was still the ANC's deputy president. Within days of this statement becoming national and international news, Zuma issued an unqualified apology.[3] In subsequent narratives of the story, the apology continues to be erased as it is inconvenient to the single narrative of how African political leaders are not reformed. In another incident, when Zuma was pushed into saying something about the conviction and sentencing of Tiwonge and Steve in Malawi by the Democratic Alliance, he wrongly stated that South Africa had already condemned the incident.[4] No information about the alleged statement of condemnation of the conviction could be found. However, the effect was that the president of South Africa had condemned the conviction in the South African parliament, which is a positive step for the country to take. Despite the inherent contradictions with South Africa's international relations 'policy' of not commenting on the domestic affairs of other countries in the region, the condemnation, which was clearly issued for the first time in parliament when Zuma was pushed, was rendered immaterial by the single story.

Similarly, when Zimbabwe's prime minister said that there were enough women for men in Zimbabwe and he could not understand why men would want to breathe on each other's ears,[5] he was vigorously condemned for this statement. When his party, the MDC, swiftly moved to issue a statement, distancing the organisation from the statement,[6] the single story would not allow the retraction to stick. This is despite the fact that arguably the largest party in the country had effectively adopted a stance advocating LGBTI rights.

Similarly, the Kenyan prime minister, Raila Odinga, wrongly referred to the Kenyan constitution as prohibiting same-sex relationships.[7] The Kenyan constitution is silent on this issue. Within days of this statement, after he was condemned, he claimed that he had been misunderstood. While he did not retract the statement he made it clear that he no longer wished to be bound by it, in public at least.

In all three instances, the danger posed by the initial statements cannot be overstated. The statements were hateful and devious. They were all talking to constituencies which they had judged to be more favourable to homophobia. Nothing in their pasts could have prepared their progressive supporters for the statements. Zuma cannot be said to have been testing waters; this is what made his first statement the more shocking. Tsvangirai and Odinga have both been portrayed in the media as progressive advocates of democracy and human rights, and their statements were shocking because they appeared to be a denial of the applicability of human rights to the LGBTI community. However, the retractions and corrections clearly show that there are social forces within and outside these three countries that have the power to control, mitigate and negate the homophobia of individual politicians. Who stands to benefit when the narratives erase the fall-out and the retractions that happened after the statements were made?

While these and other political leaders' utterances have remained firmly in the spotlight, progressive voices and other positive developments continue to be erased. In Uganda the leader of the opposition and then candidate for president, Kizza Besigye, has publicly stated his opposition to the anti-homosexuality bill and advocated the decriminalisation of homosexuality.[8] He based his objection primarily on the right to privacy, as meaning the state has no interest in what people do behind closed doors, although he also argued that arresting and prosecuting members of the LGBTI community was a waste of public funds.

Similarly, in Malawi, weeks after the legislature voted to include lesbian same-sex conduct under the provisions of the penal code, which prohibits same-sex relationships, the minister of justice and constitutional affairs, Dr George Chaponda, stated that Malawi would not change the laws to decriminalise homosexuality after Germany cut its financial aid to the country in response to its failure to do so.[9] He also argued, however, that while homosexuality remained against the law, Malawi had privacy laws that protected people from the intrusion of the state and said that homosexuals would generally not be prosecuted. While this is not the perfect solution, the use of privacy laws may be the best short-term strategy in Malawi to protect the rights of LGBTI people. And yet these statements are ignored by the single story narrative.

From these examples it can be seen both that homophobia remains strong on the continent – of this there can be no doubt – but also that there are pressure groups within African societies, within political parties and national parliaments as well as within governments, which are prepared to take on the homophobia and to pressure governments towards respecting the rights of LGBTI people.

Africa must move fast. Now!

In other parts of the world, there have been varied, complex and prolonged processes aimed at realising the rights of LGBTI people. Although there is not one formula or road map that can be cut, pasted and found to be useful for everyone, some of the strategies suggested for some countries seem to be set against a gradual and incremental development of the movement. Strategies proposed for the African movement have varied but what they have in common is the idea that movement building is surplus to requirement and that there is a quick way in which the indignity, stigma, violence and hate against LGBTI people can be remedied. It is even suggested that the answer to how to tackle the various forms of violations of rights of LGBTI people can be found in courtrooms and that the solution can be as uncomplicated as finding a lawyer, a client, writing a brief and getting the courts to declare as unconstitutional the laws that criminalise same-sex intimacy. A growing and cautious movement is increasingly being requested to be more assertive and aggressive in claiming rights. Those who argue otherwise are accused of being content with the status quo or of simple cowardice. It is part of the single story to propose a single solution for 'Africa' regardless of the levels of preparedness within countries to undertake action and in denial of the specific contexts of individual countries. The potential negative impact of such a strategy in countries that are not ready is huge. It is quite possible that legal decisions will be made at national and regional levels that criminalisation of homosexuality is both constitutional and in compliance with the African Charter. This may have a reinforcing effect on criminalisation across the continent and damage countries where local strategies are having some success in changing attitudes. This is in addition to the potentially catastrophic effect on the individuals who are chosen to bring cases in these countries.

Get sanctions!

It was only a matter of time before African countries started objecting to being bullied by Western countries to change their position on homosexuality. Politically, with homophobia the dominant narrative on the continent, this is an easy sell for politicians.

The currency called 'withholding financial aid' has clearly been overtraded. Withholding aid on behalf of a minority is a dangerous, double-edged sword as it often leads to further suffering by other disadvantaged groups, the beneficiaries of aid, and can lead to further isolation of the minority.

When Malawi rejected the Germans' financial aid because of its condition that it decriminalise homosexuality, the loser was, of course, the multiple causes that the financial aid supported. Politically, the loser was Germany for being a bully and not caring about human rights but for insisting on 'imposing Western values'. It was easy for Malawi to hold its head up high and say, 'This money is a threat to our sovereignty and undermines our political autonomy, the social and cultural values that we hold.' Regardless of how this move came about, how does this help the local LGBTI movements become entrenched in the local civil society movements that need donor funding to do a range of other activities and provide services to other causes? How does this move enable the local movements to continue dialogue with their governments when 'their issues' have cost the country so much in foreign aid? The single story disregards local processes and context and pretends that the LGBTI movement is insular and can work without local ties.

Outspoken friends

Increasingly, there is a view that the fight for 'gay rights' is more than just a fight for human rights. Western involvement is easily denounced as another form of colonialism and something that should be rejected as a matter of principle. There are various ways in which the sentiment is expressed but there is a view that the West cares more about the rights of gay people than other human rights, in the same way as it has always seemed to care about the human rights of people whose countries had oil. In January 2011, when David Kato[10] was murdered, international organisations and governments were elbowing each other onto the podium to denounce the murder. The Ugandan authorities' response was to immediately deny that homophobia had any role to play in Kato's murder. Others asked where was this display of outrage from the international community when people were butchered in the streets. If it was minorities that the West cared about, where were they when the Batwa people continued to be hunted in the Congo, the Basarwa people faced human rights violations in Botswana, and the albinos in some parts of East Africa were murdered? Where was the outpouring of support and media attention when all of that happened?

The big distinction between discrimination against sexual minorities and the discrimination that other groups are subjected to is that the law serves to authorise, normalise and legitimise the discrimination by criminalising the sexual conduct of sexual minorities. In almost all cases, governments will gladly own up to the laws and justify their existence. The other forms of discrimination are often issues that the governments themselves feel that they do not have a solution to and have taken steps to prohibit discrimination on that basis. If the governments are the perpetrators of the violations, they will still not easily admit to them. At the most, the governments will often seek to absolve the state machinery and demonstrate how they are complying with international human rights standards by launching investigations in order to prosecute those who were involved. For as long as Western involvement is seen as an instigator or sole supporter of the LGBTI movement, the growth of the movement and its entrenchment into civil society will remain elusive and the autonomy of the movements will remain in question.

Similarly, well-intentioned Internet campaigns aimed at advancing LGBTI activism can achieve the opposite. In December 2010, the co-directors of AIDS-Free World embarked on a letter-writing campaign in order to speak out against homophobia. Initially, it appeared that they were writing to institutions. They wrote to the African Union, the Commonwealth and the United Nations. Then there was correspondence between Paula Donovan and Bernice Sam, who is the regional director of Women In Law and Development in Africa (WILDAF).[11] The facts, largely drawn from the correspondence between the two, relate to a comment by Bernice Sam during the Ghanaian constitution review process. Sam is alleged to have said, 'We believe it is time for our constitution to define marriage clearly because we cannot hide from the fact that these kinds of union may catch up with us in the future. This is the time to say, we don't want same-sex marriages.'

There are many things that are concerning about the correspondence, including the tone, the language and the content. I will focus on two, the context and the issue. Ghana does not have a big LGBTI movement; the Centre for Popular Education and Human Rights (Ghana) (CEPERGH) and others are working towards building such a movement. The issue of decriminalisation has not been publicly debated. Over the past year there have been marches organised by Christian and Muslim organisations against homosexuality. A few public figures, like human rights lawyer Nana Oyeh Lithur, have been willing to publicly associate themselves with the plight of same-sex relationships. Needless to say, at this stage same-sex marriages, although required for full equality, are not yet on the agenda. Bernice Sam is a respected women's rights advocate not only in Ghana but also in West Africa and other parts of the continent. The nascent LGBTI movement is seeking to expand circles of activism with other mainstream human rights organisations. In many parts of the world, the women's movement has been a traditional supporter and it continues to be an ally of the LGBTI movement in many parts of the continent.

How is Bernice Sam's public flogging and urging to denounce homophobia helpful to anyone? Which activist asked for same-sex marriage in Ghana? Who, in Ghana, had been prepared to enter into a debate over same-sex marriages? Gay marriages continue to be contentious the world over. A big refrain by many opponents on decriminalisation is, 'If we decriminalise they'll want to get married and adopt children.' Advocates and activists have consistently said, 'That's not what we are talking about now. Let's cross that bridge when we get to it.' The UK's equal love campaign and the US's almost finished battle on same-sex marriages cannot be transplanted to Ghana. It is an untimely and non-contextual intervention. It forces local activists to answer and enter battles that are not of their making and put issues on the agenda where there is no capacity to deal with them.

Conclusion

The situation in Africa regarding the rights of LGBTI people is diverse and complicated by national and local politics, history and societal norms. While homophobia is particularly strong in

English-speaking Africa, partly as a consequence of colonial laws, it does also exist in French-speaking Africa. Some mainstream civil society organisations and opposition political parties have begun to support the movement, while others remain populist on the issue. Countries where the government feels the least legitimate are often the strongest in their homophobic rhetoric, making external criticism potentially counterproductive. Each country will need to develop its own strategy in realising the rights of LGBTI people and the single story militates against this, creating the impression that there is a simple, often legalistic, response to what are clearly human rights violations.

It will be important for local movements to interact with regional and international allies in their fight for LGBTI rights. Local, regional and international collaborations have been able to help movements to develop effective strategies. However, it will be crucial that local movements retain ownership of their struggles and that regional and international movements serve to complement and assist. In this vein it is important to ask questions about relationships with non-national civil society organisations. Are these relationships about initiating actions or supporting local movements? What can international NGOs do in countries where there are no active civil society movements? What happens if the processes are not anchored, owned or supported by local groups? How do local and international LGBTI movements interact with hostile/neutral local mainstream civil society organisations? How are progressive or neutral local politicians used to develop positive change? The single story narrative of the African homophobe does not allow these questions to be asked and answered honestly in the varied countries on the continent and therefore acts as a barrier to developing effective national strategies.

Acknowledgements

A special thanks to my friends Solomon Sacco, who provided critical feedback and insight and helped immensely in clarifying and shaping some of the ideas, and to Joel Nana, who is always available on the other end of the line to discuss, share facts and ideas, provide insight and challenge some ideas. All mistakes are entirely my own.

Notes

1   Keguro Macharia (2010) 'Homophobia in Africa is not a single story', *Guardian*, 26 May, http://www.guardian.co.uk/commentisfree/2010/may/26/homophobia-africa-not-single-story, accessed 18 June 2011.

2   iol (2006) 'Zuma provokes ire of homosexuals', 26 September, http://www.iol.co.za/news/politics/zuma-provokes-ire-of-homosexuals-1.295239, accessed 18 June 2011.

3   News24 (2006) 'Zuma sorry for "gay" remarks', 28 September, http://www.news24.com/SouthAfrica/Archives/ZumaFiles/Zuma-sorry-for-gay-remarks-20060928, accessed 18 June 2011; BBC (2006) 'Zuma apologises for gay comments', 28 September, http://news.bbc.co.uk/2/hi/5389378.stm, accessed 18 June 2011.

4   Brendan Boyle (2010) 'Zuma slams Malawi imprisonment of gays', Times Live, 27 May, http://www.timeslive.co.za/local/article474052.ece/Zuma-slams-Malawi-imprisonment-of-gays, accessed 18 June 2011.

5   New Zimbabwe (2010) 'Mugabe, Tsvangirai slam homosexuals', 26 March, http://www.newzimbabwe.com/news-2109-Mugabe,+Tsvangirai+slam+homosexuals/news.aspx, accessed 18 June 2011.

6   Sithandekile Mhlanga (2010) 'Zimbabwe PM Tsvangirai's comments on gay rights only personal opinion – spokesman', Voice of America (VOA), 26 March, http://www.voanews.com/zimbabwe/news/Zimbabwe-Tsvangirai-Said-to-Agree-With-Mugabe-on-Gay-Rights-26Mar10-89284972.html, accessed 18 June 2011; Blessing-Miles Tendi (2010) 'African myths about homosexuality', *Guardian*, 23 March, http://www.guardian.co.uk/commentisfree/2010/mar/23/homophobia-africa-gay-rights, accessed 18 June 2011; *Zimbabwe Reporter* (2010) 'MDC in damage control over PM gay remarks', 26 March, http://zimbabwereporter.com/politics/816.html, accessed 18 June 2011.

7   Bernard Momanyi (2010) 'Arrest gays, Kenyan PM orders', Capital News, 28 November, http://www.capitalfm.co.ke/news/Kenyanews/Arrest-gays,-Kenyan-PM-orders-10670.html, accessed 18 June 2011.

8   IQ4News (2011) 'Kizza Besigye condemns "kill the gays" bill', 11 January, http://www.iq4news.com/iq4news/kizza-besigye-condemns-kill-gays-bill, accessed 18 June 2011.

9   *Nyasa Times* (2011) 'Malawi refuses "homosexuality" aid condition', 9 February, http://www.nyasatimes.com/national/malawi-refuses-%E2%80%98homosexuality%E2%80%99-aid-condition.html, accessed 18 June 2011.

10 A Ugandan LGBTI activist, who was murdered on 26 January 2011.

11 AIDS-Free Africa (2010) 'Homophobia plagues Africa, correspondence between AIDS-Free World and Bernice Sam', 16 December, http://aids-freeworld.org/Newsroom/Press-Releases/2010/Homophobia-Plagues-Africa.aspx?p=2, accessed 18 June 2011.

16

Telling stories – fiction

Happy Mwende Kinyili

Shining ebony. I always think of shining ebony when I look at his face. Slender, fine features form this young lad. Elegance underscores his every movement. I watch him speak as the words elude me, and instead read his face to hear his heart break. He pulls back into himself and searches desperately for some resolution, some way to comfort himself as his heart breaks with self-loathing and bitterness. I cry.

Her eager eyes stare deep into mine as she listens to my words. She wants her hearing to change the world – her world. She moves with me, sways to the beat of my words – each staccato a stamp of hope. The sun is shamed by her radiance, hope breathes in her. She rushes out to the world, ready to tell a different story. The world kicks her out – her rendering is false, the word is clear, she is wrong and she is sin. The light is brutally snuffed out. She breaks. And breaks, again. Her eyes bore holes of hatred into her being. I cry.

I walk into church on Sunday morning. Young, progressive up and comers are gathered by the thousands, singing songs of praise and worship. They search for divinity, deity, holiness – they search for God. Your fire burns within me … burn within me with your fire. Lift up your eyes and see the glory of the Lord is on the earth, arise! Lifting holy hands in worship. Bow down and worship him, enter in … consuming fire, sweet perfume … this is holy ground. Some are moved to their knees, others to lay prostrate before their God.

The pastor steps to the pulpit. The sermon begins. I watch faces in the congregation. Most nod in agreement, eagerly in consent with the pastor. Hallelujahs and praise Gods are heard from the congregation. Yet in their midst, ignored and condemned faces drop and a tear breaks the tenuous hold and slides down their faces. The pastor's words, though intended to liberate, imprison many souls. They stare from between their prison bars to the option presented – You are a sinner, but because we are all sinners, we cannot condemn you. What we do is pray for your redemption. Let God redeem your soul. I cry.

I find young Shining ebony, standing at the beach staring out into the water. We talk. He tells me of his love of men. How each day, he wakes up and prays to overcome this love. He fasts every other month, believing that this will be the fast through which his love of men is overcome. He prays for redemption. Why doesn't God hear his plea? When will God bring him healing and redemption to walk away from his cross? When will he desire a woman as he desires a man?

I tell him my story.

I walked this earth for 33 odd years. In my lifetime, I sought good in humanity and many a time, I found good in humanity. I sought the divine in humanity and that too I found in my people. Sadly, as I walked the earth, it was clear to me that the search for divinity in the heavens had taken my people far away from the divine they sought. And so, I walked a different path and taught those who would hear. The leaders in the search for the divinity declared that I was Beelzebul[1] because my ways were different from their ways. The religious leaders of my time shunned me because I feasted with tax collectors and ladies of the night, and I had women active in my ministry on earth. Those whom the leaders called the lowest in their time, I loved and held close to my heart. I remember the time I had dinner at the Pharisee Simon's house, and a woman who had been condemned as a sinner came to me and washed my feet with her tears and precious oil, and dried my feet with her hair. Simon, in his continued condemnation of the woman, thought that I, as a holy teacher, should not let her touch my feet. It was sad to see that Simon could not understand the love she poured out to me and the love I in turn poured out to her. Simon failed to see the divine in her.[2]

Similarly, as I watch the world today, I see that there are those who have been given status and are counted as those worthy. They look at you, Shining ebony, and see your love for other men as that which is not worthy. They declare your love sin, and state that because of your love, they cannot love you in totality. They declare you less important, less valuable, less worthy to be my child. Yet, as they teach from their mega churches and mighty pulpits, they forget that which I taught when I walked this earth. Those who loved indiscriminately, I would call to my side. Those who saw the divine in all humanity, I would call to my side. They continue to forget my teaching, 'Truly I tell you, just as you did it to one of the least of these who are members of my family, you did it to me.'[3]

The charge was simple, 'Love your neighbour as you love yourself.'[4] Yet, the teachers of today declare that it is because of this very love that they shun you and declare you a sinner. They state that they cannot love you without calling out and condemning the 'sin' you live, the 'sin' of your loving another man. Yet, my disciple Paul taught them love and left no room for ambiguity. Paul taught love as patient and as kind, love as that which does not envy, boast and is not arrogant. Love is that which does not insist on its own way. It does not rejoice in wrongdoing, but rejoices in truth. Love bears all things; believes, hopes and endures all things.[5] Despite these words, the teachers of today are noisy gongs and clanging cymbals – for they speak with no love.[6]

Shining ebony looked at me as I concluded my story. His disbelief, he explained, was because while I had shifted the focus to love, I still remained silent on the teachings in the Bible used to condemn his love for other men. Despite the message of love I shared, this message did not silence these teachings. Did God not consider these messages would kill and destroy those like him as they were included in the teachings of God? Shining ebony turned away and said, 'The love you speak of is held back from me and mine.'

My heart broke. The hatred rained on Shining ebony had snuffed out the possibility of his accepting divine love. To Shining ebony, I continued my story.

My story, the story you read in the Bible, is all about divine love. People, just like you, Shining ebony, speaking out of their moment in history and cultural reality, wrote down their divine experience, and the teachings were then shared with millions of people across time and space. They wrote of war and of worship. They tell us about the birth of their loved ones and their inevitable death.

They try to make sense of their world and write of their search for certainty. Yet, what ties together their stories is their experience with divine love – the giving and receiving of divine love.

In our moment in history, we struggle to make sense of these stories and to give them appropriate importance in our daily lives. We find that we cannot live out the stories exactly as they did, and the examples offered conflict with each other or with our innate sense of rightness. Unfortunately, we often turn to these conflicts to keep down those who have been kept down across history, and to advance an agenda that does not carry divine love. Across history and in different places around the world, women, black people, economically oppressed people, homosexual people – anyone whose experience of divine love did not fit in with those who held the power at that moment in history – were condemned and declared sinners and less valuable members of society. The teachings of the bible were used and continue to be used to condemn them and deny them an experience of sanctioned divine love.

Shining ebony, my message to you is not to explain why the teachings of the bible have been used as they continue to be used – to deny others the experience of divine love. Rather, I teach of love – the love that prompted my walk on this earth to find the divine in all humanity and to share my experience of divinity with all humanity. My life was to offer hope to those who society declared hopeless, and to teach divine love through my actions. For I gave my life for all of humanity, because of my love for all of humanity, and it is this love that I continue to share with all people so that all people can love as I have loved them.

Notes

1   Matthew 12:24.
2   Luke 7:36–50.
3   Matthew 25:40.
4   Matthew 22:39.
5   1 Corinthians 13:4–7.
6   1 Corinthians 13:1.

17

'Faces and Phases'

Zanele Muholi

I decided to capture the positive images of my community in order to contribute towards a more democratic and representative South African lesbian, gay, bisexual, trans and intersex (LGBTI) history. I embarked on a journey of visual activism to ensure that there is black LGBTI visibility, to showcase our existence and resistance in our democratic society, to present a positive imagery of (especially) black lesbians and trans people. The first phase of 'Faces and Phases' began in 2006 and the series, which is ongoing, is now in its third phase.

Aside from the dictionary definition of what a 'face' is (the front of the head, from forehead to chin), the face also expresses the person. For me, 'Faces' means me, photographer and community worker, being face to face with the many lesbians and trans persons I interacted with from different Gauteng townships such as Alexandra, Soweto, Vosloorus, Katlehong, Kagiso.

Individuals in this series of photographs hold different positions and play many different roles within the black LGBTI community: soccer players, actresses, scholars, cultural activists, lawyers, dancers, film makers, human rights/gender activists. However, each time we are represented by outsiders, we are merely seen as victims of rape and homophobia. Our lives are always sensationalised, rarely understood. This is the reason for 'Phases': our lives are not just what make the newspaper headlines every time one of us is attacked. We go through many stages, we express many identities, which unfold in parallel in our existence.

From an insider's perspective, this project is meant as a commemoration and a celebration of the lives of black lesbians and trans that I met in my journeys through the townships. Lives and narratives are told with both pain and joy, as some of these women were going through hardships in their lives. Their stories caused me sleepless nights as I did not know how to deal with the urgent needs I was told about. Many of them had been violated; I did not want the camera to be a further violation; rather, I wanted to establish relationships with them based on our mutual understanding of what it means to be female, lesbian and black in South Africa today.

I call this method the birth of visual activism: I decided to use it to mark our resistance and existence as black lesbians and gendered persons in our country, because it is important to put a face on each and every issue.

'Faces and Phases: II – Siyafana', which means 'we are the same' – considers the similarities and differences within our 'black' race. Our creator might have fashioned each of us differently, but in his/her eyes we are the same species. Yet there are apparent differences and nuances that differentiate us from our neighbours.

It is this negotiation of sameness and difference that moved me to continue with my project 'Faces and Phases', where I captured photographs of different people in various countries. This had

Asanda Fanti, Stockholm, Sweden, 2011

Skye Chirape, Brighton, United Kingdom, 2010

been a way of responding, out of frustration, to the ongoing violation, rape and murder of women (especially queers) in Africa because of our sexualities and ethnicities. I embarked on the Siyafana project at the height of the xenophobic and homophobic attacks in South Africa that have led to the mass displacement of people in my country. Many died, women were raped, even small babies became victims of hate crimes, regardless of the constitution that stipulates equality and democracy for all. Far from home at the time, I was accommodated and embraced by strangers while residing in Toronto, Canada (which does not happen to everyone). I don't know what treatment my late Malawian father experienced at the hands of the past regime when he and his fellow men migrated to South Africa in the 1950s looking for greener pastures. However, the reality was not greener for these 'others'. Often they were left homeless without food and employment after their houses were burnt.

Featured in this series are beautiful, young and matured human beings from various places, from Toronto to London, Johannesburg and Cape Town. One can't distinguish who is from

'TK' Tekanyo, Gabarone, Botswana, 2010

Kasha N. Jacqueline, Toronto, Canada, 2009

Funeka Soldaat, Makhaza,
Khayelitsha, Cape Town, 2010

Tlhalefo 'Zeal' Ntseane, Mafikeng,
North West, 2011

where or how each person defines her/himself. From women
to transmen to 'whatever' – people are people. Human beings
deserve to be treated with love and respect, each and every one of
us. My aim was to capture the subtle complexities that challenge
our prejudices due to ignorance and hate. Even though we speak
different languages, at the same time there are commonalities
within our multiple identities – black/queer/women, etc.

The photos here are from 'Faces and Phases: III', which was
launched at the 2012 Documenta 13 in Kassel, Germany, and it
is this fact that is my point of departure for the third series. The
question I ask, and would like others to consider, is 'What does
it mean to have a travelling exhibition which was first shown at
Documenta?' Documenta is a specific and highly selective space
that comes together once every five years. What does it mean to
exhibit black lesbian, queer art in such a white space at the height
of hate crimes taking place in South Africa? Note that none of
the portraits are smiling. Now, there is an intensity, a piercing
of stance and of eyes. There is almost an accusation – Where are
YOU? What have YOU been doing? You look but you are always
silent – nothing but a gaze!

Twice removed: African invisibility in Western queer theory

Douglas Clarke

Western queer theory has set itself up as a leader in the field. That is to say, queer theory that is coming out of US, and to a lesser extent Canadian, academia is what is commonly thought of as being the most well developed theory on the subject of same-sex desiring, homosexuality and queer lifestyles. It seeks to shake the foundations of what is commonly accepted as 'normal' sexuality and searches out ways to create acceptance, history and intellectual property for homosexuals of all ages, classes and backgrounds (Fuss 1991, Seidman 1996, Hawley 2001). Yet, there is a distinct lack of consideration for African same-sex desiring culture. It is as if Western queer theory attempts to erase both African-ness and African-centred homosexuality. This essay seeks to address this double erasure by calling into question the practice and motives of Western queer theory and how it applies itself to what I will call the 'African question'. For a theory that seeks to disrupt power and cultural normativity, Western queer theory is firmly rooted in the West's historic and popular notions of what it is to be African and Afro-homosexual.

A note on language: because I will be arguing from a theoretical vantage point, I will refer to African homosexuality or Afro-homosexuality as terms to cover the broad expanse of Africa's 54 countries. In no way does my pan-Africanist language seek to homogenise the people or the sovereignty of the countries on the continent. My broad linguistic strokes serve only as a counterpart to the language and content of current, popular Western queer theory, which often treats Africa as a country rather than a multidimensional continent. It is a reality of theoretical discourse that the author must use language that covers a broad expanse of subjects even if it seems to be to the detriment of finer distinctions and subjectivities. With this apology and explanation in mind, I move on to define more of my terms in the hopes of creating the clearest example of theoretical literature that can be produced at this time.

This essay is a critique of the queer theory that is coming out of Western academic discourse, which is, in the confines of this piece, to be understood as the writing, discourse and dialogue about queer culture, homosexuality, same-sex desire or any other facet of non-normative sexuality being produced in academic institutions in the US and Canada. This does not disqualify or rectify the racist and 'blind' queer theory of any other country. It is only used to define the terms that will be used throughout this essay. As well, this essay will deal with 'African-ness', a created term to demarcate its subject from African Americans or North American 'Blacks'. In no way does this term mean to encapsulate an essence or essential nature of all Africans. Finally, this essay will use a host of terms to deal with homosexuality and queerness. In fairness I think that it is important to state categorically that while Western queer theory has compartmentalised queerness into several categories (lesbian, gay, bisexual, transgendered, transsexual, intersexed, etc) it would be unwieldy in an essay of this size to spell out all the categories every time that one is used. For that reason I will often refer to homosexuality or queer as a catch-all term meant to represent the sexuality of all those who do not consider themselves part of the popular majority of heterosexuality. Having set out all of my terms, I turn my attention now to a few ways Africa has already contributed to queer studies as a field.

It should first be stated that Africa has given the world a form of queer theory that largely remains invisible or 'unsaid', as Epprecht (1998) has described it. Africa, unsurprisingly, has a long history of homosexuality and queer relations. Many of these queer relationships have remained quiet as they have contravened a not-so-secret, unspoken agreement of silence between 'polite' Africans. It is transphobia, a fear not of same-sex relationships but of the lack of discretion (Epprecht 2005: 253).

What can be read in this transphobia is a tolerance of homosexual activity although not a respect for it (Epprecht 1998: 636). What I mean by tolerance is just that, a bearing with or permissive attitude that exists so long as these activities do not become public knowledge. Epprecht goes further by saying that especially in Zimbabwe there was the attitude of turning a blind eye to 'discreet, eccentric or "accidental" homosexual acts provided the proper compensation and social fictions were maintained' (Epprecht 1998: 645). So why do I bring this up? Certainly I am not advocating secret homosexual relations or specious treatment of those whom society 'believes' could be 'gay', but what is important is acknowledging that Africa has a model for queer theory that is largely unexplored in the Western world. If the cautious reader takes Epprecht at his word, then, we can see that Africa, long before the West came around, had a policy in place to tolerate homosexual activity so long as it was kept behind closed doors. No doubt, everybody wants a theory which is more progressive, allowing homosexuality to be more than tolerated even out in public, but it cannot be denied that Africa does give the West a good starting point to jump off from. Allowing people their own sexual choices does not destroy a society or cause it to fall into ruin, but it does allow advances to occur. Africa, for all the debate and erasure that has happened, does have several strong queer advocacy groups which have come to light since the 1980s, including the Jacaranda Queen contests (Black drag queens) and GALZ (Gays and Lesbians of Zimbabwe). Having briefly outlined some of the advancements Africa has made (socially and for queer theory), I can continue to the main topic at hand, how the West has attempted to erase and background African queers.

African sexuality, as a study, is a topic that is difficult to pin down; it has a long history of theoretical speculation and is fraught with many racist issues. African sexuality has been subject to anthropological research which sought to determine the sexual practices of African and other 'primitives' (Lyons and Lyons 2004: 5, Epprecht 2008: 34); it has been subjected to scholarship which oversexualised the Black man (Fanon 1967: 159–60, Lyons and Lyons 2004: 131) and most recently it has been subject to an erasure of sorts, a denial of sexuality to those who inhabit the same-sex desiring cultures of Africa (Spurlin

2001: 185, Johnson 2005: 127). Africa is marginalised in Western queer theory, which means that queer Africans are not being represented in the leading literature or theoretical frameworks dealing with sexuality. Though lesbian and gay sociology is still not as common or widely distributed as it should be (Stein and Plummer 1994: 178), African queer studies are even less so. By not having a voice that is being recognised in the emerging literature, African sexuality is being pushed past the margins into obscurity. The effects of this are devastating; whole identities are not being accepted or contributing to the overwhelmingly White and North American canon of queer theory. It also makes the job of the researcher more difficult. In pulling together the information needed for this essay, I found there was a considerable lacuna in sources that explicitly dealt with the erasure of African queer identity in queer theory. There were plenty of sources that dealt with African American sexual politics, Black sexual stereotyping and the history of African American sexual stigmas (Collins 2005, Russell 2008), but not much about African queer theory. It seemed as if the literature itself was condemning the African homosexual to the margins. What became abundantly clear was that the West was certainly in a position of control when it came to the dissemination of academic queer theory; moreover, it was White, academic North America that was in control. Many sources dealt with sexuality, queerness, homosexuality and gender categories, but few gave serious attention to the intersections of race and cross-cultural identities. This essay hopes to bring to light what is missing and draw a sharp distinction between how the West has used queer theory and how Africa can create its own unique queer theories.

To a large extent, Western queer theory has overlooked the multi-ethnic aspects of identity creation. Not only has queer theory not taken a look at the multicultural dimensions of sexuality but it has also eschewed a close look at the multicultural dimension of its own study. Focusing so closely on sexuality, Western queer theory has overlooked race and essentially 'white washed' the figure of the homosexual (Sullivan 2003: 66). This means that most of the queer theory that has been written has been written with the White homosexual in mind. At best there is a cursory treatment of cross-cultural representations and expressions of same-sex desire (Spurlin 2001: 185), which often invent the Black homosexual through the Euro-centric and Euro-American gaze. Said's (2003 [1978]) concept of positional superiority helps clarify how queer theory has rendered the Black homosexual invisible. 'Positional superiority ... puts the Westerner in a whole series of ... relationships with the Orient without ever losing him the upper hand'(Said 2003 [1978]: 7). Substitute 'Africa' for the 'Orient' and the meaning is functionally equivalent in this discussion. For the West, the upper hand is significant; it is an 'us' against 'them' mentality that has existed in many popular representations of foreigners. To lose the upper hand would simply mean the West did not have the right answer, or more specifically it would mean that the West did not have the only answer. By couching things in terms of position (upper hand), Said has drawn attention to the very way the West deals with cross-cultural issues. Superiority is invoked when the West is able to give a suitable answer to its own questions with little regard to those that fall outside of its constructed parameters. Positional superiority is nothing more than a statement claiming validity in all possible circumstances without actually testing those circumstances which are not your own.

The West has set itself up as the authority on knowledge about the homosexual experience. Those who are not part of the West can only benefit from the imposition of this structure. Africa cannot make its own way without appealing to the knowledge (and hence power) of the West. Two choices stand before the African homosexual: either disregard your identity and adopt one of a Western style or fit yourself into prearranged categories of Western fabrication. Both these choices seem inauthentic, outdated and mostly racist. Why is it that Africa should yet again adopt a Western model instead of creating one of its own? What is it about White homosexuality that Black Africans share to such an extent that they must adopt Western theories to better understand themselves? And what is it about the West that sets it apart from the rest of the world when it comes to understanding the multiple identities that come along with being homosexual? All of these questions cry out for attention and answers that are yet to be seen from the Western world. What is needed is a decolonisation of the theory that is being created, allowing new intersections to be produced.

Frantz Fanon, a Black psychoanalyst and intellectual, wrote extensively on how to decolonise a country, both intellectually and physically. Fanon spent his life in pursuit of understanding the relationship between the coloniser and the colonised, especially in respect to their mental lives. He was interested in the subjectivity of the Black body that existed in a White supremacist world (Cherki 2006: 26). Working from a largely psychoanalytic perspective, Fanon questioned colonialism and its legacy and the impact it had on individuals who lived within its confines (Gendzier 1976: 502). His theories proved important for many scholars and continue to hold influence in post-colonial studies. It is the anti-colonial and decolonisation theories that this essay will adapt to the current topic of queer theory.

For Fanon the colonised world was split in two: the colonisers and the colonised. The coloniser's world was compartmentalised, cold and sterile and the site of 'sermonisers, counsellors and "confusion-mongers"' (Fanon 2004: 4). These confusion-mongers set out to oppress by spreading the rhetoric of the colonisers. It is their job to subjugate the colonised and feed them the 'truth' as the colonisers see it. The other half of the colonised world is given over to the colonised who walk about shoeless, in shacks and on their knees (Fanon 2004: 4–5). This is a world that is fed information to keep it quiet and obedient. What Fanon has described here is nothing less than the situation of Western queer theory. The White Western academics are the colonisers, feeding the (African) 'colonised' information that they say is true and which they impose as a rule on the colonised identities. Where does this leave the identities of Afro-homosexuals? Erased, stereotyped and demonised (Nagel 2000: 123). Perhaps even worse than this, it leaves the identities split. Africa is torn between the coloniser's words, which offer a dominant Western perspective on their identity, and a uniquely African-centred approach to homosexuality as it is constructed in African culture.

The continued subjectification of the African identity to Western queer theory creates the double consciousness of Dubois. W.E.B. Dubois was an American sociologist who sought to understand the consciousness of the African American who felt himself to be both a Negro and a citizen. The Negro attempted to find a place in racist American society, which led to 'two unreconciled strivings, two warring ideas in one dark body' (Dubois 1903 [1999]: 11). How could one be both a Negro and a citizen if citizenship required you to not be a Negro? This is the problem that Dubois sought to unravel throughout his life. In much the same way this essay asks how Africans can allow Western queer theory to speak for them. Moore, theorising on both Dubois and Fanon, says that this often drives the Black body to Whiteness, to a desire to accept Whiteness (Moore 2005: 758) or in this essay, to accept Western-ness in hopes of collecting the two halves of the double consciousness. To leave the African identity split is to leave it ahistorical and susceptible to the imposition of Western ideas. What is needed is a whole consciousness which is able to understand its own history, identity and future (Moore 2005: 761).

The only way to reconcile the two halves of this split is through decolonisation. There must be a choice made between the two warring ideas. Turning back to Fanon, who states, 'decolonisation is always a violent event' (Fanon 2004: 1), it is through this violence that the colonised are able to struggle for their history and win out against the coloniser's ideas. However, this is not the type of violence that uses guns or knives; rather this is a decolonising violence which humanises and returns the identity to the colonised. For Fanon, the colonised have a right to self-determination, self-definition and decolonisation (Rabaka 2009: 168). If the colonisers violently impose their ideas from on top, then the colonised have the right to return that violence to regain what has been erased by the imposition. This violence is the type that unites the split consciousness and gives power back to those who have been marginalised and erased. Through the use of decolonising violence, the colonised learn to determine what is best for them and how to create their own identity, which is the exact opposite of erasure.

It may seem that this essay has turned violent, that it is now based on the language of fighting and destroying, but this is not the case. What is being proposed is a decolonisation of thought, a removal of the imposition of the Western way of thinking, which would allow Africa to reclaim (or create) a system of theory that would be based on African history, African culture and African identities. This new queer theory would be African from inception, not based on Euro-American models that are being debated in Western academic traditions. This essay is not able to give Africa the answer, seeing as it is being written by a Westerner, but I can give a model and tools that will guide the creation of a pan-African theory. The model and tools that follow are 'polite suggestions' that outline a theoretical framework that may be helpful in reclaiming African homosexual identities.

Epistemic decolonisation is just as violent as physical decolonisation, except that it deals with issues of theory, identity and thought. It is a rejection of what is being implanted by the 'sermonisers' of Fanon. What is needed to combat this imposition is the conviction to apply an alternate theory that neutralises the enforced system. In the 'African question' a theory is needed that allows Africa to create a structure that repels Western queer theory, which adopts the spirit of queer theory in general but does not follow doggedly in what has been written. It cannot be forgotten that what the West has set down has effectively erased African identity. What Africans need is to reclaim that identity and move forward with something that celebrates what they can bring to the table. One way of doing this is by taking responsibility for their sexuality.

Joyce Trebilcot, a philosopher and feminist theorist, takes up the topic of responsibility and how it applies to sexuality. Trebilcot says that the first thing to realise about taking responsibility for a situation is that it is not the same as taking responsibility for the cause of that situation (Trebilcot 1984: 421). Somebody may take charge of cleaning up spilled milk without actually having spilled it. In the same way she says that an individual can take responsibility for their sexuality now, without having to account for what it has been and what it will be in the future (Trebilcot 1984: 421). What can be extracted from this for the current discussion is the need for Africans to 'let go' of what has previously been theorised about their queer identities and start fresh from their own perspective. This is not to say that anybody should forget what has been theorised in the past. Specious accounts which read Africa as limited and unilinear and which reinforce basic racist assumptions will always be part of and a detriment to African history (Pincheon 2000: 40). What I am saying is that Africa can take responsibility for that history, while not taking responsibility for causing it. No doubt it is easier said than done, but with that accomplished, moving on becomes much more rewarding. Trebilcot goes on to say, 'To take responsibility for one's sexuality, broadly conceived, is to take responsibility for the whole range of erotic/sexual/gender phenomena that are aspects of one's actions, attitudes, thoughts, wishes, style, and so on' (Trebilcot 1984: 422). To add to this list I would say that it also means taking responsibility for being heard and removing oneself from the margins. If sexuality is something that can be taken charge of and an individual can be responsible for all the phenomena that go with it, then it can be epistemically decolonised by theorising counter to the imposed ideas. By acknowledging the situation and refusing to take responsibility for how it came about, the colonised are able to shrug off the weight of answering to the imposed colonial ideas. When these ideas have been cast off, the colonised are able to take responsibility for their sexuality as it stands, devoid of impositions and roadblocks, giving them the opportunity to create something that is a better fit for the whole range of their specific sexual practices and desires. Taking responsibility, then, is one such way to reunite a bifurcated consciousness, repairing history and moving forward in the knowledge of a humanising epistemic decolonisation.

One last point should be made here. This chapter is dangerously close to reinforcing the binary problem without yet having mentioned it. The binary problem exists when theories attempt to neatly package their subject matter; hence we get Black/White, Occident/Orient and gay/straight sitting in opposition without appreciating the crossover that actually occurs. I would like to take the remaining portion of this piece to address this danger. Binaries are disastrous things; by using them a theorist is able to make a strong point on the surface, but one that does not hold up under scrutiny. They hold within them unspoken similarities that are effaced or ignored in the interest of winning an argument. For example, the statement 'gays are not straight' seems valid and strong, yet how could one understand what it is to be straight or gay if the other did not exist and share some similarities. Similarities would include the notion that both gayness and straightness must exist in relation to a body, they inform something called 'sexuality' and they are both categories used to classify sexual partners. What we have seen so far in this essay is that there is a deep divide between the queer theory of the West and that of the emerging theory of Africa, but this is not to say that they are exclusive and bound only by their own borders. Diana Fuss argues that binaries are about coupling that which is inside and that which is outside (Fuss 1991: 1), meaning there are always those that it includes (inside) and those which it excludes. Further, it can mean that there are those who are able to execute said practice (inside) and those who cannot (outside). In the field of sexuality studies this binary is often invoked when speaking about those who are making the theories. Those who construct the theories often couch the distinctions in who is included in their proposals and those who are excluded. When speaking about queer theory, as we have seen, White queers tend to be the dominant subjects of Western queer theory, which immediately excludes Africans to the outside or marginal limits. This discourse also goes back to Said's idea of positionality, where we have seen Africa as a continent outside of any theory that deals with the 'Western' world. So what sets this essay apart? Did not this essay call the knowledge from the West colonial? This must mean that I have argued for Africa to be on the inside now and the rest of the West should be moved to the margins. I dearly hope that this is not the case.

Fuss goes on to say that the figure of inside/outside cannot be entirely taken away, but that does not mean that it must always stand for diametrically opposed opposites. She says, further, that any given term always depends on what is exterior to it (Fuss 1991: 1). This simply means that if we do not have something on the 'outside' then we cannot know what is 'inside'. This chapter will now attempt to make a case for this reasoning. When it comes to Western versus African queer theory, it is undeniable that the West has attempted to make theories which encompass all queer cultures without exception. These theories ultimately fail because they do not take into account the cultural differences that exist in multicultural communities or cross-cultural countries. Western queer theory also does not take into account the issue that they are imposing ideas on thinkers without giving them the ability to speak for themselves. Taken together, these issues put the West in the 'inside' position, having 'inside' knowledge and 'inside' comprehension. Yet, there would be no impetus, no reason to 'take responsibility for sexuality' if this positioning did not happen against the background of Africa being considered on the 'outside'. Being positioned on the outside certainly can be read as being a bad thing, not having insight and not being privy to the important dealings which take place at the heart of any matter. However, every interior must have an exterior which bounds it, which gives it its meaning. If there was no outside then there could never be an inside, it would just extend to infinity. Therefore I can say that without the West positioning Africa on the outside, the West would never come into the knowledge that what they are doing is imposing their colonial ideas on other thinkers. Africa, in some ways, determines the West. I have taken the notion of inside/outside and turned it on its head a bit. Many scholars will argue that so long as the language of position exists there can be no true fairness of representation. I am not saying that those scholars are wrong. My point is only that in this essay, at this time and dealing with this subject, I do not want to set up a strict dichotomy of Africa versus the West. Instead, I want to say that the inside determines the outside just as much as the exterior determines the interior. There are boundary crossings that exist on a theoretical as well as a practical level. Therefore, what I want to call attention to is the erasure that such positioning has already caused. It is not about Africa coming back to dominate the Western academic tradition so much as it is a discussion about how Africans can decolonise their thought and react with theories and identities of their own.

In conclusion I would like to say that this was not an easy essay to write. I had to balance on a fine line of post-colonial study that leads along twisting paths. Stray too much one way and it would seem that I am blaming Western theory for all of Africa's queer theory faults, stray too much the other way and it would seem that I am positioning Africa above the West. I hope that I have done neither of these things. When I started this project I sought to make a point of how dominant Western queer theory has been, how widely disseminated it is and how persuasive its arguments are. I also sought to show that being this formidable can lead to many issues, the main one for me being that it was erasing Africa and African queers. With the completion of this piece I know that I will continue to work diligently to make a stronger case for Africans to take the reins of their own sexuality and become responsible stewards for their own academic tradition. I know that Africa is slowly coming to its own and making waves in the academic community and I am thankful that I have been given this opportunity to lend my voice. Through the decolonisation of thought, Africa has a chance to break free of the margins and plant itself firmly as a theoretical force to be reckoned with. Decolonisation may be a violent affair but it is also a necessary one. It is my hope that African queer theory will be the next topic that gets discussed at Western universities, not because I think that the West can do it better but because Africa will have made such a contribution that it can no longer be ignored.

References

Cherki, A. (2006) *Frantz Fanon A Portrait*, New York, Cornell University Press

Collins, P.H. (2005) *Black Sexual Politics: African Americans, Gender and the New Racism*, New York, Routledge

Dubois, W. (1903 [1999]) *The Souls of Black Folks*, Gates Jr, H.L. and Oliver, T.H. (eds), New York, Norton and Company

Epprecht, M. (1998) 'The "unsaying" of indigenous homosexualities in Zimbabwe: mapping a blindspot in an African masculinity', *Journal of South African Studies*, 24(4): 631–51

Epprecht, M. (2005) 'Black skin, "cowboy" masculinity: a genealogy of homophobia in the African nationalist movement in Zimbabwe to 1983', *Culture, Health & Sexuality*, 7(3): 253–66

Epprecht, M. (2008) *Heterosexual Africa? The History of an Idea from the Age of Exploration to the Age of AIDS*, Athens, Ohio University Press

Fanon, F. (1967) *Black Skin White Masks*, New York, Grove Press

Fanon, F. (2004) *The Wretched of the Earth*, New York, Grove Press

Fuss, D. (1991) 'Inside/outside', in Fuss, D. (ed) *Inside/Outside: Lesbian Theories, Gay Theories*, New York, Routledge

Gendzier, I. (1976) 'Psychology and colonialism: some observations', *Middle East Journal*, 30(4): 501–15

Hawley, J.C. (ed) (2001) *Post Colonial Queer: Theoretical Intersections*, New York, State University of New York Press

Johnson, E.P. (2005) '"Quare" studies or (almost) everything I know about queer studies I learned from my grandmother', in Johnson, E.P and Henderson, M.G. (eds) *Black Queer Studies: A Critical Anthology*, Durham, NC, and London, Duke University Press

Lyons, A.P. and Lyons, H.D. (eds) (2004) *Irregular Connections: A History of Anthropology and Sexuality*, Lincoln, NE and London, University of Nebraska Press

Moore, T.O. (2005) 'A Fanonian perspective on double consciousness', *Journal of Black Studies*, 35(6): 751–62

Nagel, J. (2000) 'Ethnicity and sexuality', *Annual Review of Sociology*, 26: 107–33

Pincheon, B.S. (2000) 'An ethnography of silences: races, (Homo)sexualities, and a discourse of Africa', *African Studies Review*, 43(3): 39–58

Rabaka, R. (2009) *Africana Critical Theory: Reconstructing the Black Radical Tradition from W.E.B Dubois and C.L.R James to Frantz Fanon and Amilcar Cabral*, Lanham, MD, Lexington Books

Russell, T. (2008) 'The colour of discipline: civil rights and Black sexuality', *American Quarterly*, 60(1): 101–28

Said, E. (2003 [1978]) *Orientalism*, New York, Vintage Books

Seidman, S. (ed) (1996) *Queer Theory/Sociology*, Cambridge, Blackwell Publishing

Spurlin, W.J. (2001) 'Broadening post colonial studies/decolonizing queer studies: emerging "queer" identities and cultures in Southern Africa', in Hawley, J.C. (ed) *Post Colonial Queer: Theoretical Intersections*, New York, State University of New York Press

Stein, A. and Plummer, K. (1994) '"I can't even think straight": "queer" theory and the missing revolution in sociology', *Sociological Theory*, 12(2): 178–87

Sullivan, Nikki (2003) *A Critical Introduction to Queer Theory*, New York, NYU Press

Trebilcot, J. (1984) 'Taking responsibility for sexuality', in Baker, R. and Elliston, F. (eds) *Philosophy and Sex*, New York, Prometheus Books

NGOs and queer women's activism in Nairobi

Kaitlin Dearham

Introduction

In the past decade, the rise of the queer movement in Africa has prompted the formation of non-governmental organisations (NGOs) throughout the continent. In Kenya, some of the first NGOs working to address lesbian, gay, bisexual, transgender and intersex (LGBTI) issues were established in Nairobi. These organisations operate at a local level, while drawing on paradigms developed by transnational queer movements and struggles. This chapter is an examination of the methods and structures employed in the queer women's movement in Nairobi through the case study of an LBTI women's group called Minority Women in Action (MWA). I will discuss the phenomenon of 'NGOisation', which is the process of institutionalisation and professionalisation of NGOs. NGOisation, as well as the heavy reliance on a human rights framework, limits MWA's ability to address the needs of queer women in Nairobi. Nevertheless, MWA has been successful in creating a strong network of queer women who support each other and engage in various forms of activism.

This essay is based on qualitative research carried out for a larger project on the topic of queer women's organising and identity construction in Nairobi. Fieldwork was conducted in Nairobi during May to August 2010. Throughout my research, I worked primarily with MWA, which is a member of the Gay and Lesbian Coalition of Kenya (GALCK). At the time of research, the organisation was run exclusively by volunteers, the majority of whom were Kenyan. Research was conducted through participant observation[1] and in-depth interviews with 21 queer women between the ages of 20 and 40. The majority of interview participants were members of MWA or other GALCK-based organisations, particularly Artists for Recognition and Acceptance (AFRA), a group for queer women artists, and Gender Education and Advocacy Programme (GEAP), a transgender rights group. Some interviewees worked for organisations that collaborate with or fund LGBTI organisations. All research participants were assigned a pseudonym to protect their privacy.

The landscape of organising in Kenya has shifted since this research was carried out. More organisations have been created, some advocacy-oriented and some social. As more groups are established, sex workers and transgender people are becoming more vocal and visible. There are also more safe spaces for queer women now than there were in 2010. Over the past two years, GALCK has experienced managerial and financial problems which have strained its relationship with the LGBTI community.

Given the proliferation of human rights-focused groups, issues of accountability, transparency and oppression within the movement remain as relevant as ever.

Terminology

The vast majority of the women who participated in this research identify as lesbians. However, most held other identities – such as gay, dyke, queer, bisexual or transgender – alongside the label of lesbian. Some women refused labels altogether.

Many women noted that 'queer' was not widely used in Kenya because most people have not been exposed to the term. Broadly speaking, 'queer' refers to people whose sexuality or gender identity falls outside of the boundaries of heterosexuality. It is also used to refer to a movement which seeks to deconstruct compulsory heteronormativity[2] and stable sex/gender roles. The flexible and malleable quality of the term 'queer' is one of its most important characteristics.

When discussing specific research participants, I will refer to them using the terminology of their own preference. However, when referring to research participants or to the community as a group, I will use 'queer' rather than LGBTI, in order to acknowledge the presence of women who do not identify with any of the identities encompassed by LGBTI. In the discussion of organisations working on queer issues, I will continue to use the acronym LGBTI, since the organisations specifically target 'LGBTI' people and employ a more static understanding of sexuality.

LGBTI NGOs in Kenya

Kenya has a burgeoning queer community, which is becoming more visibly organised and is pushing for human rights. Ocholla writes that as early as the 1960s, gay men were gathering in public bathrooms and in tearooms in downtown Nairobi (Ocholla 2011: 94). Evidence of an organised political movement first arose in 1997, with the formation of Ishtar MSM. This organisation was originally formed to address the needs of male sex workers; it has since expanded to work for the health rights of all men who have sex with men, as well as transgender women (Kuria 2009: 2). A number of other LGBTI organisations have formed following Ishtar. While some focus on health, others aim to make changes in some of the legislation pertaining to sexuality in Kenya.[3] Others have a mandate to educate the public or to provide safe social spaces for LGBTI Kenyans. In 2006, the Gay and Lesbian Coalition of Kenya formed. GALCK is a coalition of six of the major LGBTI rights groups in Kenya, and works to support their goals and objectives (Kuria 2009: 5). Five of these groups, including MWA, share office space in Nairobi.

Minority Women in Action was formed in 2006, shortly after the formation of GALCK. Several women who had been part of the early organising efforts began to meet to discuss the possibility of forming a group specifically for women. Faith, one of MWA's co-founders, explained the original goals of the organisation:

> The aim was basically to fight for our rights. Essentially, to build us up, build our capacity ... to advocate to other organisations and individuals, so that they would understand where we were coming from ... and also to handle issues on sexual and reproductive health, which no one had really done before. And then, of course, to have fun.

The founders saw the need to create an organisation specifically for women, as queer women were under-represented in the existing LGBTI organisations. Many women saw this as an indication of a larger problem of gender hierarchy within Kenyan society, and the resulting relative lack of women in public and political spheres. In the following comments, interviewees speculate on the reason for the dominance of men in LGBTI organising:

> Mary: Basically, it's a patriarchal culture, so people don't really see women that much ... Maybe we're not used to being seen. Maybe it's a culture thing.

> Jake: It's a man's world ... For the gay man, when he was born, he was told, 'You're a man, this is your world, you control it.' When a woman is born, she is told, 'You have to be a good wife ... or mother. Your place will be ... serving your husband.' But for the guy, it's like, 'You have to run this country.' That's why I think there are more gay men in GALCK than lesbians.

> Rose: Even in mainstream human rights organisations, women have had to fight a lot for their place. So it's really not any different within LGBTI organisations ... it's just a patriarchal system. It's a system in which the more dominant has the voice ... and it happens that a lot of the time women are marginalised. I was hoping it would be different, because gay men [suffer from] patriarchal oppression too. But it happens not to be different within the LGBTI community ... Even in women's organisations, there's a tendency to sideline trans and intersex [issues].

Interviewees identified the reproduction of gender hierarchy within LGBTI organisations as the major reason for the need to create a queer women's organisation. Another reason given for the lack of women's voices in LGBTI organisations was that there are more queer men who are willing to be open about their sexuality than women. This relates to women's economic marginalisation, as well as the social pressures on women to marry and have children at a relatively young age compared to men. Finally, the tendency of LGBTI organisations to focus heavily on men who have sex with men (MSM) and HIV/AIDS was identified as an additional factor precipitating the formation of a queer women's organisation. While HIV/AIDS is a relevant health concern for queer women, programming and workshops generally focused more on this issue than made sense for them. The formation of a queer women's organisation meant that women could focus on the issues that specifically concerned them.

From the beginning, MWA was formally organised, developing a leadership structure, strategic plan and a constitution within a year. The steering committee is the top decision-making body of the organisation. It is elected yearly from among the MWA members and consists of eight officers with various financial, administrative and programming duties. The steering committee communicates suggestions and ideas to the rest of the members, and is responsible for organising activities, events, workshops and seminars.

NGOisation

Though the development of LGBTI rights-oriented NGOs is relatively new in Kenya and on the continent, other social movements have also employed the NGO model as a form of political mobilisation. The feminist movement saw an explosion of women's rights NGOs in the 1980s and 1990s. The subsequent 'NGOisation' of the movement has been criticised by scholars and activists alike (Alvarez 1998 and 1999, Armstrong 2004, INCITE! 2007). The organisations which formed through the feminist movement, and later the queer movement, are frequently hierarchical and highly bureaucratic. Donors, who are concerned with financial accountability, push organisations towards professionalised, formal structures which are easier to monitor (Alvarez 2009: 177). Because NGOs are so often dependent on external funding, and donors like to fund projects which have demonstrable impacts as a 'return' on their 'investment', NGOs often prioritise short-term projects with quantifiable results. This means that organisations are frequently governed by practices which are similar to those of corporate businesses (Alvarez 2009: 177).

Armstrong (2004) points out that while such practices ensure that NGOs are accountable to their donors, neither NGOs nor donors are reliably accountable to the local community. Hierarchical structures and an emphasis on professionalism, which encourages elite leadership, means that it is easy for NGOs to became alienated from people at the grassroots level (Armstrong 2004: 40). In this sense, the most marginalised community members are often unintentionally excluded. The necessity for NGOs to speak a language that appeals to donors means that they are often employing an international development lexicon which may not resonate in local contexts. In this section, I will examine the effects of NGOisation on queer women's organising in Nairobi through a discussion of the use of the human rights framework and of class issues.

Human rights

The adoption of the human rights framework by LGBTI organisations reflects a larger pattern of mirroring approaches and practices taken by 'mainstream' NGOs. MWA works within the human rights framework by working to secure the rights of LBTI women in Kenya, and educating its members on human rights principles. Yet queer women in Nairobi are divided on the applicability and efficacy of the human rights framework. Some argue that it is the most effective means of addressing queer issues. Others are more sceptical about its use in this context, questioning its efficacy even as they employ it pragmatically within their own organisations.

In the African context, morality or cultural arguments are often used to counter human rights arguments (see Cobbah 1987, Njoh 2006). Cobbah writes that human rights institutions have historically engaged in cultural imperialism, highlighting the fact that when the Universal Declaration of Human Rights was adopted by the United Nations in December 1948, the UN was dominated by Western countries, and most of sub-Saharan Africa was still under colonial control (Cobbah 1987: 316). Despite this, many argue that the human rights framework is not Western in origin. Rose, one of MWA's co-founders, explained:

> Human rights, the word itself, is Western. But ... is it to say that there were never human rights concerns in Africa before colonialism? Honestly, I do not believe that ... perhaps the words used nowadays or other superficial aspects are Western, but the concept of human rights, human dignity, treating people with dignity, a sense of justice, were there.

Nevertheless, it is very easy for homophobes to dismiss queerness as Western, particularly when it is being defended primarily through the use of a theoretical framework which is widely considered to be alien.

This is not to say that the human rights framework should be abandoned entirely. This framework can be useful when it comes to advocating changes in policy and legislation, as these frequently employ rights-based language. However, it is important for queer activists to be able to hone our arguments to particular audiences. As Khadija, who works for a social justice organisation, observed, 'I think that when we're talking to that type of [grassroots] audience, human rights language is limiting, in that it sounds very imperialist. It sounds very donor-driven.'

Khadija also pointed out the limitations of employing an exclusively policy-oriented approach, since it pushes organisations to constantly engage with state institutions. Challenging homophobic state policy is important and necessary work, but is sometimes done to the neglect of communities in which queer Africans still live and negotiate their everyday interactions. This means that a change in legislation, though always welcome and victorious, does not always reflect the reality on the ground. The persistence of human rights violations relating to sexuality, despite the wide state endorsement of treaties and conventions upholding sexual rights, demonstrates the limitations of these instruments; that is, the disconnect between international and national laws, and local lived experience.

The perception of human rights as Western and donor-driven may also alienate queer activists from their larger communities. Njoki, a lesbian poet and songwriter, and co-founder of AFRA, explained:

> There's a feeling like we as gay people are isolating ourselves from the rest of the community. The heterosexual people feel like we are fighting for special rights. When you talk about LGBTI rights, it makes them feel like we are advocating for special rights that are more pronounced over theirs.

This perception that queer Kenyans want to be 'special' or 'different' from other Kenyans serves to reinforce the cultural argument that queerness is alien and that it has no place in African communities. Leah, who is a member of MWA and works for a sexual rights funding organisation, also emphasised this danger by explaining how the human rights framework does not necessarily resonate with activists, but that they continue to use it pragmatically because it is easily understood by international donors. Leah cautioned against employing inappropriate approaches for the sake of gaining funds, pointing out that relationships with funders are easily lost as political trends change. She explained, 'Right now I think sexual minorities are like the flavour of the month, so everybody wants to work with them. But what do you do when we're not the flavour of the month, then what happens?'

Class issues

The professionalisation and institutionalisation of NGOs, as well as the emphasis on policy-oriented work, often create class divisions within organisations. In the case of MWA, though effort is made to address the needs of all members, many of the low-income members felt that the programming did not address their reality and challenges. Queer women from low-income areas experience more violence and sexual assault than women living in middle-class neighbourhoods. Though violence and rape are not exclusive to low-income neighbourhoods, economically oppressed women are disproportionately affected. In interviews, this was partly attributed to a difference in living conditions and increased dependence on family for survival. Women who shared a room with family members, or who lived in extremely close proximity to neighbours, found that their behaviour was easily policed. This policing took the form of verbal harassment, physical violence, and rape. Reverie, a lesbian from a high-density, low-income suburb of Nairobi, explained the impact of living conditions in her estate.

> In the ghetto ... the law is not really enforced and people don't really know about legal issues. They take the law into their own hands. So if they think that today you're supposed to be beaten, they do exactly that. If they think today you're supposed to be raped, that's exactly what they'll do ... And you'll do nothing about it. 'Cause the legal system doesn't really care what you're going through.

> Outside of the ghetto, I think it's different. People know, but you live in this context where others really don't care about your business ... We're a [large] population living in the ghetto. And the people, the way you live, the small spaces: it's very easy for people to get into your business.

When it comes to safety, it is more difficult for women from low-income areas to engage in risk management practices when their very living conditions heighten the likelihood of their being 'punished' because of their sexuality. Yet NGO discussions of queer women's security often do not take class differences into account.

Jake, another lesbian from a low-income neighbourhood, described the challenges of queer women in these areas by saying, 'In ghettos, you'll find queer people, and they're illiterate. They have no skills. You know, day-to-day life, it's a struggle for them. Since you don't have an education, you have nothing. The only option you have is to get married, 'cause getting married doesn't need a lesson.' Val, an MWA steering committee member, also discussed the ways in which lack of formal education and visible queerness can make it more difficult for queer women to gain employment. She explained:

> We're all queer and we all have the same problems. Maybe some more than others [because] there's also a huge gap in financial status. You find that a lot of these young girls are struggling. The toms can't really wear a frock or a dress ... and go out for an interview because they feel like they're not being who they are. Who they need to be. And what happens is that the years go by, and you don't have an employment history. And you find yourself in the same place you were at twenty. But it's no fault of your own ... life just sucks.
>
> The few of us who have made it a little bit, we may not be doing enough to uplift the ones that are not really making it ... it takes a lot of sacrifice on ourselves, to help the ones who are down. But then again you wonder how to start ... You know, when I was twenty I was in college, and for me, school was a priority. Go to school, get work. But other people don't have those opportunities, and I think that's what's lacking. I tell you, I don't know how to bridge that gap. For sure, I don't.

Though Val herself is a gender non-conforming lesbian, she was able to overcome the difficulties associated with not being 'feminine enough' because of her educational background and the opportunities this afforded her. Her comment about toms[4] being unable to find work was a common complaint among low-income, gender non-conforming women, who would often end up being unemployed or working in the informal sector.

Queer women in low-income areas are often more dependent on family for financial support, and may become trapped in heterosexual relationships and marriages to survive. It can be difficult for these women to participate in NGO-style workshops and other activities for several reasons. Such activities, which are frequently conducted in English, may be inaccessible for those with little formal education; for women who are living with or married to men, the need to attend a meeting can be difficult to justify; and meetings and other activities are often held downtown or in middle-class neighbourhoods, which can be difficult for lower-income women to access because of travel time (as low-income neighbourhoods and informal settlements are mainly located on the outskirts of Nairobi). Reimbursement for fares, however, is normally provided for women who attend MWA's workshops and activities. Alice, a former committee member, speculated, 'It would be nice if they could reach out more to the women, especially at the grassroots. Because usually the meetings we have are up-class, you know, up-town kinda meetings. And really there are a lot of women out there who have not been reached.'

Some women, both from the member base and from the steering committee, mentioned the hierarchical nature of the organisation as a stumbling block to addressing class issues. But the larger impediment seemed to be the lack of communication and dialogue on class differences within the organisation. Naomi, a steering committee member, stressed communication as key:

> I feel like what it is, is that we need to be having these conversations and we need to have them more frequently. No one's talking about it ... I feel like if we had more dialogue, we could build bridges, [break down] misconceptions, preconceived notions we have about each other. So that we could come together and have a more cohesive group.

Naomi mentioned that people were 'dug into their positions', and that political and class education was needed to resolve the issue. Rose also talked about the importance of dialogue and education in addressing the class issue:

> To deal with class differences, which are so inherent in people, it will take re-socialisation. It will take re-educating people in some of the things they take for granted. The same way we have to re-educate people on patriarchy, on women, on homosexuality, on transgenderism, on intersex people ... re-examining our concepts, which is very difficult.

Here, Rose is drawing an important parallel between class and other structural oppressions. Many interview participants expressed a common desire to address this issue – the willingness is certainly there. Nevertheless, it is a challenge for an organisation which prioritises professionalism to find a place for low-income women in the leadership structure. The struggle to include people from a diversity of economic backgrounds in the decision-making processes and leadership of organisations is common in the NGO world.

Successes

MWA has made great gains despite the difficulty of working within an NGOised environment. The women who were involved in the creation of MWA, and those who are currently involved in organising, are very dedicated to their work. Many put in long hours of unpaid work and contribute their own resources to create a more equal and safe society for queer Kenyans. In this section, I will discuss organisational successes in creating visibility and encouraging queer mobilisation.

Visibility

MWA and GALCK have a great impact on making the public aware that queer people exist in Kenya. The fact that these organisations were formed and are run by Kenyans helps to deconstruct the myth that queerness is 'un-African'. MWA and GALCK's visibility and persistent advocacy work have helped queer issues become part of public consciousness and dialogue, which is a major change from even five years ago. Rose described the impact of GALCK's participation in the World Social Forum in 2007:

> We had a tent, not even a desk. And we called it Q-spot. We had people's poems, we were showing the community's artwork. There were sessions, other organisations from around Africa also participated, there were workshops. And we had a permanent desk where we had people talking about LGBTI issues. Members of the public could come, ask questions, we'd have conversations. And it was actually very good because we got a lot of media out of it. So that at least helped to wipe out that myth that LGBTI people do not exist in Kenya, for those people in denial.

This was one of the first times that queer people appeared publicly as a group in Nairobi, speaking for themselves.

Safe spaces

The GALCK office, and other spaces which MWA occupies for events, are some of the few places where queer women feel able to relax and do not have to monitor themselves for fear of revealing their sexuality. These formal LGBTI safe spaces complement the informal queer safe spaces which queer women develop for themselves outside of organisations through personal relationships and networks. Research participants unanimously agreed that finding a social and/or activist space in which they could 'be themselves' was an enormous relief. Sam, a member of AFRA, described the first time she came to the GALCK centre: 'It felt really awesome ... because previously, I used to hide myself ... but when I met the first group of lesbians and bisexual people, I was so impressed. I felt like I have a family out here. I don't have to hide myself anymore.'

Many participants described their first encounters with MWA or other GALCK organisations as 'meeting family', or finally finding a place where they fitted in or belonged. Ruth, who is on MWA's steering committee, described how being in the presence of other queer people had the effect of normalising her sexuality: 'I could see people, they're happy... they're behaving like nothing big, just like any other normal person.' Being in a space dominated by queer people was a major step for many queer Nairobians, who may have previously felt isolated and alienated even if they already knew one or two queer people. Faith explained that when MWA was forming, 'There was a lot of excitement ... I think prior to that time, lesbians ... were all sort of scattered. But this basically brought all the lesbians together, at least the little circle that knew each other within Nairobi.'

Mobilisation

MWA and other GALCK organisations have succeeded in mobilising the queer movement in Kenya by creating linkages with other queer and ally organisations, encouraging the creation of new LGBTI organisations elsewhere in the country, and by inspiring queer Kenyans to engage in activism outside of organisational contexts. As one of the first, and certainly one of the most visible, groups working for LGBTI rights in Kenya, GALCK has been a positive example and in some cases a catalyst for others who may want to start queer organisations or do queer work in Kenya. Some of these groups have decided to employ more radical approaches in their activism.

Even for those who have decided not to engage in activism through MWA or other formal organisations, MWA has been a useful point of connection to other queer women. Those who have decided not to participate in the organisation, largely because of structural concerns, continue to engage in queer activism of various sorts. This may be formal (working with another NGO) or informal (maintaining emotional and financial support networks with other women, or articulating their struggles through art or media engagement). In this sense, involvement with MWA has been a jumping-off point of activism for many.

Coalition

The fact that several Kenyan LGBTI rights NGOs have come together as a coalition group protects them from some of the pitfalls of NGOisation. Though GALCK's member organisations are to a degree competing for funding, the organisations frequently come together to hold events as a coalition. The fact that several organisations share office space means that it is easy for their members to exchange ideas and collaborate on projects. The coalition helps maintain both movement-building and diversity by encouraging its member organisations to work together. This echoes Tsikata's (2009) observation that the formation of coalition groups among women's movements in Ghana has enabled activists to transcend some of the issues of NGOisation by coming together on matters of common interest.

Strengthening the movement

In her analysis of feminist NGOs in Israel, Hanna Herzog states that 'the strength of the movement comes from its willingness to self-criticise, as well as from its diversity' (2008: 274). In this way, women's organisations managed to remain effective and true to their feminist roots despite NGOisation. I believe that this sentiment is equally applicable to the queer movement. Queer women's NGOs must engage in self-criticism through an examination of their programmes and structure, looking at whether they are serving their membership base, and by being open to discussion and debate. It is important for members to be willing to speak up and work to correct what they perceive to be problematic within the organisation.

In the African context, it is particularly important for the queer movement not to pigeonhole itself. In Kenya, as in elsewhere on the continent, homophobic discourse often takes on a cultural bent, decrying queerness as 'un-African'. Two ways in which the NGOisation of queer movements reinforces this discourse is by encouraging NGOs to specialise to the point of isolation, and by encouraging the use of the human rights framework, which as previously stated is often perceived as Western and relies primarily on engagement with the state at the expense of focus on communities. In order to avoid isolation, it is critical to reach outside of the queer community and develop strong alliances. This means not just working with other organisations that address queer issues, as is already happening, but also being present as queer Africans in other progressive movements. Of course, the challenge behind this type of engagement is ensuring safety, since even so-called progressive political spaces are not necessarily safe enough for queer Kenyans to be open about their sexuality. One example of coalition-building in Nairobi was the Warembo Ni Yes campaign,[5] in which women from diverse backgrounds mobilised to push for the adoption of the new Kenyan constitution. This campaign brought together women from labour, feminist, queer and sex workers' movements, from a range of economic backgrounds.

Through coalition building and learning from other progressive movements, queer NGOs may also develop new ways of approaching their activism, to complement the human rights approach. While reflecting on this issue, Naomi said:

> I feel like there are different ways [of organising]. The human rights model is only one ... I feel like it's not effective enough when we're not able to answer these questions when it comes to culture, which is ingrained, deeply ingrained, even within the LGBTI themselves.

She went on to explain that we have so much knowledge in Kenya, and in Africa as a whole, which could be used to create a new framework for activism. In other words, we must use the knowledge and traditions of our own communities to inform our activism, rather than relying on what may have been effective elsewhere in the world.

MWA has done important and groundbreaking work in the establishment of a queer women's movement in Kenya. However, it is critical to acknowledge the limitations of the dominant NGO model, and ensure that the creation of organisations does not mean the exclusion of some queer women. Dialogue, self-reflection and progressive alliance-building are important tools in creating a strong queer movement in Africa.

Acknowledgements

I would like to thank all the sisters who participated in my research for sharing their lives and stories so generously with me. A special thank you goes to the women of Minority Women in Action, who welcomed me and introduced me to the community. I would also like to acknowledge the Social Science and Humanities Research Council of Canada (SSHRC), which provided financial support for this project.

Notes

1   Participant observation is an anthropological research method that
    involves taking part in daily life and activities, while simultaneously
    observing and collecting data relating to those activities. During
    participant observation, I observed group interactions and how beliefs
    and values were expressed in a relatively natural, informal setting.
2   Heteronormativity is a set of assumptions about sex and gender roles
    which legitimises homophobia and transphobia. Heteronormativity
    assumes that people fall into only one of two sexes (male or female)
    and genders (men or women), which have certain roles in life.
    Heterosexuality is assumed to be the only natural sexual orientation,
    which means that only sexual and marital relationships between a man
    and a woman are acceptable. Sex and gender are assumed to naturally
    correlate, which means that transgender and intersex people are
    excluded from heteronormative frameworks.
3   Sections 162 through 165 of the penal code are commonly interpreted
    to mean that sexual acts between people of the same sex are illegal in
    Kenya. The law is very ambiguous, referring to 'unnatural offences',
    'carnal knowledge against the order of nature' and 'acts of gross
    indecency' (Kenya Law Reports: 2010). These laws were established by
    the British government during colonial times, and have remained in the
    Kenyan penal code since then.
4   'Tom' is a short form of 'tommy', a term for an androgynous, boyish or
    gender ambiguous queer woman derived from the term 'tomboy'.
5   http://www.waremboniyes.org, accessed 15 March 2010.

References

Alice, Faith, Jake, Khadija, Leah, Mary, Naomi, Njoki, Reverie, Rose, Ruth,
    Sam and Val (2010) personal interviews, Nairobi, Kenya
Alvarez, Sonia E. (1998) 'Latin American feminisms "go global": trends
    of the 1990s and challenges for the new millennium', in Alvarez, S.E.,
    Dagnino, E. and Escobar, A.E. (eds) *Cultures of Politics/Politics of Cultures:
    Re-visioning Latin American Social Movements*, Boulder, CO, Westview
Alvarez, Sonia E. (1999) 'Advocating feminism: the Latin American feminist
    NGO "boom"', *International Feminist Journal of Politics*, 1(2): 181–209
Alvarez, Sonia E. (2009) 'Beyond NGO-ization? Reflections from Latin
    America', *Society for International Development*, 5(2): 175–84
Armstrong, Elizabeth (2004) 'Globalization from below: AIDWA, foreign
    funding, and gendering anti-violence campaigns', *Journal of Developing
    Studies*, 2: 39–55
Cobbah, Josiah A.M. (1987) 'African values and the human rights debate',
    Human Rights Quarterly, 9: 309–31
Herzog, Hanna (2008) 'Re/visioning the feminist movement in Israel', *Journal
    of Citizenship Studies*, 2(3): 265–82
INCITE! Women of Color Against Violence (ed) (2007) *The Revolution Will*

Not Be Funded: Beyond the Non-Profit Industrial Complex, Cambridge, MA, South End Press

Kenya Law Reports (2010) 'Laws of Kenya', http://www.kenyalaw.org/kenyalaw/klr_home/, accessed 15 March 2010

Kuria, David (2009) 'History of LGBTI movement in Kenya, and way forward', 6 May, http://galck.org/index.php?option=com_content&view=article&id=17:history&catid=9:activism&Itemid=9, accessed 7 May 2010

Njoh, Ambe (2006) *Tradition, Culture and Development in Africa: Historical Lessons for Modern Development Planning*, Burlington, VT, Ashgate Publishing Company

Ocholla, Akinyi (2011) 'The Kenyan LGBTI social movement – context, volunteerism and approaches to campaigning', *Journal of Human Rights Practice*, 3(1): 93–104

Tsikata, Dzodzi (2009) 'Women's organizing in Ghana since the 1990s: from individual organizations to three coalitions', *Development*, 52(2): 185–92

20

The struggle for intersex rights in Africa

Julius Kaggwa

Being intersex is a journey along the indeterminate middle ground between male and female; this variance or diversity in sex development and gender is still very controversial in Africa. This chapter highlights the extreme social, cultural and religious biases that surround this controversial ground in Africa, as well as the correlation between gender and sexuality from an African perspective.

Challenges and opportunities around sex, gender identity and sexuality in Africa are strongly linked to the family, and are frequently grounded in culture and disparate ideologies. While many individuals have used conservative ideologies to oppose gender and sexual diversity in Africa, emerging sexual rights voices have underscored common values of democracy, health and human dignity to advance them. My chapter explores the struggles involved in challenging the traditional binary sex and gender dichotomy in Africa and how culture, including religion, has been used to advance a repressive agenda as well as acting as a barrier to advancing freedom of gender and sexual expression in Africa.

It is an established fact that sexuality is an integral part of the human experience. Yet in most parts of Africa, sexuality is still greatly gendered and only discussed in terms of procreation and disease control. This is one of the reasons why most sexual health programming in Africa focuses on behaviour and attitude change, especially in the area of sexual activity and expression. Sadly, however, cultural dictates in the form of fundamentalist religious beliefs and social standpoints have meant that these interventions and messages are also gendered and exclusive to conventional sexual expressions and relations. The convention is that one is either male or female and that the male and female will in turn engage in monogamous heterosexual sex – which is the sexual activity between one woman and one man. It does not embrace atypical sex identities and alternative sexual relations, such as sexual activity among gender and sexually variant people.

Africa is vast and diverse in her cultural content and yet there are commonalities in attitudes to human sexuality and gender diversity in almost all of our countries. Variance in gender and sexuality is frowned upon and considered to be taboo in dominant African culture. Most African families – which are usually extended in composition – do not openly engage in discussions on sex and sexuality. Furthermore, sexual development, activity and expression are usually shrouded in extreme secrecy. For example, in my tribe of Baganda in Uganda, sex cannot be bluntly called 'sex'. It is alluded to in proverbial terms, such as 'pointing another to the devil's realm' (*okutunuza omuntu mumbuga za sitani*) or in a more positive light 'a private adult conversation' (*akaboozi kekikulu*). It is therefore from this fixed cultural premise that arguments around sex development, gender, sexual diversity, sexual activity and choice are considered 'un-African' and unwelcome.

In many countries in Africa, dominant gender discourse takes the strictly binary forms of woman and man. Anything outside of that is aberrant. However, even within that binary dichotomy, man remains the more privileged gender. This is also seen in HIV interventions, where pregnant women are subjected to compulsory HIV testing but not the expectant fathers, where female sex workers are blamed for fuelling the pandemic and not the men who buy their services, where it is more acceptable for genital mutilation to be done on intersex infants to make them girls rather than leave them as supposedly 'dysfunctional' boys, where there is more brutal rape of women, regardless of whether such women are intersex or not.

In many African countries, enormous resources have been, and are still being, spent to establish HIV and malaria prevention and treatment programmes and to address social justice and economic problems. However, gender and sexual variance is still a key social determinant of inequalities in accessing those programmes. Even in the wake of men-who-have-sex-with-men (MSM) and women-who-have-sex-with-women (WSW) HIV programming, a sub-culture that assumes that only gay or anal sex exists besides heterosex has ensured the exclusion of the myriad of identities in which sexual and gender expression takes many different, other forms. For example, intersex people in Africa often find themselves destitute. And when they are sick, they are not able to freely access health care. As a result, they self-medicate both for illness and hormonal medications with over the counter and often expired medicines. Often, they will even share needles. This is one of the challenges intersex people share with their African transgender counterparts. More often than not, they will not be able to determine their seropositive status and yet, due to the pressing need to survive, they seek a livelihood through sex work (usually with no protection whatsoever). Even in this industry, they are discriminated against.

Culturally and politically, non-conformity to prescribed sex and gender categories and roles is considered immoral and is vehemently discouraged and criminalised in most African countries. This deters many people from accessing social justice and services and, at the very worst, makes them rebels or criminals. Intersex, lesbian and transgender women, for example, refrain from seeking sexual and reproductive health services for fear of being harassed, ostracised and discriminated against. Sexually risky activity resulting from lack of appropriate information and interventions for this population has fuelled the incidence of hate crimes, sexually transmitted infections, HIV and AIDS among these populations in most of Africa.

In many instances, religious and cultural fundamentalism is evident in the way policymakers and medical practitioners are sceptical and scornful of the body politics of gender non-conforming people, to the extent that they craft all possible ways to exclude these populations from society as cultural and social rejects and criminals. A case in point is the anti-homosexuality bill which was tabled in Uganda by member of parliament David Bahati in October 2009.

Examples drawn from provisions in the bill include the broad fashion in which homosexuality is defined to include 'touching another person with the intention of committing the act of homosexuality'. This is a provision highly prone to abuse and which puts all Ugandan citizens of all genders at risk. Such a provision would make it very easy for a person to witch-hunt or bring false accusations at will against another simply to cause scandal.

Furthermore, if one's job is in any way related to sexual and reproductive health services, human rights activism, advocacy, education and training, research, capacity building and related areas, the anti-homosexuality bill poses a serious threat in its provision about the 'promotion' of homosexuality. The bill seeks to silence human rights activists, civil society, the media and anyone who would engage with issues related to sexual and reproductive rights. Since sexuality is a dynamic and integral part of the human experience, regardless of which gender or sex we identify as, legislation such as the anti-homosexuality bill makes all of us potential victims and criminals.

This bill shows how society and policymakers are using religious arguments to establish categories for people when they design culture and policies that reveal prejudices and biases based on homophobia, racism, sectarianism and so on. It also informs us that culture as we know it is continuously evolving and can be the vehicle that either impedes or promotes positive social and economic change. In the case of this bill, undeniably everything is being done to deny sexual and reproductive health rights to Ugandan citizens who are considered not to conform to cultural dictates of what 'normal' gender and sex classification should be. In this regard intersex people are mistakenly taken to have two sexual organs or to have the ability to have sexual intercourse with both men and women, portraying them as either gay or bisexual. Additionally, some intersex people who opt to change from a best-guess sex assigned at birth will travel a journey similar in some ways to that of a transsexual person and often face similar prejudice and exclusion.

In most African societies children born with these variations are often killed shortly after birth or, if not, they are kept hidden from social and community life. Our media and community engagement efforts around intersex health and rights over the past two years have slowly broken through this barrier and provoked constructive dialogue around broader gender and sexual identities.

It is important to note that family institutions all over Africa are undergoing significant transformation, especially in terms of the dialogue around the correlation between gender and sexuality as well as the importance placed upon sex and gender roles. There have been increasing publicity and evidence that many African people, from all walks of life, have bodies that do not conform to 'normative' male or female bodies, some of whom practice, and express themselves through, exploratory gender expressions and sexual activity. We cannot afford to shy away from the fact that there are many people who occupy the grey middle ground between male and female. The subject of debate is usually whether sexuality, sexual activity and variant sex classifications should be gendered; whether or not these people – whose sex is indeterminate at birth or at puberty – have rights to life, information, appropriate health and dignity in their chosen, forced or intrinsic gender identities and expression.

In the case of Uganda, the intersex reality challenges the extremist religious and moralistic culture that denies sexual minorities and non-conforming genders access to and enjoyment of sexual health and rights. These lived realities include (all names have been changed):

- Musa, a 16-year-old boy who lives with his mum and was diagnosed with undescended testes and hypospadias as a baby; he was operated on as a child but surgery was not successful
- Mary, a 22-year-old woman who has ambiguous genitals where a male penis developed within her vagina; she attributes her failure to find a marriage partner to this intersex condition
- John, a 20-year-old young man living with his stepmother who has had corrective surgery more than twice but who still cannot find the funds to remove the under-developed uterus, close the vaginal opening and release the penis
- Jane, a four-and-a-half-month-old child who was born with ambiguous genitals, whose doctors had reported hypospadias and genital malformation; she was being hidden by her mother and was later reported dead under mysterious circumstances
- Ivan, a 23-year-old man who was near suicide because his breasts had developed like those of a woman; he was binding them in a similar way to that done by female to male transgender people.

Social and cultural issues, just like science, are always evolving – even in Africa. We know that change and the ability to adapt to it are the ingredients of a dynamic and progressive society. And any society can resolve to adapt to any necessary changes within its social and cultural moulds in order to ensure that all the freedoms of its people are protected. In the era of searching for best practice in human rights advocacy, it is a matter of urgency for Africa to appreciate differences in sex development, gender identities and related human rights. The critical challenge is how to formulate relevant strategies to achieve this within our cultural contexts as Africans.

The critical aspect about which we need to educate ourselves as Africans is that while we need identities for the purposes of organising, intersex in itself is not an identity and an intersex person will often find themselves taking on other identities when it comes to gender, sexual orientation and choice. We must also acknowledge that dehumanising societal attitudes, under the convenient guise of 'cultural dictates' towards intersex children and people, are clearly a gender- and sexually-based violence issue.

As a mitigation strategy, the intersex movement in Uganda and the East African region is focusing on creating greater visibility and amplifying voices around intersex issues and related human and sexual rights through public education and media and community engagement.

African statement on sexual orientation and gender identity

2012-03-07
Human Rights Council 19 Session-Geneva

We African activists speak on behalf of the people throughout the continent who continually face persecution and violence on the basis of their sexual orientation and gender identity. We also speak in solidarity with the sentiments of the Women Living under Muslim Laws in their letter addressed to the President of the Human Rights Council.

We have received with joy the report of the UN High Commissioner for Human Rights Navi Pillay that highlights the deplorable state of human rights for LGBTI people.

We commend the leadership of South Africa in opening dialogue around the human rights of people with non-conforming sexualities and identities. We urge Member States to take this opportunity to engage in constructive dialogue on this important issue.

The African continent has risen and continues to rise against oppressive structures like colonialism, apartheid, despotism and dictatorships. LGBTI persons however continue to experience oppression and violence that derive from:

1. Archaic and barbaric colonial laws against adult consensual sex,

2. Colonial Victorian ideas of morality disguised as African traditional values,

3. Patriarchal notions of gender and gender expression,

4. Religious fundamentalisms,

5. Strongly held social constructs that contradict the African values of Ubuntu, acceptance, peace and shared co-existence.

LGBTI persons in Africa continually face stigma and discrimination, harassment and arbitrary arrests, alienation from family and faith, lack of access to social services including health, justice, housing, education and dignified livelihoods. All these, despite African states being signatories to the Universal Declaration of Human Rights, the African Charter on Human and Peoples Rights, particularly Article 2 and 3, and the AU values of equality and non-discrimination.

We as African LGBTI activists are not asking for any new or special rights, we urge you as our African states, to live up to your obligations under international and regional instruments and your own national constitutions; all of which recognise equality and non-discrimination for all persons.

We call upon our African states to end violence and discrimination against LGBTI citizens, abolish all discriminatory laws in existence. We call upon those states currently considering legislating such laws to cease. We call upon all African states to create legal and social environments conducive to the equal enjoyment of all rights for all citizens.

http://bit.ly/UvZzMj

Queerying borders: an Afrikan activist perspective

Bernedette Muthien

planetary piss?

i yearn to float with ducks
on open air waves
nip pluck tuck everywhere
neither here nor there
i am both none inbetween
kiss her fuck him desire
only a dream
sitdowncomic pencilling
shower songs
thru unwooded electrical storms

neutron?

i am an infinite ravine
engorged rivers erode my scar
    tissue
lickmarbling the craters
on all sides
nations in-habit my being
as i moisten for his mastery
and fingertip her open-legged
    vulnerability
all the while aware
of all our innocence
made of nothing but
air
+/- i am charged
with no sides

Any field of study only has relevance if actual people, and specifically communities of people, are able to use it in concrete ways. Hence, theorising entirely for theory's sake, however intellectually stimulating to some of us, has absolutely no relevance to the daily, lived realities of grassroots (or 'ordinary') people. One should, however, tread cautiously with such a dualistic view, a view derived from lived experience in both activist and academic (rarely intersecting) environments. At times 'ordinary' people are not seen to be 'theoretical' about their 'experience' and the theoreticals seem hopelessly devoid of being experiential – fluidly speaking, an experience is theoretical in as much as the theoretical is very much experiential. They should not be put on oppositional grounds. Simultaneously, and especially to avoid dichotomising theorising and experience, the inextricable experience–theory dance is not often slow and close, but rather loose and jagged, and often exploitative, rather than co-creational. Hence my own passionate commitment to participatory, action-based research methodologies that seek mutual skills exchange.

In the broader African context, and particularly in South Africa almost 20 years into democracy, systemic transformation is of critical importance. Questions relating to how one transforms societies from inequality, injustice and systemic violence into societies of reconciliation, diversity, justice and non-violence are issues most pertinent to many of us. Violence is a daily, lived reality for non-heteronormative people the world over, and especially in Africa, but even closer to home in South Africa in particular. Here, as is the case everywhere, lesbians are subject to what this author calls 'curative rape', the rape of women perceived of as lesbian by men, ostensibly as a 'cure' for/of their (aberrant) sexualities. Other men also, even more ironically, subject some gay men to this 'curative rape'. Hence theorising about non-heteronormativity, and lesbianism in particular, cannot be divorced from the ordinariness of 'curative' rape for many lesbians the world over, and in South Africa specifically.

Further questions to contemplate include: how relevant a field of lesbian studies is to ordinary people, what is a lesbian, and who defines lesbianism. The word 'lesbian', as are most of the concepts encompassed within the rainbow or alphabet soup of letters LGBTQI, was coined and developed outside African realities. In South Africa Nguni speakers have long (erroneously) referred to homosexuals as *stabane* or 'hermaphrodite' (intersex). The original inhabitants of southern Africa, the Khoe-San, are not heteronormative, and genders and sexualities are seen as fluid and dynamic, rather than as static binaries. This fluidity applies to most ancient indigenous peoples the world over, from Native American *berdache* to Indian *hijras*. These include people usually referred to as a 'third sex', transgender, intersex and/or anything other than the stereotypical masculine–feminine dichotomies. Definitions usually work in negative terms, which define self in relation (and usually in opposition) to an Other. Hence, homosexual means not heterosexual, and lesbian means non-heterosexual, or homosexual, woman. However, employing a linear definition of lesbian may exclude the infinite varieties of sexuality choices that are 'inbetween' and vary over time and with circumstances.

So how should one define lesbian? Many people I associate with define lesbian as the equivalent of gay homosexual, i.e. the opposite of heterosexual. While the construct queer embraces those who are non-heteronormative and includes the inbetween fluids, the construct lesbian does not necessarily include me, because I define myself as beyond binaries, as inbetween and fluid, dynamic and variable. Perhaps some may call me bisexual, but this term too subscribes to a notion of polarity – that I am both poles – when in fact I shift and change positions, not on a static linear continuum, but on an endlessly spiralling ellipse that, not ironically, is ovoid, symbolic of female reproductive power. Is lesbian defined as orientation, or as preference? Are we victims of biology, or active agents with choice?

While I do respect those who identify as lesbian, we all know lesbians who sleep with men, and lesbians who, even if they don't act on them, enjoy sexual fantasies of men. The same applies to women who identify as heterosexual and, often silently, mentally or actually, engage sexually with other women. Many African women outside South Africa who might identify as lesbian elsewhere are married with children and/or practice their same-sex sexuality in silence, due to the violence of post-colonial patriarchal homophobia. For example, a leading African gender activist's house was bombed at least once, because she worked on sexualities broadly and lesbian activisms specifically, apparently outside of the general public view. One of her tasks has been to establish discreet national networks for gay men and gay women. It is this clandestine sexualities activism that directly resulted in the attacks on her, and which warrants such extreme caution on her part. A further example was attacks on Intersex South Africa co-founder, Sally Gross, which necessitated similar personal safety measures. Personal acts of violences against non-heteronormative activists are closely tied to the generic societal violences against those perceived of as not heterosexual, including the 'curative' rape of women perceived of as lesbian, which is so prevalent that queer organisations in South Africa have entire projects specifically dedicated to this form of gender violence.

It is precisely the imperatives of heteropatriarchy that keep both lesbians and their straight sisters in the flimsy boxes of their binaried sexuality. How much simpler it is to find safety in a homogenous identity, even if all identities are more complex upon further investigation. For example, archaeo-anthropology shows that humans have always migrated across continents throughout time, and hence the idea of a homogenous race or nationality is flawed at best. We are each, all, hybridised, without any definite certainty about origins. The only thing we can ever really be certain of, at this stage, is that we are all born human, even as some ancient spiritual traditions, such as Hinduism and Jainism, refer to inter-species reincarnation.

If we assume that sexuality, like any other identity, shifts constantly on the endless circumference of an infinite ovoid, then sexuality can never really be fixed, is not predetermined and primordial, does not hold us hostage physiologically. After all, the field of physiology itself evinces that chromosomes and hormones are by nature fluid, and both 'male' and 'female' exist in all human beings. Static polar genders of male and female are therefore not scientifically accurate, and merely serve the interests of heteropatriarchy, to divide and rule, in similar ways that science has been used to divide and conquer during colonial eras and under apartheid in South Africa. As Stephen Batchelor puts it:

> Things are not as clear-cut as they seem. They are neither circumscribed nor separated from each other by lines. Lines are drawn in the mind. There are no lines in nature ... [Everything emerges] from a matrix of conditions and in turn becomes part of another matrix of conditions from which something else emerges (Batchelor 1997: 76).

Is there such a construct as an African lesbian? Is the idea of an African in a globalised world possible? One cannot forget how 54 UN-recognised national (colonial) borders cut through indigenous ethnic groups like the Dagara, who live in Burkina Faso and Ghana, as well as the Khoe-San, who continue to live in Namibia,

Angola, Botswana and South Africa. As a continent, Africa argu-ably has the world's most diverse cultural and historic legacies with up to 3,000 languages still spoken.

Africa includes the range of Lesotho's lesbian-bisexual miners' wives in Cheryl Stobie's work and Ifi Amadiume's (1988, 1998, 2002) writings of women-to-women marriages in her native Nigeria. Stobie (2003) critiques the book *Boy-Wives and Female Husbands: Studies of African Homosexualities*, which offers a range of texts from the 18th to the late 20th century, and examines a considerable number of sub-Saharan cultures, providing ample evidence of homosexual practices being indigenous over a long period. There is much fascinating material, including translations of ethnographic accounts of pre-colonial and colonial times, court records of male homosexual 'crime' in early colonial Zimbabwe, same-sex marriages, the concept of 'male lesbians' in Hausa (West Africa), adolescent same-sex sexual behaviour, cross-dressing, role reversal and women who love women in Lesotho. Also of interest is an appendix with a list of 50-odd African cultures with same-sex patterns, most of which have local terms for same-sex sexual practices or roles, and there is evidence for same-sex erotic relationships between co-wives, and between (heterosexually) married women in Lesotho.

Speaking of his native Dagara people in Burkina Faso, Malidoma Somé asserts that gender has very little to do with anatomy:

> It is purely energetic. The whole notion of 'gay' does not exist in the indigenous world. That does not mean that there are not people who feel this way that certain people feel in this culture, that has led to them being referred to as 'gay' ... The great astrologers of the Dogon are gay ... Why is it that everywhere else in the world, gay people are a blessing and in the modern world they are a curse? It is self-evident. The modern world was built by Christianity. They have taken the gods out of the earth and sent them to heaven, wherever that is... (Somé 1993).

Sobonfu Somé reflects on the ordinariness of Dagara women's sexual-spiritual intimacies:

> Sexuality, including woman-to-woman sexuality, is so inte-grated into the spiritual life of the Dagara that her people have

no word to specify 'lesbian' or even 'sex'... Like many other Africans, the women of Dagara do not sleep with their men. Women need to sleep together, to be together to empower each other ... then if they meet with men, there is no imbalance ... We have a female father who gives us male energy. She looks like a male. Anything we feel or experience that we haven't dealt with is expressed. This women's group ritual balances their male/female energy. It is so we are not completely male or female (Somé 1994).

Alicia Banks (2005) cites an article entitled 'Inside gay Africa' to describe how the Watusi still have a reputation for bisexuality. In the cities of East Africa, Zande women risked execution by pleasuring each other, sometimes with phalluses fashioned from roots and in Zaire, homosexuality had a mystical element to it while bisexuality is also quite common among the Bajun tribes of east Africa. So while the word lesbian may have ancient Greek origins, the practices it describes are certainly universal, and definitely include Africa. However, what is clear from many of the citations above is that sexualities are not necessarily divorced from spiritualities or other aspects of life and being human, as well as the fact that sexualities have always been fluid, especially in pre-colonial Africa and many other ancient indigenous societies.

Rather than a narrow focus on lesbianism, and lesbian studies, it may serve Africa better if we re-historicise and re-claim pre-colonial fluidities as at least one way of moving beyond the stranglehold of colonial, and still prevalent, binaries, oppressions and violences. In this sense alone, queer studies broadly offers a more comfortable reception, rather than a home, entirely because it offers greater inclusivity, even as it suffers the same dis-eases of power and exclusion as any other field of study. One should never forget the irony of pre-colonial being defined in relation to the colonial. As the iconic African feminist scholar, Ifi Amadiume, puts it:

Pluralism and opposition are not colonial imports. Yet there is wide disagreement on how to name society in Africa before the colonial encounter. Hybridity writers have unfortunately unleashed such virulent attacks against the idea of an authentic African tradition that many have caved in and avoid the notion of tradition in Africa, preferring to use concepts like transition and modernity. They suppose that all that was precolonial is dead and buried. *I am reclaiming the concept of the traditional in Africa to mean precolonial African cultures,* but concede a problem with a rigid time break or something static. *I argue that the traditional can also be in the present, and the traditional can be dynamic.* This is why I introduce a juxtaposition of notions of collective kinship and opposition (Amadiume 2002: 7, emphasis added).

The struggles for basic lesbian rights are still far from being globally realised, including in South Africa where the notion of 'curative' rape has gained the country renewed notoriety after South Africa entered the *Guinness Book of Records* for its high rape statistics during 1999. Gender-based violences serve as a precise reminder that heteropatriarchy should be our focus, and that sexuality studies and activisms need to be inclusive of the whole range of sexualities that have always been practised. Until such time, lesbians and gays who routinely discriminate against more fluidly queer folk perpetrate the very same cultural and other violences as does heteronormativity in modern societies.

We need to raise critical questions of how the identities we choose, or find ourselves engaging in, help us to live in practice. How relevant is identity studies to the daily lives of ordinary queer people, and indeed to the struggles against heteropatriarchy; how do queer studies help people realise their full sexual health and freedom? Homophobia sits alongside other systems of oppression, such as racism and sexism, and needs to be analysed and combated in these intersectional contexts.

Adopting and living any beyond-heteronormative identity and lifestyle is a subversion of heteropatriarchy, and hence contributes towards transforming society. If one's identities and lifestyles attempt to transcend status quo binaries, it may prove to be all the more revolutionary, even as it may be more challenging, to hold one's ground in opposition and under coercion from both perceived polarities.

In her germinal essay, 'The master's tools will never dismantle the master's house', the late Audre Lorde wrote:

Those of us who stand outside the circle of this society's defini-tion of acceptable women; those of us who have been forged in the crucibles of difference; those of us who are poor, who are lesbians, who are black, who are older, know that *survival is not an academic skill* [original emphasis]. It is learning how to stand alone, unpopular and sometimes reviled, and how to make common cause with those other identified as outside the structures, in order to define and seek a world in which we can all flourish ... In a world of possibility for us all, our personal visions help lay the groundwork for political action. The failure of the academic feminists to recognise difference as a crucial strength is a failure to reach beyond the first patriarchal lesson. *Divide and conquer, in our world, must become define and empower* (Lorde 1981 [1979]: 99–100, emphasis added).

In walking the transformative talk, may this queerly fluid and inbetween activist, who identifies as polymorphously perverse for its ironically subversive and transformative potentials, leave you satisfied with the moment, fully aware that any authenticity is merely an ideal...

I Q

u're in the centre
of your war against conflict
and yet the silences of an entire
    alphabet
around one Greek letter
closes the infinite spiral
of balkanisation
decapitating
this (in)voluntary bastard's
air
supply

31 August 2003, Women in
Black conference, Italy, for Lepa
Mladjenovic

picture perfect

there's a thumbprint
on a face without a pupil
and lines of identity
circling the frame
greyscale
with some swatches
of peach
life's a finger supper
snap

Acknowledgements

With appreciation to Engender for supporting the writing of this chapter: http://www.engender.org.za.

Bibliography

Amadiume, Ifi (1988) *Male Daughters and Female Husbands: Gender and Sex in an African Society*, London, Zed Press

Amadiume, Ifi (1998) *Reinventing Africa: Matriarchy, Religion and Culture*, London, Zed Books

Amadiume, Ifi (2002) 'Bodies, choices, globalizing neo-colonial enchantments: African matriarchs and mammy water', *Meridian*, 2(2): 41–66

Banks, Alicia (2005) 'Gay racism: white lies/black slander', in *Fito*, feminist e-zine, http://www.engender.org.za/publications/ JLSQueeryingBordersfinal.pdf, accessed 17 December 2012

Batchelor, Stephen (1997) *Buddhism Without Beliefs*, New York, Riverhead

Lorde, Audre (1981 [1979]) 'The master's tools will never dismantle the master's house', in Moraga, C. and Anzaldúa, G., *This Bridge Called My Back: Writings by Radical Women of Color*, Watertown, MA, Persephone Press: 98–101

Muthien, Bernedette (2003) 'Why are you not married yet?! Heteronormativity in the African women's movement', *Women's Global Network for Reproductive Rights Newsletter* 79, http://www.wgnrr.org (in English, Spanish and French), 17 December 2012

Muthien, Bernedette (2005) 'Playing on the pavements of identities', in van Zyl, M. and Steyn, M., *Performing Queer*, Cape Town, Kwela Books

Ochs, R. and Rowley, S.E. (eds) (2005) *Getting Bi: Voices of Bisexuals Around the World*, Boston, MA, Bisexual Resource Center

Stobie, Cheryl (2003) 'Reading bisexualities from a South African perspective', *The Journal of Bisexuality*, 3(1): 33–52

Somé, Malidoma (1993) 'Gays: guardians of the gates', http://www.oocities. org/ambwww/GAYS-IN-AFRICA.htm, accessed 17 December 2012

Somé, Sobonfu (1994) 'The lesbian spirit', *Girlfriends Magazine*, http://www. oocities.org/ambwww/GAYS-IN-AFRICA.htm, accessed 17 December 2012

LGBTI-Queer struggles like other struggles in Africa

Gathoni Blessol

Much has been written about the African lesbian, gay, bisexual, transgender, intersex-queer (LGBTI-Q) struggle to attain equality and freedom, ideally enabling acceptance and inclusion by Africa's religious, culturally diverse and traditional societies. What both our LGBTI-Q community and the larger African society tend to forget is that LGBTI-Q persons are not aliens from space or the West – like it is claimed – but are a representation of our African communities; only the concepts, definitions and ideologies that shape our struggle for recognition are foreign and estranged.

What this implies is that the LGBTI-Q communities are African through and through, are religious, are part of the rich cultural diversity and are both traditional and non-traditional people. They are daughters and sons, brothers and sisters, mothers and fathers, friends and family, neighbours and even grandparents of our African communities.

While at the 2011 World Social Forum in Dakar, Senegal, I attended one of the 'Queering Africa' sessions. Here I was introduced to a concept that left me yearning to reflect and redefine my personal struggles. The speaker was by far the most powerful queer and human rights defender I had ever seen or heard. She was also a member and activist in the democratic left movement in South Africa. I remember my contradictions being how she, considering her sexuality, had arrived at such political radicalism. How was she able to speak so eloquently on other struggles in her country? Aside from the fact that the South African constitution upholds the rights of sexual minorities, how had she won the respect, hearts and trust of people from other movements?

I took the opportunity to discuss with her my questions about her work as an activist across social movements. She told me that while her sexuality still remained a very important part of her life, there was so much more to her as a person and as an activist than her sexuality. There was the woman who is African and part of a people who are oppressed in this patriarchal, sexist, racist, class-ist and capitalist society which places the dollar over human life. While her race, gender and sexual orientation – which had constituted the basis of her oppressions – remained important to her struggle, her politics went beyond her identities.

She continued that what the LGBTI-Q community needed was the presence of a politically conscious queer movement across Africa, a movement that was aligned with other struggles to end capitalism and the social, economic and political injustices, exploitations and oppression that come with it.

This activist was so powerful that she moved not only me but also the whole audience. She was a leader in all respects and someone I wanted to emulate in the future. In fact, for the first time I deemed I needed an education in all forms of humanity.

Something else she said that remains a sad truth was that LGBTI-Q struggle is one of the loneliest struggles in Africa. It is extremely hard to demand solidarity, and this is compounded by the many divisions in the movement over variances of power, culture, tradition and politics.

In this chapter I try to relate my understanding of some of the variances discussed in the sessions to the context we have in Africa and in Kenya, for instance the power struggle between the religious extremists/fascists and the liberals.

The religious extremists in Africa, whose kingdom of heaven has been bestowed on them because of their 'righteousness', are the followers of the evangelical ministries from the West in testimonies, speech and norms, sometimes even in accent and spiritual tongue. The irony is not lost. Most of the religious practices we have here in Kenya are influenced by the Western notion of spirituality and religion, which is based on what is male, white, 'prosperous' and their God – who is a Caucasian man. Our African religious leaders preach to us these doctrines in US accents using strange spiritual tongues – *'shammah, 'nisi'* and *'eloi'* – none of which are African words to refer to God.

Our churches have been accused of receiving huge amounts of funding from their religious 'brothers and sisters' in the United States to support them in their persecution (even promoting the death penalty) of LGBTI-Q people. Please note that all this is done in the name of the Lord, as my comrades and I clearly witnessed while attending the burial of David Kato, who was murdered in his own house in 2011. At the burial a priest, a shameless one, contested the noble life David had here on earth and the efforts he put into the struggle, stating that even animals 'know' who they are supposed to 'mate/sleep' with. That 'man of God,' for whatever reasons, be it his religious madness or 'righteousness', had no right to disrespect the deathbed of another.

I felt cheated by religion and the few mad men that spread the gospel, presenting an image of a creator that is more hateful and vengeful than the holy, loving god they preach. Their double standards are obvious: the religious leaders strongly preach against homosexuality as an issue of morality while they condone murderers, rapists and capitalist oppressors, glorifying them and committing their filthy souls to the Lord to rest in eternal peace. In addition, the role of the church in conflict and war is not a secret; the hate speech in the Rwandan genocide, the supplying of weapons in the Burundi civil war or the partisan preaching before the December 2007 election in Kenya that fuelled the outbreak of brutal post-election violence are but a few examples.

The observation in my country Kenya of these same religious extremists is that they have experienced a loss of state power after the people voted for a constitution in 2011 that enhanced the proper integration of the existing Kadhi courts of our Muslim brothers and sisters into our judicial system. Secondly, the new constitution states clearly that Kenya is a secular state, meaning the separation of the state from the church.

Thus how else can they regain power other than by dictating what is morally upright, and what issue is better suited than homosexuality, which is already disdained by society?

The religious extremists' rivals are the 'liberals', those on the left who would raise questions on the universality of norms and the oppressive capitalist system, those who are supported by the pink colonialists, cupcake feminists and 'visionary' interventionists. They are the well-suited, middle- to upper-class bourgeoisie that come to Africa to 'save' the 'poor' African people. They are the college students who volunteer after graduation to 'help' and later return as board members and CEOs of NGOs and especially donor organisations with all the answers and the perfect visions. And as we have learnt by now, aid comes with a price, no matter how little, so over time the continent has seen the birth of countless NGOs that derail the processes of any progressive movement and change in Africa. They start as great organisations and end up as bureaucratic petition factories. I am not insinuating that all NGOs have ill intentions, but as Issa Shivji states in his book *Silences in NGO Discourse*: 'We do not judge the outcome of a process by the intentions of its authors. We aim to analyze the objective effects of actions, regardless of their intentions.'[1]

The end result of this catastrophic ideal, as in most struggles, has been a rise of donor-motivated LGBTI-Q activism and organisations that are 'visionary' driven, impractical, capitalistic and commercialised – mostly marginalising the grassroots' struggles, realities, concepts and solutions. Our LGBTI-Q organising has in the large part become hierarchically structured, donor mandated and limited in activism. This has left very few conscious LGBTI-Q spaces which are progressively analytical and radical or with the ability to raise awareness in their communities about issues affecting us as Africans, such as the multiple levels of oppression that come from our socio-economic or socio-political realities as first African then queer people.

This has in turn limited our thinking to what donors 'want' and how best we can acquire funding rather than how we can incorporate our struggles with the other social rights movements alongside which we live and work. As a result, the bourgeois cadre has given birth to a few 'liberators' of the LGBTI community, who again are donor chosen. They have become the public face of the struggle and are well-funded gatekeepers. This has led to further divisions around economic status and class such that one queer person cannot relate to another without considering how well known they are and the depth of their pockets. Another consequence has been the lack of a strong, passion-oriented queer movement which adheres to its own localised grassroots constituencies in Africa. All this is compounded by the religious madness that is leading to the gross and fatal human rights violations of the African LGBTI-Q community.

The contradictions in the way the LGBTI-Q movement has developed so far have added to the perceptions in the wider heteronormative society that homosexuality is a Western thing or, as a comrade of mine would put it, 'something someone picked up on their way to the city life'. Another belief, and one I heard on my way home from the World Social Forum, is that becoming gay happens when one is moving up the ladder and wants to obtain money. In the case of women, they become feminists, and later lesbians, to avoid the responsibilities of having children. I found these statements to be obnoxiously funny.

However, if the LGBTI-Q movement could re-examine historical evidence of the amazingly diverse and complex African sexual practices and expressions, they would have something to refute these misconceptions and enhance their struggle. I believe it is a crucial step in any struggle for people to gain an understanding of where they are from, where they are and where they are heading to. In fact, once you begin looking into material about homosexuality or sexual identity in general in ancient African cultures, it is incredible how many studies and stories are revealed that contradict completely the rigid notions of African sexuality that are being termed as 'African'. These studies provide historical evidence of homosexuality in pre-colonial Africa found in language, naming, drawings and religious practices that reach from the very north to the south, from west to east.[2] To name only a few, one could draw attention to the Qemant of central Ethiopia, where homosexual relations between shepherd boys were common, or the Maale in southern Ethiopia where men (*ashtime*) performed female tasks and had sexual relations with men. Likewise, the Meru of Kenya embraced men (*mugawe*) who dressed as women and sometimes married other men. Also, among the Kikuyu in Kenya, woman–woman marriages were quite common. Some scholars argue that these were more practical than sexual relationships; nevertheless the fact remains that they existed and still exist. The Hausa called homosexual transvestites *yan daudu*. The Nzema of Ghana practised marriages (*agyale*) between two men who were in love with each other. The Kirundi language of Burundi has at least five words for male–male sexuality. In Angola marriages between two men were honoured and prized and men behaving like women were called *chibados*. Among the Zande of Sudan, sex between two females is called *adandara*. And on and on I can go! This and much more shows that homosexuality existed long before Christianity came to this continent – only it wasn't bracketed as it is in the acronyms we use these days – and it defies the theory that homosexuality is un-African.

Lack of knowledge of our history is a major setback not only in the LGBTI-Q movement, which is being fought against with so much fervour, from left, right and centre, but in any movement. African history has largely been researched for us by Western scholars, causing lack of sufficient and proper documentation, for instance, the ridiculous dictations we recited in pre-school that deliberately and wrongly told us Dr Livingstone ended the slave trade in Africa and Dr Krapf discovered Mount Kenya when in fact our ancestors had lived on those lands viewing the same mountain and had named it Mount Kirinyaga. Yet we were told that it was a white man that had discovered it. Ironically, it continues to be referred to as Mount Kenya even after attaining our 'in-dependence'.

Another misunderstanding arises when the words 'African', 'constitution' and 'Christianity' fall in the same sentence in an argument against homosexuality. Christianity is not African because it came into Africa along with Islam, as a ruse for the 'civilising' mission and colonisation in the 18th century. The constitutions of African countries also came about after colonisation and were presented as British or French instruments to bind their colonies, including Kenya. Our history was dictated and fed to us by the colonialists to justify their inhumane acts, and after independence they presented us with a few of their puppets to emulate and celebrate as our heroes while they reinforced capitalism in the name of globalisation to the continent. This has left most struggles, including the LGBTI-Q one, without a discourse that is practical and African oriented.

The various struggles fight the same oppressive system they are knowingly or obliviously part of. An example is found within our LGBTI-Q advocacy spaces where we ignore class oppression, hierarchies and bureaucracies and end up narrowing our struggles down to only sexual liberation for a few. A reading of LGBTI-Q history and politics in all their complexity enables us to recognise the reality that there is more to this struggle than meets the naked eye. A more complex exploration of African LGBTI-Q history and politics along with colonialism will lead us to an understanding of the relationship between the oppression of black people in general and women and LGBTI-Q people in particular. This in turn will leave our struggle open to be studied, analysed, criticised and hopefully accepted as one of the oldest African customs in history.

The state and its political leaders are another hindrance to these struggles. Politicians tend to use the LGBTI-Q community for political mileage or to hide the real issues that are affecting our countries. A perfect example was the parliamentary confusion in Kenya at the end of 2010 when the case files on who murdered Robert Ouko resurfaced. Then Luis Ocampo[3] of the International Criminal Court (ICC) unveiled the list of those suspected of being responsible for the post-election violence, which brought chaos among the parliamentarians. This was followed by 'finger pointing', in a spectacular political show of accusations and denials, rhetoric and propaganda. I could not afford to miss the news; it was like watching a drama series.

Amusingly, as the suspense and doubt mounted among the Kenyan populace, the prime minister (PM), while in Kibera slum, ordered the arrest of gay people in Kenya. This immediately gave the Kenyan populace something to think about other than the post-election violence. While the Kenyan political elite figured out ways to fundraise to prevent their fellow goons from going to the ICC, the Kenyan populace was busy arresting and beating up people in the homosexual community, as the PM had advised. But when Kenyans were no longer distracted by such rhetoric and refused to be deterred from the ICC issue, the dirty game of politics was applied. The PM claimed in front of the international community and Ocampo that he had been misquoted and that he acknowledged the rights of the 'gays' – whatever that meant. He then repeated virtually the same gabble during Kirima's[4] burial, which was after the Wikileaks saga.[5]

The queer struggle is also situated in the socio-economic and cultural reality of people's everyday lives, a reality which dictates how LGBTI-Q people interact with and survive in the world around them. Society has interpreted LGBTI-Q lives and struggles as being nothing more than sexual deviation or disorientation, as though these people are not social, political and cultural beings like everyone else and have no rights to claim. It is on this issue of rights that the debates on sexual orientation and gender identity focus. It is a normative mindset brought about by patriarchy, sexism, capitalism, plus the gender roles assigned at birth, which ignores the intersex people living among us. As a result, gender assignment becomes problematic for society though not necessarily the individuals themselves.

We need to decolonise our minds from imperialism and capitalism to become a society which is conscious and diverse and which acknowledges that homosexuality is human, as it is African. Decolonisation creates socially progressive initiatives and spaces that do not cluster and classify issues into established norms. We need to consider different forms of engagement and education to show our people that Africa has a grounding and richness in humanity that is all-inclusive, away from the political, social and economic manipulation and rip-off that has been taking place.

The positive view is that people and cultures are never fixed but, rather, are constantly changing over time. For example, two decades ago it was seen as wrong in any context to get a divorce, or for women to wear trousers. Our societies can change over time, knowing that social, economic and political struggles intersect. These issues all seem familiar in every struggle, but there has been a void, waiting for action to take place.

While we discussed change in the World Social Forum sessions, our brothers and sisters in Egypt and Tunisia united and were making that change. They made their history, redefined the 'normal' that Mubarak was untouchable, and revolutionised their populace. I left the World Social Forum with only one concept. We need to reclaim our own histories, decolonise the minds of our people, build our own societies and with our own rules, which are African by Africans. With solidarity, comradeship and unity, let us put all our differences and personal politics aside and fight that which is oppressing us, by having a wave of movements (one that is already vibrating in Africa) that will bring that change. That, to me, is the new world I anticipate seeing.

Notes

1 Issa Shivji (2007: 2) *Silences in NGO Discourse: The Role and Future of NGOs in Africa*, Nairobi and Oxford, Pambazuka Press.

2 An excellent start to the topic is Steven O. Murray (2009) 'Homosexuality in "traditional" sub-Saharan Africa and contemporary South Africa', in *Seven Sister Study Group Reader, Volume 1*.

3 Luis Moreno Ocampo was the prosecutor at the International Criminal Court (until June 2012) who prepared the case against the alleged main perpetrators of the violence which occurred in 2007–08 after the contested Kenyan elections. Four of six suspects faced trials that are ongoing as I write.

4 The late Kirima was an infamous business person who was murdered on his way home one evening.

5 Wikileaks is an Internet platform/forum that exposed a lot of shady dealings between politicians and the United States.

Small axe[1] at the crossroads: a reflection on African sexualities and human rights – life story

Kagendo Murungi

I am an African human rights advocate who became engaged with formal human rights work in 1996, fresh out of graduate school and in need of a work visa. Years before, as a women's studies major, I had been exposed to the intersectional analyses and creative expressions of lesbian feminists of colour. As a feminist, I began to wonder whether human rights principles were being applied to the lives of continental Africans who loved people of the same gender and faced persecution for it. I wanted to know where this work was being done, whether it was part of the feminist movement and how to become involved.

During my first semester in college, as I strolled through the bookstore one morning, I had been drawn to the bright orange of *Zami*,[2] and slipped it into my cart after briefly glancing at its back cover. I remember being impressed by the low, wide stack of orange and marvelling at the abundant visibility of a publication by a Black lesbian. My research began then and there.

As a young feminist African immigrant student coming of age in the late 1980s and early 90s, I was exposed to pragmatic innovations in the application of rights frameworks to localised and transnational injustices, violations and imbalances through my campus and community anti-apartheid, anti-heterosexist, anti-racist, feminist work.

The first image of an openly gay continental African I ever saw was of a smiling Simon Nkoli, the pioneering South African anti-apartheid, pro-gay rights activist working against HIV/AIDS. My

229

first encounter with the ramifications of visibly supporting human rights for all women without regard to their sexual orientation was in 1995, during the UN Fourth World Conference on Women in Beijing. For my participation in the lesbian human rights march, I was framed in a short but highly sensationalising article in a national Kenyan daily as young, studying abroad and surrounded by a sea of arm-waving white women (read: impressionable, too far from home for too long, whitewashed, Westernised, tokenised by a foreign colonial agenda and confused). When I received a copy of the article from my father, I was too paralysed by my own fear of the consequences to really consider what my parents' experience of shock, worry, anxiety and concern must have been like at the time.

I wished then that I had emerged into a broadly recognised, obviously legitimate pan-African, democratic, postcolonial liberation movement. I would come to understand more about the actual arena and my relative position in it in the months and years to come, through my work with human rights organisations to document the lived experiences of continental African LGBTI people and to advocate on their behalf.

In hindsight, I have wondered how I could have somehow been more prepared for the complete damnation and stigma of dealing with sexual orientation, in any public way, as a continental African. There are few first-person descriptions of African lives in the transitions between isolation, shame, ridicule, threats, blackmail, violence, self-hatred, courage, hope, fear, activism and love. I still search for a tangible sense of lived indigenous African same-gender loving experiences. I want to see detailed accounts, from Africans themselves, of their successful experiences navigating personal roles and community responsibilities. I want to see how people like myself have made the journey from these spaces to wholeness.

In the mid-90s, the topic of homosexuality was introduced into the public domain in African countries at an unprecedented level. In the month prior to the Fourth World Conference on Women, President Mugabe of Zimbabwe became the first African head of state to publicly denounce and ostracise African homosexuals, with such vehemence as to bring him infamy. I learned that Kenyan President Moi had responded to the international media frenzy surrounding the Beijing advocacy for lesbian rights as women's rights by ridiculing the women's rights movement, calling its agenda into question, and belittling its great strides and concrete achievements, especially in the decade since the Third World Conference on Women in Nairobi in 1985. I lamented later news about peripheral, stigmatised communities and groupings in several African countries that had been pushed even further underground. Meanwhile, the vast majority of advocates for African women's rights kept any possible analytical proximity to these issues obscured, for fear of having their legitimate struggles as straight women undermined by association with lesbian issues. Open season on LGBTI Africans was officially under way.

The making of an activist

Following the emotional and political intensity of the women's conference in Beijing, I decided to engage with the substance of what was politically at stake in an issue that had impacted my life so dramatically. I accepted the offer of a full-time job with the International Gay and Lesbian Human Rights Commission (IGLHRC), where I would help create a regional programme, including a focus on Africa. I practically stepped out of the classroom into the vast arena of international human rights. I set out to absorb as much knowledge as possible about international human rights protocols, conventions and mechanisms; regional human rights bodies; relevant national constitutions and penal codes; allied non-governmental organisations; and useful media outlets for the work.

My first cycle of involvement in working for sexuality-related human rights from a US base exposed me to the daily rigours of working to legitimise human rights for 'sexual minorities' in regions of the world where broad-based support for them is still in its infancy. I was transformed both personally and politically through my work alongside committed organisers, in which we supported and challenged each other in countless ways to expand our approaches to realising sexuality-related human rights. The substance of my daily work included monitoring, confirming and disseminating information about human rights violations; writing action alerts and press releases; liaising with governmental, non-governmental and intergovernmental organisations; and fielding information requests from media, policymakers, colleagues and supporters.

I was fortunate to have been exposed, during my college years, to the importance of a gender perspective on human rights and its core concern with the invisibility of women's experiences in applying and developing mainstream human rights law and related United Nations mechanisms. In the historical development of human rights paradigms, women had never been conceptualised as legal subjects. The appropriate subjects of human rights law had been white, male, land-owning citizens of politically and economically independent Western nations, to whom alone the presumptions of universality and indivisibility of rights could possibly be applied. Most of the substantive norms of international human rights law had been defined in relation to individual men's experiences, and were stated in terms of discrete violations of rights in the public realm.

In order to address the equal status of women, advocates had begun undertaking conceptual shifts to explicitly and systematically address the respective socially constructed realities of women and men. The impact of culturally specific gender roles, particularly in the private sphere, had begun to be recognised as an impediment to women's full enjoyment of human rights as a condition of their equal status in society. The rights of all women to make individual sexual choices and to conceive children regardless of marital status, without the threat or reality of exposure to violence within the domestic sphere, were essential to their full enjoyment of rights to bodily integrity and health.

My involvement in the work taught me that these rights had direct implications for applying international human rights law and practice to the elimination of sexuality-related discrimination and injustice. I learned that issues of violence against women and women's reproductive freedom were inextricably linked to human rights issues related to sexuality, justice and freedom. That African heads of state have most often addressed their anti-homosexual, fundamentally anti-feminist, inflammatory messages to local women's groups was no simple coincidence. Deteriorating socio-economic conditions within African nation-states had turned LGBTI Africans into easy scapegoats, in the face of expansions in civil society, growing movements for women's rights, constitutional reform, HIV/AIDS education and prevention, affordable drug and treatment access, post-independence land rights, and anti-hunger and pro-democracy movements.

I also learned that the success of work on African sexual rights should be reflected in a practical recognition of the multi-centricity of the issues and structures needing to be addressed. This should result in a constant structural transformation of the sites from which the work is being done as fresh analyses emerge from the work itself. In the face of the global drought of African-written publications on African same-gender desire, love, relationships and communities, the application of human rights frameworks to the conditions of LGBTI Africans in independent African states necessitated linkages with African women's movements. My experiential understanding of the need for more accountable and effective applications of human rights law and practice to the lives and rights of African same-gender-loving people convinced me of the urgent need for multimedia documentation of best practices, or successful indigenous and diasporic strategies.

Working as an African immigrant on African lesbian and gay rights from a US-based organisation in the context of globalised economic inequities, prevailing patriarchal notions of indigenous statehood and citizenship, and current resurgent fundamentalisms was an experience fraught with immense paradox. For some measure of self-protection at that time, I adapted by utilising an alias for my professional work and seeking political asylum. Working for the implementation of human rights frameworks as a mobile, multiply located, indigenous African immigrant woman, crossing national borders and dealing constantly with immigration bureaucracies while speaking and acting from shifting locations, was purely exhausting and surreal. I was randomly faced with strange, harassing and threatening phone calls and emails, along with the constant threat of blackmail. These tensions and perils of negotiating, juxtaposed with erasure and overexposure from within an obscured discourse, finally led to my taking a break.

I needed time to reflect on my personal and political experiences as a human rights agent. I craved channels through which to creatively claim more of my pan-African legacy. I yearned for a deeper exploration of the new dimensions of my life path. I sought more solid grounding in daily practical responsibilities for my health and to my loved ones. I left my human rights job and began searching for ways to more evenly balance my commitment to creative political work for socio-economic justice.

With time and the patient support of friends and family, I began to understand that my isolated efforts to cope with the pressures of my experiences by fragmenting myself in practice and appearance had been based in illusion. Using my image in one place but not my name; speaking my name at one site but not my experiences; sharing my personal experience somewhere but not my full analysis anywhere – none of this had worked. Those partial identities and fractured narratives had not protected me. I had remained adrift in a hegemonic discourse on my rights, unprepared as yet to coherently contribute to shifting it. When I stopped working for the realisation of identity-based civil and political human rights, it was because that daily work was failing to sustain me in basic ways. I needed the close proximity of people who shared more aspects of my daily experience. Thus, I relocated to the north-eastern US, with its abundance of first-generation African immigrant communities. I sorely needed social and cultural infrastructural support for my whole Black African self.

In downtown Manhattan and Brooklyn, I linked up with a group of pan-African performance artist friends who were creatively expressing themselves on issues of gender, sexuality and nationality. They generously took me into their fold, and I joined them at rehearsals and discussions, primarily as an inquisitive voyeur into aspects of my own life. I attended social gatherings of pan-African friends of numerous sexualities and gendered realities, where we watched and critiqued gender-sexuality dimensions and stylistic devices in cinematic depictions of Africans; performed poetry; shared stories; flirted; danced; laughed; ate; and created community. There, so far away from 'home', many of us unable to travel for long periods due to fluctuating immigration statuses, we bravely pieced our psyches together, contemplated wholeness and created family. Witnessing my community's basic collective need for safety, trust, friendship, creative self-expression and economic autonomy, and our individual contentions with that need, reaffirmed my sense of social and cultural human rights as primary to and indivisible from civil and political rights in this country as well as our countries of origin.

This group of north-eastern artist-activists had initiated successful translocal initiatives (that is, initiatives between localities rather than across national boundaries), which continue to be supported by voluntary labour and the generous donations of our translocal networks, along with assistance from progressive international, philanthropic and human rights organisations. We are succeeding in mobilising increasing funds in support of African political and sexual dissidents displaced due to their work on sexuality-related human rights. These courageous and resourceful men and women are survivors of harassment, detention, torture and rape. The significance of our autonomous agency – our individual and collective choices as African communities – is evident, since our comrades often have no other immediate recourse to justice, even when their cases are already well documented by human rights organisations (whose missions, nonetheless, do not include the systematic release of emergency funds for sexual and political dissidents in need).

Linking the past to the future

Human rights discourses deployed in response to the current conditions of African all-sexual[3] people too easily obscure the agency of these very subjects. The decontextualised visibility of LGBTI Africans, in the absence of sustained, autonomous educational efforts, limits our local and translocal organising potential. While we remain exposed to all manner of personal policing, including the constant threat and reality of exposure to blackmail, we cannot afford to have our courageous life stories and initiatives erased, sidelined or subsumed by the well-intentioned agendas of others. We must remain vigilantly conscious of our historical relationship to movements, both in the US and in our countries of origin, that have had broader visions for social transformation.

Our historical legacy as African all-sexual people includes victories over slavery, colonisation and apartheid; and centuries of experience with multi-pronged organising for fundamental social, economic and political transformation and freedom for all. Our conceptual approaches to organising draw from the multilingual, interdependent, intertextual, intersectional strategies of pan-African, Black and Third World feminist movements. It is essential that our progressive US-based allies contextualise themselves relative to this country's history of genocidal war against indigenous peoples and enslavement of Africans, and recognise the centrality of white supremacist ideology to the maintenance of white structural privilege and US capitalist expansion.

While current mainstream LGBTI and human rights publications may provide some interesting and even useful perspectives on our lives and organising, they too casually uphold white male structural privilege. These purported defenders of our existence and rights reveal their cynicism and myopia when they apply paternalistic packaging to African all-sexual experiences without explicit and systematic consideration of our complex autonomous agency in perilous circumstances. The survival of all-sexual Africans working under life-threatening conditions in fragile coalitions urgently requires demonstrated recognition from our allies that the eradication of white supremacy and male supremacy goes hand in hand with the eradication of heterosexual supremacy.

Our daily material realities and political economies as migrants, along with our ideological convictions and political alliances as Africans, influence our social language, cultural expression and pragmatic parameters as agents for change. In September 1999, a tri-continental coalition of African, Black and migrant LGBTI people realised a timely cultural intervention at the first Africa-based International Lesbian and Gay Association (ILGA) Conference in Johannesburg, South Africa. With the support of the Astraea International Fund for Sexual Minorities (for whom I worked as a programme consultant the following year), members of our New York-based African LGBTI network, the Johannesburg-based Gay and Lesbian Organisation of the Witwatersrand (GLOW) and Amsterdam-based Black and migrant LGBTI group 'Strange Fruit The Real' planned and created a cultural free-zone dubbed 'Unifying Links', which served as a clearing house for the experiences and needs of lesbian feminists of colour attending the conference.

A group of us, hoping to inspire self-expression among global lesbians of colour and our friends and allies, drafted and circulated a list of goals and strategies for our multimedia intervention and requested input and participation from our allies. Our explicitly anti-racist and pro-feminist agenda prioritised self-empowerment, visibility, autonomous and equal participation on our own terms, the creation of space for networking and creative cultural self-representation, monitoring and documentation of the conference itself, and good old-fashioned fun. To this end, we secured and decorated a room in the conference hotel in which we screened independently produced videos reflecting our various communities, maintained tables and wall spaces where allies could display their organisational materials and creative works, and sustained a critical dialogue on issues arising at the conference as well as issues crucial to local and translocal organising by lesbian feminists of colour.

Africanising sexual rights

As we know, many African states remained colonies of European countries during the drafting of the Universal Declaration of Human Rights, and only became party to it after gaining independence during the last half-century. This is the context of the ongoing debate regarding questions of universality versus cultural relativism in the application of human rights frameworks. Global economic shifts of expanding capitalism in postcolonial African states keep them in unequal political relationships with Western industrialised nations, further complicating the application of human rights frameworks. These complexities, applied to the realisation of sexuality-related human rights, require that we utilise interdisciplinary approaches that consciously explore the multiple dimensions of social oppression. Such approaches allow us to raise the following questions (among others):

- How can we work collaboratively from a US base with indigenous community-based organisations and individuals without usurping their territory and re-victimising them?
- How can we utilise the human rights framework and its reliance on the identification of victimised individuals and groups

(in this case lesbians, gays, bisexuals and transgender people) while maintaining our critique of identity-based sexualities and the human rights framework itself?

- How can we promote geographical equity and autonomy by contributing to the greater redistribution of economic resources?
- How can we centralise issues of racist violence, xenophobia, police brutality, anti-immigrant backlash and racial profiling, all of which impact on our daily lives, as part of a two-way information exchange?
- How can we sustain autonomous networks and groups of pro-sexual rights and LGBTI people of colour as we maintain our employment in institutions with various agendas?
- How do we access various sites and channels of communication to document and publicise our lived experiences and analyses?

The human rights questions in African sexuality-related issues must be related to practical, effective anti-racist and anti-imperialist liberation politics. This requires conscious effort. One example of success in such efforts has been the application of feminist analyses to issues of women's agency and power in sexuality- and gender-related violence, resulting in the transformation of language by movements against sexual harassment and assault. The battered women's movement, in particular, has succeeded in changing the terminology from 'victim' to 'survivor' when referring to women who have been subjected to violence and abuse. Black feminist and civil rights movement analyses have also illuminated the discursive limitations and adverse collective psychic impact of referring to African Americans as a 'minority group' rather than as members of 'under-represented', 'under-resourced' and 'over-exploited' communities. These sorts of discursive shifts necessarily disassociate conditions of social, economic and political injustice from membership in particular ethnic groups or inhabitants of particular geographical locations.

The application of racial equality and the discursive empowerment of indigenous Africans, along with substantive measures to ensure gender equity, are inextricable from human rights approaches to sexual freedom. Only such multi-pronged approaches can hope to begin to surmount the obstacles of conservative cultural, religious and political constraints on sexuality-related rights. Sexuality-related human rights are not merely an issue of sexual identity. Sexuality-related human rights practices, which require a public association with sexual orientation or membership in a 'sexual minority group', must therefore be problematised. Failure to do so risks the loss of varied social, cultural and economic dimensions in meeting challenges to the general realisation of basic rights and fundamental freedoms.

In order to mobilise timely responses to the anti-homosexual witch-hunts in our countries of origin, African all-sexual human rights workers based in the US have found it strategically useful to develop ties with all-sexual organisers on the African continent and anti-heterosexist allies throughout the world. There is an increasing demand for swift and coordinated resettlement assistance for political dissidents active in sexuality-related human rights work who are fleeing from their countries of origin. Integral to this is the need for the establishment and expansion of emergency funds for sexual and political dissidents and for indigenous organisers in the sexual rights arena.

If we are to destigmatise the defence of human rights for LGBTI Africans, we must first recognise that any African who does so publicly is immediately marked as a homosexual and directly subjected to social stigmatisation. This is certainly true for Africans in Africa, but also for those of us in the diaspora. My three-year tenure as Africa/Middle East/Caribbean regional specialist at the IGLHRC made me the only 'Kenyan lesbian' easily associated with lesbian and gay rights via Internet searches, which contributed significantly to my duress at the time. This is clearly not helpful in sustaining an effective sexuality-related human rights movement. Ensuring African autonomy in self-identification is therefore crucial to this work, and requires the broad implementation of standards for security and the protection of confidentiality. These standards must include freedom in the selection of public identities, including the use of aliases as basic security prerogatives.

People-centred human rights advocacy work that protects freedom of expression should permit and encourage practitioners to frame and promote their work as they see fit. For example, when I returned to the IGLHRC as programme officer for Africa and south-west Asia, I elected to identify myself via a theoretical network (the Africa Southwest Asia Network) for purposes of identification with a collective rather than individual purpose. I also chose to identify myself as an African feminist as being more practical and strategic than public identification in terms of sexual identity in a limiting mainstream rights context. My work at IGLHRC evolved primarily into initiating locally directed, applied-research project partnerships combating violence against women ('curative rape') and between women (domestic violence), as well as fostering human rights and 'personal growth' for women of various sexualities in Africa. To identify myself more strongly with African women's and gender rights activists, I have also at the time of writing succeeded in changing my professional title to 'Africa programme officer'. Women's work for gender justice is a fine African tradition with which to ally myself as an African woman working from a US-based gay and lesbian human rights organisation.

Action networks have worked effectively as tools for postcolonial Third World feminist organising for a few decades now. Issue-based and regional translocal networks empower collaborative work, while supporting the autonomy of the respective constituencies involved. They help mobilise political will and economic resources in urgent matters; expedite communications; and offer opportunities for social, cultural and analytical support, among other things. In work on human rights issues related to African sexuality, region-identified action networks offer practical discursive and security platforms for promoting public identification with contentious issues. Political groups working on these issues are challenged to heightened creativity, in order to prevent the imposition of dangerous sexual identity labels that can mark particular subjects for discrimination and restricted mobility. Community strategies for action, such as identification and linkages with regional and issue-based networks, offer the advantages of depersonalised visibility and broader bases from which to advocate for justice.

We need to conduct basic needs assessment surveys within indigenous and diasporic African all-sexual communities. Meanwhile, other documented needs include funding, technical support, strategies for overcoming language barriers, leadership development, human rights trainings, publications on similar lived experiences, multimedia production and distribution, speaker and performance venues, development and promotion of standards for the protection of intellectual property, 'South–South' dialogues and 'Third World within–Third World without' dialogues.[4]

Bringing it all back home

My political methodology has been rooted in US-based Black and Third World feminist principles and pan-African feminist strategies for translocal human rights work. My spirit has been sustained through creative expressions of community organising and self-expression in my local neighbourhoods. Being involved in aspects of video distribution and production along with poetry writing and performance has provided me with necessary sites for community interface and grounded inspiration. If sexuality-related human rights are to be equitably realised by Africans on the continent and in the diaspora, cultural agency is a basic necessity, along with autonomously documented knowledge and sustained material support of community-building initiatives.

My experiences have taught me that efforts to link human rights issues to our communal realities as human beings are about process and perception. Our familial processes impact on community perceptions and vice versa. We must always remain critically conscious of our complex and sometimes contradictory subjective positions in human rights advocacy. Human rights advocates are a diverse body of subjects, with varied perspectives based on their communal realities. In the development of appropriate methodology, effective human rights strategies must address both the experiential needs of the subjects under consideration and the content of specific rights. As new strategies are developed and implemented, the current climate of volatility in the sexuality-related African human rights arena necessitates particular sensitivity to the inclusion of African all-sexuals in decision-making positions. In this way, the benefits of deep analysis in consciously applied knowledge, along with those of content production and distribution, can be applied to expanded rights concepts and discourses.

Confronting the stigma, silence and denial related to African homosexuality has challenged me to work to reverse the results of negative external identifications, incomplete self-definitions, fossilised attitudes and static histories by naming what is connected and what matters to me. I returned to formal human rights work after three years of creative work for economic, social and cultural pan-African human rights in a variety of geographical locations. I am blessed with a renewed sense of hope, a clearer vision of some next steps to implement, the close support of friends and new daily rituals for self-care.

This chapter was originally published in M.J Alexander, L. Albrecht, S. Day and M. Segrest (eds) (2002) Sing, Whisper, Shout, Pray!: Feminist Visions for a Just World, *Edgework Books.*

Notes

1   From a Bob Marley lyric:
    Why boasteth thyself, oh evil men,
    Playing smart and not being clever?
    I say you're working iniquity to achieve vanity, yeah,
    But the goodness of JAH JAH endureth forever.
    If you are the big tree,
    We are the small axe.
    Sharpened to cut you down,
    Ready to cut you down.
    For the full text, see http://www.bobmarley.com/songs/songs.
    cgi?smallaxe.
2   Audre Lorde (1983) *Zami: A New Spelling of My Name*, Santa Cruz, CA,
    Crossing Press.
3   'All-sexual' is a term used in the Caribbean Forum of Lesbians, All-
    Sexuals & Gays (C-FLAG) network to indicate that it considers all-sexual
    behaviour to be part of a sexual continuum in which classifications such
    as 'gay', 'lesbian' and 'bisexual' often cannot be rigidly applied. The terms
    'men who have sex with men' and 'women who have sex with women'
    are attempts to move around these rigid classifications. The term 'all-
    sexual' refers not only to biological and sexual characteristics, but also
    to social attitudes related to them. 'All-sexuals' therefore refers to same-
    gender-loving persons whose actions are not in violation of the Universal
    Declaration of Human Rights, that is to say, whose actions are not abusive
    to minors and other persons who are in dependent circumstances or of
    diminished capacity, or otherwise in violation of the rights or personal
    dignity of any person. See http://www.jflag.org/misc/allsexual.htm.

4   Third World Within (TWW) is a New York City-based network of people of colour organisations. Their purpose is to highlight 'domestic' issues resulting from US racism and economic restructuring, to educate and mobilise communities of colour around these issues, and to work in solidarity with activists, organisers and communities in the Third World and around the world to demand accountability from the US government and international institutions for their role in developing and maintaining policies and institutions destructive to the Third World and Third World communities in the US.

Nature ain't rigid – poem

Mia Nikasimo

Spanning the world
From Africa to Asia;
From Europe to Utopia
Anywhere you go
In gender identity
There are no absolutes
In gender identity
There are only relatives
Forcing absolutes
Upsets the balance
Of nature – a gradual wedlock
   of both
Brings equilibrium

this is...

Its natural from birth i was told
Botherwise; only aged three or
   four

Frontier identity gender the is
   this –
One are genderqueer +
   transgender
You be to fought be to have
   wars if
Knot a to up adds this all

I was a man
I am now a woman
I was a woman
I am now a man
I was seen as both
I am neither...
You are a man, a mob says
You are a woman, a mob says
I am a woman, i insist
I am not a man but some insist
Now both I am
Now neither am i
I am everybody
I am not everybody
I stand at the cusp
Of both and neither
And so when you
Say you know all
All you know is
Y o u r s e l v e s
Y o u r s e l v e s
Is know you all
Know you say you when
So and neither and both of
Cusp the at i
Everybody not am i

Everybody am i
Neither am i
Now both am i
Man a not am i
Woman a am i
Neither am i
Both now am i
Woman a am i
Man a not am i

Four or three aged only
Botherwise; told was i
Birth from natural its

So you told me?
Man a not am i
Woman a are you
Woman a not am i
Man a are you
Woman a am i
Man a are you
Woman a am i

Equilibrum brings
A gradual wedlock of both –
    nature of
Balance the upsets
Absolutes forcing
Relatives only are there
Identity gender in
Absolutes no are there
Identity gender in
Go you anywhere
(?) Utopia to Europe from
Asia to Africa from
all this adds up to a
Knot if wars have to
Be fought to be you
Transgender + genderqueer
Are one – this is the gender
Identity frontier

Is this

Cos

Nature aint rigid

26

On the paradoxical logic of intersections: a mathematical reading of the reality of homosexuality in Africa

Charles Gueboguo

Introduction

Scholarly friends wonder why I 'bother' to debate with anti-homosexuals and reactionaries rather than just focusing my attention, as an African scholar, on 'supporting reasonable people to help the dinosaurs die out faster', particularly when so many excellent scholars have already abundantly demonstrated the 'evidence' I am going to discuss, which is also now completely accepted by UNAIDS, all the major donors and even many African governments through, for example, their AIDS national strategy plans or their human rights reports.[1]

I would argue that, as a constructionist, I do not take social facts for granted and I do not see them as static. I keep in mind that they are dynamic in their essence, meaning every time that, as an observer, you try to address 'homosexualities' in Africa you will always have something new to discover. That is true for all social facts. Should we assume that because neocolonialism, corruption or democracy, for example, have already been addressed by well-known scholars and in a very rigorous manner, all has been said? What about the fact that science is perceived as a cumulative process of discovery (Bourdieu 2001)? The fact that same-sex sexualities have been well addressed by non-African scholars is not an excuse to stop trying to 'rethink' the social realities which still bring tragedies to the daily lives of individuals in Africa due to their sexual orientation: death, rape, blackmail, extortions (Thoreson and Cook 2011). But as we will see further, the issue that I underline here is another way of phrasing the now inner binaries between what should or should not be said regarding homosexualities in Africa. Who actually has the legitimacy to argue who can and cannot speak about homosexuality? Scientifically speaking, my answer is no one.

I therefore suggest that the ongoing dramatic situation of people on the continent who love the same sex as themselves could be addressed in different ways, and mine is an assumed theoretical position. This is because, although homosexuality has been addressed by scholars in Africa, myself included, we have still missed the answer to why the daily life of individuals is getting worse. My hypothesis is that we still need to challenge and add theory, not in the Greek sense of *theoria*, that is pure and simple contemplation, but in the sense of a philosophical position. The intention is to address and challenge the common-sense view regarding same-sex sexualities across the continent that homosexuality issues are seen as secondary to be scientifically addressed. While so doing, my aim is to attempt to re-open the field of possible interpretations.

That being said, I would like to continue to discuss in this paper the boundaries, noticed in some common social discourses in the continent, of the binary hierarchy that holds between social objects that are considered worthy and those that are considered by some people to be unworthy, particularly where the latter are consigned, along with their relevant social agents, to the margins of society. 'Homosexualities' in Africa à la Murray and Roscoe (1998), which sometimes seem to be considered unworthy, are, with some exceptions, often consigned to the margins.[2] This act of pushing such reality to the fringes of accepted social boundaries is the move that creates an initial sense of emptiness.

Here, homosexuality apparently does not exist in Africa: according to some intellectually discredited anti-homosexual individuals, it was imported from elsewhere, quite often from the West; it seemingly exists as something of secondary importance that the mostly international media exploit for their own ends;[3] and, finally, homosexuality is but a non-identity, a manifestation of 'bisexuality', whose only goal seems to be to strengthen the position of the dominant phallo- and heterocentric order.

This is to say that the root of this emptiness can be found in some common-sense discourse in a social space. The economy of this social space is characterised by a politics of confinement, contentiousness and abstraction, which remains the nature of the performative social space of compulsory heterosexuality (Butler 2005). The symbol of this space is the erect phallus. Indeed, in dominant political discourse on the continent, a distinguished place is reserved for the penis in the ways in which life, power and pleasure are symbolised, as has been shown by Mbembé (2010). A not insignificant influence is granted to the work of the phallus. While every observer can notice that this situation is not at all different from elsewhere in the world, the author keeps explaining how before, during and after colonisation, power in Africa has sought to wear the face of virility. Even more so, the formulation, implementation and understanding of power largely worked according to the idea of an infinite erection. The political community operating in this space has always wanted, above anything else, the equivalent of a male society, and this has 'always' been depicted by an erect penis.[4] Hence the hypothesis that the whole psychology of power in Africa could have been organised around the phenomenon of the swelling of the virile organ. Likewise, the whole creative discourse (*poiesis*) that produces homosexualities in the social sphere continues to reflect the way in which social systems represent homosexualities and, consequently, also the structures that render impossible its very erection as an entity not confined to the fringes of what is speakable.

It is this habitus (a system of acquired long-term dispositions) that, on the whole, when translated into an ethos of evasion, has its roots in the near-total – therefore partly speakable – social negation of a viable space for homosexuality in Africa. The structure of this position cannot be seen in isolation from the prevailing politics of confinement. For Ekotto (2010: 183), this notion translates as the impossibility of a subject feeling free to participate in the game of social interaction without feeling constrained by the race, gender or sexual orientation of another person supported by a dominant mode of interaction. The dominant mode can be understood as external forces that are oppressive and that do not allow the subject to be the master of his or her own destiny. I call this symbolic system of domination, which uses, among other things, confinement as its teleology of subjection, the phallus.

Moreover, the performance of habitus that determines the direction of individual trajectories suggests that the origin of homosexuality lies in a space belonging to the other, and also places its existence at the margins of the socialised body – which is different from a subject's normative incorporation in the form of an ethos and a habitus. Here, the socialised body expresses the idea of a social group in a process of normative systematisation, projecting the illusion of a coherent whole (*holon*) as an 'abject' fact. In this area, taboos create boundaries within a social space (Kristeva, as cited by Butler 2005: 254), at the same time as creating the basis for the formation of emptiness, although its point of departure lies at the very heart of *sociation* (society in the process of formation) (Javeau 2003). Taboos will always be pushed to the margins. Emptiness is the matrix that carries all prohibitions, things that are unspeakable: in short, socially 'unworthy' objects. These are objects that, in what Derrida called a phallocentric culture, are excluded from the spectrum of intelligibility and from what is politically visible and objectifiable (to follow the Latin meaning of *objectare*: to cast in front of oneself, in order to observe).

Drawing on mathematical logic, I would like to show how 'unworthy' social facts can be found, quite paradoxically, to intersect with 'worthy' social facts. In its performance, the intersection of 'worthy' and 'unworthy' facts within the social body can make 'unworthy' facts appear as recessive elements. Such is the case with homosexual reality in Africa. A demonstration of the logic of this recessiveness will then allow us to put forward the hypothesis that 'unworthy' facts are non-dominant, but existing. As such, these facts are also worthy of being seen as speakable facts, to be analysed and discussed in general, as can be seen in this volume. It is therefore not about a myth, an invention or the construction of a reality that apparently does not exist, for some ill-informed extremists, on the continent,[5] or which has supposedly been imported from elsewhere, from the opposite shores of the Atlantic. This is the fallacious conceptual argument that, across the continent these days, brings about the effects of stigmatisation, discrimination, intolerance, rape, physical and verbal assault, and even murder committed against people who claim to belong or are suspected of belonging to this 'pariah' category (Gueboguo and Epprecht 2011).

Whether we agree with it or not, it is necessary to recall the fact that homosexualities exist in Africa and that they can, on this basis, be a marker revealing something about an area of social reality. I will support my argument with an approach used in recessive theory as applied to the field of mathematical logic, which will highlight the paradox that can emerge out of intersectionality. This will involve analysing the intersection that holds where there is a manifestation of recessive elements, supported by mathematical logic (Nyeck 2010).

Nyeck and 'intersectionality'

In her analysis of colonial blackmail, Nyeck raises the issue of knowing how to determine the causal relationship between a number of subjects coinciding in Africa and the appropriate methodological approach to be used. In response, she proposes that a discourse resting on intersectionality as its theoretical framework be formalised. From intersectionality, she suggests that 'the understanding that socio-political issues are sometimes intertwined in a way that makes differentiation very difficult helped cover important grounds in the study of sexuality and politics'. Further on in her analysis, however, she shows how intersectionality, if it is the only theoretical framework being used, is not always sufficient as a way of drawing out the dialogue and solidarity that might exist between and beyond intersecting categories, especially when the area of intersection is a social space involving hyperbole and controversy, as we have already highlighted above.

Consequently, she draws upon mathematical logic to demonstrate how these categories interact and, in doing so, draws attention to their paradoxical nature. Her aim is to show the non-visible relation that exists between the categories of homophobia, (state) institutions and Cameroon (as a space of contention). In doing so, she draws attention to their equivalence, their state of inclusion and their intersectionality, all from a mathematical perspective. By using such an approach, she discusses the necessary paradox surrounding this intersectionality. She states that:

> While colonialism and homosexuality may intersect as distinctive discursive categories in what I call, 'colonial blackmail,' to oppose the gay rights movements in Africa, the outcome of their intersection is etymological fallacy because it is empty. This emptiness, I argue, is paradoxical and counterintuitive in at least two ways. First the outcome empty is paradoxical because it unintentionally and necessarily defeats the purpose of the strategic use of colonial blackmail as the baseline for wholesale resistance against domestic queer activism in Africa. Second this outcome is counterintuitive because it does not sufficiently suggest that homophobia alone is what hides behind this emptiness (Nyeck 2010).

Here, I will take up her method of analysis and adapt it by introducing elements of linguistics and psychoanalysis in an attempt to draw out any scientific interest there might be for researchers looking at homosexualities in Africa. By using mathematical logic, my aim is to investigate the relationship held between the French words *homosexualité* (homosexuality), *chercheur* (researcher) and Afrique (Africa).

'*Homosexualité, chercheur* and *Afrique*': mathematical logic, intersectionality and paradox

Let us consider the sets following H, A and C, which represent the set of letters (x) that make up the words *homosexualité* (homosexuality), *chercheur* (researcher) and *Afrique* (Africa), where x can only appear once. The distinct, extensional definition is therefore as follows:

H = {homsexualit};

A = {afrique};

C = {cheru}.

Here, each element x is the smallest distinct, meaningful unit in language, or what Saussure calls a phoneme. Phonemes are the distinct elements we perceive, which, when taken in isolation, define nothing at all, unless we place them alongside each other, in relation to other phonemes. From a social perspective, each element x refers to the manifestation of a particular social reality, whereas from a psychological perspective, it refers to the label of individuality: what we call the 'I' (*le je*). As such, the 'I' has no content (Dubet 1994). The 'I' can hold up without the 'me' (*le moi*) (Chébaux 1999), which is manifested in, among other things, the desire for pleasure (*jouissance*). But in fact, the 'me' combines with the 'I' and becomes a fixed, integral part of the structure-giving 'us' (*le nous*). The 'me' is the internal control for the expected roles assigned to a social agent, right up to his or her death. The 'me' (or ego) is a product of the super-ego internalising normative demands, and the 'us' is a synthesis of this, a way of relating to structured interaction that is acquired from early childhood (Dubet 1994: 129). It is possible for there to be variable failures in the enactment of this in relation to normative assessments made by the 'us', since the 'me' can actually decide to be thrust to the margins of normative standards. If the 'me' manages to derive pleasure within the receptacle of the normalised, structured world, there still remains at this level an illusion of being what appears to be the case (Chébaux 1999: 131), or better what is projected as being the case. This is why, according to Goffman (1974), the 'me' remains the interpretive structure used in the space occupied by the individual within the 'us', if we go by the behaviours expressed by that individual. In this case, there can be no 'me' without the 'us' (Mead 1963 [1934]), and no 'us' without there being an opposition to 'them' (*eux*): 'the elementary form of this relationship opposes the in-group, existing only in the constant affirmation of its difference and its distance from the out-group'[6] (Hoggart 1970 [1957], as cited by Dubet 1994: 114).

As such, the in-group appears as an autonomous 'me', which we call society. This society has an identity, has a patronym that is able to be used, has regulations that could appear as road signs, such as green lights and red lights. In short, what we have is a whole system of organisation (Touraine 1975: 605). Consequently, the idea that the 'me' is an integral part of the 'us' at the same time as lacking the concept of being opposed to 'them' is a utopian vision. Pleasure (in the homosexual sense), which is one manifestation of the extension of the 'me' (Chébaux 1999: 125), can only be understood in the context of this discursive relationship with the 'I', which can itself become a pathological relationship if, in turn, the 'I' is considered without reference to the 'us' (Elias 1973 [1932]).

If we therefore agree on the fact that each phoneme is not a phonetic but a practical representation of an area of reality (or individuality) that shapes the whole of each separate set, and therefore falls under the heading of *sociation* (in Javeau's reading of the term), in this case H = A = C if and only if each set shares the same phoneme as another set. In the case in hand, there is no relationship of equality between these sets:

H ≠ A ≠ C.

When applying her analysis of blackmail to 'homophobic discourse in Africa', in this regard Nyeck postulates that if sets of letters are not equivalent in their physical nature, they can still hold something in common. They might, for example, have the same number of variables. This cannot be verified in this particular case.

However, one could see how in French the variable *Afrique* (Africa), when set out, loses none of its particular attributes, contrary to what happens with *homosexualité* (homosexuality) and *chercheur* (researcher). This allows us to postulate that Africa remains a whole (i.e. it is non-homogeneous), that is constructed as a contentious space within which the other variables interact and give it meaning. The variables therefore play their role within the matrix of Africa, while still not being equal to Africa. However, I advance the idea that they might have something in common if we consider the cardinal number relating to their intersecting sets. But I also argue that each variable carries an element of its meaning in the form of a phoneme that is drawn from the root *Afrique* (Africa). So, we said a phoneme holds no meaning except when it is placed in relation to other phonemes, and never if it is taken in isolation. In this case, there is no 'me' without reference to 'us'.

As such, if R refers to a relation such as below:

H R A R C

this implies that:

H ∩ A ∩ C ≠ ∅.

In other words, H is in relation (R) with A and C if their intersection is not empty, which means that they do not share a common phoneme. All the possible combinations in the intersections of elements within these sets show that they are related:

$H \cap A = \{a, e, i, u\}$;

$H \cap C = \{e, u\}$;

$C \cap A = \{e, u\}$.

These sets are in relation with each other. We can even see how H (*homosexualité*) holds a strong relation with A (*Afrique*) if we count the cardinal number they have in common, which is 4, as opposed to the two other intersections which have only 2 in common. The notion that the origin of homosexuality is non-African is therefore demolished. This mathematical conclusion stands alongside conclusions drawn from work outside the field of mathematics (see Murray and Roscoe 1998; Epprecht 2004, 2008; Gueboguo 2006, 2009).

The weak proportion of relations between H (*homosexualité*) and C (*chercheur*) is significant in that, among other things, it reveals a social logic that places facts that are either worthy or unworthy of scientific attention into a binary hierarchy. As such, in the field of speakable possibilities and things that are constructed as social facts in Africa, there seems to exist a binary hierarchy between issues of the moment and matters of urgency at a particular moment in time. Issues of the moment include the set of crises undermining African societies as a whole, namely in the fields of war, natural disasters, health disasters, governance and democracy (Gueboguo 2009: 171). In common parlance, matters of urgency refer to a desire to reconnect with one's 'African' cultural heritage (especially in the way this is observed by certain members of the African diaspora) in order to better equip oneself against the challenges of a globalised world. These are objects that, through their illusory 'utilitarian' nature, appear to be worthy of interest.

The dialogic relationship that is established between these objects does not offer any possibilities to what is consigned to the margins of what is socially objectifiable and speakable. When faced with utilitarian urgencies, there is a process of political confinement that is therefore concerned with relating current events that are socially acceptable. When remarking on the submissiveness of free intellectuals who are eager to present papers on such imposed subjects of the moment, Bourdieu could therefore not help stating that this situation held 'something rather pathetic'[7] (2002: 70). What we can see here is the symbolic violence and the internalisation of masculine domination (Bourdieu 1998). What is unsaid in the eagerness of these intellectuals is confined to *illusio*, or the interest in dominating one's particular time, which makes it inevitable that one will encounter history in the making. Meanwhile, homosexual reality is perceived as not being part of this.

As such, the near-total apparently[8] social negation of homosexual reality in Africa gives rise to the phenomenon's confinement within a quaternary space – to use palaeontological terminology – and its being forced to the boundaries as something unworthy, as a stain or a blemish. Within the binary hierarchy that exists between different priorities, between urgent issues and urgent matters of the moment, to be interested in homosexual reality is seen to be digressive and seems to carry with it a sense of danger. In her critique of Douglas with regard to this stain or blemish, Butler (2005 [1990]: 253) stresses that social systems can be vulnerable at the margins. In turn, the margins of society are considered to be dangerous. What we have here is a slippery slope argument, where cracks in the socialised body lead us to fear chaos in social formations that are already in crisis. This fear is presented as being more justified than the practice of homosexuality which, belonging to the private sphere, would lead us to think that homosexuality would have failed to become part of history in the making. True history is the only version we are allowed to hear, and the only version allowed to offer solutions to the building of nation states (Hayes 2000, Epprecht 2008) and to the long-established resistance to foreign domination (Iliffe 2009 [1995]), according to the official propaganda.

This building of nation states and this resistance was begun with difficulty after independence was granted across the continent (Ela 1998). This is why for decades the only legitimate and speakable contributions to research on the continent tended only to be focused on central topics such as kinship, economy, conservation, gender, racism, colonisation, post-colonisation, war, famine, dictatorship, genocide, the animalistic way in which power is performed (Oloruntoba-Oju 2006). The binary relationship held between unworthy and worthy objects in research in this area therefore becomes a general battleground, where the struggle for supremacy over meaning is always included in the act of re-performance (Cixous, as cited by Moi 1985: 105) in scientific research. The hierarchy of priorities in question is only maintained within this relationship of struggle, at the same time that this oppositional relationship is produced. In fact, the binary difference only exists in the relationship that places worthy objects – which are to be found within the socialised body – and unworthy objects – which are also situated within this body – in opposition to each other, hence the paradox that emerges. In this way, at the point of intersection between these conflicting forces and these interests, 'African queer subjectivity should emerge as an emptied set after powers intersecting in its making lose their appearance of priority' (sic) (Nyeck 2010).

Bourdieu (2002 [1984]: 197) does not see this any differently when he stresses that one of the means by which social censure is exercised can be found specifically in this hierarchy of objects, or where such objects are considered either worthy or unworthy of being studied. Consequently, social agents will find themselves spending their lives classifying themselves by appropriating objects that are themselves already classified. However, they also classify others who also classify themselves through the reappropriated objects they classify (91–2).

This logic can also be used to explain, among other things, how according to what has been demonstrated, the relationship between *chercheur* (C), *Afrique* (A) and *homosexualité* (H) can be so weak. But we could also draw upon the explanatory variable of social organisation to reinforce our position, or even the political will of the governing authorities found on the continent. This involves discussing the ideas that politicians hold in relation to the role of researchers on the continent, both in terms of the place (within geographical and political space) and the domains (which are also politically motivated) they occupy. But let us first evaluate the outcome of the interaction between the three sets, *Afrique* (A), *homosexualité* (H) and *chercheur* (C), which results in:

$H \cap C \cap A = \{e, u\}$.

Here, we can see that there is a relation, and it involves the same weak relationship of equivalence as the relation (R) found in: $H R C$ and $C R A$. This allows us to postulate that the phonemes belonging to H (*homosexualité*) occur as recessive factors in the larger set A (*Afrique*) and, consequently, may be a concern for C (*chercheur*, or researchers in Africa). The recessive nature of a phoneme as a social fact operating within a contentious space does not therefore mean that it does not exist or cannot justify its being consigned to the margins of the macrocosm of society.

Following Dubet (1994: 75), and using sociological analysis, one might say that what is foreign (or here, recessive) is not what belongs to another culture, despite what shared representations focus on. It is in fact at the very heart of sociation and also separate from this process due to its very individuality. As has been mentioned, a phoneme holds no meaning when taken in isolation. By extension, situational categories that are pushed to the margins, outside a contentious space, are to be found in the social world, just like all other categories (Bourdieu 2002 [1984]: 12). Why is this the case? Due to the following:

$H \cap C \cap A \neq \emptyset$.

Conclusion

We have been able to define the following relation (R) between the sets in hand: H R C and C R A if their intersection is non-empty. And according to mathematical theory, a relation is an equivalence relation if it is reflexive, symmetric and transitive.

A relation is reflexive if each element is related to itself, as is the case in the following:

$A \cap A = A$;
$H \cap H = H$;
$C \cap C = C$.

It is symmetric if the fact that A R H necessarily implies that H R A.

Finally, it is transitive if A R H and H R C, and therefore A R C.

To put it in a less abstract way, this means that we might take each phoneme we have marked out as an element forming part of social reality or as an element that is representative of the equivalence relation (R) we have just demonstrated. This is to say that studying one single category is equal to studying all other categorical realities in the area of sociation, or society in the process of formation. Hence the use of the term representative for each instance of element x, which operatively we refer to here as a phoneme.

In other words, writing about and discussing homosexualities in Africa holds value in representing an area of social reality in the same way that writing about and discussing post-colonisation, democracy, governance, war, social problems and disease does. The aforementioned binary hierarchy therefore no longer has any reason for being. In turn, urgent issues and urgent matters of the time themselves become empty, if their goal is merely to place a *cordon sanitaire* around the issue of homosexuality – or any other categorical fact in society that is deemed to be of secondary importance. The concern now is to know how the issue of homosexuality in Africa might emerge from its isolation in order to operate alongside and interact with other social issues in a pragmatic and therefore concrete way. Here, it might provide answers to the whole trend towards globalisation and, thereby, the widespread social changes that are taking place.

This chapter was translated from the French by Tim Cleary.

Notes

1   See, for example, how the report by the Kenya Human Rights Commission (2011) is presented as a big breakthrough, according to my friend Marc Epprecht. He argues that human rights approaches in general and AIDS issues in particular are now used as entry points to address the realities of homosexualities where they are forbidden by laws and social norms.

2   Marc Epprecht made a very pertinent remark here, saying that I sometimes overstate my point because in the flow of the debate, while not taking social facts themselves for granted, I used to assume that everyone should know that some facts are evident, for example that South Africa is known, since 1996, to be the first country in Africa to have addressed the principle of non-discrimination in its constitution. Here I will try to correct that position by adding that there are many others that have now done the same: Cape Verde is the second country on the continent to have decriminalised same-sex relationships, in 2004. I attended the December 2008 UN meeting in New York where Gabon, Central African Republic, Rwanda and Sierra Leone were among the countries which signed or signalled their intention to support the UN General Assembly's resolution to include sexual orientation within the Universal Declaration of Human Rights. Botswana's high court is discussing the same as I write.

3   While this could be true to some extent, I am not denying there is a real sense of solidarity by LGBTI groups in the West, with the support

of Western governments and organisations such as ILGA, IGLHRC, the LGBTI chapter of Amnesty International, Human Rights Watch or amfAR, the Foundation for AIDS Research.

4   In private communications with Marc Epprecht, he subtly responded to this point by saying that when he thinks about Zimbabwe, one of his fields of work, political space at the village and chief level is circular and flat, allowing for free debates and argument. He added that if he looks at parliament buildings around the continent, they are often roundish and breast-like. Compared to banks, they do not seem very phallic. So, the debate is open: this is my input.

5   Marc Epprecht (1998, 2006, 2008 among others), in almost all his research in Zimbabwe, stated that if you go to the villages, people will say, of course we know 'homosexuality' has always been here. The same statements are recorded by Murray and Roscoe (1998).

6   Quotation translated from the French.

7   Quotation translated from the French.

8   One can see again the paradox because, as has been observed, there are associations of same-sex loving people in the majority of African countries with varying degrees of acceptance (Gueboguo 2008, 2010). And according to the United States Department of State *Human Rights Reports for 2009* (USDS 2010), for example in Gabon, 'Discrimination and violence occasioned by homosexual and transgender conduct was not a problem' or in Mauritania (where, despite a potential death sentence) there was 'no evidence of either societal violence or systematic government discrimination based on sexual orientation, and there were no criminal prosecutions during the year'. Those points are made to acknowledge and to recognise the non-deterministic situation that is drawn by some extremists within some societies. This helps to keep away from an over-generalisation that could be informed by only the worst-case scenario while there are some perceptible changes at a certain social level in some places in Africa.

References

Bourdieu, P. (1998) *La domination masculine*, Paris, Seuil, 'Liber'
——(2001) 'Science de la science et réflexivité', Paris, édition Raisons d'agir, 'Cours et travaux'
——(2002 [1984] 'Questions de sociologie', Paris, édition de Minuit, 'Reprise'
Butler, J. (2005 [1990]) *Trouble dans le genre: Pour un féminisme de la subversion*, translated from the English by Kraus, C., preface by Fassin É., Paris, La Découverte
Chébaux, F. (1999) *La question du sujet entre Alain Touraine et Françoise Dolto. Archéologie de l'acte éducatif*, Paris, L'Harmattan, 'Éducations et société'
Dubet, F. (1994) *Sociologie de l'expérience*, Paris, Seuil
Ekotto, F. (2010) 'From women loving women in Africa to Jean Genet and race: a conversation with Frieda Ekotto', interview conducted by Diabaté, N., *Journal of African Literature Association*, 4(1): 181–203

Ela, J.-M. (1998) *Innovations sociales et renaissance de l'Afrique noire: Les défis du 'monde d'en-bas'*, Paris, L'Harmattan

Elias, N. (1973 [1932]) *La civilisation des mœurs*, Paris, Calmann-Lévy

Epprecht, M. (1998) 'The "unsaying" of indigenous homosexualities in Zimbabwe: mapping a blind spot in an African masculinity', *Journal of Southern African Studies*, 24(4): 631–51

——(2004) *Hungochani: The History of Dissident Sexuality in Southern Africa*, Montreal, McGill/Queen's University Press

—— (2006) '"Bisexuality" and the politics of normal in African ethnography', *Anthropologica*, 48(2): 187–201

——(2008) *Heterosexual Africa? The History of an Idea from the Age of Exploration to the Age of AIDS*, Athens, Ohio University Press and Scottsville, South Africa, University of KwaZulu-Natal Press

Goffman, E. (1974) *Les rites d'interaction*, Paris, édition de Minuit

Gueboguo, C. (2006) 'La question homosexuelle en Afrique. Le cas du Cameroun', Paris, L'Harmattan, 'Études africaines'

——(2008) 'Mobilisations transnationales des communautés homosexuelles en Afrique : une affaire à suivre', *Anthropologie et Sociétés*, 32 (numéro hors série): 85–93, http://id.erudit.org/iderudit/000229ar, accessed 4 December 2012

——(2009) *Sida et homosexualité(s) en Afrique: Analyse des communications de prévention*, Paris, L'Harmattan, 'Études africaines'

——(2010) 'Ce qui est fait pour nous sans nous est fait contre nous! De l'internationalisation des recherches auprès des MSM en Afrique', *Outliers*, a Collection of Essays and Creative Writing on Sexuality in Africa, 3 (Spring): 36–50, http://www.irnweb.org/assets/journals/1a9bae05 99500121bb330626a4a0e239.pdf

Gueboguo, C. and Epprecht, M. (2011) 'Extortion and blackmail on the basis of sexual orientation in Africa: a case study from Cameroun', in Thoreson, R. and Cook, S. (eds) *Nowhere to Hide: Blackmail and Extortion of LGBT People in Sub-Saharan Africa*, New York, IGLHRC

Hayes, J. (2000) *Queer Nations: Marginal Sexualities in the Maghreb*, Chicago and London, The University of Chicago Press

Hoggart, R. (1970 [1957]) *La Culture du pauvre*, Paris, édition de Minuit

Iliffe, J. (2009 [1995]) *Les Africains: Histoire d'un continent*, translated from the English by Mourlon, J.-P., Paris, Flammarion, 'Champs histoire'

Javeau, C. (2003) *Sociologie de la vie quotidienne*, Paris, PUF, 'Que sais-je?'

Kenya Human Rights Commission (KHRC) (2011) *The Outlawed Amongst Us: A Study of the LGBTI Community's Search for Equality and Non-Discrimination in Kenya*, KHRC, Nairobi, http://www.scribd.com/ fullscreen/55843667?access_key=key-12w5qfcz5xyhawdyr4od, accessed 3 December 2012

Mbembé, A. (2010) *Sortir de la grande nuit: Essai sur l'Afrique décolonisée*, Paris, La Découverte

Mead, G.H. (1963 [1934]), *L'Esprit, le Soi et la Société*, Paris, PUF

Moi, T. (1985) *Sexual/Textual Politics: Feminist Literary Theory*, London and New York, Methuen

Murray, S. and Roscoe, W. (eds) (1998) *Boy-Wives and Female Husbands: Studies of African Homosexualities*, New York, Palgrave

Nyeck, S. (2010) 'Accounting for paradoxical emptiness in contentious intersections: colonial blackmail, "token causation" and sexuality in Africa', paper presented at the annual American Political Scientist Association Conference in Washington DC

Oloruntoba-Oju, T. (2006) 'Dèdè n d? ku ikú n d? Dèdè: fe/male sexuality and dominance in Nigerian video films (Nollywood)', in Kopf, M. (ed) *Wiener Zeitschrift für kritische Afrikastudien/Vienna Journal of African Studies*, 'Sexuality and Power in African Literature', 11, http://www.univie.ac.at/ecco/stichproben/nr11_english.htm, accessed 4 December 2012

Thoreson, R. and Cook, S. (eds) (2011) *Nowhere to Hide: Blackmail and Extortion of LGBT People in Sub-Saharan Africa*, New York, IGLHRC

Touraine, A. (1975) 'Autoportrait du sociologue', *Esprit*, 1: 587–605

United States Department of State (USDS) (2010) *Human Rights Reports for 2009*, http://www.globalequality.org/storage/documents/pdf/2009%20hr%20report%20sogi%20references.pdf, accessed 7 June 2011

27

Mounting homophobic violence in Senegal

Mouhamadou Tidiane Kassé

In February 2008, a wind of homophobia swept through Senegal. It continues to sweep the country, with periods of exacerbation and moments of calm. The ebb and flow is fed by information and comments on homosexuality published periodically in the local press. In a country that is 95 per cent Muslim and 4 per cent Catholic, popular disapproval remains based on religious beliefs, but it is also based on cultural and social structures which impose a strict moral order in certain areas of social life. Considered a practice 'against nature', homosexuality carries penalties ranging from one to five years imprisonment, plus 100,000 francs (about €150) to 1,500,000 francs (about €2,200) in fines.

Homosexuality has long been tacitly tolerated in Senegal. Section 319 of the penal code, which condemns sexual relations between persons of the same sex, was introduced in 1962 but has rarely been applied. Men who have sex with men (MSM)[1] have lived openly, occupying social roles where their identity as homosexuals was fully expressed. They pandered to the 'grandes dames' of Senegalese society; some of them even became stars of the jet set and social gatherings in Dakar. Besides these ceremonies, their presence was also seen as a sign of sophistication at family celebrations (baptisms, marriages, etc). They have even been noted in political circles, where their ability to mobilise and entertain community members reinforced the skills of women in those areas.

In this regard, the sociologist Cheikh Niang notes that during the colonial period *'gorjigen'* (*homme–femme* or man–woman, a term that refers to the homosexual in Wolof) played political roles alongside women in the cities formerly called the Four Communes of Senegal (Dakar, Saint-Louis, Gorée and Rufisque). The two main political leaders of the pre-independence period, Lamine Guèye and Léopold Sédar Senghor, both enjoyed the support of female leaders (*dirijanké*, or lady) who, between 1950 and 1960, surrounded themselves with *gorjigen*. Several oral sources report that the *gorjigen* of Saint-Louis played a leading role in the electoral victory of Senghor and staged his triumphant entry into Saint-Louis after his 1950 electoral campaign (Niang 2010).

The homophobic violence recorded in Senegal since 2008 therefore contrasts with the attitudes that had hitherto prevailed, as much in its actual manifestation as in its scale. Circumstantial, episodic and isolated, the phenomenon has reached a degree and form never before experienced. There has been a systematic hunt for homosexuals, in the form of harassment, stoning and lynching. The media have regularly reported these incidents. In one case, the buried body of a person alleged to be homosexual was unearthed and dragged out of a Muslim cemetery. The debate has occupied the press for weeks, including, at its extremes, calls to murder. It has been noted that some of the most hardline positions taken were from Muslim religious circles, especially from the Collective of Islamic Associations of Senegal (CAIS).

The hunt for homosexuals began following the publication by *Icône*, a local magazine, of pictures showing a gay marriage. Before the concert of indignation had invaded the press, the people identified in the images were arrested by police on 4 February 2008. With this marriage, ordinary Senegalese discovered a little-known side of homosexuality. Common representations had been limited to the image of people who were effeminate in their attitudes and had close circles of female friends. This 'marriage' was seen as an attack on a sacred institution and revealed to many that homosexuality is not an attitude, but also a sexual orientation. 'Indeed, for the Senegalese, (...) the term Gorjigen, unlike the word homosexuality, refers explicitly to gender relations, not sex' (Niang 2010).

Perceived as a trend and not an effeminate sexual orientation, homosexuality has long been tolerated in Senegalese society. Signs and acts of hostility against homosexuals were evident at times, but never reached the widespread violence seen since February 2008. Crowder (1959), cited in a study by a team from

263

the Université Cheikh Anta Diop de Dakar (Niang et al 2003), suggests that this tolerance has been noticeable since the colonial period: 'The elders and faithful Muslims condemn men for this, but it is typical of African tolerance that they are left very much alone' (Crowder 1959). This tolerance, at times an indifference to homosexuality, is no longer the norm.

Several events have taken place since 2008 to strengthen the radicalisation against homosexuality. In December 2008, nine people were arrested by the police for alleged homosexual acts. The case will carry on for a long time. The arrests of February 2008 did not result in prosecution; the five defendants were released from police custody and the matter was allowed to run its course. This time, the case ended in court. At the end of the trial, the court pronounced sentences of eight years in prison. This penalty goes beyond the penal provisions against homosexuality, and reflects a climate of rampant homophobia and the feelings of a judge outraged by the comments of the defendants. Before the bar, some of the defendants openly acknowledged their sexual orientation and practices. Their attitude was perceived as a challenge, or even an insult.[2] Prior to this, trials for homosexuality had given way to denial, regrets and tears.

The silence of the authorities

This judgment garnered international condemnation, both from the French government and organisations defending human rights. Locally, a joint statement was issued by the African Assembly for the Defence of Human Rights (RADDHO), the International Federation of Human Rights, the Inter-African Union of Human Rights and Amnesty International Senegal to say 'no to homophobia, yes to tolerance'. The text called on the state's obligation to 'ensure respect for the physical and moral integrity of persons involved ... and, more generally, to condemn in the strongest manner homophobic acts likely to undermine the physical and moral integrity of homosexuals'. Referring to article 7, paragraph 2 of the constitution of Senegal, the organisations also argued that 'everyone has the right to life, liberty, security, and free development of his person'. This provision is seen as potentially encompassing the sexual orientation of individuals.

These events passed without any reaction from the Senegalese government, leading to the creation of a climate of impunity over attacks against homosexuals. In this respect, Codou Bop points to a political weakness created by economic crisis, where popular movements are indicative of a popular mistrust towards the authorities (Bop 2009). Reminders to the government that, in addition to the laws and constitutional provisions already in place, they were also signatories of international conventions caused them great embarrassment. But faced with public pressure, they have still not taken positions in line with the international commitments they have undertaken.

Violence against homosexuals was accompanied by ferocious attacks against any rhetoric or attitude that provided an alternative view of homosexuality. When the five people arrested in February 2008 were released, public opinion was that a homosexual lobby was nestled in the heart of power. The reaction from abroad was denounced as an 'immoral' Western war against religious and moral values. Homosexuality has also been linked to the spread of AIDS in a country where this group has a very high prevalence of HIV infection – a 21.5 per cent rate of infection compared with 0.7 per cent in the general population.

These attitudes of rejection and denial stubbornly refuse to recognise the fact that homosexuality is a reality rooted in Senegal, even though the fact is particularly evident in certain quarters and references to it are not lacking. In 2002, a team of researchers at the Université Cheikh Anta Diop conducted a study attesting to the importance of homosexuality in Senegal and its frequency across socio-economic groups and ethnicities (Niang et al 2003).

Before the wave of homophobia, homosexuals were among the actors engaged in the fight against HIV/AIDS. It was decided that the current situation made it unsafe to continue their strategies for responding to the epidemic and consolidating the results achieved by Senegal in this area. To escape the violence, HIV-positive homosexuals stopped going to health facilities where they could have received antiretroviral drugs. Those groups who had animated the network for awareness and prevention of the HIV epidemic have suspended their activities. Networks through which gay organisations fighting against AIDS organised their response to the epidemic have also fallen apart; their members have left to escape acts by angry people or police operations. Moreover, the nine people convicted in January 2009 argued that they were arrested while conducting training sessions in the fight against AIDS.

The risk of losing the networks of associations for homosexuals is considered serious, as MSM are a bridge group in the transmission of HIV. Faced with homophobia, many marry and maintain heterosexual relationships to conceal their same-sex orientation. In addition, more and more young people tend to engage in homosexual practices for financial gain – a disguised form of prostitution – while maintaining their heterosexual activities.

Immediately after the arrests in December 2008, a number of NGO leaders, researchers and others involved in the fight against AIDS established an informal crisis committee. Their first action was to plead for the release of the nine prisoners. Subsequently, they engaged in a more sustained action to put an end to the 'persecution of MSM in Senegal and the promotion of greater respect for their dignity'. Their strategy for promoting an environment of tolerance towards homosexuality is based on building alliances with Christian leaders and Muslim moderates, journalists, representatives of public authorities, politicians and intellectuals. In addition, they conduct training programmes to reinforce the skills of those involved in advocacy.

Homosexuality and AIDS

The approach adopted by the crisis committee is not to frame the debate about homosexuality in terms of human rights or to advocate for the decriminalisation of homosexuality. The emphasis, rather, is on issues of public health: the safeguarding of the achievements of the fight against AIDS; respect of the right to health; and ensuring support for homosexuals through access to treatment services and prevention. It is in this dimension of public health that the committee seeks to promote religious and cultural discourses of tolerance and non-violence.

MSM are trained to enable them to handle advocacy themselves. Journalists are also targeted to inform them of the realities of homosexuality in Senegal, to allow them to reflect the issues related to the fight against AIDS, and to provide parameters for analysis that strengthen their approach to the issue. Health service providers are another group that have to be addressed, to ensure better management of MSM in prevention and treatment of HIV/AIDS. Similarly, police services accused of violent attitudes against the group and members of the judiciary system are also targeted.

Approaching the issue of homosexuality through the fight against AIDS can be explained by the fact that the visibility of this group has been favoured in recent years through their involvement in advocacy and prevention of this epidemic. Previously grouped in informal networks, in the early 2000s they began to better organise themselves together to act as partners with organisations involved in the response to AIDS. From this associative movement has emerged a trend where many of those involved openly acknowledge their sexual orientation. A study conducted by Poteat et al (2011) on the impact of repression against the gay community reported that they aspire to full recognition of their rights and more respect for their privacy. But there is a potentially dangerous trend emerging, in which prominent members of the community are for the moment opposed to these aspirations.[3]

During the International Conference on AIDS and STIs in Africa (ICASA), held in November and December 2008 in Dakar, the announcement of a proposed march to demand better treatment of homosexuality in the context of the fight against the epidemic provoked indignation and even threats from some religious circles. The march did not take place, but the crystallisation of homophobic sentiment was exacerbated by open violence which erupted after the arrest of the nine people in December which, upon their sentencing to eight years in prison, led to an open hunt for homosexuals.

The coincidence of timing between the staging of ICASA and the arrests reinforced the idea that homosexuality in Senegal was encouraged by external stances and influences. This perception has caused the crisis committee to promote reflection and homegrown reactions against homophobia and to curb the activities of foreign organisations. In February 2010 a delegation from the International Gay and Lesbian Human Rights Commission (IGLHRC), who came to Senegal for the launch of the organisation's report on homophobic violence, were persuaded not to release the report publicly. MSM who testified in the report following the violence of 2008 and 2009 shared this opinion, fearing that new condemnations from foreigners might revive the hostility towards their community. The public release of a Human Rights Watch report scheduled for November 2010 in Senegal was also cancelled for the same reasons.

Those responsible for the two organisations rallied to this position after a meeting with the crisis committee. They could, however, have met with the Senegalese authorities to present them with their reports, and held meetings with human rights advocacy organisations, as well as groups responsible for fighting against AIDS. The reports they have compiled, which include testimonies from MSM on their experiences with violence and its multifaceted impact, have become useful tools for training and advocacy.

Homosexuality and the media

Since the outbreak of violence in 2008 and 2009, things have calmed down. The same causes do not always produce the same effects. Two people were arrested, tried and convicted in June 2010 for 'acts against nature between two persons of the same sex', but the sentence passed was only three months in prison for both defendants, very different from the 10-year sentence set by a judge a year earlier (HRW 2010).

The minutes of the trial published in the media have not given rise to the expression of homophobia by journalists or in public debates in the mass media. The radical religious circles have not inflamed the issue, a fact which has gone virtually unnoticed. They had played an important role in triggering the violence of past years, a fact that has prompted Codou Bop to consider related political considerations. For her, the fundamentalist Islamic groups had an interest in disseminating such speech in consideration of local elections in March 2009, as a way to consolidate their political position by taking advantage of a phenomenon that focused media attention on them and garnered wide press coverage (Bop 2008).

In their reports, the IGLHRC and Human Rights Watch (HRW), like Cheikh Niang in his study on the processing of information about homosexuality, have accused the press of fuelling the violence triggered by homophobia between 2008 and 2009. Articles and broadcasts have contributed to this, relaying and exacerbating homophobic sentiments through their commentary. But the analysis is truncated, as much of it considers the role of the media in isolation from other sociopolitical determinants. This is not the first time the issue of homosexuality has been discussed in the Senegalese press, but such an outburst of violence was never witnessed before.

In 1999, a parade of gay transvestite supermodels, held in the Saly Portudal tourist resort, made headlines in the newspapers, supported by photographs, without provoking physical attacks against homosexuals. In 2003, a lawsuit between a homosexual and a famous entrepreneur of great renown, amid accusations of blackmail and infidelity, mobilised the media and drew huge crowds for several days of hearings, with a strong presence from the gay community, who came to support one of their own, without any violent reactions from people. Similarly, in June 2002 the newspaper *Frasques* published a special edition on homosexuality, with testimonials and pictures of people who were open about their sexual orientation.

One can also go back to the 16 September 1991 edition of the newspaper *Le Soleil*, in which an article entitled 'Homosexuals: the right to be different?' tried to consider the debate. In their anonymous testimony, three men affirmed their difference ('attracted to men'), the difficulty they experienced in living with this sexual orientation ('leave us alone...!'), but also their determination to exist ('I was always queer...').

In the 10 April 1995 issue of *Le Témoin*, an article entitled 'In the world of homosexuals' was published with a front page photo of a famous homosexual who described his experience and spoke of homosexuality as a practice of 'men like everyone else' and sometimes those of 'high class society'. The newspaper wrote:

> socially, they (homosexuals) do not make any effort to enliven entourages of drianke (ladies), to serve them selflessly without looking to their own future. When they earn their living, they are typically found managing shady 'clandos', where misfits come to drink alcohol for next to nothing, while executives with loosened ties and discarded jackets amuse themselves playing

rabbles, far from their usual circles where they are bound by requirements to show restraint.

Homosexuality is widely perceived in Senegal through such a caricature to generate, according to perceptions, contempt, rejection, indignation or tolerance.

Homophobic violence in 2008 and 2009, although fed by religious beliefs, characterises a certain social orthodoxy, manifested as a form of violence against a state deemed responsible for all forms of disturbances associated with socio-economic crises. The same resentments remain, and the Senegalese authorities are struggling to define themselves around an issue that embarrasses them. In March 2011, a member of the presidential majority, the vice-president of the National Assembly, tabled an oral question inviting the government to explain information published by a local newspaper, *L'Office*, which noted the ratification by Senegal of the Geneva Convention which decriminalised homosexual practices. In his question, he stated:

> Despite the denial made by Minister Coumba Gaye (Minister for Human Rights), this information, insufficiently disseminated, continues to make waves, to the point of inspiring talks during Friday prayers in mosques. This situation has created a stir in the country; I ask the government to come to the National Assembly, to tell its members and the people of Senegal, the truth about this case.

The information was unfounded (BlogMensGo n.d., Siberfeld 2011), but the uproar it caused is a testament to the strength of convictions feeding homophobia in Senegal. Physical attacks have ceased, but the sense of violence remains latent. MSM are determined to silence any event that makes them visible to the public and the media. They have been given the responsibility to not disturb a society that does not accept them, so as not to endanger themselves and not to expose local organisations conducting advocacy, and to restore and consolidate an environment of tolerance.[4]

Homosexuality and human rights

Among homosexual associations there has been some interest in taking on a human rights approach. But whether as expressions of resistance or claims of human rights, such reactions are rare, and even silenced by members of the community itself. It is rather through evolutionary social change, in the hope of arriving pro-gressively at a more open society, that they hope to find greater social tolerance and recognition of their rights.

In fact, even though Senegal has signed conventions and charters that underpin international norms of respect for human rights, the legal texts of the country continue to harbour provisions of law which, even beyond the criminalisation of homosexuality, render illusory the possibility of legal protection for sexual minorities claiming their rights. A climate of fear destroys the open pursuit of the promotion and protection of rights.

Among MSM, evidence abounds of the 'danger' of seeking help from security forces and the law. Their experience indicates that appeals for protection only open the door to further violence. One reports:

They [the police] were beating us morning, noon and night. We had no right to counsel and we were not allowed to make phone calls. The police were constantly telling us that we had no rights because we are impure, and cursed, and that we could not share anything with the others, not even the toilets.

Another testimony tells of the conditions of interrogation by the police: 'The police took our phones and noted the numbers of our loved ones. One of them called my mother and told her, "You know what? Your son is gay!" before hanging up on her' (HRW 2010).

The Senegalese gay scene is still marked by a lack of knowledge and understanding of the law related to sexual orientation. The evident hostility noted among the judiciary compounds the problem of legal redress for the MSM community.

All these factors constrain the involvement that homosexuals might have in the few initiatives taken to promote tolerance towards them or involve them in social debates concerning the rights of sexual minorities.

Notes

1 Men who have sex with men (MSM) is more commonly used than the French equivalent, *'hommes ayant des relations sexuelles avec d'autres hommes'* (HSH), and was used in the original text to describe homosexuals.

2 Evidence obtained from a member of the crisis committee which was established to advocate for the release of convicted MSM. After several weeks of detention, they were released after the Court of Cassation quashed the verdict due to irregularities.

3 This view was affirmed to the author by the leader of one of the main MSM associations in Senegal.

4 As of 23 March 2011, the signatories of the convention numbered 85, with Senegal among them. Other African countries which had signed included South Africa, Central African Republic and Sierra Leone.

References

BlogMensGo (n.d.) 'Un tribunal de Dakar a condamné, le 29 juin 2010, deux hommes à trois mois de prison ferme pour homosexualité', Gayromandie, http://www.gayromandie.ch/Prison-ferme-pour-homosexualite-au.html, accessed 5 December 2012

Bop, C. (2008) 'Sénégal: "homophobie et manipulation politique de l'Islam"', Women Living Under Muslim Laws, http://www.wluml.org/fr/node/4514, accessed 5 December 2012

Comité de crise (2012) 'De l'orientation en temps de crise au plaidoyer à long terme: promouvoir la tolérance et le respect des droits des groupes vulnérables au Sénégal', Dakar, Comité de crise

Crowder, M. (1959) *Pagans and Politicians*, London, Hutchison

Human Rights Watch (HRW) (2010) 'Fear for his Life: Violence against Gay Men and Men Perceived as Gay in Senegal', HRW, 30 November, http://www.hrw.org/en/reports/2010/11/30/craindre-pour-sa-vie-0, accessed 5 December 2012

Icône Magazine (2008) 20 February

L'Office (2011) 23 March

Niang, Cheikh (2010) 'Content analysis of the Senegalese media on the treatment of the issue of homosexuality and homophobia', unpublished study commissioned by Panos Institute West Africa

Niang, C.I., Tapsoba, P., Weiss, E., Diagne, M., Niang, Y., Moreau, A.M., Gomis, D., Wade, A.S., Seck, K. and Castle, C. (2003) '"It's raining stones": stigma, violence and HIV vulnerability among men who have sex with men in Dakar, Senegal', *Culture, Health and Sexuality*, 5(6): 499–512

Poteat, T., Diouf, D., Drame, F.M., Ndaw, N., Traore, C., Dhaliwal, M., Beyrer, C. and Baral, S. (2011) *HIV Risk among MSM in Senegal: A Qualitative Rapid Assessment of the Impact of Enforcing Laws that Criminalize Same Sex Practices*

Siberfeld, Judith (2011) 'Dépénalisation de l'homosexualité: 85 pays signent une declaration à l'ONU', Yagg, http://yagg.com/2011/03/22/depenalisation-de-lhomosexualite-85-pays-signent-une-declaration-a-lonu/, accessed 5 December 2012

28

Queer Kenya in law and policy

Keguro Macharia

On 28 November 2010, Raila Odinga, prime minister of Kenya, said, 'If found [homosexual couples] should be arrested and taken to relevant authorities.'[1] Five years earlier, such a statement would have elicited mainstream silence or approval. This time, however, mainstream newspapers published articles challenging Raila's statement.[2] Professor Makau Mutua, a legal scholar and chair of the Kenya Human Rights Commission, argued, 'the [new] Constitution protects gay rights'. Makau based this statement on two elements of the constitution: it guarantees equal rights and it does not explicitly forbid gay marriage.[3] It is too soon to tell whether Makau's confidence is justified. As with the US and India, sexual minority rights will probably have to be debated through Kenya's law courts.[4]

In this article, I offer one narrative about the state of Kenya's sexual minority rights by examining three intertwined enactments of law and policy: the Sexual Offences Act (2006), the National Policy on Culture and Heritage (2009) and the newly promulgated constitution (2010). In examining these documents and the debates that surround them, I track how Kenyan-ness is defined in relation to sexuality. I argue that we need to understand sexual *minority* rights in relation to sexual *majority* rights. Any attempt to argue for the former without considering the latter risks missing their mutual constitution. I build on cultural theorist Neville Hoad's insightful argument that 'homosexuality' is 'one of the many imaginary contents, fantasies, or significations (sometimes in the negative, sometimes not) that circulate in the production of African sovereignties and identities in their representations by Africans and others'.[5] And I examine how the figure of the 'homosexual' circulates in Kenyan legal and cultural discussions and documents.

The Sexual Offences Act (2006)

In 2006, the Kenya Parliament enacted the Sexual Offences Act. It represented sustained activism over more than a decade by a coalition of organisations including the Federation of Women Lawyers-Kenya (FIDA), the Coalition on Violence Against Women (COVAW), the Child Rights Advisory Documentation and Legal Centre (The CRADLE) and the Centre for Rights Education and Awareness (CREAW).[6] The Sexual Offences Bill first came to public awareness in December 2004, as it was being shepherded into the parliamentary process by nominated Member of Parliament Njoki Ndung'u. Prior to assuming public office, Ndung'u, who has a postgraduate degree in human rights and civil liberties, had worked in the public sector, as state counsel in the Attorney General's office, and in the private sector, including a stint as a political analyst for the Organisation of African Unity. She was also an active member of Kenya's civil society, as a former member of FIDA and a women's rights activist.

The bill created what Michel Foucault terms an 'explosion' of discourse around sexuality.[7] It was the first time that sex and sexuality had been discussed so openly and at length in parliament, in the mainstream media and in online forums. Kenyans discussed courtship and marriage, traditional ritual and gender violence, consent and coercion.[8] As Kenyans debated the (often tenuous) lines across welcome, acceptable and criminal intimacies, they defined (and defended) what constituted normal gendered bodies and sexual intimacies. In this section, I detail how debates around the bill established the family as the target of sexual offences, and draw out the implications for this strategy for sexual minority activism.

Early in 2005, Ndung'u outlined the expansive scope of the bill when she argued, 'it is not just girls and women who can be victims; the law must recognise boys and men too are abused.'[9] By specifying that 'boys and men' were also sexually vulnerable, Ndung'u extended the bill's province to protect a wide range of people, including sex workers and sexual minorities. Certainly, some Kenyans interpreted the bill that way. For instance, the Kenya Episcopal Conference, an association of Catholic churches, supported the bill, arguing, 'There are too many broken bodies, broken hearts and broken minds of children, women and men littering the landscape of Kenya all injured, brutalised and often enough, killed by sexual violence.' However, the conference added, 'Currently, abortion, prostitution and homosexuality are illegal. The Catholic bishops would wish to have assurance that this bill does not repeal existing laws on these matters in such a manner that these evils are introduced through the back door or by default.'[10] The conference worried that the bill might protect sexually marginal figures, prostitutes and homosexuals, and acts that were against Catholic doctrine, such as abortion. Likewise, the Council of Imams and Preachers of Kenya (CIPK) was wary of measures that would legalise homosexuality.[11] These groups wanted parliament to define the segments of the population worth defending.

In addition to religious leaders, other socially conservative groups tried to restrict the scope of the bill and argued that it should reflect Kenyan values. Notably, Wanjiru Muiruri, a member of the Kenya Parents Caucus, claimed that 'progressive human rights activists' probably viewed Kenya as 'an anathema, a pariah, for stubbornly adhering to what they consider traditional and oppressive laws that are discriminatory against gays, and la di da...'. However, laws that potentially protected sexually marginal figures would 'undermine the moral fabric of society and undermine the institution of family in Kenya.'[12] Muiruri wedded sexual practices and institutions to national identity, suggesting that the Sexual Offences Bill was as much about defining proper and improper forms of intimacy as it was about defining proper and improper forms of national belonging. She advocated what queer theorists Lauren Berlant and Michael Warner describe as 'national heterosexuality': 'National heterosexuality is the mechanism by which a core national culture can be imagined as a sanitised space of sentimental feeling and immaculate behavior, a space of pure citizenship. A familiar model of society displaces the recognition of ... systemic inequalities.'[13] Muiruri effaces 'systemic inequalities' when she implicitly claims that 'progressive human rights' risk 'undermin[ing] the institution of the family in Kenya'. In her zero-sum-game model, human rights activism cannot co-exist with 'national heterosexuality'.

In retrospect, Muiruri's implicit argument that the bill was supposed to protect 'the family' signalled a major shift in strategy around getting the bill passed. On 1 April 2006, an article in the *Daily Nation* captured this re-orientation around the family:

> [T]he ladies who met this week under the auspices of the Kenya Women Parliamentary Association had a powerful message for their male colleagues: Support us in this fight against depraved sexual predators, for if they are allowed to continue, it is your daughters as well as ours, your sisters and mothers as well as ours and, increasingly, even your little sons, who will become the next victims.[14]

The *Daily Nation* reports agreed with the parliamentarians, and ended the article thus: 'Those beasts who prey on our daughters, sisters, mothers and wives must be made to pay heavily.' Civil society activists sent SMS messages to male parliamentarians that read, 'Do the right thing by supporting the Bill. You are supporting your wife, mother and daughter and sister.'[15]

This rhetorical emphasis on 'wife, mother' and so on changed the site of vulnerability: sexual offences were no longer what were committed against potentially anonymous girls and women and men and boys; they were committed against the institution of 'the family'. In passing the bill, legislators would be affirming their loyalty and devotion to 'the family'. As queer theorist Lee Edelman has asked, who would dare to be against the family?[16] No longer were parliamentarians being asked to protect any and all people who may have been sexually abused, including prostitutes and sexual minorities; instead, they were asked to defend their kin.

However, this focus on defending the family was costly: male legislators who had opposed provisions on sexual harassment, marital rape and female genital excision argued, disingenuously, that these (and similar) provisions threatened practices of courtship and marital vitality. How, questioned some MPs, would one be able to distinguish between courtship and sexual harassment? This question exposes the contradictions inherent in the bill: legislators sought to protect the conditions that enable heteronormativity, including the formation of proper, and some claimed properly African, gender roles while simultaneously protecting marriage and family from sexual offenders. Moreover, 'traditional' practices such as female genital excision could be defended because, as some MPs argued, they helped to police gender; strategically embracing cultural relativism, advocates for excision argued that it made women marriageable. As long as gendering practices and courtship rituals could be tethered to creating marriages and defending families, they received a pass.

Nor could the bill be perceived to attack gender and sexual practices that happened within marriage. This latter argument came to the fore in debates about marital rape. Even though the provisions against marital rape had been in the initial draft of the bill, available in December 2004, the debate about marital rape gained in intensity in the latter part of April and through May 2006 – parliament passed the bill in the last week of May 2006. Marital rape gained in intensity as a problem the more the bill focused on protecting the institutions of marriage and the family. Then health assistant minister, Enoch Kibunguchy, claimed, 'This bill will break families because it says that one can rape his wife.'[17] Other MPs argued there 'was no way non-consensual intercourse could occur between loving spouses'.[18] In an absurd and tragic irony, the bill set up to protect against sexual offences had been transformed into one that protected the family. As long as the heteronormative family was the unit deemed vulnerable, it could not, simultaneously, be a site within which sexual offences took place. Discussions around marital rape suggested that the bill's ultimate goal was to protect a Kenyan sexuality realised in a patriarchal, heteronormative family.

Proponents of clauses against sexual harassment and marital rape claimed that their biggest opponent in such debates was culture, which was being used as an excuse by tradition-bound men not to change the law. This explanation is only part of the story. As the bill contracted in scope, from trying to protect all the women and girls, men and boys who were sexually vulnerable to defending the heterosexual family, it became practically impossible to include any provisions that might impede the formation of the heterosexual family or that might expose cracks in the façade of the family. The heteronormative limits imposed on the Sexual Offences Act made it impossible to criminalise acts that take place within the sacred space of the heterosexual marriage bed. In protecting the family against invaders from outside

– stranger rapists, prostitutes and homosexuals – legislators could not protect the family from dangers internal to its structure. Nor could they protect the sites of its formation – sexual harassment remains a real threat, as do other forms of gendered and sexual violence designed to create normative bodies and relationships.

From law to policy: the family

In August 2008, Kenya's Ministry of State for Culture and Heritage circulated a draft of a newly formulated policy on culture and heritage. Although not explicitly stated, the policy was clearly a response to the chaos of the post-election violence that rocked the country in January and February of 2008. The official policy was released in 2009. As the 'Overview' to the policy notes, 'Policies that aim at the inclusion and participation of all citizens are guarantees of social cohesion and a prerequisite for peace.'[19] Broadly speaking, the policy has a dual mandate: it attempts to forge unities within Kenya's already diverse communities and it seeks to control the meanings of contact with countries, practices and ideologies that are, ostensibly, foreign to Kenya. It is a proposal, then, that both imagines and tries to produce Kenyan-ness as a form of intimacy that faces internal and external threats.

More explicitly than the Sexual Offences Act, the National Policy on Culture and Heritage (2009) defines the role of the family in relation to Kenyan-ness. Chapter 4 is devoted to 'The Family,' and I cite it in its entirety:

> The foundation of the Kenyan society has always been the family as the smallest unit of society and kinship relationships. However, with the advent of modern culture we have embraced contemporary concepts of family brought about by inter marriages between Kenyans and other nationals.
>
> **Policy statements**
> The Government will work in concert with other institutions to strengthen the family and kinship relations as a foundation for a unified Nation.
>
> The Government will provide easy access to families by developing cultural facilities at local level i.e. community cultural centres, libraries, facilities for performing and visual arts for the benefit of small rural communities, increase

facilities for artistic education from young children, at primary school level.[20]

Chapter 4 is brief, slightly more than 100 words. Like the curt, declarative statements used to issue orders in the military, this brevity not only assumes but constructs Kenyan intimacy as an already decided issue. Brevity, in this instance, functions as a strategy of foreclosure – this statement does not encourage or welcome dialogue. Culture and heritage are anchored in a very specific sexual form, and there can be no legitimate debate about the form of national heterosexuality.

By claiming that the 'foundation of Kenyan society has *always* been the family', (my emphasis), this document rewrites and erases Kenya's urban histories of prostitution, class-based histories embodied in Kenya's very important trade unions, multi-ethnic coalitions that function outside of kin-based frameworks, and the violent histories of colonialism that forged unities out of disparate groups.[21] Positing this very specific intimate foundation, the heterosexual family, as the central form through which 'Kenyan society' emerged erases the innovative, creative forms of affiliation that were central to creating and constructing Kenya.

'Always' also erases the temporal markers of Kenya's emergence as a nation. Now, whether we choose to privilege colonialism or not is a matter of legitimate debate. We need not anchor the development and emergence of 'Kenyan society' to 1885 or 1952 or 1963.[22] The forms this nation has taken developed much more unevenly, in short and long bursts, and it might well be that 1922, when labour activist Harry Thuku was arrested, is more significant for the emergence of cross-ethnic alliances than 1920, when British East Africa was renamed Kenya. However, in positing 'the family' as that which works around time, as the foundation on which temporality itself rests even as it also resists temporality, this document un-writes the very urgent histories we need to understand and disseminate if we are to embrace our rich multi-ethnic, multi-political, cross-class, multi-cultural histories.

Arguing that the modern family – which remains undefined – emerges through 'inter marriages between Kenyans and other nationals', this policy builds on two assumptions. First, it presumes that marriages between Kenyan nationals do not re-define marriage, the family, or Kenyan-ness in any way. Ethnicity, race, religion and class have no intimate specificity. A marriage between, say, a Gikuyu and an Indian, or a Luo and a Kamba, raises no questions; inter-generational marriages are similarly unproblematic, raising no new questions or paradigms. These claims are simply not borne out by Kenya's history.[23] Important ideas of what it means to be Kenyan are anchored in our histories of intimate negotiations. We are constantly creating and re-creating ourselves and Kenyan-ness through our forms of intimate affiliations and filiations. Our innovative intimate lives offer paradigms of how culture and heritage are constantly dynamic and evolving. Positing intranational marriages as static, pre- or anti-modern institutions robs Kenyans of valuable paradigms.

The second major assumption of this statement is that heterosexual marriage offers access to intimate modernity. As recent scholarship demonstrates, forms of intimacy are increasingly adduced as evidence of modernity. States that embrace queer rights, for instance, are deemed to be more modern while states that still criminalise queer rights are considered primitive.[24] Consequently, in framing forms of intimacy as gateways to modernity, this policy document embeds itself within existing paradigms. However, this Kenyan policy limits intimate modernity to heterosexual intimate modernity, refusing the possibility that modern intimacies exist in arrangements quite distinct from married heterosexuality. Married heterosexuality gets defined in terms of culture and heritage, while everything else, single motherhood, abstinence, promiscuity, queer desires and practices, are implicitly marked as a-cultural, a-modern, a-traditional, contributing nothing to history, to the present, and to the future.

All this within approximately 40 words in the introductory paragraph.

It is against this a-historical background that the policy statements are set, and each one merits careful attention.

> The Government will work in concert with other institutions to strengthen the family and kinship relations as a foundation for a unified Nation.

This formulation implicitly opposes those who want to 'strengthen the family and kinship relations' to unnamed others who seek to destroy them. Indeed, this policy statement builds on and buttresses the Sexual Offences Act, by privileging the heterosexual family unit as an object of state surveillance and protection.

To be sure, this statement in support of the family is important, especially if we are to realise the rich possibilities of what it means to be multi-ethnic and multi-racial. Indeed, a concerted government effort to support national integration through intimate means is vital, especially in the aftermath of the turbulent post-election violence, which sundered intimate bonds. We need to construct a national space in which the claims of ethnicity do not have the power to break intimate attachments, a national space in which intimate attachments have the power to re-define ethnic-based politics.

However, if we are to grant intimate attachments such a foundational role in creating and sustaining the nation, then it seems both strategic and logical that our national goal should be to multiply the possibilities for intimate attachment, to recognise both the range and diversity of intimate arrangements we occupy and create. We are not all marrying heterosexuals, and to anchor the country on this foundation risks alienating the many unmarried, but still intimately attached, youth; the women and men who provide intimate services; those of us who remain abstinent or celibate; and those of us who experiment with gender and sexuality in a range of ways. We need to realise the potential of the variety and diversity of intimate arrangements we occupy, not foreclose their possibilities to produce national cohesion, or what Walt Whitman terms 'adhesion'.[25]

Unlike the first policy statement, which is relatively clear, the second is garbled, unclear, illogical even. It reads:

> The Government will provide easy access to families by developing cultural facilities at local level i.e. community cultural centres, libraries, facilities for performing and visual arts for the benefit of small rural communities, increase facilities for artistic education from young children, at primary school level.

On a purely syntactical level, the sentence lacks a clear predicate. To whom will the government 'provide easy access to families' and for what purpose?[26] Yet, to dismiss the sentence based on its syntactical idiosyncrasy risks missing what it suggests, no matter how clumsily.

Briefly, it appears that 'cultural facilities' contain families – that is where one finds them, where they are constructed, and where they circulate. The aim of cultural facilities is thus to 'contain', in the sense of restrict and seal in, ideas of what families are. It is from 'culture', as created in 'cultural centres, libraries, facilities for performing and visual arts' that we receive 'easy access' to families. In short, these cultural institutions, created or supported by the Ministry of Culture and Heritage, have as a primary mandate the creation of intimate spaces of attachment. They teach us what appropriate intimacy looks like, how families function. Cultural spaces and institutions are, thus, not designed to innovate new social and intimate arrangements, nor should they challenge our pre-conceived ideas about appropriate intimacy.

What seems especially striking about this list of cultural facilities is how they manage and circulate knowledge: from the performing arts, including local community-based theatre, to libraries that store and disseminate knowledge, to the visual arts, 'culture' should provide 'easy access to families'. Artistic, cultural and literary (in the broad sense of written) works should at all times provide 'easy access' to the family and be, to use an Americanism, 'family friendly'. If inadvertently, this section recognises the relationship between the imagination and intimate innovation: intimate acts and arrangements can be created, fashioned and re-fashioned. In contrast, government-sponsored culture seeks to arrest unruly imaginations that might foster queer inclinations. Artistic and literary depictions that challenge the form and function of the narrowly defined family are, presumably, a-cultural, and worse, challenges to producing a 'unified nation'. It is important to realise what is at stake here: nothing less than the unity of the nation. Those who critique this policy are, consequently, not only 'against family', they are against a 'unified nation'.

The scope of this statement is incredible, for these specific cultural spaces, libraries, cultural centres and museums have offered refuge and solace to many isolated queer and questioning folk. We have looked for ourselves within the pages of medical books, psychiatry textbooks, dictionaries, encyclopaedias; have recognised ourselves in Radclyffe Hall, James Baldwin, Oscar Wilde, Shakespeare; have felt intimately connected as we watched plays, movies, ballets; have learned what to call ourselves, how to name and re-name ourselves, how to occupy the world as part of it, even when isolated. To then identify such spaces as hetero-cages, spaces of containment, is to erase possibility, to magnify loneliness, to enshrine impossibility as the condition of queerness.

It is especially noteworthy that two groups are mentioned: rural communities and young children, presumably those who have not been corrupted by the deracinating effects of urban modernity, those who have not been infected with intimate otherness. As constructed, rural communities and young children bear the burden of intimate memory. Rural communities are especially important because they continue to be regarded as keepers of tradition, in memory if not necessarily practice. In this document, 'rural communities' are implicitly distinguished from those who marry 'foreign nationals' and thus innovate modern forms of the heterosexual family. Rural communities become intimate museums, devoted to maintaining 'traditional' forms of intimacy that, in this document, are robbed of their diversity and heterogeneity.

In rushing to protect 'rural communities' from the intimate disruptions of modernity, this policy erases the histories of intimate and erotic innovation that are a rich part of Kenya's multi-ethnic heritage. Gone are the gender-bending practices in which biological women functioned as cultural men; erased are the woman–woman marriages practised in a range of groups; muted are the practices of partner sharing within age groups; censored are the inter-generational relationships that are central to growing up rituals.[27] I return, once again, to the brevity of this chapter, which assumes that Kenya's intimate histories need neither elaboration nor consideration, that terms like 'family' and 'kinship' exhaust how we have lived and constructed our intimate lives. This silence renders a-cultural what should be deeply cultural, a-historical what provides texture to history, a-specific what enables multi-ethnic specificity.

By juxtaposing rural communities and young children, this policy statement implicitly aligns the two, infantilising rural communities and de-urbanising young children. Both groups, this document suggests, should be protected so that they, in turn, can protect us by modelling for us how proper heterosexual intimate arrangements should function.

Despite and because of its brevity, this chapter merits the attention of gender and sexual activists. This chapter and the policy it contains are not laws. However, enacted as official government policy, this chapter could be marshalled in creating repressive laws. Anti-feminist and anti-queer constituencies may draw on this official definition of intimate culture and heritage to advocate repressive and punitive laws.

Combining law and policy

In this final section, I return to Makau Mutua's confident assertion that the newly enacted constitution protects gay rights and re-evaluate it in light of the recent history I have outlined so far. To briefly recap my argument: since debate started in earnest about the Sexual Offences Act in 2005, Kenyans have passed a series of laws and policies that wed national belonging to heterosexuality and that pledge to protect the heteronormative family; national heterosexuality has been increasingly protected in law and promoted by policy. Heterosexual marriage and heteronormative families have been so sutured to the nation that an attack on either or both is considered an attack on Kenyan-ness. Simultaneously, law and policy have implicitly defined non-normative forms of gender expression and sexual practice as threats to the family, as that against which the family must be defended.[28]

In 2007, the year following the passing of the Sexual Offences Act, Amos Wako, Kenya's then attorney general, introduced a marriage bill into parliament.[29] Officially, as Judy Thongori, a family lawyer, explained, the bill would help to harmonise Kenya's patchwork of laws that recognised multiple forms of marriage, including religious, civil and customary.[30] Unofficially, the bill responds to the anxieties provoked by debates around the scope of the Sexual Offences Act and is a national response to international activism on gay marriage.

This unofficial capacity is made explicit in the definition of marriage in clause 2.3: 'Marriage means the voluntary union of a man and a woman intended to last for their life time.' Not once in the entire bill is same-sex marriage or any other queer variation mentioned. Mutua has argued that the absence of prohibition implicitly suggests approbation: 'As any average first year law student knows, a liberty or freedom that is not prohibited is permitted.'[31] However, an interview conducted with Njoki Ndung'u soon after the Sexual Offences Act was enacted offers some insight into the relation between the unsaid and the unlegislated: 'There were claims from some conservative religious quarters that the Bill sought to legalise same-sex relations and abortion. This surprised me because knowing the sensitivity of these topics in Kenya, I had gone out of my way to ensure that the Bill did not appear to address these issues.'[32] For Ndung'u, the unsaid is part of what Haitian scholar Michel-Rolph Trouillot calls 'the unthinkable'.[33] What is neither permitted nor forbidden is effaced as a historical possibility.

Even more telling, the language and intent of the marriage bill were folded into the new constitution. Section 45.1, in chapter 4, on the Bill of Rights, reads, 'The family is the natural and fundamental unit of society and the necessary basis of social order, and shall enjoy the recognition and protection of the State.' Section 45.2 continues, 'Every adult has the right to marry a person of the opposite sex, based on the free consent of the parties.' The juxtaposition of these two sections delimits what we mean by family, sex and gender. In the draft constitution, 'family' is not a metaphor for relations of care between individuals, but is a heterosexually reproductive institution secured through blood. The constitution does not recognise fictive kinship relations based on class and other affinities. Second, this section recognises only two gendered and bodily configurations: adults come in binary pairs, the 'man' and 'woman' mentioned explicitly in the marriage bill.

The genius of this law is that it renders in affirmative, positive terms what other forms of legislation elsewhere in Africa, Nigeria and Uganda, for instance, have tried to render in negative terms. It does not ban gay marriage. It promotes heterosexual marriage. However, this affirmative legislation echoes, in spirit, the negative legislation that has raised hackles across the world. Notice, it does not say: Kenya bans homosexual marriage. Nor does it say: Kenya only recognises the humanity of appropriately gendered and genitalised human beings. Rather, it affirms the importance of family and marriage and vows to protect these institutions.

But against whom should they be protected?

It is only when we ask this question that we understand how much these two clauses resemble proposed anti-gay legislation in Uganda. The heterosexually reproductive family must be protected against queers, against men who sleep with men and women who sleep with women and against trangender and intersex individuals who disrupt the neat gender binary that anchors the nation.

My goal in this essay has been to begin tracing how intimate life is structured across Kenyan law and policy. In doing so, I have focused not on laws and policy that are explicitly anti-queer – be that anti-homosexual or anti-trans – but, rather, on those laws and policy that, while seemingly indifferent to queer bodies, desires and practices, actually rely on those bodies, desires and practices to anchor their own normative being.

Notes

1   Lucas Barasa (2010) 'Kenya PM orders gays' arrest', *Daily Nation*, 28 November, accessed 1 January 2011.

2   See Macharia Gaitho (2010) 'Mr. PM, the Bill of Rights you fought so hard for covers gay Kenyans too', *Daily Nation*, 29 November, accessed 1 January 2011; Lukoye Atwoli (2010) 'Homophobia only serves to spread homosexuality', *Daily Nation*, 4 December, accessed 1 January 2011; Rasna Warah (2010) 'Raila owes Kenyans an apology, not denial, over statement against gays', *Daily Nation*, 5 December, accessed 1 January 2011.

3   Makau Mutua (2010) 'Why Kenya's new constitution protects gays', *Daily Nation*, 11 December, accessed 1 January 2011.

4   The ruling in India merits close scrutiny by African queer activists. The full text is available at http://www.sacw.net/article985.html.

5   Neville Hoad (2007) *African Intimacies: Race, Homosexuality, and Globalisation*, Minneapolis, University of Minnesota Press: xvi.

6   For a history of the bill-making process, see W. Onyango-Ouma, Njoki Ndung'u, Nancy Baraza and Harriet Birungi (2009) *The Making of the Kenya Sexual Offences Act, 2006: Behind the Scenes*, Nairobi, Kwani Trust.

7   Michel Foucault (1978) *History of Sexuality*, trans. Robert Hurley, New York, Vintage: 17. A copy of the final bill can be found at http://www.mzalendo.com/Bills.Details.php?ID=1.

8   See, for instance, the blog post and ensuing discussion from the blog
    'What an African woman thinks', at http://wherehermadnessresides.
    blogspot.com/2006/05/sexual-offences-bill.html; Owino Opondo (2005)
    'MPs back tough new penalties for rapists', *Daily Nation*, 28 April; Emman
    Omari (2005) 'Apprehension as MPs vote for castration bill', *Daily Nation*,
    28 April; Ory Okolloh (2005) 'Rape: focus on the victim's needs', *Daily
    Nation*, 9 May; Rosemarie M. Onyando (2006) 'Cultural values, my foot!
    This is rape', *Daily Nation*, 28 April; Odhiambo Orlale (2006) 'Members
    cast fear aside to discuss taboo subject', *Daily Nation*, 30 April; Billow
    A. Kerrow (2006) 'Islam quite comfortable with sex bill', *Daily Nation*, 4
    May; Emmo W. Opoti (2006) 'Sexual bill won't stop rape; toss it out', *Daily
    Nation*, 9 May; Chris Foot (2006) 'Sex bill unjust and nonsensical', *Daily
    Nation*, 9 May; Oyunga Pala (2006) 'Why we must embrace this bill', *Daily
    Nation*, 13 May; Alexander Eichener (2006) 'An offence against humanity',
    KenyaImagine, 30 November. All accessed 10 June 2010.
9   Mwangi Githau (2005) 'MP's campaign to stem tide of sexual offences',
    Sunday Nation, 13 March, accessed 11 June 2010.
10 Kenya Episcopal Conference, 'Statement on the sexual offences bill',
    http://www.kec.or.ke/news.asp?ID=7, accessed 3 January 2011.
11 Athman Aram and Mathias Ringa (2006) 'Muslim Council supports
    sex bill, criticises male MPs', *East African Standard*, 29 April, accessed 3
    January 2011.
12 Wanjiru Muiruri (2006) 'There's hidden agenda in sex crimes bill', *Daily
    Nation*, 28 March, accessed 3 January 2011.
13 Lauren Berlant and Michael Warner (1998) 'Sex in public', *Critical Inquiry*,
    24(2): 549.
14 *Daily Nation* (2006) 'Join Forces on Sex Bill', 1 April, accessed 3 January
    2011.
15 *Daily Nation* (2006) 'Engrossing debate as sex bill is brought to the house
    of the floor', 30 April, accessed 3 January 2011.
16 Lee Edelman (2004) *No Future: Queer Theory and the Death Drive*, Durham,
    NC, Duke University Press.
17 Kennedy Lumwamu and Tom Matoke (2006) 'MPs take sex bill war
    home', *Daily Nation*, 1 May, accessed 4 January 2011.
18 Owino Opondo (2006) 'House passes sexual offences bill', *Daily Nation*, 1
    June, accessed 4 January 2011.
19 Kenya Government (2009) *National Policy On Culture and Heritage*,
    Nairobi, Government Printer: 1.
20 Kenya Government (2009): 32.
21 See Luise White (1990) *The Comforts of Home: Prostitution in Colonial
    Nairobi*, Chicago: University of Chicago Press, and Tabitha Kanogo (2005)
    African Womanhood in Colonial Kenya, Oxford, James Currey.
22 1885 was the date of the Berlin Conference, the infamous Scramble
    for Africa; 1952 was the 'official' start of Kenya's nationalist struggle,
    in which the Mau Mau took a foundational role; and in 1963, Kenya
    achieved independence from the British.

23 Within Kenya's post-independence history, the most famous case on the complications of inter-ethnic marriage was that staged between the widow of S.M. Otieno, Wambui Otieno, and his clan members. See Patricia Stamp (1991) 'Burying Otieno: the politics of gender and ethnicity in Kenya', *Signs* 16(4): 808–45; April Gordon (1995) 'Gender, ethnicity, and class in Kenya: "Burying Otieno" revisited', *Signs* 20(4): 883–912; David Cohen and E.S. Atieno Odhiambo (1992) *Burying S.M.: The Politics of Knowledge and the Sociology of Power in Africa*, London, James Currey. More recently, Wambui Otieno has also been the focus of controversy for marrying a man several years her junior. See Grace A. Musila (2005) 'Age, sex and power in modern Kenya: a tale of two marriages', *Social Identities*, 11(2): 113–29.

24 Neville Hoad (2000) 'Arrested development or the queerness of savages: resisting evolutionary narratives of difference', *Postcolonial Studies*, 3(3): 133–58; and Cindy Patton (2002) 'Stealth bombers of desire: the globalisation of "alterity" in emerging democracies', in Arnaldo Cruz-Malavé and Martin F. Manalansan IV (eds) *Queer Globalisations: Citizenship and the Afterlife of Colonialism*, New York, New York University Press: 195–218.

25 Here, I depart from the standard queer critique that the state should get out of the business of legislating intimacy. While I acknowledge the many problems of state-sanctioned intimacy, I am also wary of approaches that alienate the state, approaches that may not be appropriate or possible in a space such as Kenya.

26 To be fair, the sentence might be complete and coherent, but my disbelief at its naked heterocentrism forces me to read it as incoherent. This is what is properly called an 'interested' reading.

27 See Wairimu Ngaruiya Njambi and William E. O'Brien (2000) 'Revisiting "woman–woman marriage": notes on Gikuyu women', *NWSA Journal*, 12(1): 1–23.

28 Even non-identity based categories, such as men who have sex with men (MSM), threaten the family, as Andil Gosine (2009) explains in 'Monster, womb, MSM: the work of sex in international development', *Development* 52(1): 30:

> The transgressions of the MSM are many. He breaks legal codes forbidding sodomy and homosexuality, undermines the institution of the heterosexual marriage through his participation in sexual acts that undermine it (since many, if not most MSM, are married men), and he disrupts hetero:homosexual frameworks, through his refusal to perform or attach himself to a fixed sexual identity. These practices are all requirements of dominant Euro-American forms of sexual regulation. Indeed, what is particularly interesting about development work conducted in the name of protecting the MSM (or protecting society from him) is its emphasis on protecting key features of Euro-American sexual regulation practices: the

heterosexual couple, the public declaration and reification of identity and state-mediation of sexual practice.

29 A draft of the bill is available at http://www.mzalendo.com/Bills.Details.php?ID=40.

30 Caroline Njung'e (2009) 'Kenya marriages face drastic makeover', *Daily Nation*, 1 May, accessed 7 January 2010.

31 Mutua (2010).

32 *Reproductive Health Matters* (2007) 'Legislating against sexual violence in Kenya: an interview with the Hon. Njoki Ndungu', 15(29): 150.

33 Michel-Rolph Trouillot (1995) *Silencing the Past: Power and the Production of History*, Boston, MA, Beacon Press: 70–107.

Nhorondo – mawazo yetu: tracing life back: our reflections – life story

Zandile Makahamadze and Kagendo Murungi

We are old friends. We met at the first African International Lesbian and Gay Association (ILGA) conference in 1999, in Johannesburg, South Africa. We came from different backgrounds but ultimately have the same purpose; our futures became woven as we went on to build what has become a life-sustaining family friendship. Our story begins at the point of our meeting, with the issues and circumstances that led us both to be in Johannesburg that September 1999.

Zandile Makahamadze is the ex-chairperson and advocate for women's involvement and programmes at Gays and Lesbians of Zimbabwe (GALZ), and Kagendo Murungi is the founding Africa programme officer at the International Gay and Lesbian Human Rights Commission (IGLHRC). It is our hope that our shared lessons from the past 15 years as lesbian, gay, bisexual, transgender and gender non-conforming (LGBTGNC) African activists will increase the visibility of US-based activism and specific formative moments in organising on the continent. We also seek a grounded sense of unity with fellow activists and initiatives in Africa and are inspired to participate in the creation of resources for the sustained development of versatile movements.

The mid-1990s marked our entry into the realm of social justice activism for African LGBTGNC liberation. Our entry points were different, Zandile then having been based in Harare, Zimbabwe, and Kagendo in New York, US. Zandile became involved with GALZ through the process of exploring her sexuality and was active with the organisation from 1997 to 2002. Kagendo, having joined the IGLHRC contingent to the UN Fourth World Conference on Women in Beijing, China, was one of the organisers of daily activities at the lesbian tent at the NGO forum in Huairou, China, and subsequently took a job at IGLHRC, where she served alternately as a staff member and consultant between 1996 and 2003.

Zandile served as a board member and Africa regional representative at the ILGA from 1999 to 2002, while Kagendo served on the International Grants Panel of the Astraea Lesbian Foundation for Justice between 1996 and 2001. We both have a history of involvement in Uhuru-Wazobia, an African LGBT organisation based in New York, of which Kagendo was a founding member, and with Liberation for All Africans (L4AA), an ad hoc committee of African LGBTGNC people and allies in New York.

Past work

Kagendo: Why did you join GALZ and what was the impact of your participation as a black lesbian?

Zandile: Where I grew up you were either a woman or a man and had to be married to the opposite sex. I didn't fit into those categories so I was always curious and wanted to find out more about myself. I discovered GALZ in 1995, by coincidence at the Zimbabwe National Book Fair. President Mugabe had referred to homosexuals as 'lower than dogs and pigs' and called for them to be banned from the fair. Circumstances prohibited me from joining GALZ until 1997. I was in a very violent situation, living with the father of my two children who had raped and impregnated me with my first child at 14. No one could take care of me and this man forced me to live with him. I was dealing with a lot of trauma from being raped and abused mentally, physically and psychologically. In 1995, the Zimbabwe Women Writers offered me a full-time job, which helped me financially to get out of my situation, and two years later I was involved with GALZ. I joined because I was looking for people who identified like me in terms of my sexuality.

It was very exciting because that's what I had been looking for. I made a difference for other women, by making the place more accommodating, comforting and enjoyable. But it wasn't easy because GALZ had its own ways of operating; it didn't really welcome black lesbians or women in general. It had its own judgments, which proved to be stressful when I got more involved with the organising. I consoled myself by saying, 'I am here now, it can't get any worse.' I knew what I wanted and was going to get it despite not having support. Keith Goddard, the head of GALZ, was a white man and maybe it was hard for him to embrace lesbians because his views were like most straight men.

Prior to the IGLHRC, had you worked with any lesbian, gay, bisexual, transgender (LGBT) organisations?

Kagendo: At Rutgers University I had been a member of student organisations like the Women of Colour Collective, with Cheryl Clarke as our advisor, and a student-staff person at the Center for Women's Global Leadership. I was also blessed to have had Abena Busia as my thesis advisor. These teachers exposed me to Black and African feminist theory, African women writers, lesbian poetry and global gender rights organising, so I had a strong identity as an African feminist.

My undergraduate thesis was on representations of African lesbians in literature by African women writers. I struggled to find evidence of African lesbians and the first documented gay African I found was Simon Nkoli, in an IGLHRC newsletter. I also managed to find a statement by an African lesbian from Mozambique who had testified before the UN in the late 1980s.

In 1995, when I went to the UN Fourth World Conference on Women in Beijing as part of IGLHRC's contingent, I became even more politicised on African lesbian issues, as a coalition of lesbian organisations from around the world lobbied the UN to recognise discrimination on the basis of sexual orientation within the conference platform for action. I then took a position at IGLHRC and began to learn how to apply a human rights approach to LGBT liberation on the continent.

Were there specific strategies that you brought to GALZ and did you have support from any regional or international allies?

Zandile: The strategies that I implemented were from my life experiences. Part of it was also the knowledge I got in GALZ during my early days as an executive member, as well as a vice-chairperson and then chairperson.

I attended my first ILGA conference in South Africa in 1999, and was nominated as a board member to represent the African region. This was my first exposure to international lesbian and bisexual women's workshops. I gained more knowledge and ideas about strategies for women's involvement. I also learned ways of lobbying international alliances to find support within Zimbabwe because our platform as GALZ wasn't working. We wanted to reach out to other organisations and work together. Some organisations started to inform us about public demonstrations they were holding. My work resulted in the increase of women's participation and inclusion of women's programmes in GALZ.

What challenges did you face in your work to establish the IGLHRC Africa programme as an African located outside the continent?

Kagendo: In founding the Africa programme I had inherited a couple of folders containing materials mainly from southern African LGBT organisations and letters from African lesbian and gay individuals scattered about the continent. A lot of LGBT groups outside southern Africa were organised as HIV/AIDS organisations and even 'gay and lesbian' organisations seemed predominantly gay. No real continental network existed yet, so I had to build bridges.

Since the most visible writings about African homosexuality at that time were anthropological texts by white men, I began to collect these writings along with writings from Sister Namibia and other colleagues in Africa and created a bibliography for research on issues of homosexuality and LGBT rights in Africa, which we circulated to university libraries and LGBT allies in the US.

I prioritised reaching out to African women's, HIV/AIDS, human rights and development organisations throughout Africa in an effort to build support for LGBT African issues, even though a lot of times their responses made me feel like a spectacle, when they did respond.

Why did you move to the US and did that change your relationship to organising in Zimbabwe and with international LGBT organisations?

Zandile: My life was threatened because I was so involved in lesbian/bisexual women's rights advocacy. Not realising how much l was endangering myself and my family, I attended events as

GALZ's chairperson and gave public speeches that non-gay people attended. Many people knew of my direct involvement, and wanted to silence me. I relied on public transportation, so they followed me everywhere, shouting profanities, telling me to quit GALZ or else they would get physical. Strangers called on my phone, verbally abusing me with all these threats. I had to change my residence three times to avoid harassment. When my home was attacked I immediately decided to leave the country. I was doing this work as an individual, but my family was also paying the price. I didn't want them to keep paying the price, so I left.

I was living in Waterfalls with my girlfriend when we got attacked, and we went to the police to file a report. The officers refused to take our report; they said that they knew we were lesbians, and told us that they already knew where we lived. They accused us of causing these attacks on ourselves and said they weren't going to waste their resources by letting us make a report. I asked them how we were causing these attacks, and they said it was because of how we lived our lives. They also said that if we lived like everybody else, whatever was happening would stop. They asked why we were sleeping with women, and also said because of that they were not going to protect us since we were instigating these attacks.

Without protection it became impossible to remain in an unsafe country; I finally visited my sister and her husband and told them about my decision to leave Zimbabwe. I asked them if they could take care of my children since I couldn't depart with them. They agreed and made arrangements for them to continue schooling. I resigned my job and went to the Netherlands ILGA conference in 2002. I was heartbroken that my family was now apart and I knew that it was going to take time for us to reunite.

My decision also affected my relationship with GALZ. I was still willing to work with the organisation as an active member outside the continent. I had proposed several ways to Keith, who had originally agreed, but all of a sudden he changed his mind. I was shocked because I didn't know how the change came about. When I contacted other GALZ members they didn't respond. I then realised that they didn't want to have anything to do with me, and was hurt. I felt so abandoned by this organisation and all that I had done for it.

As an African regional representative, I wrote a resignation letter to the ILGA. The secretary general, Kursad Kahramanoglu, was very supportive and told me that I didn't have to resign. I told him that I needed to step aside and focus on rebuilding my life and then return later. I contacted several organisations in the USA, but I realised that their politics were more advanced than mine. They were in the stages of lobbying the government, while I was still struggling to be recognised by the Zimbabwean government. I decided to focus on myself, with my life, and without certain worries.

Did you encounter difficulties because of your African identity while working as a staff person at an international LGBT human rights organisation?

Kagendo: It was mind-boggling managing all the contradictions I faced. In the context of human rights advocacy, the people whose rights are being advocated for are cast as the content providers (African LGBT victims) and the advocates are cast as the authoritative producers of knowledge from that content (white and/or male citizens of the US or Europe). In this paradigm, to be an African immigrant human rights advocate is self-contradictory.

As a staff person at a US non-profit, I was compensated for my movement work. I didn't realise how challenging it would become to generate resources to maintain a tangible ongoing relationship to LGBT organising in Africa as an African in the US working outside the non-profit industrial complex.[1]

How do you view your role in the African LGBT movement as an African in the US?

Zandile: In their eyes we don't exist, but we can play a very vital role when it comes to African LGBT issues. I remember in 2007 we went to the South African consulate in New York to protest against the rape and murder of two South African lesbians in Soweto because of their sexual orientation. We had to protest about how wrong it was that these women had been tortured and killed and yet South Africa is the only African country that legalises same-sex marriages. I would like to do something more than just react to what is happening.

What were your experiences as an immigrant in international human rights advocacy?

Kagendo: As an immigrant, movement building was central to everything that I did. There were times when this felt at odds with human rights advocacy as far as it privileges lobbying governments, regional and international bodies. While protective legislation is critical, I kept witnessing LGBT lobbyists from the continent facing tremendous repercussions including being murdered in isolation upon return to their local communities.

I have no doubt that my movement-building approach as an African immigrant in the US at that time helped direct critical resources to activists and organisations in Africa and supported the growth of regional networks. My work at IGLHRC along with my US location led to my term on the international grants panel at the Astraea Lesbian Foundation for Justice.

Present reflections

Kagendo: Based on your history, why is it important for you to have been included in a queer continental publication like this one and what do you think the impact of your visibility will be?

Zandile: The higher authorities in Africa don't acknowledge our existence as LGBT people, so if they hear our views they will look deeper into history and realise that we have always existed in Africa. The publication will be authentic to our existence. It also strengthens those who are going through similar struggles.

As Africans it's important to our work, it also gives hope to many activists. We can't stay in the closet anymore, neither can we be silent about these injustices. We can't let people abuse us. They have to know that we have a right to be.

What do you feel should be prioritised in advocating for change in the African region?

Kagendo: Cultural production is critical because as Africans part of the process of colonisation was the attempted destruction and erasure of our cultures. Part of what was made invisible is the legitimacy of different family structures and sexualities within our traditions. Since bigots and opportunists use 'culture' to erase our existence, part of decolonising 'culture' means creating our own dynamic culture by participating in productions like this publication, which are documenting contemporary African voices on gender, sexuality and liberation. Bringing together more instances of documented African experience and analysis is very important. Creating channels for LGBT African activists to share analysis and strategise without the intrusion of any external 'expertise' on our lives is essential.

Did you have any help when you sought asylum and what have your main sources of support been as an immigrant?

Zandile: I did source a lot of support and am very grateful to have had your personal support throughout this process. Upon my arrival I was helped by a couple in San Diego with room and board. I tried to seek asylum there but couldn't find an attorney to help me. You, Kele and Nguru Karugu from Uhuru-Wazobia, an African LGBT group in New York, sent me some money, which enabled me to relocate to Chicago where another Uhuru-Wazobia member tried to help me to seek asylum, but was unsuccessful. You also asked a staff person from IGLHRC's asylum project to send me a Zimbabwe asylum information packet. Some Uhuru-Wazobia members wrote me letters of encouragement, including Kelebohile Nkhereanye, who used to call me as well as send messages. I contacted Pradeep Singla from the Lesbian and Gay Immigration Rights Task Force, who referred me to my attorney Heather Bertz from the Lesbian and Gay Refugee Advocacy Project. I was in contact with Anjana Suvarnananda from the Astraea Foundation, who referred me to her friend in Connecticut who was going through a divorce and needed someone to care for her 18-month-old son. After three weeks I relocated to Connecticut to take care of him and started my asylum process. I will always appreciate Heather for advocating for me, as well as all those who helped me. My family has been a big source of support throughout my struggles and my eldest sister has always been my source of inspiration. She and my friend from Belgium helped me buy a ticket to the US. My sister, her husband and family as well as my children helped me to stay stronger. They encouraged me to believe in myself.

What price did you pay working as an LGBT African activist in isolated and possibly hostile environments?

Kagendo: There were many sacrifices related to the need to be adaptable and creative for the sake of balancing the personal with the political in the fast-changing, highly charged climate of fighting for LGBT rights in Africa.

As a feminist, it was important that my experiences along with the documented needs and growing knowledge base of LGBT Africans inform the directions and strategies in my work. At one point I found it strategically necessary to use an alias in my work. This sort of autonomy in our self-identification is essential for our own sense of protection and peace of mind as LGBT African activists and should be a standard in research, documentation and advocacy on these issues.

At another point I chose to identify by my first name without my surname to symbolise my taking the responsibility of my visibility on myself without implicating my family. I confronted the appearance of being a lone lesbian African activist by claiming the Africa Southwest Asia Network (ASWAN), which appeared on my business cards along with my first name for a strategic, community-identified visibility. I think I was also wrestling with a battle-weary feeling of unbelonging and seeking ways to engage with my co-workers and the broader movement about what experiences and knowledge legitimately inform the strategies we choose in our work.

Have you been active since you have been in the US and can you share any examples of victories and challenges in your work?

Zandile: I have managed to advocate for my asylum case, which was granted a year after my arrival. You and I participated in Uhuru-Wazobia; it didn't last long because I was interested in activism and the space was for social networking. We also formed Liberation 4 All Africans and worked out a plan of action to protest against the ongoing rapes and killings of South African lesbians. We were able to advocate for the South African consulate in New York to receive our letter of grievances, in which we asked the government to intervene and bring the culprits to justice. Lots of individuals and some organisations came out in full force in our support.

What role have others played in helping balance your place in the movement?

Kagendo: We had formed Uhuru-Wazobia, a continental African LGBT support and advocacy group, in New York in 1995, and I was able to seek refuge and solace there while building community. The group was made up of mostly gay men, a small group of lesbians and a few gender non-conforming and transgender people. The recurring internal ideological clash was between those who wanted to be more politically active and those who wanted to remain a social support space. My most grounding relationships were with the feminists in the group, who helped sustain and develop my political analysis, the few men who understood the necessity for organising for gender equity and my fabulous transgender and gender non-conforming folks who kept pushing the boundaries and redefining gender.

A handful of gender non-conforming people formed L4AA, an ad hoc committee to address a spate of rapes and murders of lesbians in South Africa in 2007. The committee expanded to include None On Record, Less AIDS Lesotho and IGLHRC. L4AA co-organised a rally outside the South African consulate in New York with the Audre Lorde Project and a large group of trained activists of colour.

Why do you think it's so difficult to qualify for funding as a queer African activist in the US and how do you think this affects our ability to work in relation to the continent?

Zandile: It is difficult because of the standards set by the funders. They need to understand that we have nowhere else to go for funding, we are here, and we are also Africans. We should qualify for something so that we can advocate. Our limited funds should be considered as a high priority because we want to fight for the same issues we have been fighting for while in Africa. There is a limitation to what can be done without funding. Financially we have nothing, we can't keep on taking away from our basic necessities. For our work to be successful we should do it with an open heart, not with reservations. For example, anti-gay legislation in Uganda and all state-sponsored homophobia throughout the continent need to be challenged. We don't have the resources to protest about such injustices, but every issue needs a voice. The voice becomes stronger when it's coming from all corners of the world.

Do you feel like you agree with the current LGBT African struggles as opposed to the struggles in the US? How do you advocate in both movements?

Kagendo: Aside from all the general similarities of walking in the world as Africans, we are ultimately fighting for the same thing: to de-stigmatise our existence and popularise our struggle in our communities for the sake of equality, justice and peace. We're working to create autonomous resources for change, develop new ideologies and empower ourselves. I feel that while we have similarities, we haven't compared notes yet. Our everyday challenges may be different, depending on individual class positions, for example, but the philosophical and ideological challenges we face are the same. I think the big obstacle is that we haven't had a chance to reveal the actual substance of ourselves to each other and exchange ideas directly to discover how much we share in common, identify and understand what is really different, and discover a whole new set of resources with which to move forward jointly.

When I think about how I advocate in both movements, the main way that I've always advocated is by finding different ways to be visible, to make sexual orientation visible, to make gender identity visible, advocating for the right to dissent, the right to advocate, the right to self-determine and to continue to fight tooth and nail for direct connections between Africans in the diaspora and Africans on the continent.

Practical tools

Kagendo: What do you think the link is between spiritual practice and social change?

Zandile: The two interlink because spiritual practice advocates for social change. Spirituality always considers the well-being of others and also becoming better people. Society has set itself up to ensure it has the final say; it punishes those who don't abide by its social 'norms'. This approach affects anyone who doesn't fit its categories of normal. That's why we advocate for change so that society will change its ways.

I sustain myself as a spiritual being through following the Christian beliefs with which I was raised. I read the Bible and pray. I also try to live in harmony with myself, as well as my surroundings. I hope that one day we are all going to embrace each other and be non-judgmental.

How did you stay grounded and focused in your initiatives as an advocate for human rights and social justice?

Kagendo: I realised in a conversation with one of my spiritual teachers, a Ugandan Buddhist monk named Bhante Buddharakkhita, that for many years I hadn't been breathing. In doing human rights work, you have to react to so much negative energy every day.

When I started doing that work, my self-care was out of balance with my work since I was working sometimes 16-hour days because I was overwhelmed by the sheer volume, violence and urgency of the cases and the knowledge that my community was under attack. I realised that I had to work an eight- to nine-hour day and build relaxation and movement into my weekly schedule or I was going to keep burning out at shorter intervals.

The thing that really hit me when I started meditating is that you can't possibly advocate for someone else's justice when you don't have peace in your own mind. So meditation and studying the Dhamma is part of my practice of staying mindful, focused and grounded, and telling stories is also part of it.

How have you healed from personal and political crisis over the past 15 years, and have you found networks of support for yourself both in Zimbabwe and the US?

Zandile: I have healed myself by acknowledging that I did my best to create changes in Zimbabwe's LGBT movement and also through sharing my struggles with family and friends. I wrote short stories, and drew self-expressive sketches about these struggles. I was able to get counselling during the asylum process, which was a great step forward. Counsellors helped me to replace maladaptive behaviour with new habits. I networked and got support from others, mostly from you, Kagendo and Kele. You both restored my faith in the movement and made me realise that there are other things to focus on rather than being angry. My sister visited to strengthen me; I mostly called and emailed her to talk about my crisis. She taught me to meditate and take long walks for health reasons. My family was the most powerful tool; they helped me come to terms with my struggles. My partner Davita and the kids love me and that's the cream that tops it up. I am still working on better and healthier ways of furthering my activism.

How have you grown as an advocate of change considering your experiences and accomplishments over the past 15 years?

Kagendo: Possibly the main thing I've learned is a true sense of responsibility to myself, my family (birth and chosen), country and continent and as a citizen of the world. There is a sense in which my personal development occurred alongside the growth of the LGBT African movement so that the movement's coming of age has marked different stages of my adulthood. Through my changing relationship to advocacy I became more and more proactive in structurally supported ways, either by shifting the structure or building a whole different structure. I learned to always apply my lived experience in my approaches to the work, and that utilising the same techniques without trying any new ideas won't fundamentally change the movement in ways that we want. I learned that I had to keep finding ways to bring my own experiences to the work and make myself visible in African liberation: my movement and my passion.

I have learned that it is important to detach in order to regain perspective when bitterness or frustration takes root because that internalised anger too easily becomes self-destructive, feeding isolation and fear. One of my spiritual teachers, a *sangoma* named Prudence Mabele, always reminds me that it's not a matter of evil people versus good people but rather negative energy versus positive energy, both of which can be accessed by anyone.

Another of my teachers, Jacqui Alexander, taught me that if the suppression of our spirituality was involved in the process of our colonisation and enslavement as African people then spirituality must be part of our liberation movements as well.

If you're breathing, conscious and mindful enough you can choose what energy to direct in response to anything external that occurs. I learned that it's important to take time away from the intensity of the work and spend time with trusted friends, get enough rest, meditate, take long walks on the beach, swim, dance and create art. I have to remember that I'm a daughter, sister, cousin, aunt and grand-aunt and I need to give energy to understanding my role and responsibilities as a whole person.

Have you had access to spaces and resources to develop your activism and learning as a queer African activist in the US?

Zandile: I had to find help on my own, especially from friends and family. My friends Lauren and Carol informed me about educational programmes where I acquired a high school diploma, and was able to get a government grant for an associate's degree programme. I will be graduating at the end of this year. I am still working on international publication.

What mechanism did you use to cope with the isolation and lack of access to resources?

Kagendo: One of the biggest ways I've coped with isolation is by finding tools to overcome my own sense of fear when it arises, a fear that would keep me from continuing to push myself and other Africans to fight for equality. At different points you get tired of pushing endlessly and receiving the same kind of ignorant backlash, knowing that it's coming from the state, the media, religious institutions, and even your own family. So I committed myself to using video to document my existence and that of all my communities.

As for inaccessible resources, I think we've been really creative as a community over the years, from personal loans to and from friends including yourself, to fundraising parties, and a couch to sleep on when the need arises. These expressions of the resources we generate from our own labour always challenge me to rethink the definition of movement resources because money itself is just another form of energy that is exchanged. This conversation with you is opening my mind to just how much of a critical resource the work we're doing right now in interviewing each other is for me.

When you look back, is there something that you might have done differently?

Zandile: Maybe I could have tried highlighting differently the importance of lesbian and bisexual women's issues to gay men in Zimbabwe. I could have asked for gender-sensitive workshops; it might have been easier to bring awareness that way, than when everyone is criticising you.

I wish I had better ways of communicating with the African region, and being more connected with them while in Zimbabwe. Probably they could have had better outcomes of their plights; but because of limited funds and resources it was very hard to communicate with them.

I also wish I had had more information about the asylum process before coming here; it would have been less stressful for me.

When you look back, is there something you wish you could have done differently?

Kagendo: I've really been thinking about it and I realise that I would do it all over again because this work has made me who I am. It has transformed my life through intense joy, tremendous pain and endless soul searching. I welcome it as part of my destiny and understand the experiences of this work in the context of all the events in my life since I was born.

Before I got into international LGBT human rights advocacy, I was studying social documentary production. It's not a regret but I wish I had found a way to keep this practice in my life throughout that time. Keeping a video diary of my experiences would have been cathartic and viewing it might have nurtured a better balance between my work and my personal creative life and kept me in touch with a medium that I love.

Note

1   For a definition of the 'non-profit industrial complex', see http://www. incite-national.org/index.php?s=100.

30

Tell the sun not to shine – fiction

Diriye Osman

It was Eid and I had no one to celebrate it with. I needed a sign to point me either east or west. The sign came as a leaflet through my letterbox. It was an invitation to Eid prayer at Peckham mosque. The sign pointed south so I headed there.

At the mosque, everyone was in their Eid best. The Asian and Somali men wore their best *khamiises* in grey and white. The Nigerian men were dressed like *sapeurs* – shirts the colour of flamingos, shoes made from crocodile leather. The Asian and Somali women wore their best *garbas* and *jilbabs* in grey and black. The Nigerian women were dressed like beauty queens – dresses the colour of Fanta, shoes with clear heels. The children all ran around with Nike ticks and leaping Pumas on their backs.

I went to the taps outside to perform ablution. An Asian kid in a dove-grey *khamiis* guided me.

'Go like this,' he said, washing his hands and wrists three times. I noticed he had bite marks on his toffee-brown wrists. I copied him.

'Go like this,' he said, rinsing his mouth three times. I noticed his bottom lip was purple and fat like a plum. I copied him.

'Go like this,' he said, drawing water into his nose and then blowing it out three times. I noticed his nose had a cut the colour of pastrami across its bridge. I copied him.

After ablution, it was time to pray. 'Go,' the boy said. So I went.

I placed my shoes by the door. The mosque smelt of feet, cologne and samosas. The carpet felt like moss and the walls were white. A chipped chandelier hung from the ceiling. The men sat near the imam's podium. There was a partition for the women at the back. I crouched next to a man with *jheri* curls. He had six toes on his left foot. When he wriggled his toes, the sixth one didn't move.

'Eid Mubarak, my brother,' he said.

'Eid Mubarak,' I said.

'I hope you find peace,' he said, sensing my sadness.

'I hope so too,' I said. I wondered if his sixth toe gave him a sixth sense.

The imam called out, 'Allahu Akbar! Allahu Akbar!' Everyone stood up and raised their hands to their ears. Even though the imam's back was turned to me, I recognised his voice instantly. It was Libaan. He was wearing an egg-white *khamiis* and skullcap. His baritone was still as smooth as water.

As he said, 'Allahu Akbar' once more, I remembered the first time we'd met. He had come from Somalia to spend the summer with us in Nairobi. I was 14, he was 18.

The loudspeaker crackled as he now recited Surah Al-Fatiha. His voice swooped and dived like a kite around the Arabic syllables.

I remembered him towering over me. His skin was dark like Oreos. He had two gold teeth. He introduced me to cigarettes. I would choke on the smoke and he would say, 'You'll get there, kid.' Now I smoke 20 a day.

After Al-Fatiha, he recited Surah Lahab.

I remembered giving him my bed and sleeping on the floor. We would stay up late and he would tell me about being a goatherd in Somalia. I told him about my school in Nairobi and how everyone there called me a refugee. 'Next time,' he said, 'I'll come to your school and beat them up.'

When he said, 'Allahu Akbar!' we all bowed.

I remembered the first time I saw him naked. He was sleeping and his bed-sheet had slipped down, revealing his buttocks. My heart pounded. I leant closer. I wanted to touch him but was terrified. I sat next to him on the bed and he didn't wake up. I touched his buttocks with trembling fingers and ran out of the room. When I came back he was still sleeping. I squeezed his buttocks gently and ran out of the room. When I came back he was still sleeping. I tried to finger him but he jumped up and said, 'For fuck's sake! I'm trying to get some sleep!' I ran out of the room.

My face heated up now as he stood up and said, 'Allah hears those who praise him.' I said, 'Praise be to you, our Lord,' in a low tone.

I was afraid he'd tell my parents. But instead the next day he had offered me a Malboro. We snuck out of the back of the house and smoked in silence. When we were done he ruffled my hair and smiled a gold-toothed smile that said, 'Let's not mention this.' I couldn't look him in the eye.

Now he boomed 'Allahu Akbar' and the whole congregation prostrated. He said 'Allahu Akbar' again and we prostrated once more.

Instead of going to bed that night Libaan had lowered himself onto my mattress and slid his hand under my blanket. His hand gripped my penis. I was hard. His movements were slow, deliberate. His palms felt as smooth as buttermilk. He smelt of cigarettes and cherry bubblegum. He stroked me until my thighs were moist, throat dry. When I came, he wiped his hands on his trousers and crawled back into his bed. I went to sleep, satisfied and scared and hopeful.

Libaan called out 'Allahu Akbar' and began reciting Surah Al-Fatiha.

The next day we'd played football with the neighbourhood kids. Libaan kept passing me the ball. Every time he did this, he smiled a gold-toothed smile that said, 'Nothing happened.' He was trying to dodge a life of complications. But at night, he would place his hands, lips, tongue inside my world of complications. We would catch strokes until it was time for morning prayers. And then we would go about our day, wondering if the previous night ever happened.

As the prayer came to an end, Libaan drew his face to the right and said, '*Asalamu aleykum wa Rahmatullah*' and then to the left and did the same. We followed suit.

On the night before he returned to Somalia we lay together on my dirty mattress. I pressed his palm on my lips. He kissed my collarbone. We were desperate to prolong the moment. In the moonlit room I could see him smiling a gold-toothed smile that said, 'Nothing even matters.' As the time for morning prayer came he whispered in my ear, 'Tell the sun not to shine.' I whispered, 'I will if you promise to stay.' He boarded a plane to Somalia the next day.

Now he turned around and gave a lecture but I wasn't listening. All I noticed was his belly, which was round like a basketball. All

I noticed were his cheeks, which drooped like a bulldog's jowls. He still had two gold teeth but the rest were black. His beard had been hennaed until it resembled a bush on fire.

'May Allah bless you and your family on this joyous day,' he was saying. 'May you find peace and comfort and a sense of fulfilment. *Amin.*'

'*Amin,*' the congregation said before getting up and heading for the door. As people filtered out I felt an urge to speak to Libaan.

I wanted to tell him that I once dated an Irishman named Simon.

I wanted to tell him that I saw his face whenever I made love to Simon.

I wanted to tell him that my parents disowned me when I came out to them.

I wanted to vomit these words out.

But before I could, a woman in an ink-black *jilbab* and a young boy dressed in a *khamiis* walked up to Libaan. He hugged the woman and lifted the boy onto his shoulders. That's when he saw me. He tried to smile a gold-toothed smile that said many things: 'Not here, not now,' 'I'm sorry,' 'I'm scared.' But before he could do it, before he could break my heart a million times over, I did what I knew best.

I ran.

31

What's in a letter?

Valerie Mason-John

Using Western labels to identify a queer sensibility is problematic when we try to place the same labels onto the continent of Africa. You cannot look through a Eurocentric lens at Africa and begin comparing. For example, same-sex relationships in Africa often look different to what they look like in North America or Europe.

Most Africans do not have the luxury to leave a heterosexual culture and set up home as two men or two women openly living together in a same-sex relationship. What we may deem to be bisexuality can look different in African countries. It is common for women or men to stay in a heterosexual unit while in a same-sex relationship, not because they necessarily want to, but because if they were to set up home with their lover, they could be attacked, at worst killed, or lose all financial subsistence.

But it is also important to acknowledge that there are African men and women who have created their same-sex communities and do live with their partners discreetly. Ironically, while many of us in the West have the choice to be out or in the closet, it is the same West, specifically England, which introduced homophobic laws in many of our African countries. The Malawi couple who threw a party in December 2010 to celebrate their engagement were under threat of 14 years in prison due to an archaic British law on unnatural acts and gross indecency.

Homosexuality is illegal in at least 37 countries on the African continent. In Uganda,[1] lawmakers are trying to introduce an anti-homosexuality bill that has often been called the 'Kill the Gays Bill'. If passed, this bill would mean that someone found guilty of aggravated homosexuality would receive the death penalty, and any other homosexuality offence would mean life imprisonment. It is therefore impossible to discuss, lesbian, gay, bisexual, transgendered and intersex issues within the same context as in the West.

The immediate concern in many African countries is often about survival, how one can manage to survive in such a hostile climate. The immediate concern for us in the West is same-sex marriage and transgender rights. In countries such as Australia, America, the United Kingdom, Germany, France, Denmark and a few others, where there is some tolerance of same-sex relationships, labels have been a defining part of that culture. These explicit labels, I believe, have been a result of many people having the opportunity and courage to come completely out of the closet. These people can wave a banner, be on television, speak on radio and shout out loud about what their sexuality or gender is and not fear for their lives. This is not the case in Africa. Those who come out of the closet often put their life and family at risk.

I am a second generation African born in England. Although I have visited my country Sierra Leone, and have enjoyed the underground queer community, I can hardly speak of it. I am calling it queer, but in actual fact it is called a gay community, and there are far more men out of the closet than women.

I have grown up with labels all my life. The first I remember was orphan, the second, wog, the third, nigger, fourth, coon, and then it became a bit of a blur. The first queer label put upon me would have been when I was aged seven. I was called a tom boy, and I loved it, was proud of it. It meant I could do anything as well as or even better than some boys. I was a better goalie than most boys of my age, and could climb trees just as high as any boy, and do some of those dare-devil games boys did. I could walk hand in hand and arm in arm with my female friends.

I knew clearly from the age of eight that I never wanted a man near me. I didn't know what it meant then. But after a black male tried to ram his penis inside me, I knew I didn't want it near me again. Of course I had boyfriends as a teenager, but I never had sex with them. I wasn't interested. I was having too much fun with my mates.

When I was 13 I fell in love with a girl who sat in front of me at school. I prayed to God to stop me thinking such evil thoughts. Somewhere I had learnt that this was bad, but I had also learnt that if a boy kissed you and touched your breasts at the same time you could get pregnant. So I had a lot to relearn.

I fell in love aged 18 for the first time with a married woman. I entered into a relationship with her while she stayed in her marriage. I lived in the marital home, with their daughter, and it was at this point I needed to start exploring.

My best friend clocked on and took me to my first lesbian club. It was her way of telling me what I was. But when I entered the bookshop Gay's the Word in London and I saw the word lesbian on the book shelves I felt repulsed. It was like someone was saying I had a disease. The word looked so clinical on all the books that stared back at me. I had an aversion to the word, and could not identify with it. And why should I? The word lesbian derives from a patron god called Lesbos, a whole Greek island was named after him. Admittedly this was where Sappho was born, but the fact remains, we are Lesbians because Sappho was a Lesvian from Lesvos, just like all the other inhabitants of Lesbos who are Lesvians (the V is pronounced as B in English). And so my gut was right; I don't want to be named after a man.

I went to Leeds University in the mid-1980s, and this opened a door to separatism, feminism and left politics. I soon became a dyke – I liked that term. It resonated, and later I learnt that dyke derived from the American word 'bulldyke', and that the word probably came from the African American culture because the word appeared in blues songs of the 1930s, for example Bessie Jackson's 1935 recording of the song 'BD Blues'.

For me the word dyke meant I was up front and in your face about my sexual politics, and I was not going to compromise and wear butch clothes. I could be as femme as I wanted and still be a dyke. There were many of us, and of course it confused the heterosexual community as well as some of the lesbian and gay community. How could we want to sleep with women and wear dresses or fancy clothes? We must be bisexual.

Interestingly, white lesbians coined the term 'lesbian chic' during the mid-1990s, but I had been chic in the 1980s. Many black lesbians had always been chic; they had known no other because in black communities in the UK you had to look good on the streets, whether you were butch or femme or indeed heterosexual.

The black lesbian and gay community in London was most definitely different from the mainstream white lesbian and gay community in the 1980s and 1990s. We listened to reggae, ragga, lovers and dub. We dressed up and rarely down, and we created our own clubs, which were black only. Some of us were tired of being refused entry to gay clubs, and did not want to spend the whole night listening to white music.

The lesbian separatist movement also caused a division between black and white women. The call to curfew all men was not welcomed by the black lesbian community. Our black brothers and fathers were already being regularly hassled on the streets by the police. To bring a curfew against all men would just exacerbate the racism against black men on the streets. It would be inevitable that black men would be singled out if a curfew was introduced.

However, while at university I was a separatist for a while, lived with women and only ever socialised with women. At the centre of my life was a lesbian separatist politic. Then black lesbian separatism confronted me, and I felt torn. I had already let go of some great male friends, and now I was to let go of white women. This was too limiting for me, I think because I had been transracially placed in foster homes and orphanages and had grown up with white carers.

Once I left university and moved to London I became more immersed in the black women's scene and began thinking about my dyke identity within a black British context. In 1982 the late Audre Lorde wrote her autobiography *Zami: A New Spelling of My Name*. Some black British women ditched the labels lesbian, dyke, butch or femme, and took on the new label 'zami'. Audre Lorde had finally given African-Caribbeans a name for their sexuality. In those days I was passing myself as a Caribbean due to the stigma of being African from the continent, but zami didn't really work for me. I liked it but I was happy with my dyke label.

I soon became aware of how attached I was to the labels: black, woman, dyke and feminist. My whole life centred around these labels. They were fixed and dictated how I felt, what I thought, what I ate and who I socialised with. There was a thought police in the community, and to be a dyke I had to be vegetarian and have left politics. To be a black dyke I had to stop socialising with the enemy – white people – and only date black lovers. So I became aware of how limiting my life was becoming.

During the late 1990s I became exposed to queer politics. 'Queer' was initially reclaimed by predominantly white lesbians and gay men as a self definition. 'Queer politics', which was typified by activist groups such as ACT UP and Queer Nation, developed out of anger against the strategy of gay assimilation into mainstream society, which had still failed to win basic rights.

The early 1990s witnessed a wave of queer politics in the UK, with men and women organising together. Separatism was beginning to lose its attraction among the younger generation, and a new lesbian and gay identity was being formed. I was supposed to be liberated. I could go out, pack a dildo down my pants and go out cruising gay men for the night, and have 'raunchy sex'. And I could still have my lesbian politics and not be classified as bisexual. 'Bisexual' was a dirty word once upon a time among the lesbian community, and you hid it or suppressed it through fear of being ostracised in the community.

Queer politics was perhaps the end of the lesbian police, those academics who wrote papers about how lesbians should have sex and who stated penetrative sex was aping heterosexuality. Queer was the beginning of a new lesbian identity within the white communities that many of us black lesbians were part of. Queer politics were liberating for many and it is not surprising that in the UK we began to see a whole drag culture develop.

Drag culture was fun. I could dress up, go on a Diane Torr workshop[2] and learn how to imitate or impersonate a man. Then, everything became serious and some of my mates and lovers were taking it one step further: they could take hormones and experiment with being a male. Some happily transitioned while others flirted with the idea.

Terms like lesbian and dyke began to fall off the agenda. They were restrictive and the community was beginning to discuss gender. The lesbian and gay community included trans men and trans women, and people still wanted to socialise and do politics together. Separatism was becoming something of the past, and some of us were dating trans men. How did that define us? Which category did that put of us in? When your friends or lovers become men you have to make a world where you can all happily exist. The women and men who were transitioning began to create the spaces for all of us to co-exist. Queer seemed the most appropriate label for all of us.

The younger generation, kids in their teens, are happily identifying as queer. The teens I work with tell me that queer means different. You can be lesbian, gay, bi, tri, trans and het and be queer. I feel like queer has gone full circle. As a child growing up in the 1960s and 1970s, queer meant different, odd. It was a word adults used to describe people who didn't live conventional lives. So I was very much aware of queer as a child. The two elderly women who had lived together for years, the man who had been single all his life, the man who was effeminate, were all queer, including the famous Dame Edna Everage.[3]

I began identifying as a Buddhist during the mid-1990s, but soon realised I had just let go of a bunch of labels and had attached myself to yet another. I didn't want to be defined by a label. I wasn't a package that could be put up on a shelf and sold. I just wanted to be me. When someone asks is she or he gay, is that person trans, is this person queer, or are they intersex, these labels and the answers to these questions tell me very little because within them there is much fluidity and flexibility. What does 'he' mean or 'she' mean? They are not fixed, but we try to fix them, and I wanted to unfix myself.

Up until now the most fluid of labels has been queer, I think because it embraces all sexual identities. But then of course there is a danger of forgetting those of us who are oppressed within the queer label. So queer sits comfortably with me for now in terms of defining a lifestyle – but I am more than a lifestyle or, indeed, a sexuality.

No label does it for me. And does it matter? Who are we defining ourselves for? The authorities? The census? Why are labels so important? Once upon a time I was in the category of gay and lesbian, then it changed to lesbian and gay, then lesbian, gay, bisexual, then it became lesbian, gay, bisexual, transgendered, and today it is lesbian, gay, bisexual, transgendered and queer. Labels like zami, mati, which came out of the African-Caribbean culture, never made it onto the mainstream list. But for some black women they were first lesbian, dyke, womanist, woman loving women, zami, mati, afrekeke. The younger black generation seemed to have embraced the label queer, and the ageing politicised too. But of course some are still holding onto the old labels.

In 50 years will the letters SD, and H, be added to the mainstream list? What's in these letters? Sexual deviant and heterosexual. Not sure I will live long enough to find out, but if I do I will definitely be curious with what's in a letter.

Notes

1   theGrio (2010) 'Ugandan anti-gay pastor airs gay porn in church', 18 February, http://www.thegrio.com/news/ugandan-anti-gay-pastor-airs-gay-porn-in-church.php, accessed 10 December 2012.
2   Diane Torr is known for her man-for-a-day workshops. She is an educator, drag king expert and male impersonator.
3   Dame Edna Everage is a TV character created and performed by the Australian comedian Barry Humphries.

Does the label fit?

Liesl Theron

Introduction to cisgender

I would like to start by introducing 'cisgender'. Defining cisgender is to attribute the term to people who are conforming or agree with the gender assigned to them by society, matching their gender identity with their sex at birth. The term cisgender is mostly known and used in the transgender community.

Trans through the eyes of scholars, feminists and others

Transgender, transsexual and gender non-conforming people face oppression in the most tangible way, being on the peripheries of our gendered society. Living in an invariable struggle to validate their existence, and many times being rejected by their loved ones, transgender people constantly face marginalisation. Some feminists critique transsexual people where on the one hand female-to-male (FTM) transsexuals are portrayed as seeking to escape oppression and gain (male) privileges, and on the other where male-to-female (MTF) transsexuals are never fully accepted into womanhood – as their appropriation of femininity is only an act. These notions stem from the approach that a gendered experience or identity can only be allocated to a given sex (Butler 2004: 9). Butler goes on to say that this kind of feminist thinking is ignorant of the risks, discrimination and humiliation trans people endure in their day-to-day lives, from public harassment, lack of access to services and opportunities, to loss of employment and more severe forms of discrimination such as violence and hate crimes.

'Thinking Sex' (Rubin 1999 [1984]) is often seen as one of the foundational texts in queer studies, as Rubin integrates the politics of organising sex and sexual identities and behaviours in society with the hierarchical systems of accepted practices. This value system of approval of sexual behaviour by 'ranking' sexual activity in groups, classes or hierarchies, whether by conservative, liberal religious, secular feminist or patriarchal sectors, finds itself under the critical eye of Rubin's interrogative lens. In Rubin's theory, five ideological formations are used by societies to regulate sex and bodies in addition to sexual essentialism. Intrinsically, transsexualism and transvestism are found at the far edges of all these models, beyond the margins of inclusion. Rubin argues that feminist thought about sex is profoundly polarised and has resulted in many struggles between sub-groups within the larger feminist debate. Sexual liberation has been and will always be claimed as a feminist goal.

In the same light Wilchins argues (2004: 125) that feminism as a 'movement founded to counter the marginalisation and erasure of women – ends up in the paradoxical position of installing its own margins and erasures'. Various individuals have sought shelter and support from the women's movement and feminists, only to later find that their identity as stone butch, transsexual men and women, cross-dressers, intersex, queer youth and many other ways of self-identifying are the grounds for their exclusion (Wilchins 2004: 125). Similarities of antagonism towards trans people have been found in recent queer, LGBTI, women's and feminist spaces in South Africa and the region. Matebeni (2009) concurs with this view in her account of the feminist politics evident during a feminist leadership seminar held by the Coalition of African Lesbians (CAL) in Mozambique in 2008. Trans men and masculine-identifying people who were present at the meeting said that they endlessly joined the struggle for women's rights and LGBT visibility and fight continuously for the issues of the marginalised, yet receive no support or recognition from feminists. It became apparent that African feminism needs to revisit its way of working and offer new solutions to women's movements and feminisms in our continent. 'A clear take-away from the gathering is that the notion of feminism is still both problematic and contentious' (Matebeni 2009: 8).

During events such as at the CAL institute, and at workshops and in informal discussions, it is easy to fall into the trap of imposing on trans people how they should be defined. Without any knowledge or experience of their lives, we dare to set the boundaries of their transition (Cook-Daniels, 1998: 1). Loss of community is a real concern, both for the transitioning person and the partner (Cook-Daniels, 1998: 1), who in the case of male-identifying trans persons is often a mixed-orientation dyad where the FTM's orientation is heterosexual and his female partner defines as lesbian (Brown 2009: 3).

Dangers of homonormativity

Heteronormativity reinforces the ideology of the binary system, where one of two opposites is the only possibility for identity formation. Men/women, heterosexual/homosexual are embedded in such a society. Furthermore, it is based on the assumption that heterosexuality is the only desirable option (Steyn and van Zyl 2009: 3). With this creed goes the appropriate behaviour of the bodies 'trapped' in it, living their daily lives in this either/or world. In August 2007 a woman in Umlazi, KwaZulu Natal was stripped naked and her shack burned down, to 'punish' her for not conforming to rigid gender norms and the expectations of womanhood – she was wearing trousers. She was not lesbian, nor trans. Too little was said and written by women's organisations, LGBT organisations and feminists about this. It did not receive much media coverage either. This incident occurred shortly after the murder of Salome and Sizakele, two lesbians who were tortured, raped and murdered because they dared to transgress the expected sexuality norm. Women's bodies are the site of heteronormative control and 'nature' or 'natural' becomes the tool to organise normativity (Steyn and van Zyl 2009: 3–5). Vulnerable and minority groups are on the receiving end of the invisible power of patriarchy.

The danger of heteronormativity to vulnerable groups and minorities is evident as much as I want to argue that homonormativity leaves a direct threat to transgender, transsexual and gender non-conforming people. The 'acting straight' phenomenon is one of the ways to exclude transgender and transsexual people; many trans people succumb to the pressure to act straight, resulting in self-hate and eventually internalised genderphobia (Wilchins 2004: 17) among gay and lesbian people. The classic expression of some gay and lesbian folk who do not want to affiliate with queer events, such as Pride marches or festivals due to the 'drag queens who are "over the top" and will make us all look like that' syndrome, just shows how embedded transphobia is within gay and lesbian communities. The dismay coming from a butch woman or dyke towards an FTM translates into the same inner transphobia which reveals itself as a sneering remark that trans men are betraying womanhood and that they will lead to the false impression that 'all lesbians want to be men'. Trans people are often excluded from activities and programmes run by LGBT organisations, which conveniently follow the trend of reporting on the diversity of their constituency to donors in a politically correct manner without any understanding of trans issues among their staff and volunteers (Wilchins 2004: 29; Smit 2006: 286, 287). Namaste argues (2005: 51–54) that transsexuals and transgenders are silenced within the gay and lesbian communities unless they agree to the ideologies or promote gay and lesbian agendas.

The lack of trans services programmes in LGBTI organisations is balanced by the (finally) new trend among donors: long-awaited transgender funding. In the past two or three years, more and more (of the limited LGBTI donors) have realised and explicitly decided to fund transgender organisations, programmes and initiatives. This has led to the more opportunistic organisations scrambling for much needed funds by developing new transgender projects and programmes in a very short period. This is commendable. However, one still needs to weigh up the impact of ad hoc, haphazard programmes for transgender constituents juxtaposed against no programming at all. Naturally, one does not want to criticise the newly found enthusiasm for transgender programmes at LGB(TI) organisations, yet one must wonder how good they can be if they are (only) financially motivated. Will these programmes be developed, implemented and managed by transgender people? Will transgender people receive skills, training and guidance on how to run these programmes? Are there top management transgender staff employed at these LGB(TI) organisations? Do they have trans board members?

Looking for transgender role models, when there ain't any

Lesbian and gay people worldwide have over the years been blamed for claiming trans role models and personalities in their history making. It is no different in South Africa. In one of the earlier works on the subject, *Defiant Desire: Gay and Lesbian Lives in South Africa* (Gevisser and Cameron 1994) one reads about the story of Gertie Williams, which dates back to 1955. The chapter was written using extracts from historical newspaper and maga-zine clippings. In these Williams related a strong desire to be seen as a man, mentioned praying to God every night to be merci-fully changed into a man so as to avoid the risk of an operation, and said that no pain would be too high a price. Williams also abandoned dresses and make-up, declaring to family members she would have no more use for them: 'I wanted to be a man, and nothing was going to stop me' (Chetty 1994: 131). Although this material was directly quoted from the *Golden City Post* of 1956, when the current language around transgenderism had not emerged, the authors in 1994 did not think to add any footnotes, recognising or acknowledging the possibility of a trans identity. This is why Smit (2006: 283) righteously mentioned: 'much of South African trans history would have to be reclaimed...'.

In December 2006 South Africa became the fifth country in the world, and the first on the continent, to allow people of the same sex to marry. It was a huge accomplishment for LGBT activism and equal rights for queers in South Africa. As much as this was celebrated, including among transgender South Africans and their partners, the new Civil Union Bill and its implementation with regard to the old Marriage Act of 1961 did not make provision for a number of transsexual people. Trans couples, in any combination of their sexual orientation, could now marry, regardless of whether they defined themselves as same sex or heterosexual. The problem involved couples who were previously married under the Marriage Act as heterosexual couples where one partner had decided on transition. Regardless of the amount of love the two persons declared for each other and their intention to stay together, they were forced to get divorced in order for the trans partner to reregister his or her documentation at the Department of Home Affairs. This proved to be a very traumatic experience, as Christelle explained: 'all the dignity your relationship is provided with is taken away' (Judge et al 2008: 337).

The gender and gender identity of trans people and their partners are often pronounced as having multiple dimensions (Lenning 2008: 86, 87), which at times is confusing, complex and needs time to self-analyse. Besides time to adjust, the two parties in the relationship need to negotiate and discover what they are willing to compromise about and what will not be acceptable (Lev 2004: 289).

It is also important to acknowledge that relationships where one partner comes out as being trans are challenged with uncertainty (from both partners) at many levels. Keketso confirmed this (Theron 2009: 156) when she acknowledged her confusion when, as a heterosexual woman, she was first attracted to her partner. It was difficult for her to say she was lesbian, she could not get her head around it until, after a while, she learned he was trans and about to transition to male. Things then began to fall into place for her.

Sexual orientation is not only a concern for the heterosexual partners of masculine-identifying trans people; lesbians also scrutinise their orientation (Cook-Daniels 1998, Mason 2006, Lenning 2008, Brown 2009). Redefining or questioning one's sexual orientation is complex. Some lesbians are well established and 'out' in their communities and are challenged by many prejudices, with an accompanying sense of loss of community (Cook-Daniels 1998, Lev 2004, Brown 2009, Theron 2009). As the male-identifying trans partner's transition progresses and he becomes well adjusted in society as male, it challenges and stigmatises the lesbian partner who wants to continue claiming her lesbian identity. One lesbian noted that being with an FTM changed her identity from being a lesbian to the partner of an FTM (Cook-Daniels 1998). Two years after that relationship (with a trans man) ended, there were still lesbian activists and friends who did not accept her back as a lesbian. Even after she started dating her current partner, who is lesbian, 'we had many questions to answer explaining about her not being trans and to verify that I am actually a lesbian' (Theron 2009: 160). It is a constant challenge for lesbian partners not to lose their own identity as lesbians, while not outing their partners as trans. This challenge requires ongoing sensitisation and training within the lesbian community and beyond. 'I can't figure out how to be "out" without jeopardising his right to be out/not out when he wants to, because he passes most of the time now' (Cook-Daniels 1998). Kayt relates a similar challenge (Cameron 1996: 106) when hanging out with lesbian friends, who might end up asking if she is seeing someone. It is hard to talk cryptically, avoiding pronouns, and friends do not expect a major educational session on a social evening out. And it feels too complex to her, being a lesbian to say she is with a 'he'.

In many cases the lesbian partner was not only out as a lesbian in her community but also known for being active as a volunteer or activist. Having to shift an identity in its totality not only erases a history of her activism and community participation, but may also lead to devastating emotions such as depression (Cook-Daniels 1998: 1).

Becoming the partner of a transgender person

In 2009 I did my honours research focusing on the female cis-gender partners of masculine-identifying trans people. One of the key focuses of this research was to determine whether the sexual orientation of the cisgender female partner of a masc-uline-identifying trans person, or their understanding thereof, had shifted. I will not delve here into the nuanced detail of the research outcomes, but will instead illuminate the intricacies of what the female cisgender partners experienced by looking at their responses when asked how they defined themselves before they entered into the relationship with their masculine-identifying trans partners.

I interviewed eight female cisgender partners of masculine-identifying trans persons from different ethnicities, language groups, and cultural and class backgrounds. Four women were black, of whom two were Xhosa, one Zulu and one Tsonga. Of the four white women, three were from an English upbringing and one was Afrikaans. They ranged in age from 25 to 53 at the time of interview. Although only one partner has indicated they preferred a pseudonym, I have decided to allocate pseudonyms to all females and their trans partners.

Three partners used a variety of ways to describe themselves on a bisexual continuum. Of the two heterosexual women, one said she was 'heterosexual with a past' and two of the partners described themselves as lesbians. Two of the couples were married, one with the lesbian partner and one with the bisexual partner. The couple where the cisgender partner was bisexual were married according to the old Marriage Act, whereas the other couple utilised the civil union.

Does the label fit? LGBTIQD

A person's sexual orientation is understood to predict the gender to which a person will feel attracted. Becoming the partner of a transgender person radically complicates the cisgender partner's experience of their sexual orientation because being in a cisgender –trans relationship challenges gender norms and sexual identity expectations, queering both heterosexual and homosexual spaces.

Although the group of cisgender partners of masculine-identifying trans persons I interviewed were all female, they represented a whole array of sexual orientations. Sexual orientation and identity are complex and people sometimes refer to themselves outside the categorisations of lesbian, bisexual or heterosexual offered by mainstream discourses on sexual orientation. It becomes apparent that the definitions or labels accepted and used by academia and the organised LGBTI sector are not necessarily the descriptions people use when self-identifying, even where that language is available to them. Individuals also find different ways to manoeuvre sexual orientation or identity around experiences of bisexuality.

Within the interview material, claiming labels to identify themselves in terms of sexual orientation, and therefore partner choice, proved to be an ongoing process of manoeuvring and self-negotiation. For some interviewees, especially those who were more politically minded, it became a layered process even before their relationship with a transgender person.

The interviewees had very diverse and complicated ways of thinking about their sexual orientation. None of the interviewees described a change in their own sense of their sexual orientation, but their understanding of what gender can encompass and mean did evolve during their relationships with their partners. The research findings also show how the perception of sexual orientation is concerned with sexual norms, based on bodily realities. Although strong arguments persist that gender is a social construct, the negotiations of most cisgender female partners in navigating their sexual orientation was hinged on (their understanding of) their trans partners' bodily composition.

The notion of being bisexual is based on the assumption that there is a two-sex binary of sexual orientation. Busi reflected on her bisexuality in exactly that way. However, before she was in a relationship with her trans partner, Busi constructed her own notion of bisexuality:

> I came to the realisation that what had attracted me to my previous partners had not been first their gender or whatever, it had been the self. I had either been attracted to a personality trait or one thing or the other and then ... how we had sex, but sex usually comes after the attraction.

Starting on this research, I anticipated finding at least some cisgender female partners sharing a shift, insignificant or more obviously experienced, in their sexual orientation. Conspicuously, though, at the point at which they were being interviewed, no one expressed any difference from the way they had identified their sexual orientation before they met their trans partners. As mentioned above, some challenges and (self) negotiations took place, which brought them to the point of realisation that although their understanding of sexual orientation had broadened, they had in fact not shifted their own sexual orientation. Strikingly, most of them had, however, expressed some shift in the way they generally viewed sexual orientation, gender and gender identity. This manifested itself in different ways for different female cisgender partners. Because Lebogang was confused by the fact that she started dating a female-bodied person, while refusing to see herself at any time as a lesbian, she did experience some shifts in understanding gender through the realisation that although her partner was (currently) female-bodied, he was transitioning to male. She managed to compare herself, as a heterosexual woman who was in a relationship with a female-bodied person, with a lesbian through the lens of physical body and biological sex. When she realised that he was 'no more a lesbian', a shift occurred in her understanding about the construction of transgender identities, which also removed, to her relief, her own identity as a lesbian.

Amanda also thought through the transition's effect on her sexual identity and expressed her sexual orientation based on the body of her partner: 'I mean because he would go for surgery if it was viable … and then that would take me back to being with a man?'

Susan conflated gender identity and sexual orientation when I asked her in the interview about any shift in her own sexual orientation. She did not experience any shift in either the way she viewed gender (roles or identity) or her own gender expression (or roles):

> I've never seen the major line between male and female. There is no difference to me. If you're useless in plumbing, then you're useless in plumbing. It doesn't make you 'not a man'. I'm a terrible cook, but that doesn't make me even less of a woman. So, gender as such hasn't changed for me in any way at all.

Busi also expressed a different understanding about being bisexual. Her identity did not shift, but she gained much more knowledge of the whole kaleidoscope of gender/s and orientations, which broadened her mind. Where she previously described bisexuality based on only two sex options being available, she subsequently felt that bisexuality was a description which did not fully encompass all the varieties in-between of people who were 'available' to fall in love with. She notes, 'It's really changed, you know, the geography of my sexual orientation quite a lot.'

On many different occasions Nosizwe had spoken about the ever-growing LGBTIQ acronym and concluded that in the perceived opinion of other lesbians, she might have to add the letter 'D' – for Disappointment.

Conclusion

I used two lenses to look at the well-named LGBTI alphabet soup. With the first lens I scrutinised the way feminists, scholars and LGB look at T. The second lens magnified how female cisgender partners of masculine-identifying trans persons grappled with identifying their sexual orientation before they entered their relationships with their trans partners. These two viewpoints raise serious questions as to whether the LGBTIQ label is useful and how far the acronym will be extended before it reaches its expiry date.

References

Brown, N.R. (2009) '"I'm in transition too": sexual identity renegotiation in sexual-minority women's relationships with transsexual men', *International Journal of Sexual Health*, 21

Butler, J. (2004) *Undoing Gender*, New York, Routledge

Cameron, L. (1996) *Body Alchemy: Transsexual Portraits*, San Francisco, Cleis Press

Chetty, D. (1994) 'Lesbian gangster: the Gertie Williams story', in Gevisser, M. and Cameron, E. (eds) *Defiant Desire: Gay and Lesbian Lives in South Africa*, Braamfontein, South Africa, Ravan Press

Cook-Daniels, L. (1998) 'Trans-positioned', *Circles Magazine*, June: 16–22, http://www.forge-forward.org/handouts/Transpositioned.html, accessed 27 June 2009

Gevisser, M. and Cameron, E. (eds) (1994) *Defiant Desire: Gay and Lesbian Lives in South Africa*, Braamfontein, South Africa, Ravan Press

Judge, M., Manion, A. and De Waal, S. (eds) (2008) *To Have and to Hold: The Making of Same-Sex Marriage in South Africa*, Johannesburg, Fanele – an imprint of Jakana Media

Lenning, E. (2008) 'This journey is not for the faint of heart: an investigation into the challenges facing transgender individuals and their significant others', unpublished dissertation, Western Michigan University

Lev, A.I. (2004) *Transgender Emergence: Therapeutic Guidelines for Working with Gender-Variant People and Their Families*, New York, The Haworth Clinical Practice Press

Mason, M.E. (2006) 'The experience of transition for lesbian partners of female-to-male transsexuals', dissertation, Alliant International University, San Francisco

Matebeni, Z. (2009) 'Feminising lesbians, degendering transgender men: A model for building lesbian feminist thinkers and leaders in Africa?', paper delivered at the Gender Justice and Body Politics conference, Cape Town

Namaste, V. (2005) *Sex Change, Social Change: Reflections on Identity, Institutions and Imperialism*, Toronto, Women's Press

Rubin, Gayle (1999 [1984]) 'Thinking sex: notes for a radical theory of the politics of sexuality', in Parker, R. and Aggleton, P. (eds) *Culture, Society and Sexuality: A Reader*, London and Philadelphia, UCL Press

Smit, E. (2006) 'Western psychiatry and gender identity disorder (GID): a critical perspective', in Shefer, T., Boonzaier, F. and Kiguwa, P. (eds) *The Gender of Psychology*, Cape Town, UCT Press

Steyn, M. and Van Zyl, M. (eds) (2009) *The Prize and the Price: Shaping Sexualities in South Africa*, South Africa, HSRC Press

Theron, L. (2009) 'SOFFA perspective', in Morgan, R., Marais, C. and Wellbeloved, J.R. (eds) *Trans: Transgender Life Stories from South Africa*, Auckland Park, South Africa, Fanele – an imprint of Jacana Media

Wilchins, R. (2004) *Queer Theory, Gender Theory: An Instant Primer*, Los Angeles, Alyson Books

33

Human Rights and Legal Implications of the Same Sex Marriage Prohibition Bill, 2011 for Every Nigerian Citizen

A briefing Communiqué for His Excellency, the President of the Federal Republic of Nigeria & The Senate and the House of Representatives of the Federal Republic of Nigeria

An analysis prepared by Nigerian civil society organizations, human rights organizations, feminist and women's rights groups, social health workers, social and economic justice activists and NGOs

This is the third time a Bill prohibiting same sex marriage is introduced by the Nigerian parliament. The proposed law is titled "Same Sex Marriage Prohibition Bill, 2011", however, it goes well beyond the title to criminalise every Nigerian person(s), individual and group who may be suspected of any trace, exhibition, association and or characteristic of same sex relationship, friendship, association or gesture.

It is very important when Bills are proposed by members of parliament that all Nigerians look closely into them to see what implications they would have for every Nigerian, irrespective of gender, sex, religion, creed, culture, sexuality, tradition, origin, ethnic group and political opinion. Often, when laws are introduced, most Nigerians do not understand their provisions and implications for their daily lives as citizens of Nigeria. Civil society organizations in Nigeria have a duty to inform and educate the citizens, as well as lawmakers, about oppressive and dangerous implications in potential legislation.

The proposed Same Sex Marriage Bill 2011 was passed by the Senate on the 3rd reading on 29th November, 2011. It also passed through a first reading at the House of Representatives on 7th December, 2011. This analysis seeks to analyse and highlight its grave implications on the daily lives of every Nigerian.

With this bill Nigeria and Nigerians will be shown to be untrustworthy and incapable of upholding and domesticating international treaties and conventions which they have signed and ratified. From the perspective of foreign investors, the inability to uphold international agreements raises the question of whether their investment and personnel can be safe in the hands of such [an] untrustworthy partner. At a time when the country is on a drive to attract direct foreign investment, this bill also stands as a threat to the economy.

According to the 2010 UNGASS (United Nations General Assembly) report on Nigeria, 3.6% of the population is comprised of people living with HIV/AIDS – i.e. more than 5.5 million people. The bulk of the support to curb the spread of the virus and support those already infected or affected is coming from international donors. Many of the people living with HIV/AIDS are heterosexuals and if organizations geared to help them are barred, as in this bill, this will have a catastrophic effect on stopping the rate of new infections and helping those already infected.

It is worth noting for all Nigerian citizens that the proposed bill aims at:

a) prohibiting any form of de facto cohabitation between two individuals of the same sex or gestures that connote same sex relationship directly or indirectly. If this bill becomes law male-male or female-female holding of hands, touching each other, making eye gestures, hugging or any display of affection will be evidence for conviction and 10 years imprisonment.
   The Bill also aims to:
b) restrict the right to freedom of expression;
c) restrict the right to freedom of association;
d) restrict the right to freedom of thought, including the freedom of conscience and religion;
e) target human rights defenders who speak out for the human

rights of individuals and communities, as well as advocates for sexuality, reproductive rights and the right to health;

f) and, ultimately, target the rights and safety of persons who either identify as lesbians, gays, bisexuals, transgenders, or, who simply do not fit conservative gender roles and stereotypes, as well as anybody who is related to them or sympathetic of them;

g) promote widespread social control, intrusive to individual privacy.

h) Finally it targets any legal defense and representation for persons or groups involved in in any real or perceived same-sex related case.

Thus if the proposed legislation is passed into law Nigeria would violate many of its obligations under our own constitution, our own laws, and, international human rights law.

Violations of international human rights law which would result from the bill, include of Article 22 (freedom of association), Article 19 (right to freedom of opinion and expression) of the ICCPR (International Covenant on Civil and Political Rights). Similarly they would violate Article 9 (freedom of expression), Article 10 (right of free association), Article 11 (right of assembly), Article 12 (right of residence) and Article 8 (the right to have one's cause heard and to a defense – including by the counsel of one's choice) of the African Charter on Human and Peoples Rights (ACHPR). Since the ACHPR was adopted into Nigerian law in 1983, the provisions of this bill violate our own national laws also.

Of principal concern for all Nigerians is that Sections 5 and 7 of the revised and final copy of the bill reach far beyond its scope to attack freedom of assembly and speech, among other rights. The bill, as currently revised, is extemely likely to encourage discrimination against all individuals regardless of their sexuality, and in fact constitutes an incitement to violence, ill-treatment and torture.

Specific sections for concern to all Nigerians

SECTION 4 (2) of the proposed Bill

In a very tactile society as ours, where people of the same sex frequently hold each other's hands, wrap their arms around each other's waists, embrace each other warmly, it will be difficult, if not impossible to know when such actions are a display of amorous relationships or expressions of human intimacy and affection that are devoid of any sexual intention. This provision of the bill opens up the possiblity for witch-hunting and vindictive accusations which could impact on every Nigerian, and create a climate of fear and repression.

SECTION 5 of the proposed Bill

The prohibition of "gay clubs, societies and organizations," and of any person involved not only in registration, but even in sustenance and meetings, registration, participation even in private, directly or indirectly, and the further prohibition of publicity, procession, and "public show of same sex amorous relationship" may potentially affect anybody and any group; for example:

a) Any Muslim or **Christian women's rights group** teaching the Qu'ran or the Bible could be targeted as a "lesbian group" and persecuted by those who do not appreciate women understanding for themselves the liberatory potential in religious texts. In general, any women's rights group could be easily targeted by those who do not support women's empowerment.

b) Any member of any **same gender organization**, even students in **same gender schools and clubs (like the boy scouts or girl guides)**, could be targeted by anyone holding a grudge against members of the group or opposing the aims of the group.

c) **Any person who does not fit the conservative understandings of traditional or social norms** of his or her community, such as an unmarried person in his or her 30s or 40s, or even a woman who happens to be in trousers could be easily accused of being gay or lesbian.

d) Section 5 could also be a powerful tool in the hands of unscrupulous politicians and aspirants against their **political opponents** and thus undermine the electoral process and the democratic development of the country. For example, any politician or candidate could be maliciously accused of privately supporting either same sex amorous relationships or gay societies or of being gay. And whether proved or not in court, even being accused under the law would likely ruin that person's political career.

e) Any **journalist, newspaper, radio, or television station** reporting objective information related to gay issues could easily be accused of promoting publicity of same sex amorous relationships. The bill could be easily used as a tool of censorship for political purposes.

f) Any human rights, civil rights, women's rights or health advocacy group, including those working on HIV/AIDS prevention, could be accused of indirectly supporting same sex amorous relationships just by applying international human rights and health standards. **Groups doing controversial work on any topic** could be attacked with the excuse that they also support gay rights or promote same sex sexual relations. This law could potentially affect a wide variety of **civil society activists and/or organizations** in the country.

g) If this bill became law, nobody could even **advocate** against the human rights implication of the law itself without being found guilty of indirectly supporting same sex amorous relationships. This would be an **inherent contradiction for a democratic system**.

h) Under the proposed law no **lawyer or paralegal** will be able to **offer legal representation or support** and in fact such a lawyer or paralegal personnel could be criminalized for representation, defense or support of any case perceived to be same sex related.

SECTION 7 of the proposed Bill

Rather than simply defining marriage as an act between one man and one woman, Section seven's sweeping inclusion of any two people of the same sex living together allows anybody to be targeted, even when they do not have any sexual relationship at all.

a) Many people in Nigeria share their housing for economic reasons. If two roommates are of the same sex they could be accused by anybody with whom they have a personal or public dispute of "living together as husband and wife" and be prosecuted under the law.

b) Their relatives, friends or visitors could be accused of indirectly supporting in private a same sex amorous relationship just by visiting them.

SECTIONS 1(3) and Section 2(2)

Section 1(3) and 2(2) states that even if there are valid same sex marriages or civil unions entered into outside Nigeria, they will not be recognised in Nigeria. This may be aimed at non-Nigerians – it would clearly discourage same-sex partners from visiting or working in Nigeria (or investing in Nigeria). But there are also Nigerians living in the diaspora who are married to same sex partners or planning to do so. Many talented Nigerians live in the diaspora openly as gays, lesbians, bisexuals, and transsexuals. They contribute positively to the development of their country of residence but are afraid to come and contribute to the development of our motherland because of fear of victimization. Nigerian LGBTIs living in the diaspora do not want to be isolated from home, family and childhood friends – this bill would virtually enforce that.

Furthermore, criminalizing same sex relationships will force many Nigerian Lesbians, Gays Bisexuals and Intersex (LGBTI) to leave the country and become refugees and asylum seekers in other countries. This also affects Nigeria by contributing to brain drain.

In summary, the implications and effects of the bill, will go far beyond the prohibition of same sex marriage (which is discriminatory in itself), and will result in widespread human rights violations, censorship, impediments to open and democratic process, fear, repression and the break up of family relationships, as well as the loss of talented and patriotic individual[s] – for all Nigerian citizens irrespective of their sexuality. In fact, even though this Bill is still only potentially law, there are increasing reports of people being harrassed, intimidated, discriminated against and physically aggressed, on the basis of their actual or perceived sexuality already.

In recogniton of this, we make an **Urgent call for action to His Excellency, the President of the Federal Republic of Nigeria, members of the Senate and House of Representatives of the Federal Republic of Nigeria.**

We, the undersigned members of Nigerian civil society organizations, human rights defenders, women's rights activists, media advocates, social health workers, and concerned Nigerians hereby ask His Excellency, The President of the Federal Republic of Nigeria, and Distinguished members of the Senate and House of Representative to:

1. Withdraw immediately the proposed Same Sex Marriage Prohibition Bill, 2011 due to its implications for gross human rights violations of all Nigerans irrespective of their sexuality and the likelihood that it would bar Nigeria from the community of democratic nations.
2. Take measures to stop extrajudicial actions taken by law enforcement and other state agencies which are human rights violations – including all those directed against individuals who may be (or are suspected of being) LGBTI.
3. Ensure that law enforcement and other state agencies address and stop individual and mob action aimed at or resulting in the intimidation, inhuman and degrading treatment of people and individuals on the basis of the actual or perceived sexuality.
4. Take immediate measures for consultation with the human rights commission, civil society and stakeholders in the preparation, review and amendment of all proposed legislation to consider their implications for human rights and democratic process.
5. Uphold democratic principles and parliamentary procedures for ensuring balanced and diversified debate from all sectors – ensuring no shortcuts of process.
6. Take into account the report of the Integrated Bio-Behavioral Surveillance Survey (IBBSS)-2007 conducted by NACA which further stresses the importance of integrating Men who have sex with men (MSM) into HIV/AIDS programming in Nigeria (which based would become criminal if this Bill was [passed]).

List of Organisations and Individuals who are signatories.

APPENDIX

CONTENTS AND CRITIQUE OF EACH CLAUSE OF THE PROPOSED BILL

A BILL FOR AN ACT TO PROHIBIT MARRIAGE OR CIVIL UNION ENTERED INTO BETWEEN PERSONS OF SAME SEX, SOLEMNIZATION OF SAME AND FOR OTHER MATTERS RELATED THEREWITH by the Senate of the Federal Republic of Nigeria as follows.

Clearly the new bill is totally unnecessary because since same-sex sexual conduct between consenting adults is already prohibited and criminalized under the Criminal Code, the Penal

334

Code and various Shari'a Penal Codes, consequently, same-sex marriages are already unlawful in Nigeria.

It is also unnecessary, because there has not been any demand for same sex marriage in Nigeria.

The proposed law will violate several fundamental human rights enshrined in the 1999 constitution.

35(1) Every person shall be entitled to his personal liberty and no person shall be deprived of such liberty...

Although several countries have chosen not to allow same sex marriage by defining marriage as the union between a man and a woman, Nigeria would be the first country in the world to prohibit same sex marriage with criminal provisions.

If this law passes, every Nigerian could be at threat, or liable under the law, whether they are in real same-sex relationships or merely perceived to be so, or even know others who are in same-sex relationships.

1. Prohibition of Marriage or Civil Unions by Persons of Same Sex.

1(3) A Marriage Contract or Civil Union entered into between persons of same sex by virtue of a certificate issued by a foreign country shall be void in Nigeria, and any benefit acruing there from by virtue of the certificate shall not be enforced by any court of law in Nigeria.

The scope of these provisions is unclear. Since same sex marriage is not allowed by the legal definition of marriage, clearly any same sex marriage however celebrated is legally void and there are no legal consequences and effects. Therefore, these provisions are redundant.

The provisions concerning the prohibition to recognize same sex marriage validly contracted abroad are unnecessary also. Under international private law, the obligation for state parties to the Hague Convention of 14 March 1978 on Celebration and Recognition of the Validity of Marriages to recognize same sex marriage validly celebrated abroad is highly disputed and rejected so far. In any case, Nigeria has not signed that convention: this means that Nigerian authorities have full jurisdiction with regard to the definition of marriage under domestic law. Nothing in sections 49 and following of the Marriage Act 1990 makes possible the recognition of a marriage celebrated abroad which is contrary to domestic law.

2. Solemnization of same sex marriage in places of worship.

(1) Marriage or civil union entered into between persons of same sex shall not be solemnized in any place of worship either Church or Mosque or any other place or whatsover called in Nigeria.

(2) No certificate issued to persons of same sex in a marriage shall be or civil union shall be valid in Nigeria.

This provision violates article 18 of the ICCPR, as it would restrict the right to freedom of religion of those groups that might choose to bless same sex union, even if no legal consequences are attached to such unions. This has been the case of several Christian churches and Jewish temples in several countries, and the state prohibition clearly interferes with such a freedom.

The exception of article 18(3), with reference to the protection of morals, does not apply in this case: the interpretation of the Human Rights Committee to the notion of morals, General Comment no. 22 (1993) on article 18 clearly states that the notion of morals "derives from many social, philosophical and religious traditions; consequently, limitations on the freedom to manifest a religion or belief for the purpose of protecting morals must be based on principles not deriving exclusively from a single tradition" (8).

Finally General Comment no. 22 explains that the right to freedom of religion must be interpreted broadly, precisely because article 18 recognizes the exercise of such right "either individually or in community with others and in public or private" (4).

This provision is therefore unconstitutional under the Nigerian Constitution as it violates article 38 that recognizes the freedom of religion, and constitutes the basis for separation between state and churches. It also violates Article 8 of the African Charter on Human and Peoples' Rights and therefore also Nigerian domestic law.

3. Recognized Marriage in Nigeria.

Only marriages contracted between a man and a woman shall be recognized as valid in Nigeria.

Again this replicates existing law and is therefore redundant.

4. Registration of Homosexual Clubs and Societies.

This provision raises the most serious concerns in terms of violations of human rights obligations by Nigerian authorities under the ICCPR, the African Charter and the Nigerian Constitution.

4(1) The Registration of Gay Clubs, Societies and organizations, their sustenance, processions and meetings are hereby prohibited.

The prohibition of LGBTI organizations to be registered under Nigerian law, especially in the light of the criminal offense introduced by paragraph 1 of section 4, is **contrary to Article 10 of the ACHPR (which is domesticated as Nigerian law), and Article 22 of the ICCPR** which reads:

> 1. Everyone shall have the right to freedom of association with others (…).
> 2. No restrictions may be placed on the exercise of this right other than those which are prescribed by law and which are necessary in a democratic society in the interests of national security or public safety, public order (ordre public), the protection of public health or morals or the protection of the rights and freedoms of others. (…)

As explained above, the exception of the protection of morals is not acceptable according to the Human Rights Committee in Toonen, where they concluded that the derogation to the right to privacy could not be justified in the name of the protection of public health, in particular to prevent HIV/AIDS spread. The Committee argued that the ban on same-sex sexual conduct might have an impact on HIV/AIDS education and prevention, causing in fact the spread of the disease among certain stigmatized groups.

Similarly, the provision would violate article 10(1) of the African Charter establishing that *"[e]very individual shall have the right to free association provided that he abides by the law"*, as well as the Resolution on the Right to Freedom of Association (1992) that was later drafted by the African Commission on Human and Peoples' Rights stating that:

> [t]he competent authorities should not override constitutional provisions or undermine fundamental rights guaranteed by the constitution and international standards;

2. In regulating the use of this right, the competent authorities should not enact provisions which would limit the exercise of this freedom;

3. The regulation of the exercise of the right to freedom of association should be consistent with State's obligations under the African Charter on Human and Peoples' Rights.

For the same reasons, this provision would be unconstitutional constituting a violation of article 40 of the Nigerian Constitution. *4(2) The public show of same sex amorous relationship directly or indirectly is hereby prohibited.*

As already indicated, Section 4 breaches article 19 and 22 of the ICCPR by criminalizing any activity *directly or indirectly* related to LGBT issues or same sex amorous relationship. The restriction is so severe that it reaches activities carried out and thoughts as well as opinion expressed in private.

The gravity of this violation is certainly confirmed by several reports issued in the past 10 years, starting from 2001, by the U.N. Special Rapporteur on the promotion and protection of the right to freedom of opinion and expression. The reports highlight and criticise cases of censorship, restriction and criminalisation of rights to freedom of speech, as well as abuses, attacks and restrictions by state authorities against LGBTI advocates or individuals whose behaviors do not conf[o]rm to conservative social norms and expectations of acceptable gender or sexuality.

The criminalization of any form of expression and association related to LGBTI rights therefore exposes all human rights defenders operating in the fields of sexual rights, health rights and LGBTI rights. Abuses, especially of LGBTI human rights defenders have been extensively reported by the Special Representative of the Secretary-General in the past 10 years. This Bill would increase that abuse. It would result in a situation contrary to the Resolution on the Protection of Human Rights Defenders in Africa (which Nigeria has signed) and would expose the Nigerian authorities to the scrutiny of the Special Rapporteur on the Situation of Human Rights Defenders established by the African Commission on Human Rights.

Section 4 will also have a significant impact on social rights, such as right to sexual health and HIV/AIDS prevention. General

Comment no. 14 of the Human Rights Committee, on the Right to the Highest Attainable Standard of Health recognizes that the principle of non-discrimination of Article 2(2) "proscribes any discrimination in access to health care" on grounds of, amongst other things, health status (including HIV/AIDS) and sexual orientation (**Article 12 of the International Covenant on Economic, Social and Cultural Rights – ICESCR**). The right to the best attainable state of physical and mental health is also protected by Article 16 of the African Charter, and thus also in Nigerian domestic law.

As repeatedly underlined by the U.N. Special Rapporteur on the Right of Everyone to the Enjoyment of the Highest Attainable Standard of Physical and Mental Health, discrimination and stigma would certainly restrain the access to health and sexually transmitted disease prevention for all Nigerians, irrespective of their gender and sexuality.

Finally, these provisions in particular might seriously endanger the lives of all Nigerians who are real (or perceived to be or simply accused of being LGBTI); exposing them to increased risk of degrading, inhuman and cruel treatments and punishments, torture, extrajudicial executions, arbitrary deprivation of their liberty. It is precisely because of incidents of human rights violation against LGBTI defenders that the Special Rapporteur's report states that "discrimination on grounds of sexual orientation and gender identity may contribute to the process of dehumanization of the victim." The fact that even private forms of expression, speech and association would be subject to the scrutiny of the criminal law promotes rigid social control, even by non state actors, as well as the concrete risk of a political use of this legislation

5. Offences and Penalties

(1) Persons who entered into same sex marriage contract or civil unions commit an offense and are liable and are each liable on conviction to a term of 14 years imprisonment.

(2) Any person who registers, operates or participate in gay clubs, societies and organization, or directly or indirectly make public show of same sex amorous relationship in Nigeria commit an offense and shall each be liable on conviction to a term of 10 years imprisonment.

(3) Any person or group of persons that witness, abets and aids the solemnization of a same sex marriage or civil union, or supports the registration, operation and sustenance of gay clubs, societies, organizations, processions in Nigeria commits an offense and shall be liable on conviction to a term of 10 years imprisonment.

The fact that the bill explicitly confines the jurisdiction with regard to the application of the law does not mitigate the seriousness of the human rights violation and the concerns about a wider social control and abuse that constitute the reasonable consequences of the enactment of this law.

2. Interpretation

"Civil Unions" means any arrangement between persons of the same sex to live together as sex partners, and shall include such descriptions as adult independent relationships, caring partnerships, civil partnerships, civil solidarity pacts, domestic partnerships, reciprocal beneficiary relationships, registered partnerships, significant relationships, stable unions, etc.

The bill is unnecessary to prohibit same sex marriage in Nigeria: section 27 of the Marriage Act 1990 already implicitly defines marriage as the union of a man and wife, whilst all the Criminal and Penal Codes of Nigeria already make same-sex sexual conduct non-permissible.

"Same Sex Marriage" means the coming together of persons of the same sex with the purpose of living together as husband and wife or for other purposes of same same sexual relationship.

The proposed definition of same sex marriage goes far beyond the notion of same sex marriage as accepted in those countries that have legally recognized the marriages between persons of the same sex. This definition actually refers to *any* form of same sex relationship, including de facto cohabitation of same sex couple. This is inconsistent with international and foreign legislation, case law and legal literature.

This provision clearly violates the ICCPR. Although the Human Rights Committee has established in *Joslin v. New Zealand*[1] that the ICCPR does not recognize a fundamental right to marry for same-sex couples under article 23(2), in *Young v. Australia*[2] the Committee itself recognized that different treatment between unmarried same-sex and different-sex couples may constitute a breach of state parties' obligations under the prohibition of discrimination of article 26, which includes discrimination on the basis of sexual orientation. As a consequence, the ban introduced by the bill, by reaching out to any form of cohabitation between individuals of the same-sex, is contrary to ICCPR Article 26.

Also, because the bill bans the intimate and emotional choices of consenting adults, it is extremely intrusive of the privacy of those persons whose behaviors do not conform with conservative gender and social roles. Such a definition of same sex marriage and the provisions that follow go far beyond the boundary established in *Toonen* and violates Article 17 of the ICCPR and, consequently, the constitutional provision of article 37. Furthermore, in practice, the Bill also would implicate the likelihood or simple resemblance of such choices (by defining same sex marriage as "other form of same sex relationship for the purposes of cohabitation as husband and wife").

By criminalizing any form of same sex relationship the bill does not protect family and traditions as required by Article 18 of the African Charter, but rather jeopardizes individual dignity and security, respectively protected by articles 5 and 6 of the Charter. It also clearly withdraws protection from LGBTI people and their families who under Articles 5(2) and 5(3) may find themselves imprisoned for 10 years if they do not denounce family members who are LGBTI.

This intrusiveness into the private sphere in fact promotes stigmatization against individuals and groups already at risk of marginality, exposing them to violence and abuses both by local authorities and non state actors. Both the U.N. Special Rapporteur on Extrajudicial, Summary or Arbitrary Executions and the Special Rapporteur on the Question Of Torture and Other Cruel, Inhuman or Degrading Treatment Or Punishment have, over the past years, extensively reported on how discrimination, marginalization and the failure of states to protect gays, lesbians, transgenders and other groups that do not fit with "sexual norms" have been the cause of killings by non state actors and state authorities, as well as tortures and other abuses by state authorities. They have thus held governments responsible for the violation of article 6 and 7 of the ICCPR. Similar conclusions have been argued by the Special Rapporteur on Violence against Women, Its Causes and

Consequences, as well as by the observations of treaty bodies, such as the Committee against torture in its interpretation of the Convention against Torture (CAT) in the past 10 years.

[1] Communication No. 902/1999, UN Doc. CCPR/C/75/D/902/1999 (1998).
[2] Communication No. 941/2000, UN Doc CCPR/C/78/D/941/2000 (2003).

http://bit.ly/U8xQQB

34

Deconstructing violence towards black lesbians in South Africa

Zethu Matebeni

Introduction

The claim to a black lesbian identity in South Africa, and in the African continent as a whole, is an important but contested claim. The lesbian category, as an identity and a social and political group, highlights sexuality and gender as well as the interplay between these and other identity categories such as race, nation and class. This interplay, I argue, recedes and resurfaces in the ways in which the lesbian category is made to 'disappear' through various forms of injustice, the use of language and through violence in contemporary South Africa.

South Africa is well known for its high rates of violence generally and towards women in particular. As a group of women (I take Monique Wittig's (1993) arguments seriously here) or female-bodied persons, black lesbians have been increasingly framed as victims of specific forms of crime and sexual violence perpetuated on their bodies – what certain groups have termed 'corrective' or 'curative' rape. Undoubtedly, violence against lesbians is part of a broader scourge of violence towards women. Even though it may seem difficult to separate anti-lesbian violence from broader violence against women, there are differences between the two. Lesbians are targets of violence because of their sexual orientation, gendered expressions and identity. Moreover, they are considered to be transgressing and disrupting gender/sex norms. By suggesting and positioning sexuality independent of men and reshaping gender structures, lesbian sexuality and gender challenge dominant sexual and gender orders. Masculine or butch lesbians are targeted because their visible masculine traits disrupt the gender hierarchy by symbolically claiming male privilege (Gontek 2009, Gunkel 2010). Femme lesbians, who remain 'invisible' in society as they are deemed 'heterosexual', are violated because they invert their feminine attraction and eroticism to other women, and not men. Regardless of where one fits within the lesbian paradigm, the mere existence of black African lesbians, in particular, remains contested.

In various, often violent ways black lesbians in South Africa, even with the progressive pro-gay rights laws, live under harsh conditions that attempt to 'do away' with their sexual subjectivities. The form of corrective or curative rape mentioned earlier is one such example. In the next sections I address the ways in which this language of rape and sexual violence has contributed to the branding and framing of black lesbians as 'special' victims of widespread rape and sexual torture towards women in South Africa. This is a complex and difficult position to take because on the one hand, as presented earlier, lesbians are attacked because of their perceived and real disruption of the gender and sex order. On the other hand, by framing black lesbians as special victims of a form of rape, the language of corrective rape locates black lesbians in the townships of South Africa outside the wider gender, class, sexuality and racial struggles of social justice in South Africa.

The language of rape as 'corrective/curative'

Black lesbians living in the townships (and thus presumed 'poor') in South Africa have been increasingly seen as victims and survivors of what has been termed curative or corrective rape. This victim narrative of black lesbians is a problematic, limited view of how we as black lesbians experience the fullness of our lives. The concepts of curative/corrective rape arise out of lesbian and feminist activist circles in South Africa (Muholi 2004, Mkhize et al 2010). One of the first published pieces of activist research to introduce the term curative rape, entitled 'Thinking through lesbian rape' by Zanele Muholi (2004), credits Donna Smith, the then CEO of the Forum for the Empowerment of Women (a black lesbian organisation in Johannesburg) for defining the phrase.

Muholi's (2004: 118) piece referred to the testimonies of 47 lesbians in the Gauteng area, the majority of whom had been 'raped explicitly' because of their sexuality or gender non-conformity. Many others had been assaulted or had survived rape attempts, various forms of abuse and abduction. Among them less than half had reported their experiences to the police and many had little faith in the police or the criminal justice system.

Organisations working with black lesbians in South Africa continuously report numerous cases of black lesbians experiencing curative/corrective rape because of their sexual orientation and identity (Muholi 2004, Bucher 2009, Mkhize et al 2010). Curative rape is defined as the 'rape of women perceived of as lesbian by men as an ostensible "cure" for their (aberrant) sexualities' (Muthien 2007: 323). The term has become synonymous with the 'poor' black lesbian experience in the township. Outside the notion that this term limits this kind of experience only to a certain class of black lesbians, there are a number of reasons why I suggest that it presents a problematic reading of violence towards lesbians. According to police records and accounts of crimes in South Africa, corrective rape does not exist. All rape is recorded and categorised the same way. In a documentary film investigating rape and lesbians in South Africa, a police official states when asked about the phenomenon of 'corrective rape' (Schaap and Gim 2010):

> What is corrective rape? I'm not sure what corrective rape is. As far as we are concerned – corrective rape is not a problem here in South Africa. Based on the way the crimes are reported – if somebody reports a crime of rape, it is investigated as rape. We don't have a phenomenon or a crime category called corrective rape that will be able to tell you that this is reaching alarming proportions...
> Vishnu Naidoo, South African Police Service spokesman

Strategically, the use of such a term has been effective in activist circles as it captures and highlights the extent of injustices and violence perpetrated on black lesbians because of their sexualities and identities. Beyond such circles, it remains unclear how useful the deployment of this term has been. The language of rape as curative in this regard, I argue, does more harm than good to black lesbian groups. Marking certain groups as victims of a special kind of crime can make them vulnerable to unintended further victimisation. Knowing that a victim has experienced curative rape immediately identifies her as lesbian, a category many (including certain institutions) still treat with disdain. In this sense, this language and terminology can unintentionally work against what it set out to do.

Describing the intention and action of the perpetrator as curative can mean, or be misinterpreted to mean, to implicate the victim as 'deserving' of the crime. Such language positions her (all cases of such reported rapes are women) as being cleansed of something that is unwanted, abnormal and outlawed in society. Through corrective/curative rape, lesbians then become cured and normalised. In the twisted mind of the rapist, taking claim over a woman's body through a violent process of 'teaching her to behave like a woman' (Reddy et al 2007: 10) only makes sense as a way of advancing patriarchal gains. There is nothing corrective or curative about rape. On the contrary, rape is very damaging, it 'causes anger. It destroys and wrecks lives. It causes divisions and it damages an innocent soul' (Reddy et al 2007: 11). Seen from the vantage point of the survivor or victim, such terms can be offensive and debilitating. The use of such language (or the reading of violence as curative) suggests an elevated status for the perpetrator who is seen as 'curing' and 'correcting' for the good of the dominant culture, while stigmatising and branding the survivor. Thus the blame shifts from the perpetrator to the victim, who is seen as having transgressed societal norms.

Without getting trapped by the use of language, let us consider the possible ways in which terminology can assist us in achieving its intended functions. Phumi Mtetwa's (2011) latest welcome contribution in *Amandla* offers an alternative to how the term corrective can be used in our society. Mtetwa inverts the term correct by redirecting it away from lesbians (or rather in relation to rapes committed on lesbian bodies) and to homophobes. Her piece 'Correct the homophobes' leaves the term 'correct' permanently in inverted commas throughout to show her own ambivalence to it. She does not shy away from problematising the term in this piece and further challenges those who are against homosexuals, and those who are yet to join the struggles of all the members of our society, to be correct. She argues that they must 'correct' their ways by directing our society towards social transformation and justice and not towards damaging individual lives.

The use of this term may have been effective at one time, but I suspect it might have reached its expiry date. Recently a group of activists who are members of civil society organisations in the national task team on violence towards lesbian, gay, bisexual and transgender people in South Africa have had to battle with a number of questions relating to the use of the term corrective rape. Among many questions, we had to consider the reasons a separate category of rape was developed when it was and remained unrecognised as such. Additionally, we had to interrogate the usefulness of labelling rape in this way. These questions have only been partially answered by a call to do away with the term altogether. The response to that has been to find a replacement term that similarly captures corrective rape. Currently, this group has proposed that violence and rape should not isolate specific groups or individuals. Instead, violence should be thought of in its broad sense while also being specific about who is targeted. It is hoped that the move to finding alternative language or terminology about violence towards LGBTI people will capture both their sexual subjectivities and gender non-conformity.

Finding new terminologies and language that highlight various forms of violence and injustice is essential but also time-consuming. Experience from deploying the term curative rape has shown that terminology can hurt the same people it was designed to help while also excluding some within similar groupings. Above all of this, it is important to guard against contributing to forms of patriarchy that aim to blind and silence us through violating our bodies and through the use of language, while advancing patriarchal gains.

The erasure of lesbian identity

Many of us rely on the justice system for justice. However, there remain a significant number of cases that go unreported or under-investigated for a number of reasons. In Muholi's piece (2004) most of the women she talked to never reported their cases to the police, and many of the reported cases remain uninvestigated.

For many black lesbians justice is deferred or not obtained even when they know the perpetrators and continue to live among them. This troubling reality is one sign of how black women receive short shrift from the criminal justice system. Even when cases make it to court, we are often reminded of how flawed and limited the justice system can be. The effects of this can be felt in very personal (and therefore political) ways.

To illustrate this I will make reference to one of the few well-publicised cases, that of Eudy Simelane, a 31-year-old black lesbian and national soccer player murdered by four young black men in her township. Unlike with many other murders of a black lesbian woman, Eudy's case may be regarded as highly successful as it reached court and there has been a conviction. In similar cases, arrests of the perpetrators have been unimaginable for various reasons, including no police investigation, claims about lack of evidence, a lack of material resources to follow up on cases and various other delays and limitations.

Like many activists, I followed this case and many others very closely, particularly inside the court. It is to the court proceedings of Eudy Simelane's case to which I refer in this section. It is the events of the proceedings on 12 February 2009, a cold Thursday morning in Delmas, that have left me and many others baffled, not knowing how to make sense of the role of the court and the judiciary in parts of South Africa.

Delmas court, about 80km from Johannesburg in the East Rand, is known for the Delmas treason trial,[1] one of the longest-running political trials in the legal history of South Africa. This was the site of the prosecution of the celebrated gay rights icon and anti-apartheid and AIDS activist Simon Nkoli, together with the then prominent ANC-aligned political leaders. It may be said that like the treason trial, Eudy Simelane's case was political. Outside the court was a group of more than 150 angry protesters, mainly young black (lesbian) women. There were a handful of white women, mainly from outside South Africa. Young black lesbians had come from as far as Durban and Cape Town to show solidarity in yet another case of what has been increasingly understood as 'hate crimes towards black lesbians'.

The trial was scheduled to begin at 10am, but due to delays, it had been postponed. A crowd had gathered outside the court singing and protesting against this delay and what some activists called 'delayed justice'. Many of those in the crowd had been in Delmas the previous day, too, but were all sent home 15 minutes after arrival because one of the accused had been summoned to another trial in a different court for a series of other crimes. Turning up at court only to be subjected to yet another delay was described by some of the protesters outside the courtroom as being 'drawn up and down, called to court every now and then and then justice delayed'. Emotions ran high as many of those in the crowd regarded it as a very personal case. For some, the outcome of the case would determine how and when they could utilise the everyday public spaces in their communities, whether they could walk safely in their streets or be able to go to a park.

Eudy's murder had taken place in KwaThema, a township well known in the past for being accommodating to gay and lesbian people and which had generated many politicised groups of gays and lesbians. For residents in KwaThema, such a murder challenged their own sense of safety and suggested that their township was not as safe as they had imagined it to be. For the many black lesbian protestors outside the court, Eudy's murder implied that the streets of the township were not safe for black lesbians. Their unmasked visibility outside this court was in one way a reclaiming of their space and demand for justice; they were willing to face the four accused head-on inside the court.

It was accused number four, Mpiti, whose statement rattled many of us in the court. Reading his statement, Mpiti seemed relaxed. He pleaded guilty on the counts of murder, robbery with aggravated circumstances and being an accomplice to attempted rape. Part of his statement included the following: 'Eudy recognised Themba (another co-accused). Themba gave me the knife and said I "must do something" as she recognised him and could see who he was. He confirmed that she knew him and Themba said "she will get us arrested", so I "must do something…"'

Upon cross-questioning after reading his statement, Mpiti claimed that he did not know the deceased before killing her, that her identity was revealed to him only after his arrest: 'I was informed after my arrest of her name and where she is from. I was told she was a Banyana Banyana soccer player. I also heard about her sexual orientation, while I was in custody.'

By this time all of us paying attention to the court proceedings had already noted what the judge chose to miss. Mpiti had acknowledged that his co-accused (Themba) had been recognised by Eudy. Later, he claimed not to have known Eudy prior to killing her. It is also undoubted that Eudy was a well-known figure in her township. It is not common for a young black women who plays in the national soccer squad to go unnoticed by her community. It is similarly uncommon for members of our societies not to see forms of gender expression that challenge popular gender norms. Not only was Eudy a well-known community figure, people recognised her as a lesbian and a 'butch' lesbian.

It was the judge's intervention that angered many of us in this court. The prosecutor had proceeded, questioning the accused about his knowledge of Eudy's sexual orientation. Judge Mavundla quickly interrupted this line of questioning and authoritatively stated: 'There is no significance of the victim's sexual orientation in Mpiti's crime.' The prosecutor, forced to withdraw his line of questioning, exhaled and, seemingly defeated, sat down.

The unjust protector

Judge Mavundla's assertion during Mpiti's cross-questioning was a disturbing and damaging intervention from the highest person in the court of law. His intervention made sexual orientation and identity an invisible and insignificant part of Eudy's life and the lives of the many people in the courtroom. He denied common knowledge that Eudy was known by the perpetrators and many others in the community to be a lesbian. Judge Mavundla foreclosed the possibility that Eudy was targeted specifically because she was a lesbian, an important factor that makes many lesbians feel vulnerable and unsafe in their communities. Mostly, I want to argue, the judge committed a serious injustice by silencing sexual orientation and identity, silencing it also as a motivating factor in the murder. Through his power and position, he committed a painful and further violation of many lesbians and of Eudy's family.

The judge's failure to recognise the importance of sexual orientation and the multiple identities of the victim illustrates what Amartya Sen calls a 'solitarist approach to human identity'

(2007: 4–6). Thinking that any person or victim of crime possesses only one identity during that crime limits the possibility of seeing the myriad of identities found within each individual. It is a flaw not to recognise that Eudy was a young, black lesbian woman in the township without the means to feel protected in her own community while providing for her family. Instead, during this case, we were made to listen endlessly to how Mpiti was a young unemployed man, a struggling father of a small baby, a partner who couldn't take care of his girlfriend, a son whose ill mother needed him; the list was endless. In short, Mpiti was a victim of circumstances that led him to criminal behaviour, circumstances that were beyond his control. At the same time, we were prevented from seeing Eudy's multiplicities and interwoven identities. She was only to remain unnamed, faceless, without identity and just 'the deceased'.

As Sen puts it, 'in our normal lives, we see ourselves as members of a variety of groups – we belong to all of them' and all of the time (my addition). The same person can, without any contradiction, occupy different subject positions. Thus, asserting that sexual orientation has 'no significance' was not only an undesirable moral or ethical judgement, but it was also a limited description or a 'solitarist approach' (Sen 2007: xii) to understanding and describing the many ways people live their lives. Therefore, to rob an individual of the multiplicity and intersectionality of her identities is problematic. It is problematic because we inhabit the world with a myriad of identities and associations. These do not cease even in the case of murder or violence (Sen 2007: xii). Thus, when a case is being dealt with, at least at the level of the court, it is expected that all the reasons a violation took place would be taken into account. Therefore, by his intervention, the judge foreclosed the opportunity to explore the multiple reasons[2] a violation and murder occurred.

The judge was wrong, but it may not have been entirely his fault. As Sally Kohn (2001: 225) argues, society:

> generally is premised on a hierarchy of social classes – based on race, sex, sexual orientation, gender identity, age, wealth, education level and so on. This social hierarchy transfers to the legal realm … those accused of offending someone above them

in social status are likely to be handled more severely than those offending someone below them.

Given the socially unequal, heteronormative and patriarchal society we live in, it is not entirely surprising that our lives as middle- or lower-class black lesbian women, even in the context of the court, a progressive constitution and a human rights discourse, will remain in the lower ranks of the social hierarchy or even unrecognised.

Efforts at redress have been numerous, including a call for appropriate legislation to facilitate the legal proceedings. However, what is paramount is sensitising the primary sources of justice. From the moment the victim enters a police station or is seen by a member of the police force, her experience with the different ranks of the justice system should not deter her from seeking further help. The point of entry into the justice system should be sensitive about the victim's subjective experiences of violation. It is through such added efforts that our lives and experiences as members of race, class, gender and sexual identity formations will cease to disappear.

Notes

1   Simon Nkoli was arrested in 1985 and charged with treason. He was in detention for alleged terrorist activities together with 21 other activists. The Delmas treason trial was one of South Africa's most protracted court cases, ending in 1988 with Nkoli's acquittal.
2   I am indebted to Sarai Chisala for this insight and for her illuminating arguments.

References

Bucher, Nathalie Rosa (2009) 'South Africa: law failing lesbians on "corrective rape"', Inter Press Service (IPS), 31 August, http://ipsnews.net/print.asp?idnews=48279, accessed 27 July 2010

Gontek, Ines (2009) 'Sexual violence against lesbian women in South Africa', *Outliers, A Collection of Essays and Creative Writing on Sexuality in Africa*, 2 (Spring): 1–18

Gunkel, Henriette (2010) *The Cultural Politics of Female Sexuality in South Africa*, New York, Routledge

Kohn, Sally (2001) 'Greasing the wheel: how the criminal justice system hurts gay, lesbian, bisexual and transgendered people and why hate crime laws won't save them', *N.Y.U. Review of Law and Social Change*, 27: 257–80

Mkhize, N., Bennett, J., Reddy, V. and Moletsane, R. (2010) *The Country We Want to Live in: Hate Crimes and Homophobia in the Lives of Black Lesbian South Africans*, Pretoria, HSRC Press

Mtetwa, Phumi (2011) '"Correct" the homophobes', *Amandla: South Africa's new progressive magazine standing for social justice*, 20 (July/August): 20–1

Muholi, Zanele (2004) 'Thinking through lesbian rape', *Agenda*, 18(61): 116–25

Muthien, Bernedette (2007) 'Queerying borders: an Afrikan activist perspective', *Journal of Lesbian Studies*, 11(3): 321–30

Reddy, V., Potgieter, C.-A. and Mkhize, N. (2007) 'Cloud over the rainbow nation: "corrective rape" and other hate crimes against black lesbians', *HSRC Review*, 5(1): 10–11

Schaap, Jeremy and Gim, Beein (2010) 'Female athletes often targets for rape: E:60' (video documentary), http://sports.espn.go.com/espn/e60/news/story?id=5177704

Sen, Amartya (2007) *Identity and Violence: The Illusion of Destiny*, London, Penguin Books

Wittig, Monique (1993) 'One is not born a woman', in Abelove, H., Barale, M.A. and Halperin, D.M. (eds) *The Lesbian and Gay Studies Reader*, New York, Routledge: 103–9

35

Zanele Muholi's intimate archive: photography and post-apartheid lesbian lives

Kylie Thomas

> The ones who fear me think they know who I am.
>
> Minnie Bruce Pratt[1]

This paper focuses on the work of South African black lesbian photographer Zanele Muholi and raises the question of how experience that is deemed unspeakable can enter representation. If we always read images through 'codes of connotation', through what Roland Barthes terms the '*studium*' of our knowing, how is it possible to overturn ways of seeing that render lesbian subjectivity invisible?[2] And if lesbian subjectivity is made visible through suspending the structures of recognition, what are the political implications of occupying such an 'outlaw' position? How does being beyond recognition open or close the field of political possibility? My reading of Muholi's portraits that constitute her 'Faces and Phases' series explores how her photographs work with the ambiguities of 'passing' – passing away, passing between states of gendered being, and passing through the prohibitions against making lesbian experience visible and mourning lesbian loss. In this way this chapter argues that Muholi's most recent body of work 'queers' both the conventions of memorial photography and her own earlier representations of lesbian subjectivity.

Zanele Muholi is one of a handful of black women artists who figure prominently in the visual art field and her work has been shown both in South Africa and abroad. She is certainly the most visible black lesbian artist in South Africa and has received numerous awards for her work. Her photographs have also generated a great deal of controversy. In August 2009, South Africa's Minister of Arts and Culture, Lulu Xingwana, walked out of an exhibition that contained several of Muholi's photographs on the grounds that they were 'immoral, offensive' and worked 'against nation-building'.[3] This has placed Muholi's photographs at the centre of a national debate about homophobia, freedom of expression and queer experience.[4] I will return to the significance of Xingwana's comments later in this paper in my discussion of the tactics Muholi employs in her photographs of black lesbians who have been subject to 'corrective rape' and who have died of AIDS-related causes or who were murdered as a result of hate crimes. I read these images as works of mourning that invoke conventional tropes of memorialisation to circumvent precisely the socially normative prohibitions so dramatically performed by Xingwana in her role as an authorised voice of the state. The paper offers an analysis of the transformation in Muholi's mode of working that occurs when she addresses the question of how to represent loss. In particular I trace how her current work draws on the conventions of memorial photography in order to secure a place for queer subjects within representation. At the same time I show how this complex working with and against the 'structures of recognition' signals a departure from her earlier and more narrow conceptualisations of lesbian subjectivity.[5] In order to do this I begin by describing some of the ways in which her photographs can be understood as engaged in the task of 'differencing the canon', before turning to a reading of her most recent series of portraits, 'Faces and Phases'. The work of South African feminist theorists Desiree Lewis and Pumla Dineo Gqola and curator and artist Gabi Ngcobo has drawn attention to how Muholi's photographs render the complexity of lesbian lives visible.[6] However, this brave and politically necessary task is not the sum of her work. The import of her current photographs lies in how they both lay bare and contest the ways in which the lives of queer subjects are made invisible and their deaths ungrievable. 'Faces and Phases', I argue here, works at the limit of the speakable, and Muholi's photographs mark that limit even as they pass beyond it.

Disrupting visual codes

In *Encounters in the Virtual Feminist Museum*, Griselda Pollock presents an approach to the history of art that embarks on the work of what she terms 'differencing the canon'.[7] She swiftly lays to rest the notion that the canon is quite 'differenced' enough already by noting that '[n]ot only have we had to struggle and still struggle on to ensure equity in the representation of all women as well as all men in our cultural archives, but now our very struggle is being written out of history, brushed off as a passing irritant.'[8] Pollock begins her reflections on the place of women in the history of art, in the museum and in the archive, by relating her encounter with a series of postcards that depict *The Three Graces*, a neoclassical sculpture by Antonio Canova. She notes how the prevalence of the female nude in the art museum is so naturalised that we no longer see its strangeness, and as longstanding signifier of Western art the naked female form becomes a placeholder for women in art – the place of 'woman' in the museum, a stony limit point for feminist art practice and theory. Her book goes on to produce 'a virtual feminist museum' through a constellation of images exhibited in what she terms 'rooms' at the beginning of each of her chapters, all of which unsettle and recalibrate the archive of art history. Pollock's work reminds us that 'Archives matter. What is included shapes forever what we think we were and hence what we might become. The absence of women's histories in world archives has defined a vision of the human on the pattern of a privileged masculinity.'[9] Pollock's approach to reconfiguring how we think about visual culture is suggestive and her archival feminist aim resonates with the work of Zanele Muholi in several ways. Muholi's project is also an archival one and is concerned with many of the same issues of visibility and invisibility that have consumed feminist scholarship since the 1970s. In her artist's statement which appears in the catalogue for the 'Innovative Women' exhibition, she writes: 'As an insider within the black lesbian community and a visual activist, I want to ensure that my community, especially those lesbian women who come from the marginalised townships, are included in the women's "canon".'

A cursory survey of Muholi's work thus far reveals the intensity of her commitment to producing a visual archive of black lesbian experience. Her photographs have appeared in group exhibitions since 2002, her solo exhibition 'Visual Sexuality' was held at the Johannesburg Art Gallery in 2004, and since 2006 she has been represented by Michael Stevenson, a commercial art gallery in South Africa. She has held four additional solo exhibitions there: 'Only Half the Picture' (2006); 'Being' (2007); 'Faces and Phases', first exhibited as a series in 2009; and 'Indawo Yami' (2010). Her exhibitions in Europe and North America include solo shows in Vienna and Amsterdam. In 2007, together with white South African lesbian photographer Jean Brundrit, Muholi facilitated a series of photographic workshops 'to gather diverse opinions and diverse lesbian experiences in South Africa' with eight aspiring photographers.[10] While the artist is now firmly positioned within the commercial art world, she continues her work with the Forum for the Empowerment of Women, an organisation that she co-founded, and to teach others to take photographs.[11]

Muholi's photographs open new spaces of representation in South African visual culture but follow in the tradition of feminist/lesbian art-making practices established over time by artists such as the US-based Judy Chicago, Cindy Sherman, Laura Aguilar and others. In her oeuvre there are numerous works that proclaim their transgressive, disruptive stance, and these are perhaps the images that are easiest to categorise, easiest to dismiss – as some critics have – as 'not very good art' that nonetheless makes an important political point.[12] Some of the images in Muholi's book *Only Half the Picture* and some that appear in her more recent 'Being' series are among those that invoke conventional tropes of lesbian/feminist representation to contest the bounds of what is considered proper for women and for art. 'Dada, 2003', a black and white photograph of a bare-breasted black woman strapping on a dildo, her face beyond the frame of the image, the 2005–06 'Period' series and the 2009 'LiZa' series can all be read as testing the limits of propriety in art and as a straightforward claiming of a visual space for embodied black lesbian experience. And through these works Muholi's project can be said to be aligned with the mainstream feminist position that Pollock articulates in *Encounters in the Virtual Feminist Museum*. For in this conceptualisation of the production of a new form of feminist archive that makes the experiences of women visible, it is of course necessary that the women who are represented are recognisable as women. Muholi's project, one that she articulates on her website as 'mapping and archiving a visual history of black lesbians in post-Apartheid South Africa', also engages and affirms a particular form of identity politics in order to lay claim to a place within an existing order of representation.

At the same time, Muholi's concern with securing a place for lesbian experience within 'the women's "canon"' signals that what constitutes lesbian subjectivity is by no means decided. Her words testify to the ontological insecurity of the category of being that is 'lesbian' in a context where corrective rape is practised as a way to 'restore' lesbians to womanhood. Bringing the work of Zanele Muholi into conversation with the feminist position Pollock articulates also opens a way to consider what the limits of 'differencing the canon' might be. What happens when radical and disruptive forms of subjectivity seek to enter representation? Does the canon hold? Does the archive seize up, prohibit entry? What kinds of silences remain?

Light writing in dark times

Muholi's first monograph, *Only Half the Picture*, carefully works with the aesthetics of the body, a complex holding of traumatic histories encoded in skin together with a celebration of lesbian desire and the promise of pleasure. Through Muholi's lens black female bodies are resignified; framed as the subjects of and for lesbian desire, they make visible an erotics of longing, of sexual intimacy and of community. At the same time, many of the photographs carry resonances of photographs of black female bodies drawn from a long history of racist iconography and which map the continuities of black female oppression over time. In the cracked toenails of the women in 'Triple III', for instance, there are signs of hardship, in the dark markings along the outer edges of the thighs of the reclining figures there is a shadow of darkness, of violence, bruises or stains.[13] Read in conjunction with the other photographs in the 'Triple' series that portray the interlocking legs and buttocks of three women and that bring to mind the erotic nudes of Edward Weston or Imogen Cunningham, the ambiguities of 'Triple III' are largely erased. Its erotic dimension comes to the fore. The pose of the three women speaks of the stillness of sleep and shows the protective tenderness of bodies curved around one another. And yet there is something disturbing about the arrangement of these bodies on the floor. They are shown to be resting on a strip of carpet, its detail in the foreground so close-up it becomes a strange terrain and then fades to merge with what appears to be a stone floor that extends behind them. The marks on the limbs of these women evoke the history of slavery, summon photographs of the bodies of those killed in the Rwandan genocide, provide a visual echo of the legs of schoolgirls who have been tear-gassed and who run from the police in Soweto in South Africa in 1976. The larger context of Muholi's book, one that includes photographs of women after being raped, raises the question of how it is possible to read black lesbian desire outside of the violence of both the past and present. I want to say that inside the frame of 'Triple III' there is no fear, only kinship, intimacy, love. But if this is so then fear is just beyond the borders of what is made visible here and haunts this beautiful assemblage of bare forms. Here, as in the works that form part of her series portraying lesbians who have been subject to hate crimes that I discuss below, Muholi is masterful in her portrayal of the vulnerability of the human body and the complexity of embodied experience.

In 'Ordeal, 2003', there is a line of fury that runs through the arm of the woman who crouches at the edge of an enamel basin scrubbing her hands into a blurred frenzy, moving so fast and so slick with water they appear unskinned.[14] At the centre of the photograph in which everything else remains still these hands are rendered unrecognisable, a pulpy mass, an internal organ exposed to the air, an aborted foetus or placenta. Something that cannot be washed clean.

This is the first of a series of photographs in *Only Half the Picture* that depict the survivors of hate crimes. It is followed by a double-page spread of a case-number, a crumpled piece of lined paper depicted against a black ground, issued by the South African Police Service in Meadowlands, Soweto. Handwritten on the page are the details of a case – the date of the incident, the name of the inspector assigned to the case, a phone number and an official stamp. There is also a line that reads 'ATT. Rape + Assault G.B.H' [Grievous Bodily Harm]. The photograph that appears overleaf casts light on why this hastily written case-number should be accorded so much space. 'Hate Crime Survivor I, 2004' is a closely cropped portrait of a woman visible from her waist to just above her knees. The vertical lines of her hospital-issue pyjama pants angle slightly in towards the centre of the photograph and draw the viewer's eyes to her slender wrists and hands which are positioned on her lap, her curved finger and thumb forming a dark hollow, a point of entry into her body, a metonym for the violated parts of her we cannot see. Around her wrists are three identifying tags that signify her in-patient status but here also read as manacles, handcuffs. And suddenly her striped clothing resembles a prison uniform, and the posture of her body holds the echo of countless images of incarcerated men who stand with their heads bent, their hands and feet bound – a stance of guilt. The implication is that in spite of the indisputable archival evidence represented by the photograph of the case number that immediately precedes this image, lesbians who are raped are often not believed and are treated as criminals both inside and outside of the justice system. The juxtaposition of these two photographs makes visible the ways in which those who are subject to rape are also often accused of having brought violence on themselves. The concept of corrective or curative rape is often read as premised on the idea that lesbians have done something wrong to begin with and that rape is that which will set things right, restoring the natural order. Muholi articulates how rape is used to punish and correct lesbians in South Africa: 'Curative rapes, as they are called, are perpetrated against us in order to make us into "real" and "true" African women – appropriately feminine, mothers, men's property.'[15] Yet as Muholi's photographs show, understanding the psychic mechanism that underlies curative rape as an act that restores the order of patriarchy through affirming relations of power between men and women is to grant a kind of sense to senseless acts of hate. Her series depicting survivors of hate crimes shows how the act of curative rape is fundamentally tied to a desire to murder.

One of the most painful photographs in Muholi's oeuvre is 'Hate Crime Survivor II'. It appears alongside the photograph of the 'criminal/survivor' and powerfully undoes the flawed and fatal logic that seeks to blame lesbians who are raped. In a hospital ward on a high bed covered with a white sheet is a figure under a heap of dark bedclothes. In fact it is only the caption that accompanies the photograph which renders the figure legible – without the single line that tells us that what we are looking at is a person, a 'survivor', there is no way to know for certain that the shape on the bed is a human form. The camera angle renders the bed enormous and foreshortens the figure so that the person appears shrunken, barely there. The photograph portrays how the human form is overcome by the trauma of psychic collapse. Here the effect of rape is shown to be ontological erasure, the annihilation of subjectivity. The person who we know to be there but whom we cannot see has not been made 'woman' but has been altogether unmade as a subject.

'Aftermath, 2004' portrays a woman standing, and in this sense contrasts the collapsed figure on the hospital bed on the preceding page.[16] However, the large scar that extends down the length of this woman's thigh signifies that there can be no easy moving beyond the trauma of rape. The scar is a sign of a much older wound but serves here as an outer manifestation of her more recent physical and psychic wounding through corrective rape. The scar itself, an elongated teardrop, an opening into her body now closed, like the curled hand of the woman depicted in 'Hate Crime Survivor I', serves as a metonym for her violated vagina. There is something unbearable about the positioning of this woman's hands. They seek to shield her, to protect her, in this instance from our gaze as much as from the traumatic memory of attack, but at the same time they are passive, they are hands that speak a history of defeat. If there is a *punctum* here it is not the scar that we cannot fail to see, but the light as it catches the thumb of this woman, her curled fingers, the vulnerability of her being that is encoded in her hands.

Muholi's hate crimes series asks us to think differently about how we understand sexuality and subjectivity, and this is not restricted to thinking what lesbians are or might be. They show us that to be lesbian is not to perform desire in a way that transforms/queers an underlying essential being that is 'woman'. Instead they show, through laying bare the painful way in which the corrective rape of lesbians restores absolutely nothing at all, the emptiness at the centre of the fiction that animates all forms of gendered being.[17]

Queering the archive

The ways in which Antonio Canova's sculpture of the three graces might be read as pregnant with lesbian/transsexual desire is surfaced in a photographic work by British artist Della Grace/Del LaGrace Volcano.[18] The black and white photograph shows three women, naked but for their jackboots, standing in the pose of *The Three Graces* with their arms around one another and their heads shaved, their bodies scarified, pierced and tattooed. I first saw LaGrace Volcano's reworking of the sculpture in Parveen Adams' book *The Emptiness of the Image* and Adams' reading of the photograph is a provocative one. For Adams the image disturbs the conventional modes of representation of woman to such an extent that she argues: 'These women are beyond recognition.'[19] She goes on to explain:

> Recognition is a process that may be looked at from two sides. Women who are recognised as such are recognised by a rigorous template of definition. If we do not recognise, in this photograph, these women, it is not because they are recognised as something else. It is rather because the structure of recognition has been suspended.[20]

What Adams draws attention to here is the way in which LaGrace Volcano's photograph inaugurates a way of looking that undoes our gendered gaze. The transgressive power of the image lies in the fact that we cannot simply substitute 'woman' for another recognisable category of being – whether that is 'lesbian' or anything else. Adams' reading provides a way to account for the absence of LaGrace Volcano's *The Three Graces* from Pollock's virtual feminist museum. Her analysis of how the photograph works to suspend the structures of recognition raises the question of what it means to be positioned outside the realms of the legible. And this returns us to the significance of the archive, which, as Pollock notes:

> is pre-selected in ways that reflect what each culture considered worth storing and remembering, skewing historical record and indeed historical writing towards the privileged, the powerful, the political, military and religious. Vast areas of social life and huge numbers of people hardly exist, according to the archive.

> The archive is overdetermined by *facts* of class, race, gender, sexuality and above all power' [my emphasis].[21]

Indeed, the archive produces these 'facts' as much as it holds them and seeks to secure them. The archive is also (and I think this is the sense in which Zanele Muholi employs the term) a site of struggle for legitimacy. A certain kind of entry into the archive will mark queer lives as deviant, perverse and criminal. Another mode of entry, one that Muholi's work seeks to find, is that which will guarantee visibility within the social that is not at the same time a form of erasure. Central here is the question of what the archive itself demands – what are the conditions of entry into the archive of legibility? If 'the archive is the law of what can be said', what is the place of outlaw subjects who are not merely beyond or outside the law but who signify the law's very undoing?[22]

It is in a space of suspension, a kind of limit zone between recognition and invisibility, that Muholi's most powerful photographs are situated. The ways in which Muholi carefully forces the boundaries of the archive's frontier is the subject of the remainder of this chapter. I explore how, through a process that literary theorist Ross Chambers terms 'genre-hijacking'[23] and that I draw on and recode here as 'passing', Muholi's work performs a complex negotiation of the limits and possibilities of and for queer subjectivity within representation.[24]

Mourning and/as masquerade

> Ultimately, Photography is subversive not when it frightens, when it repels, or even stigmatizes, but when it is pensive, when it thinks.
>
> Roland Barthes[25]

In *Camera Lucida*, Barthes defines his concepts of the *studium* and the *punctum*, key terms for thinking about how photographs are read. Most photographs belong to the *studium*, that which I have learned to see by acculturation and that which cannot really reach me. And then there are those photographs that arrest my gaze, photographs that disturb the *studium* of my knowing, photographs that wound me, photographs that I love. This element within the photograph is animated through the particularity of my gaze. It is this Barthes terms the *punctum*: 'The second element will break or (punctuate) the *studium*. This time it is not I who seek it out (as I invest the field of the *studium* with my sovereign consciousness), it is this element which rises from the scene, shoots out of it like an arrow, and pierces me.'[26] Barthes' concepts of the *studium* and the *punctum* set up a method of reading photographs that illuminates how all readings are cultural – but at the same time legitimate a deeply subjective mode of response. The concept of the *punctum* allows Barthes (not to mention all those who have followed in his wake) to cast his emotional, poetic responses to photographs as a theory. I draw on these concepts here to grant a kind of legitimacy to my readings of Muholi's photographs. At the same time I am struck by how thinking her work in relation to Barthes' influential terms casts light on the implications of 'queering the gaze' beyond gay and lesbian studies. In other words it is not simply that Barthes' method offers a productive mode of reading Muholi's photographs, but Muholi's work shows that reading with and for the *punctum* can be understood as a mode of queer reading, an openness to ways of seeing that disrupt the heteronormative patriarchal hegemony that limits and structures our gaze.

In *Camera Lucida*, Barthes writes of how 'to give examples of *punctum* is, in a certain fashion, to give myself up'.[27] To reveal the ways in which I am affected by a photograph is to be exposed, describing what I see is an act that 'outs' me, one that positions my intimate self in a public sphere. 'Giving myself up' before a photograph is also to occupy a subject position beyond or outside of my own. What might the minister have seen had she stayed to look at Muholi's photographs? The incendiary quality of the works Xingwana did and did not see lies in how they make possible a space for us to acknowledge our own (queer) desire, I want to argue, in how they provide an entry point into an intimate archive, one that is embodied, one that is formed through love.

There is a second *punctum* that Barthes identifies as he studies the photographs that move him and attempts to identify the secrets of photographic affect. That *punctum* is time. Photographs make visible the passage of time and they mark our inability to halt its passage. This relation between photography and time is central to understanding how photography, and portrait photography in particular, is linked to mourning. In *Camera Lucida* Barthes reads

Alexander Gardner's 1865 portrait of Lewis Payne, a young man who was photographed in his cell while awaiting execution for attempting to assassinate Secretary of State W.H. Seward: 'The photograph is handsome, as is the boy: that is the *studium*. But the *punctum* is: *he is going to die.*'[28] Barthes quickly comes to see that all photographs make visible our being-towards-death. 'I read at the same time: This will be and this has been; I observe with horror an anterior future of which death is the stake. By giving me the absolute past of the pose (aorist), the photograph tells me death in the future.'[29]

The photographs that make up the 'Faces and Phases' series exploit the relation between photography and mourning to great effect. All the photographs in the series are shot in black and white, almost all the subjects face the camera, 'returning' the viewer's gaze, most are half-length portraits, and several depict only the head and shoulders of the subject. Each photograph is captioned with the name of the person portrayed, the place in which they were photographed, and the date the image was taken. The uniformity of the images indicates that they form part of a single body of work. The seeming regularity of the series also serves another end – it operates as a visual sign of a shared experience, of a community of being, and is a common practice in photography that aims to memorialise.

Muholi's artist's statement for 'Faces and Phases' overtly articulates her desire to assert black queer presence in contemporary South Africa and frames that desire in relation to the ever-present threat of violence, both discursive and material: 'It is important to mark, map and preserve our mo(ve)ments through visual histories for reference and posterity so that future generations will note that we were here.'[30] In her description of the work she intends the series to perform Muholi writes: 'Historically, portraits serve as memorable records for families and friends as evidence when someone passes. Faces express the persons, and Phases signifies the transition from one stage of sexuality or gender expression and experience to another.'[31] Here Muholi uses the term 'passes' in the sense of 'passed away' or 'to die'. An analysis of the work 'Faces and Phases' performs also reveals how 'passing' operates in another way through these photographs that make visible the passing away of lesbians as a result of hate crimes and AIDS-related diseases and a form of passing between fixed gendered positions. These portraits simultaneously permit these lesbian lives to pass into an archive of mainstream visual representation through their 'hijacking' of the generic conventions of memorialisation. Ross Chambers has developed this idea in relation to the work of gay writers who have testified to their experiences of living with and dying of AIDS. 'Genre-hijacking' makes use of established generic conventions to speak what culture has deemed unspeakable. In the case of Muholi's work in South Africa, what is unspeakable is both lesbian desire and loss. 'Faces and Phases' mobilises the conventions of memorial portrait photography to open a space for mourning and at the same time queers that space by juxtaposing images of the dead with multiple portraits of living queer subjects.

The question of what is at stake in this act of passing marks the fine line between passing as a strategy of survival, a mechanism that allows one to appear, and passing away, becoming invisible as a queer subject through one's entry into the realm of the legible. This invisibility can be psychic, a metaphoric loss of subjectivity, and can take material form through the threat of murder that affects lesbian being everywhere in South Africa today. Muholi's artist's statement draws attention to the portraits of those who have died but at the same time positions them among the portraits of the living. Here the presence of the dead signals the precarious position of the living and the living remind us of the subjectivity of the dead:

> 'Phases' articulates the collective pain we as a community experience due to the loss of friends and acquaintances through disease and hate crimes. Some of those who participated in this visual project have already passed away. We fondly remember Buhle Msibi (2006), Busi Sigasa (2007), Nosizwe Cekiso (2009) and Penny Fish (2009): may they rest in peace. The portraits also celebrate friends and acquaintances who hold different positions and play many different roles within black queer communities – an actress, soccer players, a scholar, cultural activists, dancers, filmmakers, writers, photographers, human rights and gender activists, mothers, lovers, friends, sisters, brothers, daughters and sons.[32]

Positioning the portraits of the dead among those still living implies solidarity with the dead, a community that traverses the boundary between life and death. The rhetorical force of this pairing of the living and the dead powerfully refuses the dehumanisation of black lesbians that led to the deaths of the women memorialised here. This positioning which insists on the relation between the living and the dead also means that we necessarily read each portrait in the series as haunted by the possibility of violence, rape and murder.

The photographs in the series of women who have died – Busi Sigasa, Penny Fish and Nosizwe Cekiso – make use of the recognisable codes of the obituary form but read in relation to the other portraits in the series these codes are undeniably queered. Witness the juxtaposition of 'Nosizwe Cekiso, Gugulethu, Cape Town, 2008', and 'Gazi T Zuma, Umlazi, Durban, 2010'. What results is a form of queer memorialising that makes lesbian lives and deaths visible without sacrificing their queerness. It is the particularity of these deaths as lesbian deaths that Muholi will not allow to pass even as they 'pass' into the memorial structures of recognition. The photographs that make up 'Faces and Phases' negotiate the line between passing and death, visibility and invisibility. For in these images what we see is not 'woman' and yet we cannot recognise these subjects as lesbians either, for a moment, in looking, the fixity of our gendered look cannot hold.[33] 'The structure of recognition has been suspended.'[34] All that is thought to separate black lesbians from 'human' subjectivity is simultaneously present and absent here. The photographs insist on the particularity of the black lesbians they portray at the same time as they insist on their sameness – to other women, to other embodied subjects, to the human. Through these 'straight' portraits we bear witness to queer lives. Muholi's photographs move us through and beyond our perceptions of what lesbian subjectivity might be and at the same time challenge us to reconceptualise the bounds of what is thought to constitute the human. Must the passage between invisibility and visibility entail giving up queerness? In their complex defamiliarising of the conventions through which we recognise the human, the portraits that constitute 'Faces and Phases' suggest this does not have to be so.

Muholi's photographs claim a place for queer subjects in the field of visual art. Through this act of 'claiming', her work testifies to the complexity of queer experience in post-apartheid South Africa and at the same time constitutes a demand for political recognition. Muholi's photographs, which bear witness to the experiences of lesbians who have been subject to hate crimes, as well as some of the responses her work has generated – like that of Xingwana – illuminate that this demand has yet to be met.[35] The inclusivity of the South African constitution is often the starting point for debates about gay and lesbian rights in the country; however, as many of Muholi's photographs show, to be queer is still to be subject to multiple, and often violent, forms of erasure.

This essay appeared in a slightly longer form in the journal Safundi *in 2010.*

Notes

1 Pratt (1990: 114).
2 Barthes (1981: 26).
3 Van Wyk 2010. For the media statement see Xingwana (n.d.). It is also instructive to read the minister's statements on art that does promote nation building. See, for instance, her address (Xingwana 2009) at the launch of the Moral Regeneration Month.
4 I employ the term 'queer' to open a way of thinking about sexuality and subjectivity that crosses and seeks to undo the bounds between categories of identification such as 'gay', 'lesbian', 'straight', 'bisexual' and 'intersex'.
5 I draw the phrase 'structures of recognition' from psychoanalytic theorist Parveen Adams (1996). The term implies socially constructed ways of seeing and modes by which one becomes recognisable as a subject, as well as the psychic dimension of the operations of the gaze.
6 Lewis (2005), Gqola (2006) and Ngcobo (2006).
7 Pollock (2007: 13) and also Pollock (1999).
8 Pollock (2007: 13).
9 Pollock (2007: 12).
10 A selection of photographs by the participants at the workshop, a description of the project and some of Jean Brundrit's own very interesting photographic work which, like Muholi's, engages with lesbian experience, (in)visibility and the archive is collected in Brundrit 2008.
11 For more information about Muholi's visual activism, see her projects on her website www.zanelemuholi.com.
12 See the critiques levelled at Muholi's early work by reviewers such as Smith, and reprinted in Muholi (2006: 90–1); and Hogg, cited in Lewis (2005: 17).

13 The image can be seen on the Michael Stevenson Gallery website (Muholi 2005).
14 See this and other images at Muholi (2005).
15 Muholi (2009a: 19).
16 For other readings of this photograph, see Lewis (2005) and Gunkel (2010).
17 The key text for thinking gender as performative remains Judith Butler's *Gender Trouble* which asks, among other things, how 'language itself produce[s] the fictive construction of "sex"' (Butler 1990: xi).
18 Della Grace is now Del LaGrace Volcano, a gender-variant visual artist. See www.dellagracevolcano.com.
19 Adams (1996: 123).
20 Adams (1996: 138).
21 Pollock (2007: 12).
22 Foucault (2002: 145).
23 Chambers (2004: 29). See also Chambers (1998) for an excellent study of how writing the experience of living with and dying of AIDS tests the boundaries of autobiographical writing.
24 Natasha Distiller's essay 'Another story' (2005) offers a critical reflection on the limits of and for lesbian experience within representation. Interestingly, Muholi refers to Distiller's argument in her discussion of her motivation for producing 'Faces and Phases' and states: 'I wanted to resist the heterosexual representation of lesbians through portraits' (Muholi 2009a: 26).
25 Barthes (1981: 38).
26 Barthes (1981: 26).
27 Barthes (1981: 43).
28 Barthes (1981: 96).
29 Barthes (1981).
30 Muholi (2010).
31 Muholi (2009a: 27).
32 Muholi (2010).
33 For a representative selection of images, see Muholi (2009b and 2010).
34 Adams (1996: 138).
35 See, for example, the recent incident at the United Nations Human Rights Council in Geneva where South Africa's representative Jerry Matjila objected to the inclusion of sexual orientation in a report on racism as to do so would be to 'demean the legitimate plight of the victims of racism' (Fabricius 2010: 3).

References

Adams, Parveen (1996) *The Emptiness of the Image: Psychoanalysis and Sexual Differences*, London, Routledge
Barthes, Roland (1977) *Image, Music, Text*, Glasgow, Fontana
Barthes, Roland (1981) *Camera Lucida: Reflections on Photography*, New York, Farrar, Straus and Giroux
Brundrit, Jean (2008) 'A Lesbian Story: an Exhibition Project by Jean Brundrit'

Butler, Judith (1990) *Gender Trouble: Feminism and the Subversion of Identity*, New York, Routledge

Chambers, Ross (1998) *Facing It: AIDS Diaries and the Death of the Author*, Ann Arbor, University of Michigan Press

Chambers, Ross (2004) *Untimely Interventions: AIDS Writing, Testimonial and the Rhetoric of Haunting*, Ann Arbor, University of Michigan Press

Distiller, Natasha (2005) 'Another story: the (im)possibility of lesbian desire', 63: 44–57

Fabricius, Peter (2010) 'SA fails to back efforts at UN to protect gays', *Cape Times*, 23 June: 3

Foucault, Michel (2002) *The Archaeology of Knowledge*, London, Routledge

Gqola, Pumla Dineo (2006) 'Through Zanele Muholi's eyes: re/imagining ways of seeing black lesbians', in *Zanele Muholi: Only Half the Picture*. Johannesburg: STE Publishers: 82–9

Gunkel, Henriette (2010) *The Cultural Politics of Female Sexuality in South Africa*, New York, Routledge

Lewis, Desiree (2005) 'Against the grain: black women and sexuality', *Agenda*, 63: 11–24

Muholi, Zanele (2005) 'Only Half the Picture: 29 March–29 April 2006', archived exhibition announcement and images, Michael Stevenson, Cape Town, http://www.michaelstevenson.com/contemporary/exhibitions/muholi/muholi.htm, accessed 5 July 2010

Muholi, Zanele (2006) *Zanele Muholi: Only Half the Picture*, Johannesburg, STE Publishers

Muholi, Zanele (2009a) 'Mapping our histories: a visual history of black lesbians in post-apartheid South Africa', self-published essay, http://www.zanelemuholi.com/ZM%20moh_final_230609.pdf, accessed 14 December 2012

Muholi, Zanele (2009b) 'Faces and Phases: 9 July to 8 August 2009', archived exhibition announcement and images, Brodie/Stevenson, Johannesburg, http://www.brodiestevenson.com/exhibitions/muholi/index.htm, accessed 5 July 2010.

Muholi, Zanele (2010) 'Faces and Phases', artist's statement and images, Michael Stevenson, Cape Town, http://www.michaelstevenson.com/contemporary/exhibitions/muholi/facesphases.htm, accessed 5 July 2010

Ngcobo, Gabi (2006) 'Introduction', in *Zanele Muholi: Only Half the Picture*, Johannesburg, STE Publishers: 4–5

Pollock, Griselda (1999) *Differencing the Canon: Feminist Desire and the Writing of Art's Histories*, London, Routledge

Pollock, Griselda (2007) *Encounters in the Virtual Feminist Museum: Time, Space and the Archive*, New York, Routledge

Pratt, Minnie Bruce (1990) *Crime Against Nature*, New York, Firebrand Books

Van Wyk, Lisa (2010) 'Xingwana: homophobic claims "baseless, insulting"', *Mail and Guardian*, 5 March, http://www.mg.co.za/article/2010-03-05-xingwana-homophobic-claims-baseless-insulting, accessed 18 June 2010

Xingwana, Lulu (2009) 'Address by the Minister of Arts and Culture, Ms

Lulama Xingwana, MP, at the launch of Moral Regeneration Month',
Polokwane, 11 July, Department of Arts and Culture, http://www.dac.gov.
za/speeches/minister/2009/11Jull09Speech.html, accessed 2 July 2010
Xingwana, Lulu (n.d.) 'Statement by Minister of Arts and Culture Ms Lulu
Xingwana on media reports around the innovative women exhibition',
Department of Arts and Culture, http://www.dac.gov.za/media_
releases/2010/04-03-10.html, accessed 2 July 2010

The portrait – fiction

Pamella Dlungwana

Jabu stands, heads and shoulders, with her father, in a portrait that hangs in the lounge. They look like siblings, actually, her father fit and older and Jabu lean and younger. The only difference is the degree of hair and hairlessness on their faces. Her father has a beard, it's hard and black, it could be bushy and thick but the way it catches the sun makes it hard and scratchy looking. I've just decided Jabu is a she; we've not had this madness before. Silly, really, when you factor the reality that we've been dating for three months now. Jabu has simply been Jabu. In Zulu Jabu has managed to avoid the discomfiture that we've just experienced at the Pick 'n Pay.

'Savings or cheque ma'am?' the cashier asks.

This question is met with a vacuous silence, a fumbling through Jabu's pockets and a scratching of the head by me.

'Cheque please,' is Jabu's short but firm reply.

On our way to the car I want to ask what the cashier meant by her question, why Jabu answered her and didn't correct her at first. The silence I thought we'd left in the check-out queue has followed us into the car and all the way into Jabu's flat at the Berea.

I stand there, between the fridge and the sofa, in Jabu's lounge, staring at the portrait of father and daughter, father and son, and ask myself over and over, what I aim to do with this discovery. Jabu spends the rest of the afternoon in bed; she's suddenly not feeling well. I unpack the groceries solo, the portrait on the wall boring holes into my back. Father and daughter, father and son, monitoring my every move.

I peek into the bedroom before I leave; Jabu is asleep, I think. I lock and post the key under the door. The neighbours are cooking dinner, beans and beef, maybe. I should be home cooking mush and mush for my family too. The walk from the Berea to the train station is obese with men and women, boys and girls. Women in dresses, long skirts, short skirts, in combinations of blouse-shirts-vests and headwraps and braids and wigs and afros. Men in pants, shorts, Bermudas and golf shirts, tees and vests, short hair, cornrows and dreadlocks. Men in thick shoes with big footprints in the sand and women in dainty heels and sandals and cute sneakers.

Jabu's hair is soft, cornrowed neatly and like her father's beard it shines in the sun. Jabu wears pants, clam diggers and short shorts with basketball tops and sweaters. In clam diggers her calves are like beach boulders tucked into blue-black flesh and her feet peek out from masculine Nike slops and Air Jordans. I'm relieved that her hands aren't calloused paws and remember that they are big, in the way the rest of her is generally big. I love Jabu before I love her and him together, before I wonder why we never take off our tops when we have sex.

I walk faster to the train, going through the inventory of my mother's freezer. I'll cook chicken and rice; I'll make a quick curry, maybe fish. I'll use some of that curry paste my sister bought.

I get to the train station late. I'm the only person in school uniform. The train is full, it's the sardine can I'll rip open later, spilling fish onto a clean white plate to gut and debone it better. Men smell, they have a heavy odour. A fat man pinches me against a pole, his arm extended above my head. His armpit is in my face and his belly presses against my ass. I assume he has deodorant on but there's a sweaty meatiness about his scent; his armpit is breathing directly into my nose. Jabu always smells fresh; Calvin Klein bottles sit proudly in her bathroom. I spray some of it on my blazer once a week. I sniff myself between classes when I miss Jabu; it feels a bit like if I were to turn I would find Jabu standing behind me.

I stare at the fat man's face and suddenly his moustache starts growing in my direction, long hairs spaghetti reach for me. I feel sick and wonder when we'll reach Thembalihle station. I need to get home to cook tinned fish and rice and watch my family eat it.

At eight Jabu calls. She wants to know if I got home safe, her tone is flat, anaesthetised of any emotion. I'm fine, I got home ok. Cool, then. Bye. Bye.

I go to bed early and can't fall asleep. The image of Jabu as I left her in bed follows me and I don't know what to ask when we meet again. The portrait hanging in her lounge is hurtling towards me like Mr Fat Tum's hairs did on the train home.

In the morning I expect to get Jabu's call. It doesn't come. I don't have money, my mom's forgotten to leave us lunch money again and I don't have a cell phone. I don't know if I'll see Jabu in the afternoon and so drag my feet as I prepare to leave the house. Her sister calls just minutes before I leave. I must go to City Hospital on my way to school. Jabu's not well. She hangs up.

The hospital is a block from my school. I jump off the train and walk right past my school, even though I'm running 15 minutes late and the gate is closed and the elders I'm meeting along the way are giving me strange looks. The hospital's ground floor has a receptionist; she's seen me here before. I've spent a few days on the lobby, waiting to see my aunt who has asthma. We've chatted on all those occasions.

'Is your mom not well again?' she asks.

'No, she's fine. I'm here to see a friend,' I reply, rushing past and pressing the lift closed. I avoid her questions, if my aunt falls sick again I don't want this woman telling tales. I'm hiding Jabu. I've never hidden Jabu before. Am I hiding Jabu or avoiding answering questions about ditching school? I don't have an answer to that. I'm alone in the lift but the many me's staring back don't look too proud.

Jabu is in a female ward, a ward for women. The walls are a curious pastel pink. The nurses at the nurses' station curtly inform me of the visiting hours. I tell them I've brought a patient toiletries. When they ask who it is I'm visiting I give them Jabu's name. Both nurses look at each other then at me and tell me how to find Jabu.

'The patient has cut her breast ... something like a razor. Yeah, with a razor, I think. It was a smooth cut. No accident. The pictures we've taken of her breasts show other cuts, along the armpits and the breasts themselves. This is not the first time. The scars on the patient's...'

City Hospital is no University Hospital. It's semi private, there shouldn't be so many people in lab coats standing around Jabu's bed. There shouldn't be people talking around Jabu, about Jabu. I am hesitant to walk, though: it's not visiting hours, Jabu and I aren't family. She's sedated, she's bound by medication and she can't speak. I lean hesitantly against the doorframe, silently hoping the whole scene disappears, that Jabu be fine, at lectures at ML Sultan and not lying in bed being analysed.

The talk of pictures taken of the patient at admission the night before continues. These strangers have seen Jabu's breasts. They have a folder full of pictures of them somewhere in the hospital premises. I imagine them passing these pictures around later, casually tossing them from one person to the next as they pontificate on why any sane person would mutilate themselves so. So engrossed in their little enclave are they that my presence still hasn't been noticed.

Jabu turns slightly; he's been awake all this time. He's been awake whilst these seven or eight lab-coat-wearing, gossip-starved academics have been poring over his file.

'Hi, excuse me. May I speak to him alone, please?' It comes out like that, like I've practised it for hours, like it's something I get to say often. They look at me, in my uniform, with my backpack. I must be the sister, one of many. They clear out, sort of. They stand aside, let me in and I'm standing at Jabu's bedside.

It can't be that bad, I want to offer. I don't know why but that idea dies in my throat. I have no idea what it must be like, good or bad. I stand there, like a jelly mould, inanimate and purposeless.

'I hate English,' Jabu manages. He lifts his hand and reaches for mine. We are locked like that a while, our hands clasped together, my school bell ringing in the background. His hands are bound in bandages much like the type he keeps on his bedside table. His thumb rubs at the centre of my hand, we chuckle.

The medical gossip squad exits stage left. I set my bag on the floor, grab a chair and spend the rest of the morning talking to my partner.

Seeing beyond colonial binaries: unpacking Malawi's homosexuality discourse

Jessie Kabwila

Introduction

The debate on gayness and lesbianism, usually referred to as homosexuality, is mainly polarised between two competing discourses that are largely colonial in origin. On one side, there is the minority voice, speaking through legal structures, cautiously fighting for homosexuality to be legalised, advancing arguments that are mainly steeped in the human rights discourse. On the other, there is the majority, louder voice, vigorously rejecting this call and spearheaded by churches, traditional leaders and government officials. What this chapter looks at is the predominant lack of indigenous and home-grown ownership in the arguments advanced by either camp. Using my participation in Malawi's constitutional review process, reactions to the 'Malawi Gay and Lesbian Society' email on the Chancellor College listserv, the *Malawi Daily Times* captions of Minister of Information Patricia Kaliyati and *Nyasa Times* articles on the Malawi Gay Rights Movement, I argue that given the level of hiv and aids[1] that Malawi is facing, and the imperial, parasitic and vulture character of the human rights discourse, 21st century Malawi has to own this discourse. The decision whether to legalise or keep homosexuality illegal in Malawi needs to be made on Malawian and indigenous terms. Postcolonial Malawi needs to have this conversation on decolonised terms that neither follow the prescriptive and colonising human rights discourse nor the essentialised Malawian culture discourse that ends up being a proxy for the Western colonial discourse of Western and Eastern organised religion and class elitism. The discourse needs to spin on an axis that:

- Accepts and values difference, diversity and openness of voice
- Interrogates the pros and cons of legalising it for the daily life of the majority and average Malawian across class, gender, sex, ethnicity and other categories
- Determines how homosexuality as a category engages with whatever we define as being a Malawian
- Defines and traces historically what sex and homosexuality mean to Malawian citizenship from precolonial times to date, accounting for the changes.

Approaches anchored on polarised binaries will only problematise and increase tensions in Malawi. On the one hand are arguments steeped in political expediency that often bastardise the concept 'culture', employing colonial and imperial products such as Christianity and Islam. They construct a hegemonic form of cultural essentialisation. On the other are Western voyeuristic and Darwinian concepts that exoticise Africa, Africans and African sex. They portray legalising homosexuality as yet another Western discovery, a gift to the dark and primitive continent and proof of an African modernity.

Since this chapter mainly draws from print media sources, it starts by giving an overview of the coverage of print media,[2] focusing on the years 2005 to 2007.[3]

Homosexuality in Malawi's print media

In general, the Malawian reaction to homosexuality as reported in the media has been negative, ranging from intolerance to outright homophobia. Compared to 2003 and 2004, the year 2005 saw a significant increase in the public media of debates on issues such as homosexuality, cross-dressing and transvestism.

The Malawian media, especially print and radio[4] (television is not widely in use), treat homosexuality, transvestism and cross-dressing differently. Homosexuality is the issue that is mostly debated. The discussions mainly centre on its morality and most submissions oppose it on the altar of religion and culture. Transvestism is rarely discussed while cross-dressing is often not linked to homosexuality or transvestism. The kind of cross-dressing that is visible in the Malawian media is the one that happens during traditional functions such as weddings, funerals, initiation rites and entertainment gatherings that might be indigenous or cosmopolitan or a mixture. There is also an increase in popular artists taking on female stage names such as Anne Matumbi. TVM, Malawi's television station, has even run documentaries on boys who dress like women to entertain. When these musicians are asked why they do this, they report that it is for commercial reasons; it makes them more famous than others and weaves a sense of intrigue and suspense around them, thereby enhancing their sales. The Malawian media feature men dressed like women and vice versa at weddings and even during funerals for some ethnic groups but this is not treated as a practice indicative of sexual 'deviance' or homosexual tendencies. All in all, the media imply that transvestism is absent in Malawi as it is not even discussed. Cross-dressing is portrayed as a practice that is not linked to sexuality, sexual identity or identity issues but as a tool of entertainment that either sex can practice. Homosexuality, on the other hand, is generally seen as a new menace, an alien 'sin' that needs to be rooted out very fast before it spreads and contaminates Malawians. Discussions on homosexuality in the public media sometimes spill over into the online discussion forums of the University of Malawi.

The Chancellor College listserv

Early in 2005, the listserv of Chancellor College, the main constituent college of the University of Malawi, carried a posting from the 'Malawi Gay and Lesbian Society' said to be based in South Africa. It outlined their legal status and stated that they planned to table their request for legalisation in the next constitutional review, scheduled to take place later in the year. I was interested to monitor the response to this issue for three reasons: as a participant in the constitutional review process; a feminist academic activist who has seen the card of culture, ethnicity, gender, regionalism played in her struggles against patriarchy,[5] especially on issues concerning violence against women;[6] and as an activist and the president of a union which had a member who was gay and who was constantly verbally persecuted.[7]

I was interested to see how 'learned' Malawians were going to react to this issue which had been thrust into their faces. I wanted to see if the discussion would be investigatory, condemnatory, participatory and/or dismissive. It was an issue that made several rounds in the senior common room[8] but now the homosexual community[9] had put pen to paper and prompted a response.

What followed were views that cited religion and culture as grounds for legitimising the largely homophobic stands. To start with, the responses threw everything in – gays, lesbians and paedophiles were all lumped into one boat. Comments ranged from labelling homosexuality non-Malawian, non-human and illogical, some even invoked Zimbabwe's President Mugabe: calling a homosexual person a thing, labelling homosexuality something that is not even done by animals, in effect, branding it subhuman. The Bible and Qu'ran were quoted, in a bid to prove that homosexuality is not a human act. Two emails were direct verbal attacks on the member of staff widely believed to be gay and explicitly expressed disdain for the person and anyone 'who does what he does'. Other emails labelled the practice as something understandable when done by prisoners, but not by free Malawians. The operative word that was used to link this practice with the prison was *matanyula*, a derogatory term that refers to men who participate in anal sex. One of the emails lamented why any man would not want to sleep with the numerous beautiful women while another expressed joy that the more gay men there were, the more women there would be available to him. In general, heterosexuality was labelled as the norm, anything outside it portrayed as an anomaly and therefore a deplorable and unfortunate mishap and disease.

The *makwerekwere* card

This reaction reminded me of the way I experienced Batswanas'[10] reaction to hiv and aids in 1994 to 2003. This reminded me of my experiences as a *makwerekwere*[11] in Botswana, where I was an expatriate teacher for eight years, before I returned to be a lecturer in African feminist literary theory at Chancellor College, University of Malawi.

379

When hiv and aids gained visibility in Botswana, the public opinion of Batswana interviewed on Botswana Television (BTV) and local radio stations cited this disease as a foreign one, brought in by *makwerekwere*. A good number of foreigners used to be castigated and it was very common to hear locals call for them to be sent back to their homes because they were peddling this horrible disease. What is interesting is that categories of race and nation were applied in this castigation. White and light-skinned Africans, especially those from well-to-do African countries like South Africans, were not part of the *makwerekwere* peddling hiv and aids; it was dark African 'others' from poor countries like Zimbabwe, Malawi and Mozambique who were the main targets of this blame game. I experienced this first hand. My contract to teach at Moshupa Senior Secondary School required me to take an hiv and aids test and I knew a good number of African black expatriates who had been declared jobless and sent packing home, after testing positive. I was infuriated at the clearly racist character of this policy, especially when I found out that a fellow expatriate teacher, a white Englishman, was not being asked to take this test. I decided to register my disgust with my employer, the Teaching Service Management. This Englishman, who happened to be a friend and neighbour, agreed to accompany me as he was flabbergasted at the difference in our treatment when we had the same employer and were teaching the same students. We were told to our faces that it was government policy that the test be taken by 'black' (read black African as Euro-western and African Americans were not required) expatriates.

So when I got home and heard arguments that labelled homosexuality un-African, a foreign and vile importation, the resemblance of how I had been suspected of peddling hiv and aids, mainly because of my geopolitical origins, came to mind. There was a striking resemblance in the way I had seen Batswana and now Malawians 'foreignise' a practice they found negative and hurtful, and which they did not approve of, as if all bad things are imported and the indigenous is perfect and good. The blame-the-foreigner syndrome did not stop there.

A disease brought by foreigners

In an article entitled 'Malawi government reaping peanuts from tourism' (Jomo 2006), Patricia Kaliyati, the then minister of information and tourism, went on to 'bemoan' the 'problem' of homosexuality that she said was rampant in Chintheche Inn and was fast infecting Lake Malawi's resorts (Jomo 2006: 1). She quickly played the culture card: 'Our culture does not condone homosexuality. These tourists when they come they should be learning our culture not introducing to us a bad culture like homosexuality, that is uncalled for in Malawi' (Jomo 2006: 1). She went on to blame tourists who splashed out money on young Malawians in return for homosexual favours.

On the 25 January 2007, the leading print media houses in Malawi ran a headline that captured minister Kaliyati closing yet another tourist resort on the basis of it being connected to homosexuality and drug abuse. The article went on to explain that she had gone on to lambast senior chiefs who had approached her, begging the minister to open the tourist resort because it was their main livelihood. In this article, there was no report of current or future plans for the minister to engage with the chiefs and people of this community. One wonders why, given the belief in her culture she attested to earlier, a culture that prides itself on communality, that the honourable minister did not sit down and discuss this issue with the community and the chiefs[12] instead of resorting to the top-bottom approach and using her state power and status to arbitrarily close the resort. She behaved like a colonialist who 'came, saw and conquered', going on to prescribe what was good for the people and what should happen. Through Kaliyati, the government demonstrated that when it comes to homosexuality, it does not engage with the people concerned in order to understand the issue before taking a stand.

The parliamentary take

The same minister had spoken out about homosexuality earlier while she was part of a gender training workshop in August 2006 in which I was participating. This was a joint Scottish Executive and British Council initiative to empower Malawian female parliamentarians, by linking them with civil society on gender issues.

She was one of the participants although she did not attend the whole workshop or the particular session in which I brought up the issue of homosexuality. The day before she issued her tirade about homosexuality, I had introduced the issue of sexuality and how important it was that female leaders were well informed before they rushed to say anything to the media so that they would not have to retract their views when research to the contrary surfaced. I cited the Mary Nangwale saga[13] as an example to illustrate that public political speeches by female politicians are more scrutinised for accuracy than those made by male ones.

I used the way professionals had reacted to the gay and lesbian email on the listserv discussed earlier, I asked how they as parliamentarians would handle such an issue. A good number reacted in the usual 'homosexuality is a sin' manner. But as the discussion went on some, an MP for one of the constituencies in Lilongwe, for example, wondered why the homosexuals did not come out to fight for their sexual rights, why they were writing anonymous letters. I pointed out that some of the contributory factors were that homosexuality is a crime in Malawi and the ostracism and stigma it carries.[14] I found that when one presents the facts obtaining on the ground, the parliamentarians open up and ask questions to understand this issue better. Some of them even give examples of gay and lesbian people they know, citing historical examples of such people they were told of by their grandparents. At the end of the discussion, some of the parliamentarians appreciated my presentation. The general view was that much as they can ask and open up about the issue, the bottom line is they cannot endorse that which infuriates and is seen as taboo by their constituency and party leadership. At the end of the day, they carry the views of the people whose votes they depend on for their jobs. I still emphasised that they, as individuals, need to read into this issue and take an informed position.

Minister Kaliyati's comments on homosexuality came a day after this session and I used her apparent failure to distinguish homosexuality from paedophilia to emphasise the point I had made in the previous training sessions. Kaliyati had homogenised and lambasted the practitioners of both, calling for their arrest wherever they were found in Malawi. Kaliyati was not the first politician to call for the arrest of homosexuals. She was, of course, taking her cue from President Mugabe of Zimbabwe, who in 1993 angered some participants at the Zimbabwe book fair by 'flamboyantly branding gay people as "worse" than dogs and pigs' (Grundy 2006: 1) and went on to call for their arrest in Mutare, Zimbabwe. Mugabe went on to argue that same-sex marriages were a threat to mankind and condemned churches that blessed gay unions (Grundy 2006: 2). His speech was applauded by Anglican priests in the audience and Zimbabwe is heavily Anglican. Mugabe's views found a home among the clergy of Zimbabwe and Malawi.

The Henderson rejection

The religious voice of Malawi is very audible in the debate about homosexuality. In order to appreciate the weight that this voice carries, it is important to know the religious composition of Malawi. Malawi has a population of about 18 million. Muslims and Christians account for 93 per cent of the population. There are 7.9 million Christians (80 per cent), 1.3 million Muslims (13 per cent), 305,000 belong to other religions (3 per cent) and only 423,000 are either non-believers, African traditional religions or atheists (4 per cent).[15] While addressing homosexuality and the issuing of condoms to Malawi's prisoners, Pastor Gibson Nachiye of the Deeper Life Church and Bishop Andrew Dube of the Assemblies of God 'issued a stern warning against legalising homosexuality' in July 2003, arguing that: 'Homosexuality is a sin before God, therefore, such acts as distribution of condoms would only encourage immorality' (Gmax 2003: 1).

The rejection of Bishop Dr Nick Henderson, who in July 2005 had been elected by the Lake Malawi diocese to serve as its bishop but who was challenged by conservative members of the Anglican Church, epitomises the reaction of the church on homosexuality in Malawi. In September 2005, the *Herald* reported that Bishop Malango had delayed the confirmation hearing of Bishop Henderson, because of reports that he was gay, claiming that Henderson's support of gay rights was out of step with African values. Malango was not alone is arguing that being gay goes against African values. Bishop Nathaniel Yisa of Nigeria argues that: 'The bible refers to homosexuality and condemns it outright. In traditional African society there is no room for men who want to have sex with men. As for women who want to have sex with women – to most people in the rural areas, it is unimaginable' (Grundy 2006: 2).

The argument that homosexuality or being gay is not African is an issue I take up in an article in *Feminist Africa* (Kapasula Kabwila 2006). I argue that regardless of whether one accepts or approves of cross-dressing and homosexuality, what is clear is that both practices have history and precedence in Africa. The article challenges binary thinking and substantiates its stand by providing evidence from documents on African literature, artefacts and rituals from countries such as Ghana, Kenya and South Africa. Indeed, there is a growing body of African research that illustrates homosexuality as an indigenous, home-grown practice.

Legalise homosexuality – MHRRC's plea

The argument for legalising homosexuality in Malawi is sparse but noticeably growing. In an article, Frank Namangale (2005) reports that the Malawi Human Rights Resources Centre (MHRRC) on 28 January 2005 put a proposal to the Malawi Commission to legalise homosexuality in the country. The centre said it wanted this proposal to be considered during the national constitutional review, arguing that the penalties provided for in the penal code violated the right of a person to freely choose his or her sexual orientation. The argument that was further advanced by the centre is what is most interesting: '[This is] a recognised *international* human rights standard. Discrimination of persons in many forms is prohibited and all persons are, under any law, guaranteed equal and effective protection against discrimination on grounds of race, colour, sex, including sexual orientation' (Namangale 2005: 1, my emphasis).

The centre's communications officer, John Soso Phiri, went on to say Malawians should accept that there were gays and lesbians in their community and they needed to be allowed to come out in the open and live freely. This could not happen until the centre '*open* people's minds' (Namangale 2005:1, my emphasis) and that was why the proposal was made.

The foreign gift syndrome

Starting with the MHRRC, the two words that are highlighted above, 'international' and 'open', epitomise the problematic nature of that view, whether you agree with the speaker or not. When one is trying to reach out, to be understood by the Malawian nation – a people who were colonised by Europe and who are battling various forms of Western imperialism – a request for them to follow international trends is asking for trouble. Given what usually happens to Malawians and Africans when they follow the lead of the Western-driven international world, asking Malawians to make a paradigmatic attitudinal change on an issue on the basis of what is happening internationally is unwise, wrong and dangerous. To start with, the use of the word 'international' anachronises and infantilises Malawi, insinuating that Malawi is lagging behind the times and it has no agency to chart its own path on this issue. Phiri needs to remember that this is the exact trope that was used to legitimise imperial acts like those of the slave trade and colonialism, and the trend continues to this day. Phiri needs to remember that the word 'international' connotes the West to many Africans and Malawians. Not only is it insulting to tell me as a Malawian to mimic the West, frankly, it is like asking me to follow the ways of the person who bought the handcuffs that are chaining me. Walter Rodney (1972) and Adu Boahen (1987) have convincingly illustrated how the so-called 'international' giants are the ones to blame for much of what Africa and Malawi are battling with.

The opposite of 'open' is 'closed' and when Phiri says the centre wants to open people's minds, it implies that their minds are and/ or were closed, waiting to be opened by people like him and the likes of his centre. Such an approach is hinged on power dynamics and insinuates that Malawian issues need to be engaged with the yardstick of those who champion the human rights discourse that is used by Europe and North America. In an interview with me (April 2007), Nkiru Nzegwu warned against engaging Africa in a manner that did not regard it as an equal of other continents, a way that was not respectful of its people, and which instead placed the West at the centre of the world and made it the venue of and measurement of knowledge. She gives the example of how European artists learnt abstraction from African art. Instead of acknowledging that, they turned around and labelled it tribalistic and primitive art. She goes on to explain how the sophisticated African art that they came across was labelled to mimic theirs or just glossed over. When one takes into account such views, it is evident why Phiri's views can be problematic to the Africa of today, which is struggling to stand on its own feet, facing so many 'international' obstacles in its bid to define itself and decide its own destiny. When one looks at how the West has benefited from primitivising and exoticising not only African identities but African sexualities, Africans are justified in distrusting a discourse that suggests, even remotely, that the international stand on sexuality is to be paid attention to. The international includes the Europe that in colonial times defined the African as the oversexed man and woman (Salo 2001). The people of Africa and Malawi in this case are battling an image of being anachronised[16] by the West as diseased, helpless and backward. Asking them to follow the international is dignifying the racist portrayal of Africa by the West. This issue of opening the mind of Malawians makes the approval and/or recognition of homosexuality seem to be an issue prescribed by the outside. It gives it the image of a gift that is coming from an international, enlightened and selected few people, the biblical three wise men of the East, or in this case, West. The historiography of the West with Africa, not to talk of the present day problematics, make it very difficult for Malawians to receive any 'gift' from the West. The words of Nuruddin Farah in his book *Gifts* eloquently illustrate the argument I am attempting to make here. Talking about the European languages that have been argued to be a gift that can unite Africans, Farah points out the reason for Africans mistrusting so-called gifts from the West: 'To know who I [an African] am and how I have fared, you must understand why I resist all kinds of domination including that of being given something' (Ngaboh-Smart 1996).

Racist labels

It is crucial that those arguing for the legalisation of homosexuality avoid racist labels as that will only problematise the way Africans read their cause. Richard Kirker, the general secretary of the small but vocal Lesbian Gay Christian Movement, had this to say when reacting to the split that came about when the American

Anglican church appointed Bishop Gene Robinson: 'Personally, I'd rather see a split within the ranks of the Anglican community than for people of principles to bow to the demands of homophobic Africans.'

What exactly is meant by the label 'homophobic Africans'? What if Akinola (the Archbishop of Nigeria) had been European and white, would it have made a difference? Is the problem homophobia or the epidemic capital of the owner of the homophobia, to quote Steven Gregory (2007)? Such a statement races the discourse, thereby aggravating the situation.

Engaging with homosexuality on Malawian terms

If we examine the stands taken by those for and against legalising homosexuality, it is evident that most of the arguments are externalist in nature. Malawi needs to examine this issue on Malawian terms. Instead of rushing to talk of culture as if it is a pure concept, we need to reach within ourselves as a people and find how sex is defined and has been defined before colonisation, and the role that sex and sexuality play in the Malawian parameters of citizenship and personhood. How do we define deviancy in sex? Is homosexuality an issue amongst us now or not? How is it linked to the hiv and aids we are battling? Our agenda and priorities should be based on what we feel, think, believe in and stand for with each other and collectively. Unless the identity 'Malawian' does not exist anymore, we need to be sure that the debate on this issue is owned and participated in by Malawians in their diversity instead of anchoring it to heterosexual hegemony, Christianity and Islam.

The first reality to accept in Malawi is that although we have prisoners that we give condoms to we say homosexuality is not Malawian. Surely the condoms are not for blowing up as balloons, and Lucius Banda's submissions of 13 May 2007 attest to the presence of homosexuality in prisons. Evidently, we need to recognise that reality instead of moralising and prescribing what we think sex is and should be in Malawi. We need to interrogate this moralising and prescriptive trope that runs through the arguments of those who are against the legalisation of homosexuality.

We need to ask ourselves if Malawian culture defines and polices sex the way Christianity does. I am asking this knowing how 'Malawian culture' has been quoted in the discourse on prostitution, single mothers and unmarried women in feminist literary theory. A good example is the way definitions of 'loose women', 'stray women', 'outside children' and 'bastard' have come up and been debated (Kalipeni and Zeleza 1999). In Kabwila-Kapasula (2007), Nzegwu illustrates how women's sexuality in postcolonial Africa has been policed in matters that it was not in precolonial Africa. Using the example of her Igbo society, Nzegwu (2006) illustrates how the Christian definition of loose morals and children born out of wedlock is used to police and socially ostracise women in postcolonial Igboland, unlike in precolonial times. When one goes into an African community today that has adopted the colonial definition of 'good woman', which is often modelled on Victorian ideals and was used to police European women's sexuality (Pateman 1989), it is easy to buy into the way Western categories are being normativised. It is easy to buy into categories like 'bastard' and 'prostitute', yet this was different before the Victorian-driven colonialists came to Igboland.

If homosexuality is to be rejected on the basis of it being alien, we can only do that after we have examined how we defined homosexuality before the coming of colonialism and its attendant identities, processes and institutions. We need to investigate our Malawian past, if ever it is possible, and then verify if we truly did not have homosexuality. Then again, how many things do Malawians do today that they did not do before? The issue of homosexuality needs to be unravelled and interrogated by us as people today, taking into account our yesterday. We need to weigh and see how we as a people have felt and feel about it.

We need to ask ourselves how we define sex, if sex as an act has and is ever defined in diversity. It is important to examine our different communities in their various versions of matriarchy, patriarchy, patri- and matrilocality, and see what weight is given to sexual intercourse and how that intersects with citizenship in the village and urban setting. We need to know if the way one has sex affects the definition of who is a Malawian or not. We need to unpack the interface between the way one has sex with access to resources and citizenship. In my literary studies of Malawi and the SADC region, I have yet to see proof of a community that sanctions a person, disqualifies them from being a member of the village or community on the basis of how they have sex.

Conclusion

It is important for Malawians to be engaged on their issues as an equal with other nations. We need to avoid privileging colonial logic and Eurocentricity in the conceptualisation of our problems and solutions. Those arguing for the legalisation of homosexuality need to engage with Malawi as a mature, independent and knowledgeable nation. They should not present homosexuality as an issue that the whole world has woken up to while Malawi lags behind. In an interview with the author, Nzegwu emphasises that any society and especially an African one, given its historicity, needs to be engaged with respectfully, as an equal. It needs to be approached with an attitude that reads it from the inside, not one that passes prescriptions and says 'I have come to tell you what to do' (Kabwila-Kapasula 2007: 174). Malawi needs to use its home bearings to find a solution to problems of its home because, east, west, north or south, home is best. It is imperative that Malawi wears homegrown glasses to see homosexuality beyond colonial binaries of religion/culture and human rights. The homosexuality discourse needs to be grounded in homegrown and owned discourses.

Notes

1 This paper adopts Zillah Einstein's stand on not capitalising letters that attain a hegemonic presence on others (1996) and applies this to not capitalise hiv/aids, in a bid to emphasise that while hiv/aids is real in Africa, it does not define the people of Africa. It is a way of illustrating that they are living their lives heroically in the face of such a chronic disease. Life is going on and Africa is not a story of squalor, victimhood and dependency, as the Western media would have us believe.

2 The modern state of Malawi has a population of about 18 million and gained its independence in 1964. Its low literacy levels and economic challenges make the radio the most extensively used form of media. Literacy rates are 49.8 per cent for women, 76.1 per cent for men, compared with Zimbabwe where the figures are 87.2 per cent for women and 94.2 per cent for men (UNICEF (2007) *The State of the World's*

Children).

3   I returned to Malawi in 2003 after working as an expatriate teacher in Botswana for eight years.

4   Malawi's main radio station is the Malawi Broadcasting Corporation (MBC), and the main newspapers are *The Daily Times* and *The Nation*.

5   The hegemonic force that works in various forms, including physical, ideological, institutional and processes, advocating the creation and maintenance of male dominance at individual and/or collective levels. This power is used by men of any age, race, class or religion to dominate women.

6   I initiated a project to fight violence against women in the university (UNIMA) and saw how hegemonic forces such as patriarchy masquerade, reinvent and mutate themselves, especially when under attack. This is a university where a fellow feminist academic activist (Professor Isabel Phiri) had to leave after doing some research that exposed the prevalence of various forms of violence against women in the campus I teach in.

7   I was the president of the Chancellor College Academic Staff Union (2004–06) and in our battles against the administration for visionary leadership and with the government over salaries, I had seen first hand how capitalism protects its own and fights ferociously when attacked to protect profits, inventing categories of ethnicity, gender and age.

8   A place where academic staff and their spouses meet and socialise, and discuss academic and other issues. Its membership includes university teaching staff from the lowest in rank to the highest, from staff associates to professors.

9   I believed the email came from the underground homosexual community of Malawi. This was debatable as the email stated that the members of the association were in South Africa and this made some people doubt its authenticity. I put the subterfuge down to fear of being identified given the legal status of homosexuality.

10 People of Botswana are called Batswana.

11 A derogatory term referring to black African foreigners in Botswana. I employ a subject-centred approach to its spelling, the spelling that I, the Chichewa/Shona Mukwekwere living in Botswana owned, to authchonise and contextualise the term.

12 I am well aware that the role and definition of Malawian chiefs has been very influenced by colonialism, multiparty politics and the so-called democratisation of the neocolonial state. I employ the precolonial definition of chief in Malawi.

13 The handling by the media and political system of the parliamentary debate on the first female inspector general of the Malawi police. Another example is the media's treatment of Vera Chirwa's bid to run for president. She was labelled as too old when she was the same age as Bingu wa Mutharika, then president of Malawi. There are so many examples that evidence the gender bias in political leadership globally and in Malawi.

14 Some of the parliamentarians and fellow civil society members did say they were disappointed by my choosing to discuss the issue of homosexuality, with one pointedly lamenting that this time, I had gone too far in my radicalness.

15 This is based on Reverend Dr Chakanza's paper on 'Religions Percentage of Population – Country Overview' (2004).

16 A term used by Fanon (1963), Boahen (1987) and McClintock (1995) to refer to the way the West cast Africa as a dark, backward and helpless place. Coming to it was seen as going back in time, while going to Europe was seen as going to light, development and to the world.

Bibliography

Boahen, Adu (1987) *African Perspectives of Colonialism*, Baltimore, The Johns Hopkins University Press

Chakanza. J. (2004) *African Ancestors' Religion: Chipembedzo cha Makolo Achikuda*, Zomba, Kachere Series

Fanon, F. (1963) *The Wretched of the Earth*, New York, Grove Press

Gregory, Steven (2007) *The Devil Behind the Mirror: Globalization and Politics in the Dominican Republic*, Berkeley and Los Angeles, University of California Press

Grundy, T. (2005) 'Africans set to found rival Anglican church', http://palmettoanglican.blogspot.com/2005_09_01_archive.html, accessed 5 November 2007

— (2006) 'Mugabe fuels "Reformation" against gays' http://scotlandonsunday.scotsman.com/index.cfm?id=1045722004, accessed 5 November 2007

Gmax.co.za (2003) 'Churches condemn condoms in Malawi prisons', http://www.gmax.co.za/look/07/11-malawi.html, accessed 6 November 2007

Hilson, M. (1996) 'Homophobia and postcolonialism', http://www/english. emory.edu/Bahri/Homophobia.HTML, accessed 5 November 2007

Jomo, F. (2006) 'Malawi government reaping peanuts from tourism', Blantyre Bureau, http://www.mask.org.za/prinpage.php?id=1141, accessed 6 November 2007

Kabwila-Kapasula, J. (2006) 'Challenging sexual stereotypes: is cross-dressing "un-African"?', *Feminist Africa*, 6: 68–72

— (2007) 'Celebrating Africa House: an interview with Professor Nkiru Nzegwu', *JENdA: A Journal of African Women's Studies*, 10: 171–6

Kalipeni, E. and Zeleza, P. (eds) (1999) *Sacred Spaces and Public Quarrels: African Cultural and Economic Landscapes*, New Jersey, Africa World Press

Kerr, David (1987) 'Unmasking the Spirits', http://allafrica.com/stories/200610161202.html, accessed 12 May 2007

Malawi News (2003) 'Churches to condemn condoms in Malawi', http://www/malawinews.co.za/look/o7/11-malawi.html, accessed 6 November 2007

McClintock, A. (1995) *Imperial Leather*, London, Routledge

Namangale, F. (2005) 'Legalise homosexuality says human rights body', *Daily News*, accessed 5 November 2007

Ngaboh-Smart, Francis (1996) 'Dimensions of gift giving in Nurrudin Farah's *Gifts'*, *Research in African Literatures*, 27(4): 144–56

Nzegwu, N. (1994) 'Gender equality in a dual-sex system: the case of Ontitsha', http://www.jendajournal.com/vol 1.1/nzegwu.html, accessed 1 February 2007

—— (2006) *Family Matters*, Albany, NY, State University of New York Press

Pateman, Carole (1989) *The Disorder of Women*, California, Stanford University Press

Phiri, A. (2006) *African Women, Religion and Health*, New York, Orbis Books

Rodney, Walter (1972) *How Europe Underdeveloped Africa*, London, L'Ouverture Publications

Salo, Elaine (2001) 'Talking about feminism in Africa', Women's World, http://www.wworld.org/programs/regions/africa/amina_mama.htm, accessed 7 November 2007

The Eastgarden (2003) 'Malawi, information for homosexuals in Malawi', http://www/geocities.com/WestHollywood/2144/1-malawi.html?200711, accessed 5 November 2007

The Herald (2005) 'Election of a gay bishop in Malawi shocks Anglican Church in Zimbabwe', accessed 5 November 2007

United Nations High Commissioner for Refugees (UNHCR) (2006) *Malawi Country Report*, UNHCR, http://www.unhcr.org/home/ RSDCOI/445620472, accessed 12 May 2007

Van Breda, S. (1995) 'President Mugabe condemns homosexuality', http:// www.qrd.org/QRD/world/africa/zimbabwe/excerpt.of.mugabe, accessed 5 November 2007

365gay.com (2006) 'Mugabe threatens to arrest pro-gay clergy', http:// www/365gay.com/Newscon06/022606mugabe.htm, accessed 5 November 2007

The Movement Building Boot Camp for Queer East African Activists: an experiment in revolutionary love

Jessica Horn

Memory

> *Recordar*: To remember. From the Latin *re-cordis*, to pass back through the heart.
>
> Eduardo Galeano (1991), The Book of Embraces

> Here, at the end of a soul-shaking experience of the MBBC with its emotional mountain tops, and emotional valleys, co-creating new ways of understanding self, and politicising debates on everything from bodies, to economies, to loss.... Seeing now so clearly that queer Africans are at the cutting edge of African progressive social movements, and that feminist solidarity gives air to this work.
>
> Personal diary entry, 28 March 2011

Of all the activist spaces I have engaged in since my days as a feisty feminist teenager, I have never been in a space as personally and collectively transformative as the Movement Building Boot Camp (MBBC) for Queer East African activists.[1] The MBBC was a year-long learning process organised by Fahamu and UHAI – The East African Sexual Health and Rights Initiative – in 2011, with the aim of nurturing new leadership among lesbian, gay, bisexual, transgender and intersex (LGBTI) activists by exploring and developing a deeper theoretical and political base for activist work. This formal mandate of movement building was given wings by the will of these two organisations to genuinely shift activist energies in the region, allowing for the creation of a maverick, passionate and experimental training methodology and a reflexive learning community. In practice, something electric was born between us in the MBBC process; something profound shifted in our ways of doing and structures of feeling. The experience was as momentous, in the view of one lesbian participant, as 'the moment that I realised that I was beautiful, and I was queer, and I was African, and had a consciousness'. So what was the MBBC?

This essay represents an act of retrospective analysis. It is a provisional attempt to understand the unexpected space, languages, community and transformative energy we found ourselves collectively creating in the MBBC. It is necessarily subjective, in that it is my memory and my understanding of what occurred, punctuated with resonances and reflections of others involved. It includes moments of re-membering experience (literally, the act of putting the body of my emotions back together), and engaging a theory that we lived through practice in creating the MBBC space. I write this acknowledging that it is vital that we engage what I have called elsewhere the 'politics of the process' (Horn 2009) in our work given that we spend the majority of our time in the doing, and not necessarily in the briefer moments of victory or achievement. In feeling my way back through the MBBC process, I am also constantly engaging the broader significance of the space that we created and methodologies that we developed in the landscape of an NGO based on human rights and social justice. For while we protest shrinking funding for NGO activism, we also need to appreciate the tremendous resources we do actually have at our disposal, including the potential for inter-country learning processes and on-site learning and exchanges in the comfortable surroundings of hotels. How do we best use these learning possibilities that we already have to meet the activist pedagogical imperative of nourishing deep political transformation?

Birthing ideas

In mid-2010 Hakima Abbas, an African feminist working for the Pan-African social justice organisation Fahamu, approached me with an idea to work on developing a curriculum for a training programme for East African LGBTI activists. The idea was to create a 'boot camp', drawing on a military metaphor but applying it in the sense of engaging our political development as activists with the discipline seen in revolutionary movements. In Hakima's words:

> from the first idea, the MBBC was a collective process ... it came out of conversations with comrades where the feeling was that there needed to be a re-injection of politics into the LGBTI movement, and a holistic way of looking at that movement ... and a recognition that many of us are tired and that there are great and wonderful ideas out there that are not being explored because we are taking up a lot of space.

I understood the yearning, to use Amilcar Cabral's phrase, for a 'return to the source', to re-embrace the value of rigorous political thought and debate about our political visions and the methodologies and ways that we engage and use power to instigate change. With that intention, and tremendous latitude given by the host organisations, I worked on the written curriculum.[2] We surveyed activists in the region to identify learning priorities, and combined these with our own sense of key areas to explore or introduce into African queer debate. One such area was well-being, which we prioritised as an issue to explore in both political and practical terms, as central to sustaining activism.

The learning process itself was to take place in two residential sessions, each of a week and a half, with the months in between dedicated to applying learning and ongoing discussions on key issues through an email mailing list. In planning to actually create the process, I was joined by fellow facilitators Phumi Mtetwa, a South African queer, socialist feminist who has been active in a range of intersectional struggles around sexual orientation, race, class and gender as well as the student anti-apartheid movement; Solome Nakaweesi-Kimbugwe, a feminist activist and entrepreneur who has been a vocal ally for women's, LGBTI and sex workers' rights; and Hakima Abbas. Together we formed the core facilitation team. All core facilitators were African but also, unintentionally, all were women and all firmly positioned in feminist politics, although with a variety of perspectives on this. Other facilitators joined during the process, including Najia Sabeen, a Kenyan psychologist and energy healer, who participated full-time for the second residential training. While not all facilitators were queer-identified, all shared a solidarity with queer struggle. In selecting participants, Fahamu and UHAI chose LGBTI and sex worker activists, those who represented what Hakima Abbas describes as 'people who have not necessarily been deeply entrenched in the NGO-isation of the movement but have shown commitment in a broad sense to taking risks, making things different, and who have a passion for people'.

Grounding

> You can never forget who you are and where you stand in the struggle.
>
> Bob Marley and the Wailers, 'So much things to say'

> To deny the importance of subjectivity in the process of transforming the world and history is naive and simplistic. It is to admit the impossible: a world without people.
>
> Paulo Freire (2005 [1970]: 50)

The MBBC learning space was initiated in residential training in the green surroundings of a lodge outside of Nairobi, Kenya. On the first day of the training we had organised a dialogue session, with a few members of the facilitation team sharing their own experiences and lessons from activism. The session was interesting enough, but that evening we met as facilitators and shared what was a common uneasiness about the power dynamic we had created. Paulo Freire suggests that in a liberatory teaching practice, '[e]ducation must begin with the solution of the teacher–student contradiction, by reconciling the poles of the contradiction so that both are simultaneously teachers and students' (Freire 2005 [1970]: 72). It is, of course, one thing to say, and another to make happen in a learning space. East Africans are heir to a colonial education system based on hierarchical obedience to an omniscient teacher – learning is by memorising, only speaking if asked to, and with a fear of making mistakes. Obedience is often enforced through corporal punishment, the literal enforcement of knowledge hierarchies through physical violence. In addition, even in our adult activist learning spaces we also tend not to deeply consider the silent hierarchies of class, gender and language, and how these play out in who engages and what we consider to be 'knowledge', and who ends up speaking. As we reflected as facilitators on the first evening, we realised that we had in fact re-enacted the 'teacher–student contradiction'. Although we sat in a circle, we had very much sustained the vertical hierarchy of 'knowledgable older activist who speaks versus younger activist who listens' that we had intended to subvert.

We opened the next day in a circle again, but now asking everyone in the room the question, 'How did you come to activist consciousness?' The next few hours were witness to a gentle, deep – and at moments incredibly painful – mutual sharing of realisations about evolving understandings of self, moments when homophobia or gender norms were violently enforced, political inspirations from parents or mentors, and the desire to seek liberation from the brutality of marginalisation. We allowed each other space to cry, space to run out and get air, and the opportunity to hold and be held. From that point we remained conscious, as facilitators, of the need to open space for participants to engage us all as 'teachers' too, and share their respective knowledges and wisdoms from their personal and collective activism. This revised sharing circle helped establish two critical axes of our learning community: *co-creation* and *embracing subjectivities.*

In that moment of deep sharing we encountered a new challenge as facilitators. We had felt the weight of pain in the room, and had responded as best we could. However, we were cognisant that we might not have the emotional resources to hold it all throughout our time together, given all else we were responsible for in keeping the process moving. We acknowledged openly to participants that we had struggled to find an appropriate counsellor who we felt we could trust to be non-biased. In response a participant (who was himself a trained counsellor) offered to show us a simple method of group support. He asked us to form a circle, with each person standing behind another. He then asked us to take note of the person we stood behind, and to offer to be their 'angel', looking out for them during the process and responding first if they were facing any difficulties. We also each agreed to be looked out for by the person who was standing behind us; they would be our angel. By offering this small ritual, the participant not only gave us a practical framework to manage the emotional landscape of the MBBC, he also actively redistributed the responsibility of revolutionary love horizontally, respecting each person's need for care and their capacity to give care to another. This created another foundational axis of our learning community – *mutual embraces.*

Once we had situated our politics in the context of our own life histories, we went through a layered process of situating ourselves in what we knew of the history of oppressions and liberations across the African continent, creating a visual timeline with all of the key moments that we felt had contributed to establishing – or shifting – power relations for us as Africans and in each of our other class and gendered identities. Through engaging political theory in sessions and evening reading groups, watching films about activism across the world, and sharing social movement culture such as the South African protest dance of *toyi toyi* and poetry open mics, we located our activist politics and actions firmly within existing lineages of struggle. And so we constructed another axis of our learning practice – *historicised debate.* This may sound self-evident as activist practice; however, it is surprisingly absent in enough of the NGO-based activism we have all experienced to be cause for concern.

The facilitation process: channelling flow

Seeing the classroom as a communal place enhances the likeli-hood of collective effort in creating and sustaining a learning community.

bell hooks (1994: 184)

I checked in at the boot camp as an individual who would wait for a call for proposals. I came out a researcher, poet (and check me out, I can write!), as an activist, armed with the Queer African Manifesto. It is my time to give back to the people I represent.

MBBC participant, reflection by Essy on her blog

As facilitators we worked to enter the MBBC residential and online spaces open, actively listening and engaging with the group as we began to learn about personalities, preferences and politics and notice how different people interacted. We were also open to each other, and the many different styles with which we managed sessions and presented content. Participants joked that we had 'PowerPoint and non-PowerPoint sisters', as we each brought out different facilitation and knowledge-sharing styles. We kept exploring a facilitation practice that was flexible enough to punctuate discussions on the radical potential of open source technology with choreography to Lady Gaga and Miriam Makeba songs. The guest facilitators who joined for short sessions, including a medical doctor, open-source software developers and an activist working with political theatre, shared in that spirit of radical teaching and facilitated in ways that were very much in keeping with the rhythm of the process (in fact at one point, I recall exclaiming that the MBBC process had been blessed by the ancestors, as it was so clear that whomever engaged in it came with the right energy for the space).

In the practice of co-creation, we formally drew in participants to lead sessions. In a sexual health session, a male-identified sex worker guided us through the art of safe sex, in an aesthetically astounding demonstration of engaging a sexual partner using condoms, lubricant and other tools of safe and pleasurable sex. In another session, a participant facilitated a debate on the ethics and power relations of public health research, opening space to discuss issues such as HIV vaccine trials, which some of our community members had participated in as research subjects.

In the MBBC process we also celebrated the power of eros – in the sense that African American lesbian feminist Audre Lorde (1989: 55) explores:

> [t]he very word erotic comes from the Greek word eros, the personification of love in all its aspects – born of Chaos, and personifying creative power and harmony. When I speak of the erotic, then, I speak of it as an assertion of the lifeforce of women; of that creative energy empowered, the knowledge and use of which we are now reclaiming in our language, our history, our dancing, our work, our lives.

In true East African dancing tradition, we engaged in ample provocative dance in between sessions and at the close of some days (leading to an affectionate renaming of the boot camp as the 'booty camp'), and we welcomed self-expression in the safe space of our open mics where people spoke of queer love, desire and sexual experiences. We all encouraged a participant and fabulous Ugandan drag queen with music, jewellery and a floor to 'do his thing', including in a closing celebration where other hotel guests were present. To engage this power of eros in our learning space was to meet ourselves as full human beings. It was a profoundly political act of acknowledging desires that are otherwise censored or forced into the shadows.[3] As Hakima Abbas offers, 'We were flaming in our queerness, and it was liberating to be able to be ourselves, to be fabulous, to walk and know that your brothers and sisters have your back.'

We were not always loud. In fact there were many moments where we made space for quiet. Every day of the residential process had a reflective element, including meditation, yoga and massage. We explored many practices of self-reflection that we then shared in the group, including gathering together at the end of the day to each share a thought on something that had inspired us, and ending both residential trainings with everyone writing affirmations to each other. And we had unexpected reflective practices too. One morning I was caught up in finding medical assistance for a participant, and so another facilitator (not known for her monk-like qualities) had taken it upon herself to lead the morning reflection. She had done it in the best way she knew, by playing a song from the opera *Farinelli*, asking participants to close their eyes and 'feel the music'. It was as hilarious as it was profoundly moving. With my eyes open I could see a room full of primarily young queer Africans sitting in silence and beginning to absorb the unusual and evocative sound of operatic Italian melody. In all of these moments we shared our delicateness and desire for stillness. As Kevin Everod Quashie (2012: 9) offers, 'In humanity, quiet is inevitable, essential. It is a simple beautiful part of what it means to be alive.'

For me personally, it was a new experience to engage men in this deep a facilitation process. While I was used to very personal sharing among women in the feminist tradition of embodied political consciousness raising, I had never facilitated the development of safe space in mixed-gender groups. It turned out not to be too great a mountain to climb, in that we all worked to meet each other as we were (including in our varied gender transgressions, male femininities, female masculinities and trans identities). Some men also spoke to their experiences as fathers and carers, as well as experiences of witnessing domestic violence against their mothers, with acknowledgements of women's roles and inequalities in the family. However, and perhaps expectedly, subtle patriarchies did present themselves at moments. A memorable example was when one group worked on mapping a woman's body, and the men in the group could not accurately locate all of the parts of women's anatomy (it was not the case for women in the group drawing a man's body). In some respects the flamboyance of gay men's culture also manifested more openly than lesbian cultural expression in the ways we engaged and celebrated each other, and ways that we expressed ideas of what it meant to be 'queer' (for example with many drag queen but no drag king performances). These are, of course, all learned hierarchies and very much part of the work of changing consciousness and constructing new gender norms.

Queer ubuntu

> Ubuntu ... speaks of the very essence of being human. It is to say, 'My humanity is caught up, is inextricably bound up, in yours.' We belong in a bundle of life. We say, 'A person is a person through other persons.'
>
> Desmond Tutu (1999: 31)

If I go inside the emotion that MBBC creates in my body, I know that the magic of MBBC lay in the rich, and maybe even a little unanticipated, sense of nurturing community. Creating community is work. It takes emotional labour to listen and embrace each other, as much as it takes political labour to explore disagreements and hold each other with mutual respect. Creating community also requires establishing clear ethical boundaries around ways of being and doing in communal space. During the first residential process a number of women-identified participants reported to facilitators that they were being harassed by a particular male participant. We felt that this was absolutely unacceptable and against the ethics of the space, engaged him and mutually agreed that he would not continue with the programme. Another participant had been very non-engaged from the start. We spoke with her as facilitators, and in the end she herself failed to attend the second residential training. We were fine with the decision, knowing that political work requires individual will as well as active choice, and that not everyone stays the journey. Participants also took collective ownership of the process in different moments, convening meetings to discuss how they were engaging and contributing to sessions. As a facilitator, these were beautiful acts of affirmation that the space was shared in its management and not only in the content of what was being explored.

Host institutions and facilitators agonised over the ethics of money. We are all distressed by the entitlement culture that has emerged in NGO-based activism. On the first day of the residential MBBC, some participants expressed disapproval that they would not be receiving per diems, and that the training was not held in a five-star hotel or close to urban nightlife. Representatives of the organising institutions took time to explain their political choice not to support the idea of being 'paid to learn', and the deliberate choice to situate us in a place where we could connect to the natural environment and focus on the work at hand. Participants accepted the principles, and soon enough the debate on money shifted to questions of economic justice for all. During the second residential training, participants led sessions on cooperative economics and starting collective businesses, a shift that we all noted as groundbreaking. In both residential trainings we also woke up early many mornings to jog, practice yoga and meditate outdoors.

Throughout the MBBC process we have devoted considerable time to exploring theories of power and change that have inspired various social movements in Africa, including Marxism, feminism, Pan-Africanism and black consciousness, queer theory, liberal human rights and anarchism. Participants established reading groups and read critical texts. We determinedly worked through the often difficult language of revolutionary theory. We deconstructed biblical texts on homosexuality with the help of theology-student-turned-grantmaker Happy Kinyili, and covered issues of relevance to our communities from drug use to debates on violence and non-violence as tools of struggle. In the best tradition of transgressive thought, we also kept working to make space for dissent, dialogue, contradiction and refinement. After all, if political theory is meant to inspire movements, then it also has to move.

One of the most politically rich processes was coming to individual and then collective definitions of freedom. We began by asking the following questions: Who am I? From that vantage point am I free or not free? If I do not consider myself free, what would it take for me to be free? We collated individual participants' responses into a visual map, out of which a collective politics of liberation emerged which fully embraced intersectionality. For all of us, there would be no freedom separate from economic justice, from a roof over all of our heads and a transformed position in our society and the world economy. There would be no freedom without the freedom of women, and of other constituencies marginalised by normative power relations. Freedom for African queer people, in our liberatory vision, requires engaging the earth and environmental justice as much as it does laws on sexuality. By recognising the complexities and hence diverse axes of our own oppressions we were able to fully embrace the relevance of a broad transformative politics that would make possible the basic call for LGBTI equality.

I was constantly amazed and enlivened by the energies that participants brought into the space. In the closing process of the first residential training, a Tanzanian participant created his own ritual of thanks. He had written words on individual cards that were relevant to him and his life. As we stood in the circle he handed a card to each of us, engaging us one by one with each word, in a poetic narrative linking us to elements of his body, soul, life history and survival. As he did so he wove a magical and radical political connection between us. It was the expression of a queer ubuntu: I am as you are. You are me. And I am you.

In another instance, a participant had offered to screen a documentary about homophobia in East and Southern African which featured some of the participants. We watched in excruciating anger as some of our own friends were shown being hounded by homophobic thugs, and expressed our outrage to them as the film ended. In the film we also viewed footage from the case of Malawians Steve and Tiwonge, arrested for allegedly attempting to have an illegal same-gender marriage. And as Tiwonge took the stand in the witness box, one of the participants sitting next to me whispered quietly to himself, 'That is me!'. Again, a queer ubuntu: I am as you are. You are me. And I am you.

Who, how, with what words...

> Speaking, writing, and discoursing are not mere acts of communication; they are above all acts of compulsion. Please follow me. Trust me, for deep feeling and understanding require total commitment.
>
> Trinh T. Minh-ha (1989: 52)

The MBBC process was not without its difficulties from a pedagogical standpoint. There were indeed a number of serious conceptual and process challenges, situated in large part in the context of how we currently manage activist spaces. The first major challenge was the question of who to include. Fahamu and UHAI intentionally chose people who were not the 'usual suspects' of East African NGO-based activism in a move to recognise the breadth of existing activist leadership and new activist voices. This did create difficulties for some participants, who had to navigate the politics of entitlement in NGO-activist space and returned to jealousy and anger from colleagues in their organisations and questions about who chose them as representative of activism in their respective countries. Despite active efforts on the part of the organisers to have trans inclusion, we initially did not have any transgendered participants, (the participant who worked in a transgender organisation was not trans-identified). During the second training one participant came out as a trans man, an act in itself that demonstrated the fluidity of gender identity and the potential for the gendered composition of our space to shift. In the second residential process a trans woman also joined us as part of the logistics and facilitation team.

The second major challenge was language. To begin with, the teaching, texts and films were all presented in English. English is, of course, a lingua franca for East and Southern Africans and as such a 'tool' for enabling a collective conversation and the possibility for everyone to participate in our space. However, it has its limits and exclusions, including in the fact that not all participants speak the same 'kind' of English (notably the English of academic theory). Some participants were deliciously fluent in Kiswahili but could not articulate the same texture of expression in English. Without being asked, other participants immediately jumped in to act as interpreters, translating what their fellows said from Kiwsahili into English and in some cases vice versa.

Language was also complex in the sense of the terminology and discourses that we used. In the MBBC space, differences in political perspective meant that there were inevitable differences between our languages of resistance and the languages we use to speak about issues such as sexuality, power and change. And, indeed, some of the debates we engaged in were precisely in the domain of language, for example about self-identification as a human rights defender and the notion that human rights are the most powerful language through which to express dissent. The word 'queer' was relatively new for most people in the group, and it took time to become comfortable with and understand the political intention behind the word and its relevance to our discussions around opening up and challenging binary conceptualisations of gender and sexuality. We even considered that if the term 'queer' was an act of reclaiming an insult used against sexual and gender non-conforming people in the UK and USA, then perhaps we should reclaim the word *shoga* (a derogatory term in Kiwsahili for a gay or lesbian person) and begin to articulate a *shoga* theory, grounded in East African experience. In one exercise we divided people into groups according to the African languages that they spoke and then asked them to explore all of the terminology and expressions for gender and sexual orientation, providing interpretations in English. This was a fascinating exploration of the diversity and similarities in gendered conceptions across East African languages, which also considered the existence of concepts of same-gender desire and the continuum of gender identity in many cultures.

As part of the work of developing a common yet diverse language, we also welcomed the expression of other languages, including African languages such as Kiswahili (spoken eloquently by some of the participants, to the envy of others), the language of dance, the language of visual self-representation and the language of healing touch in the massage sessions, which also enabled different kinds of 'voices' to be expressed, heard and responded to. We did not have visually or hearing impaired people in the group, which would have again pushed us to consider language, and probably would have exposed the limits of our own linguistic dexterity.

Heartbeat

> We need a revolution of the mind, we need a revolution of the heart, we need a revolution of the spirit. The power of people is stronger than any weapon... We need to be weapons of mass construction, weapons of mass love.
>
> Assata Shakur in d'bi young's song 'Revolution',
> played during the MBBC

None of what was created, shared or inspired in the MBBC could have happened without passion, vibrant political commitment beyond the 'day jobs' of NGO activism, formal facilitation or participant roles – and certainly not without love. When I speak of love I don't mean love in the romantic sense of the word. I mean love in the sense of a liberatory emotional energy; love as the political-emotional connection that we develop between each other that makes us wilfully want to contribute to sustaining each other's lives. It runs deeper than a surface identity politics, or theoretical political affiliation. Revolutionary love is what ultimately keeps us together, makes us feel so committed to each other, and manifests as a creative and replenishing breath in facing what can be complex landscapes of compromise and loss.

This energy of revolutionary love was expressed evocatively by a participant, Rena, on the final day of the residential training process. In her words:

> This day I shall appreciate all around me and breath out love, breath in love. I want to appreciate all the pashas of the day. I want to take one long last look of everything around and see them in a way I have not for the past 12 days. I want to breath deep the love they will breath out. Loving the movement. There is always beauty behind the bridge.

Revolutionary love is also evident in the solidarities shown during and after the formal MBBC training process, including in economic and emotional support for participants who had been evicted or whose houses were burnt down in homophobic attacks, and organising around a case of police brutality against the child of one of the participants. We have continued to be there for each other online and in person, where possible, in marking birthdays, expressing condolences for loved ones lost, linking people to opportunities for growth and further learning, and in joyful celebration of people's achievements. On the MBBC email mailing list, a participant shared the words of Mozambican liberation leader Samora Machel that 'solidarity is not an act of charity but an act of unity between allies fighting on different terrains toward the same objectives'. In the MBBC community and in full embrace of our diversities we certainly sustain this solidarity, with an overarching objective of reaching 'destination liberation'.

Notes

1 Participants came from Kenya, Uganda and Tanzania.
2 The full curriculum, including additional texts and contributions by MBBC facilitators and others, is available online at http://www.fahamu. org/mbbc.
3 One of the facilitators, Happy Kinyili of UHAI, did generate a debate about how queer activist space often becomes so overtly sexualised, raising a fascinating garden of questions which she will no doubt explore further.

References

Freire, Paulo (2005 [1970]) *Pedagogy of the Oppressed*, New York and London, The Continuum International Publishing Group

Galeano, Eduardo (1991) *The Book of Embraces*, New York and London, W.W. Norton

hooks, bell (1994) *Teaching to Transgress: Education as the Practice of Freedom*, New York and London, Routledge

Horn, Jessica (2009) 'Through the looking glass: process and power within feminist movements', *Development*, 52(2): 150–4, Society for International Development

Lorde, Audre (1989) 'The uses of the erotic: the erotic as power', in *Sister Outsider: Essays and Speeches*, New York, The Crossing Press Feminist

Minh-ha, Trinh T. (1989) *Woman, Native, Other: Writing Postcoloniality and Feminism*, Bloomington, Indian University Press

Quashie, Kevin (2012) *The Sovereignty of Quiet: Beyond Resistance in Black Culture*, New Jersey, Rutgers University Press

Tutu, Desmond (1999) *No Future Without Forgiveness*, London, Rider

The most fabulous place on earth
– poem

A poem in many voices

Rena

I live in a world where laughter is the song of the day
laughter until we cry
smile until we have become smiling machines
embrace until the soul sweats
love unconditionally
I live in the world where family consists of all and friends are all
I live in a world every word spoken creates, restores, and loves
I live in the world of woman power, woman sweetness, woman
    charm, women are the seducers, seducers of women
I live in a world that we have babies, don't have them, marry, don't
    get married, fall in love with my fellow women, with men, with
    me, with both women and men, with none. Yes I live in a queer
    world and I love it
I live in a world where we embrace difference and I love to live in
    this my world

Jessica

Against the amethyst evening of my world
we decorate sky, fearless
as we shine like fireflies
fall on lovers bathed in moonlight
raining laughter as they step
my world is radiance and sweat and love
raging rebellious through the hearts of its people

My world is movement
its soil, its family like roots
of a never ending vine
my world births shape shifting babies
boygirlgirlboyboygirlboygirlgirl
my world knows no rich or poor
only nourishment, it has no fury
only birdsong and drumbeats, the collective pulse
of a people breathing ... out ...

Nicole

I breathe in ... in deep, deep down in my soul
in my soul where I love, where I yearn, where my passion resides,
my passion for Africa, for my femininity, for my freedom,
freedom to love, make love to, make love with,
to sing and dance rhythms of my soul and watch as those around
    me admire, follow suit,
Looking at me
    my BIG, BEAUTIFUL body
move, African, unique,
FREE YOURSELF
my comrades
I beg ... let it go,
liberate your spirit
    Go, go, go...
run into the world where all that matters is love,
loving, holding, embracing, rubbing, kissing, feeling
    my world is love...

Jia

If queer is loving, then I must be queer,
for I love with passion,
unending devotion,
soaring madness.

In this world, in her world, in their world, in my world…
I have been them and they have been me in many ways
just like now… I am them and they are me

We are all One
you are love
I am you
and if that is so,
then I must be love
divinely present,
presently divine,
queerly divine
If queer is loving,
then I am queer

Jay

I love me,
I care a lot
every evening I sit outside and look at the sky,
I look at the moon and stars,
and thank God for all the beauty on earth.
I always relate all this to the day I will ever be free

The day I will be me without anyone questioning me who I am.
The day I will be free from oppression.
The day I will exercise my rights fully.

I know I can't do everything,
but I can do something
the way
I am

Essy

When she touches me, my heart misses a beat,
The feeling of her breast pressing on my chest feels like
The morning dew on my feet,
we communicate by looking into each other's eyes,
Her soft, wet lips are the reason I wake up every morning
God loves me that's why he brought her to me,
when we are together I am peace
like the river in the morning,
How can this love be wrong
if what I'm feeling is right?

Nicholas

Some people will try to make me
feel bad about being a gay
will try to convince me that
am incapable or inferior.
I don't believe it.
This is my life,
and I can do anything
I want to do
I don't have to
follow someone else's
expectations of who I should be.
I'll never let anyone convince me otherwise,
and never set limits upon myself,
because am a gay.
I can admire the same
qualities in myself
that I admire in other people.
Remember that am strong,
intelligent, and capable
Am dedicated to
any endeavour that I undertake

I am gay, and I have power
I can follow my dreams
and dance to the beat
of my own heart.

I don't have to go
through life dangling
from the clouds
instead I can fly to
the stars and claim
one for my own.

Hakima

I live in the world where every *body* is a testament
to the defiant mockery of conformity,
is goddess herself.
Where no *body* is illegal
and I wonder if there is enough gold
to pay for his perfect form.

I live in a world where the sweet cry of my orgasm
is a warrior call to resistance
Where he/she become obsolete in the face of you/I
Where they cannot box
we

I live in a world where your eyes erupt my freedom-fighter-mother
    instincts to cry
from the pit of my stomach
for a soul too beautiful for this world.
Where our child understands the power of love
and has too many answers for her textbook's question
is 'the baby a boy or a girl?'

I live in a world where labour is valued over capital
and all that you have is the spark in your eye
I live in a world
where your power is in the poetry of your smile

Pade

Doctors and counsellors
mentors, comrades and friends,
you are all artists by birth,
fighters and defenders of the LGBTQ,
so let your talented skills flow forth
and match to the world
head bold
Since you are like the Light to all of us,
our shining North Star
always makes our spirits soft,
and wash away our fears,
like the angel one drop of tears,
that cleans our souls...

Muhaari

I live in a place where others consider a forest,
I live in a place where others would fret at the shadows that come
  alive,
I live in a place where a coloured necklace could become a poisonous snake
or a poisonous snake a coloured necklace,
I live in a place where the need for others to validate how I feel is
  non-existent, a place where my internal locus of validation and
  evaluation is all that matters,
I live in a Utopia, yes, I am an ogre, full of mystery
able and ready to transform to fit
without losing my identity.

Yet others think me ugly,
yet others still think me evil,
yet others ostracize and condemn me for who I am,
yet others think me a misfit, a misnomer, not worthy of their
    approval,
yet I live, and love, and play and pray and prey, like everyone else.

Yes, my life is sweet, and my joy complete,
for I am an ogre,
comfortable in my forest,
happy to care and share,
here I am, here I will stay
no wonder what others say.

Dismus

I live in a world of mystery
where freedom is felt
religion does not discriminate
there is no privilege, no oppression
empowerment is ours

Barbra

I am. I am because,
I live, work, play as I wish,
Resilient queer African,
active
activist

Soloh

Darlings, darlings, darlings,
As I say to you all, be fabulous and live with each other
live in harmony as the world is chaotic
live as if freedom is the next second
to all my LGBTI friends,

to our partners,
to all our allies,
to our families,
to our neighbours,
we live and let live because we are living
for the departed Brothers and Sisters in our course, we are living for
    you,
for the community, rise above all because we are who we are

be sassy, be fierce,
   be what makes you glow
For freedom is seconds away
welcome to my LGBTI island of love and freedom
the most fabulous
place
on
earth

This poem was a collective contribution by the activists involved in the Anglophone Movement Building Boot Camp in East Africa organised by Fahamu and UHAI and discussed by Jessica Horn in Chapter 38 of this volume.

Crimson waves – fiction

Hakima Abbas

There is blood. Why is there always blood in a coming of age? Slowly, as the razor cuts through the skin, the crimson appears first as a drop, then a trickle until a trickle is a pool and my head feels light. But I wouldn't say it is unpleasant. I started this determined, stubborn – you should know this about me, I am very stubborn – but, now I am watching as if my hands, my motion, this transformation, were happening to someone else. As if I am watching from somewhere else. The pain has gone, my mind is at ease. The determination still keeps me concentrated but from afar, tired and light. Somehow I feel old as my ancestors. As if in water, the sights and sounds around me are muffled. I am floating and watching and remembering.

Remembering yes, because this has been a journey. And I have started from the end, which is really only a beginning. So, let me start from what everyone seems to want to know – who am I?

Well, I have many names, some more pleasant than others, some more true than others, but I have learnt to feel nothing about names. Who I am is not in my name or a name. But the world is hell-bent on naming and defining. Where did we get this from? This obsession with defining. Some say the *wazungu* gave it to us with their 'science'. That, before our subjugation, we were fluid; that we embraced contradiction and complexity. But that sounds like romantic hogwash to me. Surely the Avatar myth is also a European construct of the primitive other. I laugh. Whatever the case, we have certainly internalised this need to define, judge, normalise, conform, and that is the Africa I live in. That is the Africa that wants to know what I am. Constantly, the more unpleasant question: what are you? I laugh. How can one even begin to answer that question? What am I? I've learnt to ask it back. What are you?

I digress, and the thoughts are becoming cloudy. Somehow the lightness is filling up. Heavy like a rain-filled cloud. I still float, and yet there is a throbbing in my head. Just here on the right side. A rhythmic pounding like waves crashing to the shore.

I have always thought that waves are such teases. They arrive with perfect drama, with an arrogance, an impending doom, like a woman walking tall or, better still, like a transwoman, pouting, one eyebrow cocked, head down but looking straight at you, swinging her hips under tight-fitting clothing and killer heels. Just, just as she reaches you, close enough to touch you, she slowly smiles. That is how I imagine the waves, but they are teases. They enter the room, the shore, just like that. With style! With drums beating, with crowds cheering. And then, at the climax, just as they crash to prove their power… they retreat! What is that about?

But maybe I am being harsh on the waves. Maybe they are just shy after all. And who am I to talk? Because I am not that kind of shero. I am not that woman. Stubborn, certainly, and bold, only in my own way. Otherwise, I am quite ordinary. Ordinary looking: neither beautifully striking, nor pretty, not even ugly enough to stand out, just plain. I dress, well, ordinarily – no bright colours, tight clothes or high heels. I just couldn't pull it off. I speak quietly and cover my mouth when I laugh. Ordinarily shy.

Even my preferred name is ordinary. At least where I come from. My name is Njeri. One of the many Njeris in Kenya, especially in Thika where I live, where I come from, where I've always been. The town is ordinary. My life is ordinary. It's interesting to think of my life. The only time I have really felt alive was when I let the waves wash over me. Unabashedly, unashamedly, alive.

I was young then. I still am. But, really then, a hopefulness still gleamed in my eyes for everyone who cared to see. I had just graduated from high school, I came third in my school district. My father would have been proud of me. Only for the small mistake that made me the only girl in a boys' school. He refused to understand or even look at me. He always averted his eyes in disgust when I entered a room. But I didn't mind so much. Besides, I hardly saw the man. I had been in boarding school for years. He and my mother had parcelled us all off as soon as we entered secondary school. My two younger brothers were in the same school as me and they didn't seem to mind. Nobody really did. I kept to myself, studied and got good grades. Sometimes a new boy would arrive at the school and think it interesting to harass me for a bit. They would call me '*shoga*'. Mostly I would just shrug and keep walking. Because I knew I was not gay. I am not gay. I am a girl who likes boys, which, in your world of definitions, makes me straight, 'normal'. But I didn't bother telling them. I would just shrug. I think they learnt to ignore me, or tolerate me because it got boring. Or it might be because I got a reputation after the assembly incident. Ha, I am giggling now, remembering the assembly incident. I had forgotten.

One morning, like every morning, our dorm was woken by the dreadful sounds of the older prefects banging on pots and pans through the hall to make sure nobody was still sleeping. Why waking into a new day should be brutal is beyond my understanding, but… Anyway, this was a morning like any other. Ordinary, you might call it. But, when I went to the sink to splash the freezing water from the only tap for 40 boys onto my face and to look at myself, briefly, fleetingly enough to make sure I didn't have toothpaste glued to my face, but not long enough to see the painfully short hair and chiselled jawline I loathed so much, I saw it. Or rather, I felt it. I felt the stubbly, but still soft, growth on my chin. It was bad enough when my upper lip began to be crowned with thickening feathers, but, this... the spread, like a disease, of hair follicles on my face. Announcing impending doom, like the waves. I looked closer into the cracked mirror, finding the only two-by-four spot in the glass where you could actually see a reflection, and confirmed that hairy stubble was threatening to spread across my jawline and my face. I almost cried. Standing there. Silent. Until I was nudged by the next boy wanting to use the sink. I breathed in deeply. Swallowed hard and pulled back my tears. Walking on the cold slabs back to my bunk pulling my uniform over my head. Doing my tie, I asked myself, like every morning, if it were not ridiculous for a girl to be dressing like this. But this morning, my internal question was not convincing, not even to myself. My heart heavy, I followed the line of screeching, running boys towards the assembly hall. I always wondered how boys, without yelling, because that would be against the rules, could make so much noise. But this morning,

I didn't care. I could hardly hear them anyway. I had drowned out the sounds so successfully that I hadn't heard the taunts. Behind me on the flat benches we occupied to face the principal, a new boy was whispering in my ear: 'Patrick is a shoga, eh, Patrick, you like fucking boys, eh.' He laughed, looking at his pals for their approval. 'You don't have to lie to me, I've seen you looking at boys in the shower.' His words were merely sounds, in the cacophony of words around me. 'Shoga!'

Then he spat. Rancid, vile, bile. I felt a pellet land directly between my shoulders on my spine. My body jerked subtly. My jaw locked. Sweat on my palms. I saw crimson as I gently shut my eyes. My mouth dry, all my thoughts had evaporated.

I found myself rolling my shoulders and stretching my back, before turning to face this boy. Rage. This was my first time. It wouldn't be my last. Before even I knew it, I had pounded that boy bloody. His mouth, lips, nose, who knows, the source, the end, of the blood. All I know is that I was straddling him and plunged each punch into his not-so-long-ago-laughing face. Each punch landing with a satisfying thud. 1–2–3–4, how many punches, I am not sure. Like now, I was floating, from afar, watching the bloodied scene. It took four older boys to pull me off him.

Inevitably, I was punished. Caned in fact. But, I didn't mind so much. Besides, I think the principal was soft on me because I had never been punished before and was a good student. The lashes landed softly, the pain pale in comparison to the throbbing bruises of my hands where I had hit that boy. I don't even know what happened to him. I heard his parents transferred him to another school after he was released from hospital. Poor boy, I almost feel sorry for him now. I bet he didn't see that coming! I laugh.

That is where I learnt to be quiet and go unnoticed. Where I cried myself to sleep every time I was awoken to a new horror in this/that body. Because it is different now, this body. Today will be another step. A beginning. Ah, but I didn't tell you about that life, about the waves.

After my results came out and I was preparing to enter university to study biology, my older sister, who was then married and pregnant, invited me to visit her in Kisumu. We had always got along, me and my sister. She looked after me when I was little, defending me from the other kids in the neighbourhood and even, as much as she could, from my father. I would spend hours in her room watching her and her friends. It was fun. To my sister, I was just her baby and still am. Sometimes, when she looks at me lovingly, I see a sadness in her eyes. Not pity, because that would be removed. But a sadness for us; for the world maybe. She took my face in her hands once and told me that I was too beautiful for this world and that I should forgive them for not being able to understand. A single tear rolled down her cheek. 'Don't let them get to you, do you hear me,' she said firmly, strengthening her grip on my chin before releasing me suddenly, and turning away to wipe her eyes. Before I could answer, she was saying, 'Twende, let's go,' leading me out of the room for dinner. I miss her. It is not the same now that she is married and has four children. I still visit her and I love my nieces and nephews, they look just like her. But a weariness has blanketed her face. She has 'a good job and a good husband', so they say. Yet her spark has been extinguished. I'm not sure from what. My sister never tells me about her life and her feelings. When I ask, she says, 'Hush, are you my age-mate?', rhetorically. So, I hush.

When I visited, she was pregnant with her first-born. Very pregnant. And she looked beautiful carrying her oversized belly around ungracefully. She would plod around the house, shoeless, in a bra and a loose wrap tied below her waist to accommodate her extended belly protruding firmly out like a watermelon. When visitors arrived, she would simply throw on an oversized t-shirt and waddle to the door muttering about how she told everyone she didn't want visitors, why could people not listen! Then, in an instant, she would be smiling politely at whomever arrived bearing gifts and good will.

I heard her arguing with her husband one night about me. He was concerned about how she behaved in front of me. She laughed loudly, raucously, at him. So he yelled that it was inappropriate and that he didn't want his wife behaving that way, full stop! Only barely keeping herself from giggling, I heard her say soothingly: 'Don't worry about Patrick, trust me, he doesn't even notice, don't worry about Patrick.' Her husband has always looked at me suspiciously, but not much more than most men, so I haven't minded so much. Sometimes, when I take the children out, he grunts, as if disapproving, but my sister ignores him, so I do too. I have fun with those kids. The eldest reminds me so much of my sister. Curious, quiet, stubborn and very intelligent. She is my favourite. But of course, I don't tell them that.

That month I spent with them was the first time I had been to Kisumu. A melodious vibrancy overbears the tempered melancholy that sits subtly in the city air, often stopping me in my tracks. The heat can be excruciating so one of my tasks was fanning my oversized sister while she slept or watched TV. She was always complaining about the heat. 'It's so damn hot, in this place. So hot, you'd think the devil had moved in next door. Haiya, it's hot.' I laughed. I liked doting on her and the baby in her belly. I was excited about the new life she was carrying and, somewhere in the back of my mind, even excited about my new life: the possibility of starting fresh at university in a place where I didn't know anyone and far away from my parents. Maybe there I could be myself, the true self I longed to be. Kisumu seemed like the first step towards that life and I embraced it.

One day, when I was out buying groceries for the house, I stopped at a kiosk to buy sodas for my sister who, for some reason, was drinking at least four Fanta Oranges a day. I kept telling her it was bad for her, but she wouldn't listen. At the kiosk, a young man on his bicycle rode up to ask for a stick of Sportsman. As he waited for his cigarette he looked at me. Curiously but without the malice that I sometimes feel. He just stared. I got nervous and looked away, asking the woman behind the metal grilles for the sodas and clumsily lifting my bag to return the empty glass bottles. The man was wearing only a pair of knee-length khaki shorts. Though slim, the muscles on his dark skin were defined. Every motion caused a ripple through his tendons and muscles as if he were a biology experiment and I were observing every stimulus create a response. I didn't dare look at him, but watched from the corner of my eye as he lit his cigarette and stood there taking deep puffs. I was aware, through the dizzying smell of freshly burning tobacco, of his smell. A deep scent of man's sweat. Not the smell of boys so familiar from my dorms, but the musty, overwhelming scent of a man.

As if he had nowhere else to go or nothing else to do and as if it were perfectly normal for him to still be standing there, I could feel him watching me take my soda bottles and pay the woman behind the metal grilles. Saying thank you quietly and looking purposefully at the ground, I walked away. I could feel him watching my every move. I felt clumsy and foolish, aware of every part of my awkward body. I had taken only 12 steps, which I had counted resolutely in order to keep my balance, when I heard the metal clank of his bicycle. As the sound drew nearer, I stuttered 'Thir-t-t-een, four-four-t-een', not even sure what I was counting any more. 'Psst,' I heard. I have never understood why men call out to women like that. Am I a cat? 'Psst,' he said again, I assumed to get my attention. I didn't turn around – stubborn even in the tensest situations – but I gently slowed my pace until I could smell him beside me. 'Sasa,' he said, casually greeting me.

'Fit,' I responded.

'Where are you going?'

'Home.'

'You live around here?'

'My sister does, I am visiting,' I said hurriedly.

'Ah.'

I didn't know what else to say but I didn't want the conversation to end. I hadn't yet looked up from the ground and I could feel beads of sweat forming on my brow.

'What is your name?' he asked.

'Why do you want to know?' I said, sounding irritated. I just hadn't known what to say.

'I was just curious,' he said quietly, sounding deflated. I looked up and saw for the first time the gentle questioning eyes and the expectant hesitancy in his raised brow betraying the confidence of his stately body. I softened.

'I have many names. But I haven't found one I like yet,' I said softly.

He smiled, nodding faintly as if he understood.

I smiled back.

He had one foot on the pedal of his bicycle and used the other to push it along. We walked like that side by side, silently, until I was at my sister's gate.

'This is where I stay.'

'Sawa, then, I will be seeing you.'

'OK, bye,' I said awkwardly, hoping that it was not really goodbye. Fishing for something more to say, a way to make the moment last longer, a way to see him again.

He pushed his bike forward and threw his other leg over the saddle.

'I have a name, by the way,' he yelled back at me. 'It is Omondi.'

I watched him cycle into the distance, his lean form obscured under the golden dust he was lifting with his bicycle. Omondi.

As I entered the house, I exhaled deeply and realised I had been holding my breath. 'What is wrong?' my sister called out, sounding irritated.

'Nothing,' I called back.

'Did you get the sodas?'

'Yes, I'll put them in ice.'

'Good, it's so damn hot in this place, I'm dying here,' she said, fanning herself vigorously in a futile motion as if beating the stiff air.

'Omondi,' I thought to myself.

The following week was excruciating. Every day, every hour, every second, I wondered if I would see him again. I went to the kiosk more times that week than was humanly possible. Even the anonymous, emotionless woman behind the metal grilles started looking at me suspiciously. I didn't know what to do. How could I find this man? Who was this Omondi? I couldn't ask anybody because I didn't know anything about him and looking for an Omondi in Kisumu, well, is like looking for a Njeri in Thika! I drove myself mad conjuring up scenarios about when I would see him next, what I would say, how I would behave, even what I would be wearing! But there was no sign of him anywhere. And I began to wonder why I wanted to see this man again. I didn't even know him and for all I knew he could be a psychotic killer. But then I remembered those eyes. And I knew that all I wanted was to be looked at like that again. To be enveloped in that cool, non-committal body and held close in those gentle eyes telling me for the first time by a grown man that I am visible and worthy of tenderness. His eyes held promise.

And, as I say that now, my pessimistic self wonders how that is possible, in one look from a 21-year-old stranger in Kisumu. But I knew then, that that is how I felt it. The faint smell of lake in his hair and clothes gave him a permanent landscape. Like a set, a backdrop. And of course, as with every love, I gave him a theme song too. But I'm jumping ahead. I finally did see him again. A week later, he knocked on my sister's door. Somehow when I heard the uncouth thump at the door, I knew it was him. My heart leapt as I stood over the sink where I had been washing dishes. I heard my sister muttering to herself as she walked heavy-footed to the door. Then I heard his voice, unsure: 'Hello, madam. I, I was wondering if there is someone who lives here. Um, my age? You see I don't have a name, but, well, we met last week. Um…' My sister stood there looking down at him, frowning with her eyebrows and her lips. Head tilted as if bemused. Watching him curiously but irritated, her hands akimbo. I came bounding out of the kitchen wiping my soapy hands on my jeans. 'It's OK, Chico, it's for me.' And stepped in front of her to shield him from her stare. I closed the door behind me, with her still standing there, now also looking at me incredulously but saying nothing. After a second, I could hear her muttering again, this time almost as a giggle, breathing heavily as she carried her weight back inside.

'Hi,' I said.

'Hi,' he said. 'Thanks for rescuing me, I am so glad you live here, I had no idea what I would say!' he blurted, breathing out as if he too had been holding his breath since the last time we saw each other.

He laughed, deeply, a mix of amusement, nerves and relief. I laughed with him as we sat on the steps to the house. It was suddenly so easy. We talked and laughed and joked and teased. Well, he teased me, I can't say that I really teased him. And we sat there for what seemed like hours until the sky turned orange and the mosquitoes took turns sucking at my flesh. 'I should go,' he said softly, looking at me searchingly. He put his hand on my knee and gazed ahead as if the horizon might hold an answer. 'I would like to see you again.'

'Me too.'

'Can I take you on my boat?'

'When?'

'Tomorrow?'

'I would like that.'

We both laughed.

The next day I waited for that thump on our front door. My sister hadn't said anything about my visitor. She had just looked at me with a half-smile on her lips and a question in her eyes throughout dinner. I avoided her gaze but knew that my half-smile responded to hers with all the answers she needed. So, when the thump finally resounded throughout the house the next day, I heard her laugh freely before shouting, 'Your friend is here,' waddling to the door.

I came out of the bathroom where I had been brushing my teeth for the fifth time that day and heard her asking him: 'So, do you have a name, young man?'

'Yes, madam, my name is Omondi,' he said looking at his feet.

Once more, my sister laughed a full, unrestrained laugh, looking Omondi up and down.

'Hi,' I said standing at the door.

My sister placed her hand on my shoulder and looked straight into my eyes, again with that question. I looked at her as if not knowing what she was asking. 'What?' She smiled. 'Nothing. Have fun.' And then as if remembering something profound, suddenly worried. 'Oh, but...' she said.

And then walked back into the house, asking me to follow.

'Omondi, take a seat, I need to talk to Patrick.'

Omondi smiled hearing that name for the first time. I cringed, wanting to interrupt, to say, 'But no, that is not who I am. Patrick is not my name.' Instead I was led to the kitchen by my sister.

'Patrick,' she said severely.

'Yes, Chico.'

'OK, I don't know how to have this conversation. And I definitely didn't think I would have to do it now and in a rush like this. But anyway, look. You know the work I do. I tell you what I see.'

I cringed, suddenly realising what she was about to talk to me about. And stayed silent hoping she might not.

'So, Patrick, do you know how to be safe?' she said matter-of-factly.

'Hmm, yes,' I said, though I wasn't sure I did.

'And, do you have, you know, do you have the equipment?'

'Hmm, no,' I said embarrassed. 'But anyway, why are you asking me this now Chico, what are you talking about?' I said, trying to divert the conversation.

'Patrick,' she said, looking at me dead in the eyes. 'I'm not stupid and this is important. I want you to listen to me. Nothing, I mean it, NOTHING happens without being safe. Do you hear me?' she said firmly, slipping something into my back pocket. 'This is life and death, Patrick, and you are my baby.'

'OK Chico,' I said, shocked by her insistence. 'OK.'

'Promise?'

'Promise.'

She let out a deep sigh of relief. 'OK, now go, your friend is waiting for you,' she said, leaning back onto the counter. 'Remember what I said, Patrick. Always,' she said, with her head bent forward as if reciting a mantra, a prayer.

My heart felt heavy. I didn't know if it was my sister's warnings, or the fact that I was suddenly aware of the possibility of sex. I didn't even know if it was possible. How could we do it? In my head, my fantasies, well, it was like in the movies – a handsome man, I'm a cute girl, one thing leads passionately to another, as simply as it seemed. This possibility was new to me. Confused, I suddenly panicked. What if he didn't know that I, well, that I had a boy's body. Of course he knew, everyone knew, right? Then I realised I was being silly. He was a man, of course, he didn't want to have sex with me, he thought I was a man too, didn't he? I hadn't told him yet that I wasn't, so he probably assumed, right? So, we were going to hang out. Like friends. On his boat. Gosh, Chico is so crazy, why did she scare me like that?

And that is what we did. We rowed out on his boat. Well, he rowed, I sat prissily on the boat with my hands between my knees. I offered to help but, winking, he said that it wasn't a job for me. I smiled silently, looking into the water. Watching and feeling the waves carry us forward with every curl of his forearms. Now it seemed as if the stimulus and response from his body extended to the oars, the water, the waves, the boat, all as one. Rhythmic, pounding. When we reached what seemed to be the very centre of the earth, or at least the centre of the lake, Omondi stopped rowing. He put the oars into the boat and lay a blanket on the bottom, motioning me to sit. We sat and talked and laughed, letting the boat rock us to and fro between nowhere and elsewhere. I didn't know why I was so comfortable, but it felt delicious to feel lost, far from the realities of the shore. I was aware of his body, his scent, his sweat, the delicate touches between us. I was aware of his breath close enough for me to feel him laugh. Aware of his toes touching mine. Aware of the breeze carrying our laughter and shifting the distance between us. We talked about nothing and everything. And nothing else mattered. Then in a comforting silence, watching the clouds move swiftly across changing skies, he pulled me softly towards him. I lay under him as he looked questioningly with those hesitant black eyes into mine. And, as if finding a truth, he smiled and brought his lips forward to touch mine. I closed my eyes. This is where I wanted to be. In this moment, at this time, this was the end and the beginning. Gently he kissed my face, my neck, my mouth and I sank into him, aware of the growing bulge in his shorts.

His hands began to search my body with a coarse urgency that abruptly changed the rhythms in my soul. His change of pace shook me from the intensity of being lost in his scent, touch, energy. I opened my eyes and searched his face but he was too busy looking for the buttons on my trousers. Feeling me watching him quizzically he looked up and smiled. A superficial, fleeting, barely appeasing smile. I watched as he pulled my trousers to below my knees, as he unbuttoned his shorts. I watched as he kissed me, hurriedly, before searching for his entry. His hand caressing my chest was the only sign of the touch that brought me here. And then he pulled me close in one slow thrust, the pain shooting through my spine reaching the tip of my head. I held my breath again, immobilised. Then I felt the wetness, the blood. And slowly his grip loosened, he moved in and out, quickening his pace, in and out, the pain blinding, but yet bearable. Confused, I awkwardly tried to catch up to his movement, to ease to his touch. Until it was over.

We lay there in the bottom of his boat. His arm and leg limply slung across me, as he sunk into sleep, seemingly gratified. My mind was blank. The motion of the water cradling my soul. Part of me wanted to cry, part of me wanted to laugh. I wanted to hold him and was at the same time repelled by his heaving body. Then, opening my eyes suddenly as if struck by an epiphany, I turned to kiss him. I found the answer. I kissed his lips, his cheek, his neck, his earlobe. Kissed his eyes and his mouth, waking him from his slumber. I ran my hands and fingers over the muscles of his arms, his back, his neck. Slowly, gently, he rose. Opening his mouth to mine, merging to my touch, mimicking the strokes on my body. Our bodies sinking into one another's movements until we found ours. And then I held him to me, remembering for the first time my sister's caution. Too late. Too late. But still, this time I wanted to do it right. Undressing and locking eyes with his, I slipped the condom from my pocket, clumsily finding a way to open it one-handed. We laughed and there I found the eyes that I longed for. He looked at me as if he could see me whole and met me with acceptance, warmth and desire. 'Let me,' he said taking the packet and enveloping the condom over his penis with one expert motion. I laughed again, unaware that I would, but amused by my own ineptitude. He then lifted my shirt and circled my nipples with his tongue. I could see his throbbing growing stronger and thicker, and I sank into my own bliss. He began to undress me, and, suddenly aware of self, I stopped his hand. 'It's OK,' he said, turning me slowly to the side. I let him meet me. And the pain was bearable, the touch smooth, his kisses warm, my body easing into his rhythm whose crescendo slowly rose to a roar. Our waters fused, his waves crashing against my shore. Unabashedly, unflinchingly, unashamedly. We laughed.

As we lay holding each other I wondered: did he experience it as I did? Would he remember it as I would? 'We should go, it's getting dark,' he said, kissing me lightly, fleetingly. Putting his clothes back on and handing me mine, I watched this boy, wondering silently.

'I'll see you soon,' he said, as we reached my sister's house. And the realisation that I would never see Omondi again washed over me with resounding sadness. I kissed him, right there on my sister's doorstep, and mustered a smile before saying: 'Thank you.' He faintly smiled back, touching my hair with the tips of his fingers. And, there, I saw the heavy sorrow in his face, as if the realisation had unfurled over his spirit as well. We stood there. Fixed by the unattainable. Unable to freeze time. We stood there. Our fingers meeting slightly as if by accident.

Sometimes I wonder about the possibilities, of me for me of love of companionship of connection if it were all different. A utopia where I can be fully embraced and embracing. It is a futile exercise. My light has been long extinguished. I am not even sure I would recognise the being of that time, that soul, if she fluttered before me now. It's only been six years since Kisumu. My sister moved after Kathambi was born. I have never been back. But I can sometimes smell the lake in the air, suddenly in the middle of a conversation, or waiting for a *matatu* in town and I smile somewhere inside.

And now. As I make my seventh circle. As my body weakens, my sight blurs and my eyes shut, I smell the lake in the distance, hear the waves crashing closer and closer and know that if I reach long enough I will touch them.

African conversations on gender identity and ICD classifications

This conversation began following the forwarding of a statement by an advisor at the World Health Organization (WHO) on a mailing list server which included the following on transsexualism and the International Classification of Diseases (ICD): 'A third function of WHO is to establish and revise, as necessary, international nomenclatures of diseases. [...] The 11th version of the ICD is scheduled to be presented to the World Health Assembly (WHO's Governing Body) in May 2015. Although homosexuality is no longer included, other issues that may concern us remain, such as transsexualism as a mental disorder. How can we ensure that we address the health care needs of transgender populations without further stigmatising them? I hope that transgender people and the transgender movement can help us in addressing this challenge invoking the key human rights principle of participation – "nothing for us without us".' An email conversation ensued between comrades of diverse identities in East Africa on gender identity and ICD classification...

Audrey

Good morning everyone,
Transgender Education and Advocacy (TEA) will send a letter requesting WHO to retain transsexualism in the ICD classification. TEA does not see any reason to have it removed from ICD or DSM-V.[1]

Furthermore TEA sees a gay-isation trend here: the current issue is to have transsexualism removed as a mental disorder (the classification of homosexuality as a mental disorder was removed in 1990). So what if homosexuality was removed from ICD and DSM? There is a difference between homosexuality and transsexualism. There is no relationship whatsoever and it is rude to associate these two issues.

By the way, remove it from ICD for what? What alternative do you propose to have? Am glad some groups are talking of having it as a medical condition, which is okay with some of us, but we abhor the way cisgender LGB are handling this matter: having transsexualism removed from ICD and DSM because homosexuality was removed. I want to pass this information as a friend: don't jump into our issues haphazardly for the sake of being seen to be working on T issues.

Please assist in reaching out to some individuals and organisations in making them see the sense of respecting T's space. If the LGB community want to help then let them follow our lead, but not acting as our mouthpiece on such a sensitive issue as this. We can't manage to adequately get medical services for gender transition and then you find people trashing the only diagnosis we have to get the little we have?

I think the best way to deal with mental disorder-related stigma is to educate society about mental disorders, and not by erasing mental disorders from the ICD-10 or DSM- IV. Why not leave this issue to trans folks – we have our own thing and that kind of thing.

Audrey – T36,000

Hakima

Dear sis,

I completely concur with you around the stigma with mental-related disorder.

And I would like to suggest another way of looking at things, if not at the world. In my world view, there are no binaries. I do not believe that the form (e.g. gender, sexuality, etc) or content (e.g. how these manifest physically, spiritually, intellectually, etc) of our beings are linear, binary or able to be neatly categorised (I know you are a scientist so you won't like that at all). I think the mistake we make is to try to create these binaries to understand the world.

And we do it even in our movement: e.g. I am man, or woman,

or trans, or intersex. I feel that my gender, gender expression, gender performance and gender identity are all much more complex than what we understand by gender or sex or the interaction between the two, e.g. the roles I play in my family, in the street, in the sheets, how my body functions, how it doesn't, what is expected of me, what I fulfil, how I carry myself, etc and I don't believe that any two people of similar categorised gender identities have all of the same things going on (physically, spiritually or by socialisation). Indeed, I think the biological myth of binaries of sex is blown away by intersex folk – who again the dominant world attempts to categorise (even the word 'inter' implies between two things) – but who occupy a physical space of resistance against these categorisations.

I know you don't care about this part, sis, but the same is true, in my view, about sexuality. There are many things that move us sexually and there are many ways we express our sexuality that may or may not have anything to do with what we do in bed with ourselves, one or many partners. We have attempted to say we are straight, gay and lesbian to avoid the good (but much more complicated) fight of saying that sexuality is plural. I don't think men who call themselves gay are solely turned on by other men, or that lesbians don't have sex with trans men or that a gold star lesbian can't desire a gay man, etc.

This complexity/plurality of gender, sex, sexuality, identity (as well as a lot of other categories of the world – some of which I struggle more to see this way) is a political position which can allow us to fight the good/complex fight as, what I would call, queers.

'Queer politics is anti-assimilationalist, inclusive and diverse.' 'Queer is not seen as a single way of being, but rather as a dissident stance with great respect and room for difference.'

As you will see, therefore, from this point of view the ideas of gender identity disorder (or gender dysphoria) as categorised for trans folks or, as I just saw somewhere, congenital disorder (as suggested for intersex persons as a physical 'disorder') don't make much sense. I don't think that 1) these are disorders or 2) that there are cisgendered persons (when do I decide that my identity 'matches' what is expected of my behaviour or role?).

Again, the more complex route for advocacy may not be the one we choose, but maybe for the longer term of creating the world we seek, it would be better. Or, maybe I'm just off the wall and we can continue working from the same TIBLG framework! Because, sister, I understand that I say this from the privileged position of not having my gender choices oppressed daily and, as you suggest, I would always take the lead from trans folk while I walk in solidarity. And this is not to say that you and other trans folk don't daily suffer the oppressions of this binary world and sometimes as we struggle we must fight within the existing framework/binaries to dismantle it (e.g. in regards to race, I only understand this approach). Also, in the spirit of my political African Queer anarchist position, I value our plurality of opinion, so I hope my sharing was useful to get the mind juices flowing and that we can continue to discuss.

Hakima

Barbra

Hi everyone,

I was thinking about this conversation when I was coming to work today. I'm sorry if I jump up and down in my thoughts.

When I discovered I was trans, it was like a lightbulb moment. I had been told all sorts of things, and mostly I was told I was gay (or at that time: homo). I knew clearly that I wasn't that, even from a young age of 12. For me, when I heard that there was a diagnosed cause for my 'pain', it was an 'Aha' moment. I had something to tell people and I wasn't alone, I wasn't imagining things.

I think this discussion is sensitive because on one hand we know (I presume) what a relief it must be to hear someone telling you that what you're going through is not your own doing, that it is actually a documented 'disorder'. But then again, the naming of it as a disorder brings in so many other issues of 'Am I crazy? What will people think?', and so forth.

While the cause for removing GID/GD from DSM-V or ICD-10 sounds good, I wonder what actual trans persons feel. I honestly am not sure. I haven't been treated as a mental case at all and I've not suffered significant mental breakdown or depression or what have you due to my 'dysphoria'. However, by me being me, and being 'diagnosed as having GD', I have been able to access hormones and surgery and therapy.

Comparing transsexualism to homosexuality cannot happen. Homosexuals don't need hormones or surgery to be their true self. For one to love another, you don't need a doctor giving you injections or modifying parts of your body. However, for a transsexual to be who they truly are, these are real tangible things they need. Sometimes I actually see why trans and intersex correlate: because for them it's not merely 'I love this person, I'm attracted to that person', it is a physical, mental and social thing. Very tangible! That's how I see it. And that's why I'm hesitant to join the 'Stop Trans Pathologisation' campaign. Because I am not seeing them answer these questions.

I don't want to be treated as a mental case, I want to be treated as a person in need of certain medical attention that is specific to me and my condition.

I stand to be corrected though.

Barbra

Your silence will not protect you ~ Audre Lorde

Julius

Hi all,

I do echo some of the thoughts Barbra has expressed. In my view, there is a need to reflect deeply when considering individual needs vis-à-vis collective needs. Often, different people who may identify with a common situation will feel differently about the situation and will even have different approaches to the situation. The critical question for me is: does the individual have the right to make choices and adopt approaches which will meet their perceived need and give them the desired result?

Bringing my thoughts closer to the conversation in question, I would be very hesitant to raise the 'Stop pathologisation' flag without being very sure what the implications are for everyone else who may not be standing in the same political and socioeconomic space as I am. To me, the word 'disorder' in itself would not be a problem but how it is used, and if the use of it can give people like myself access to the health care and medical interventions they require.

At the risk of sounding pathological myself, I dare say there is actually something 'not quite right' or 'not quite in order' with either the way our bodies have been formed in utero (in the case of intersex individuals), or the way they turned out to be (male/ female, in the case of trans individuals). How one chooses to term that 'not quite right' body outcome is pretty much a personal matter, depending on the needs of the individual. However, when we talk about medical tests, surgeries, hormone replacement therapy (which in many cases is life-long and requires continued health monitoring) and possible health risks, it may be quite impractical to assume that we will interact with only those medical practitioners who are comfortable to modify a body which has been diagnosed to have no anomaly whatsoever. It is therefore in some way a Catch 22 situation.

A gender or sex development disorder is certainly NOT an illness or mental sickness. It is simply that – a 'body' condition that displays something 'not quite IN ORDER' for the individual who is dealing with it, and requires some medical intervention NOT to 'fix it' per se but to turn it 'right' for the concerned individual. If I am realistic with myself, this realisation opens more doors than it closes – even in regard to self-determination and esteem. I say this because if I say there is nothing OUT OF ORDER, then I have subsequent questions that will haunt me, such as why then don't I possess the body that corresponds to who I believe I am – how the heck did I get into this kind of body, which I hate with a passion? Where did these breasts come from, which should not be there and which I hate so much? Why am I growing this beard when I should have and want to have a smooth 'feminine' face, etc?

Like Barbra, I stand open to other people's thoughts but this is my two pennies' worth on the conversation.

Warmly,

Julius

Guillit

Hi all,

I'm really not sure where to begin with the 'mental disorder' thing. First I do not stand corrected but I accept and respect people's opinions. I agree with Barbra and Julius, NOTHING IS OUT OF ORDER, period. I want to share a story that shows how I believe something is wrong with society, not with us as IT [intersex and trans] people. I witnessed the cruellest discrimination and stigma on 21 March 2012. I'm writing a story about it and hope all of you in this list will chip in some ideas on what is the next step and how to help this person get out of this lifelong humiliation.

I have witnessed how cisgender persons can stigmatise someone with silence and discrimination with a capitalist mindset. Eric is an intersex person with whom I've recently experienced some of the gender discrimination that he's been facing all of his life. I only experienced it for one day, but already I was traumatised. I can't imagine how he's survived with it his whole life. After my observation, I think some of Eric's siblings might be gay and it's scary to them so they react to him with rage and ignorance.

Nothing is wrong with Eric; he was born fine with unique genitals. However, his genital uniqueness has made his family and neighbours try to kill him more than once, beat him and report him to the police every time he talks to women because he's not taking up the role they believe he should play. The community has turned against him, schoolchildren ridicule him in his home area, questioning who he is while analysing him head to toe. This is the magnitude of ignorance and society molesting IT persons.

I have also experienced some of these things, but not to that extent. It was hard for me to love myself fully in the beginning because of the way I used to feel. Knowing the G-man, wondering why He let things like that happen to me. Religious people don't understand that being trans has nothing to do with whatever is written in the Bible – hell, it's not even in the Bible! Science and medicine are classifying me as having a 'mental disorder'.

The cisgender people don't know and will never experience their body and mind not coordinating. So since they do not understand IT persons, the next easy step and way out is to call it a 'mental disorder'. Let's start there – aaaha! – and use research to judge people for who they are. They forgot to ask IT persons how they feel and relate to their shitty social norms, and if they want to fit at all. Who is normal anyways? What criteria make one normal?

This might sound pathological but it's not. I have to nip and cut 'mental disorder' out of the DSM-V and ICD-10, and even people's thoughts and ideas of classifying and labelling people without their consent. I know I'm queer as they come, if it ever comes in a package with a red ribbon on it. If the cisgender people must have me identified, stamp a sticker on me, I'm it, trans boi and part of both sexual and gender minority categories. Health care is my right. I shouldn't have to accept someone else's label for me to access it.

Classification, I do not need be in research labs to label myself according to final results. Why do we feel the need to fit everything in this world to scientific recommendations, forgetting that nature and time are constantly changing us? Society does not embrace any change without categorising and giving it a name and without a tussle! Just so that it can be filed and accessed for everyone to fit into their selfish social norms and patriarchal roles.

UP^2 is working with a social worker with a hospital in Kayole. She offers IT persons in the UP organisation refuge in seeking medical services privately, thus avoiding doctors' stigmatising and judgment in examination rooms. The people giving trainings in doctors', nurses' and social work courses should add gender into their curriculum to sensitise medical fields on IT people. And we should have posters in pharmaceutical institutions like chemists saying, 'It's not a taboo to be born ambiguous whether in mind or body. To be intersex or transgender is not an illness but a condition.'

I agree with Hakima that gender is fluid and you can and should be anything you want to be, without labels. But is this reality? Do self-definition and fluidity even happen, with visible stigmas brushing against each other during activities or events? Most of us, even trans and intersex, still try to fit into the categories of 'man' and 'woman', 'straight' and 'gay' and other binaries. We need to expand our own understanding and options for different ways of identifying and defining ourselves.

I will finish by mentioning that my emotions, thoughts, deeds and making informed choices are what make me Guillit, and changing my name has nothing to do with it. Come to think of it, why do society and its patriarchal norms have to gender names? But I feel the need and can relate to the name I chose for myself, not like the imposed or given names that I force myself to fit into like every other thing, including the DSM and ICD classifications.

I will design how to live and what is the best fit for me and be part of bringing positive changes, whether benefiting me personally or someone else. It won't be easy but I will be in the positive struggle for free choice, to love myself, and to make life liveable for myself and others who the world is not designed for. Science and the G-man may disagree but I will still craft my life to suit me; time and death are the only limits I have, though man is fighting to stop my dreams. We can only bring to life our differences, learn from one another and build each other without tearing each other down.

Solidarity,

Guillit

Notes

1   DSM-V is the fifth edition of the *Diagnostic and Statistical Manual of Mental Disorders* compiled by the American Psychiatric Association (APA), due for publication in May 2013. It supersedes DSM-IV, which was published in 2000.

2   Ushirikiano Panda (UP) is a Kenyan organisation whose mission is to create safe spaces and increase the well-being of intersex and transgender (IT) people in Kenya. The group is led by IT people themselves, and strives to develop a country in which all citizens are free to determine and express their own gender. Since this conversation, UP has changed its name to Jinsiangu, which comes from the Kiswahili words *jinsia yangu*, meaning 'my gender'.

Remember me when I'm gone

Busisiwe Sigasa (23 December 1981–12 March 2007)

In April 2006 Busi was raped by a young man near her home. A few months later she discovered she was HIV-positive. Busi was already suffering from diabetes and although she was receiving ARVs she was never really well and often struggled with her days. Not only had she to come to terms with being raped and HIV-positive, she had to live with seeing her rapist walk the streets and even be faced with him at the HIV clinic. On 12 March 2007 Busi, who had been trying to work a few days a week, came home and immediately went to her room to sleep. A few hours later her mother came by and woke her up to take her diabetic medication. Busi said OK, but she must have fallen asleep and from then she never woke up. This is one of the many poems she wrote and shared before she died, and is taken from her blog: http://latifah.wordpress.com/.

Wrote stories for the nations to read
Stood without fear and told my story
I smiled and greeted without judging
I influenced positive living to the sick
I planted seeds of hope to the hopeless
I groomed and glowed the younger ones whose parents died
I created artistic designs with my hands
I crafted and drew beautiful pictures
I installed educational reasoning to some
I taught represented the minority to the majority
I made nations aware
I wronged some and made some happy
I survived against odds

I swallowed my medication even as hard as it was it was sometimes

I did so to remain strong and to live my life regardless of my status

I fought for women to be taken into serious consideration by our government

I wrote and said 'my' spoke word

I fought and showed many that there's nothing wrong with being diabetic, epileptic and HIV

I represented many of the HIV infected lesbian sisters

I told the truth never mind the judgements

I lived and I'm still living

I loved and prayed to my GOD

I prayed without hesitation, for, I believe/d

I was a big sister to my younger sisters

I listened to my mother's teachings

I became friends with father

I'D DIE FOR MY FAMILY, I LOVED THEM SO!

I captured moments with my camera

I brought forth what was unseen to the nations through the power of image, pen and paper

I struggled to make it life

I was taken for a ride by some whom i thought were friends

I showed my rapist how strong i was regardless that he poisoned my blood with his HIV

I believed and prayed

I stood low and respected all regardless of their age, colour and size

I say along with others

I had a unique voice

I had a message to deliver and a vision to see

I tried, i fell and i never succeeded sometimes

I was patient while to some i was strange

I was loved by some and was hated by some, STILL i did my thing

I loved and appreciated beautiful women

I loved her more than life itself

Some would say...

I am full shit! but spiritually i was full

I was fed with GOD's glory that's why I praised HIM

I praised HIM more than i praised friends

I am my mother's daughter

I made history and marked historical books of this world

SO.........

REMEMBER ME WHEN I'M GONE!

FOR...without no doubt i'll and i am in peace with my maker and
creator.

AMEN!

Index